THACKERAY: THE CRITICAL HERITAGE

THE CRITICAL HERITAGE SERIES

GENERAL EDITOR: B. C. SOUTHAM, M.A., B.LITT. (OXON.)

Formerly Department of English, Westfield College, University of London

---

Volumes in the series include

JANE AUSTEN	B. C. Southam
BYRON	Andrew Rutherford, *University of Aberdeen*
DICKENS	Philip Collins, *University of Leicester*
HENRY FIELDING	R. Paulson, *The Johns Hopkins University, Baltimore* and Thomas Lakewood, *University of Washington*
HENRY JAMES	Roger Gard, *Queen Mary College, London*
TENNYSON	J. D. Jump, *University of Manchester*
THACKERAY	Geoffrey Tillotson and Donald Hawes, *Birkbeck College, London*
TROLLOPE	Donald Smalley, *University of Illinois*

THACKERAY

THE CRITICAL HERITAGE

Edited by

GEOFFREY TILLOTSON

Professor of English Literature
Birkbeck College, University of London

and

DONALD HAWES

Senior Lecturer in English, The Polytechnic, Regent Street, London

LONDON: ROUTLEDGE & KEGAN PAUL

NEW YORK: BARNES & NOBLE INC

Published 1968
in Great Britain
by Routledge & Kegan Paul Limited
and in the United States of America
by Barnes & Noble Inc.

SBN 7100 2943 8

Printed in Great Britain
by W & J Mackay & Co Ltd, Chatham

To
GORDON N. RAY
who has done so much for Thackeray

General Editor's Preface

The reception given to a writer by his contemporaries and near-contemporaries is evidence of considerable value to the student of literature. On one side, we learn a great deal about the state of criticism at large and in particular about the development of critical attitudes towards a single writer; at the same time, through private comments in letters, journals or marginalia, we gain an insight upon the tastes and literary thought of individual readers of the period. Evidence of this kind helps us to understand the writer's historical situation, the nature of his immediate reading-public, and his response to these pressures.

The separate volumes in *The Critical Heritage Series* present a record of this early criticism. Clearly, for many of the highly-productive and lengthily-reviewed nineteenth- and twentieth-century writers, there exists an enormous body of material; and in these cases the volume editors have made a selection of the most important views, significant for their intrinsic critical worth or for their representative quality.

For writers of the eighteenth century and earlier, the materials are much scarcer and the historical period has been extended, sometimes far beyond the writer's lifetime, in order to show the inception and growth of critical views which were initially slow to appear.

In each volume the documents are headed by an Introduction, discussing the material assembled and relating the early stages of the author's reception to what we have come to identify as the critical tradition. The volumes will make available much material which would otherwise be difficult of access and it is hoped that the modern reader will be thereby helped towards an informed understanding of the ways in which literature has been read and judged.

B.C.S.

Contents

CONTENTS

CONTENTS

CONTENTS

Preface

Almost all the fifty-six items printed below are reviews. One or two are parts of private letters, and one was appended to an edition. The text of all but one of the printed pieces is taken from the first edition, usually that of magazine or newspaper, with the correction of obvious misprints and the standardization of titles of books, stories and other literary works. In the nineteenth century most reviews were anonymous, and in reprinting them we have added in square brackets the names of their authors where we could find them. Since many of the writers are, and perhaps were, obscure, we have given a few biographical facts about them in the headnotes. What correcting of texts has been called for—that of misprints or misquotations from Thackeray's text—we have done silently, but have left them as they stand when the author has adapted them to suit the run of his own sentence. We have not reproduced the long quotations that were designed to give the prospective buyer or reader a sample of the novel under review, but have replaced them with a reference to Thackeray's *Works* (in the Oxford edition in seventeen volumes, 1908). When we refer to *Letters* it is to Gordon N. Ray's edition, 4 volumes, Cambridge, Mass., 1945-6. We have given the source of quotations when we knew them, except for those too well known to need it.

The chronological order which is surely obligatory in a collection such as this has, when the topic is a novelist, an appropriately narrative interest. This is especially striking when the same reviewer—G. H. Lewes is the salient example—reviews a series of books, and builds his further comments on those made already, even sometimes repeating a *bon mot* he had either forgotten he had used before or hoped his readers had. Reading them in something like the order Thackeray read them in, we see that they achieve a shape, the biological shape of a progression.

GEOFFREY TILLOTSON
DONALD HAWES

London
30 November 1966

Acknowledgments

For permission to reprint copyright material we are grateful to Mrs. Edward Norman Butler and Professor Gordon Ray for our excerpts from Thackeray's letters, and to Sir Basil Blackwell for those from Charlotte Brontë's. We wish to thank the editors of those periodicals that are still flourishing for their kind permission to reprint the pieces we have taken from *Blackwood's Magazine*, the *Cornhill Magazine*, the *Quarterly Review*, *The Scotsman*, the *Spectator* and *The Times*.

G.T.

D.H.

Chronological Table

Introduction

Ignorance is a soft cushion, and it is just as well that we critics and
would-be critics of nineteenth century literature are ignorant or we
should be uncomfortable. Our growing interest in exploring that
literature could not go on so happily if we had the suspicion—which
the present volume confirms—that our red-hot views are those of at
least some of our great-grandparents. Our discoveries are rediscoveries.
The great writings of the mid-nineteenth century received in their
own day the criticism they merited, criticism as sound and spirited as
any they are ever likely to receive. One of the interests, then, of the
present volume, and of any that are made on the same principle, is that
it brings to light those 'forgotten worthies', the critics of the great
literature of their time who were anonymous and obscure, and that
it suggests the original context of those whose names are known and
honoured. Some of the forgotten worthies we have brought to remembrance are American, which in the mid-nineteenth century still
mainly meant New England. Thackeray's writings were known there
almost as soon as in England, and indeed it was there that some of his
series of periodical writings first became books—at this date and for
long after there was no international copyright law. It was only after
Vanity Fair (1847-8), that he was acclaimed in America, and nothing
more of his was much noticed till after his first lecture tour in 1852-3.
We have included in our selection three prominent American reviews
of his novels, and they will perhaps encourage American scholars to
go further than they yet have in detailed study of his American reception. Thackeray made his first lecture tour in America ten years
after Dickens visited there, and was greatly preferred because of his
amiability, which tempered the fear that the author of the novels
might be too horribly critical of everything he came up against. We
may also note here that many of Thackeray's writings were soon translated into French and German, not surprisingly—their ethos, unlike
that of Dickens, was from the start as much European as English.

One of our American reviewers hoped that the import of Thackeray's sort of civilization would not spoil the American sort, and his fear of Thackeray's must have been very like his fear of the European. A decade or two later Henry James was to be less fearfully receptive of both Thackeray and Europe.

A hundred years ago, Arnold saw that even a great writer might misemploy his powers in vain attempts to write good poetry and good novels when all the time he could have been successfully writing good criticism. Two of the writers Arnold instanced were English.

'Is it true,' he asked,

that Johnson had better have gone on producing more *Irenes* instead of writing his *Lives of the Poets*; nay is it certain that Wordsworth himself was better employed in making his *Ecclesiastical Sonnets*, than when he made his celebrated Preface [to the *Lyrical Ballads* of 1800], so full of criticism, and criticism of the works of others?

Two of the writers whose criticism of Thackeray is drawn on in the following pages are also great writers of the literature we call 'creative' —to use a term that is useful rather than exact, for there is more creativeness when Coleridge speaks of the 'angelic strength and happy valiancy' of Shakespeare's style in *Antony and Cleopatra* than in all the many novels of Nokes or Stokes, and this means that literature itself competes with life in the prompting of great thoughts and descriptions, often crystallized in great phrases. Those two creative writers are Trollope and Henry Kingsley. Some of the rest tried their hand at novels and even poetry, and what Arnold said of the authors of *Irene* and of the *Ecclesiastical Sonnets* may be said of them also. They were better employed in writing their excellent criticism—Lewes in writing for the *Leader* rather than adding to his novels, Roscoe in writing for the *National Review* rather than in writing more poetic drama.

Another interest of this collection, as we have suggested already, is the comparative obscurity of many of the reviewers. What 'general reader' has ever heard of Robert Bell, who wrote the review of the completed *Vanity Fair* (No. 15), or of Samuel Phillips, who in his attack on *Esmond* and Thackeray's works in general writes what is surely one of the most vigorous and brilliant critical pieces in the whole range of nineteenth century reviewing (No. 32). It seems a hard fate that condemned the anonymous Samuel Phillips to wait for Dr. Gordon Ray to hail him by name, and for us to reprint him.

Most nineteenth century reviews, as we have indicated, were

unsigned, but there is another, and more important difference between a mid-nineteenth and a mid-twentieth century review, whether signed or anonymous—a difference of scale. It is true that mid-nineteenth century books, even great ones, were sometimes briefly reviewed in the periodicals, especially in the weeklies and dailies, which had their use for what we now call the short notice. But whereas the reviews that are counted long in present-day periodicals run to 2,500 words or to about two or three pages the size of this, the long reviews of a century ago are the size of pamphlets, some even the size of short books. In the *Westminster Review* of 1839 John Sterling's review of Carlyle's *Critical and Miscellaneous Essays* and *Sartor Resartus* is some seventy pages long—the pages quite big and the print small—and Elizabeth Rigby's review (No. 18) of *Vanity Fair* and *Jane Eyre* ran to thirty-two pages. The long reviews of the mid-nineteenth century were treatises, and a good one was proclaimed and discussed as a treatise would be. Accordingly reviewers had room for spreading themselves, for discussing and formulating the principles on which their criticism proceeded, perhaps comparing on an adequate scale the writer and the book under review to other writers and books. And they had enough space to examine the book before them as closely as a don examines a postgraduate thesis—witness that arch-examiner Samuel Phillips (No. 32). To set about writing one of these reviews was like setting about preparing a public lecture. It is only fair to say that some of their space was expected to be used in giving sizeable quotations, on the principle that the prospective buyer or even reader of a book is entitled to a sample.

II

With ample space available they were doubly blessed in often being able to use it for reviewing the many masterpieces of our mid-nine-teenth century literature, and in particular the many masterpieces written in a form that had only recently been established, a form that invited experiment as the old epic form, which it replaced, had not. As far as England went, the novel had now at last got completely clear of the tale and the romance, and of the subterfuge that it was biography and memoirs. That the process of its complete emancipation was slow is evinced by an uncertainty still lingering as to nomenclature. What should the writers of things like *Nicholas Nickleby* and *Vanity Fair* be called? The term 'novelist' is found as early as 1728, but it is invented by a writer who thought of novels as short tales of gallantry.[1] That both 'novelist' and 'novel' should fit writers of the greatness of Dickens and Thackeray and stories of the greatness of *Nicholas Nickleby* and *Vanity Fair*, was as yet unthought of. A century or more later the terms still had rivals. There was still much use of 'humourist', 'romancist', 'romance-writer' and so on—Thackeray favoured 'humourist', 'biographer' and 'historian'. Whatever the name of the new sort of writer, however, he was now duly honoured as the maker of literature supremely worth attending to. And the sense that his wares were of a kind created recently prompted reviewers to try to define and analyse the form, and to weigh up the claims of its constituent parts.

Like any great literary form, the novel partly defies generalizations. The only adequate definitions of it, having to include so much, tell us so little (e.g. 'a fiction in prose of a certain extent'). But this simply meant that the business of generalizing still beckoned the critic. In his essay, 'The Art of Fiction', Henry James finally demanded only one thing—that a novel should be found 'interesting' (presumably by those the novelist had in mind as its readers). Whether or not used as a critical term, 'interesting' was a fairly recent new-comer. Its modern sense may not date back much earlier than Wordsworth's Preface of 1800. David Masson had already brought it into his discussion of the new form: 'It is by the originality and interest of its characters that a novel is chiefly judged' (No. 25). And again a little later on, in a sentence that James may have been recalling, 'the aim of all fictitious literature is primarily to interest the reader'. Whereupon Masson proceeds to try to make his remark more pointed:

in a certain deep sense, it may be maintained that no kind of literary composition whatever is valuable that is not interesting, [and yet] it would . . . seem as if recently the determination to achieve that special kind of interest which consists in mere amusement, had prevailed too largely among our writers of tales and novels. We do not often see now that effort at artistic perfection, that calm resolution to infuse into a performance the concentrated thought and observation of the writer, and to give it final roundness and finish, which did exist in old times, and which supreme authorities have always recommended.

This brings in a matter that must always concern a critic when a form is as widely favoured as the novel has proved to be—the question of its

[1] It is Joseph Morgan who coins the word, and he does so cautiously: '. . . Novelists, I mean Novel-writers . . .' (*A Complete History of Algiers*, 1728–9, i, 239).

status among fellows. For one great novelist it was clear that the form she had chosen to write in stood as high as any could possibly stand: in *Northanger Abbey* Jane Austen, after picturing a young lady interrupted in her reading, and shamefacedly confessing 'Oh! it is only a novel!', goes on:

'It is only Cecilia, or Camilla, or Belinda;' or, in short, only some work in which the greatest powers of the mind are displayed, in which the most thorough knowledge of human nature, the happiest delineation of its varieties, the liveliest effusions of wit and humour are conveyed to the world in the best chosen language.

From the whole passage we infer that the brisk demand for novels was already amply being met. We also know that, by the time of Thackeray, many more of them were being demanded and published. The result of this multiplication was that Jane Austen's splendid claim for the masterpieces often seemed in danger of being swamped by the third-rate. Works of fiction that emboldened James to call the novel the 'most magnificent' of literary forms were in danger of disgrace because, now as never before, novels were being addressed to the nation at large. R. S. Rintoul indicated the range of their readers by his casual opposition of 'the idle sort' and 'the very busy' (No. 23). This latter class numbered men like himself, for he was the busy editor of the *Spectator*. The novels of the day had many readers among the busy great men—and the busy great women. It will be enough to name as nineteenth century novel-readers Shelley, Macaulay, Darwin, Huxley, Tennyson, Newman, Matthew Arnold, Elizabeth Barrett Browning (who described herself as 'a thick and thin novel reader'), and Florence Nightingale. And the category of the busy included many others than the great or even the less-than-great members of the professions. Dickens and *Jane Eyre* were read by the busy high and mighty, and also by busy charwomen, though most charwomen had to have the reading done aloud for them by the (slightly) more literate. Lucky the novelists—of whom Dickens was the supreme instance—who could please them all, and please them, as Shakespeare did, with the same work! That surely is one of the literary triumphs of the mid-nineteenth century—that the work of at least one great poet and of at least two great novelists pleased universally, and so even more widely than Pope, Jane Austen, Scott and Byron had pleased. The greatest of all achievements for a novelist was to write for all, but if that was out of the question the charwomen had to be sacrificed to the educated, then and later. It was for the educated that Thackeray wrote, as was noted by at least one (No. 30) reviewer. Even his ten thousand readers took some winning. It was inevitable that they should; for his highest hope, when he began, was that he should achieve a *succès de scandale*. Assured of brilliance, he set up as a rebel, as the great Carlyle himself had done. In the last of our exhibits (No. 56) Leslie Stephen well describes the literary context into which the early writings were catapulted. Thackeray was what the Elizabethans would have called a 'University wit'—there were several of them in the mid-nineteenth century, conspicuously Newman (author of the *Tamworth Reading Room* and the novel *Loss and Gain*) and Matthew Arnold. This Masson saw (No. 25).

III

In his early work especially Thackeray adopted a method that was more of the eighteenth century than of the nineteenth—that of choosing his matter according to a moral principle. As we should expect, his method had an explanation in the literature he most admired—the poetry of Horace and, compendiously, the poetry and prose of eighteenth century England. In the satires of Rome and eighteenth century England he found a deliberate narrowing and at the same time an amassing of material. Some of our reviewers saw that the example afforded him by a great eighteenth century artist who was also a great moralist helped explain the method now being adopted by a moralist who was writing not in the old form of the satire, which was now obsolete, but in the new form of the novel. In a moral picture such as 'Gin Lane' Hogarth's method was simplicity itself. If his picture was crowded with vicious people that was because he had collected together as many examples as possible of the ill effects of one thing, gin. He was out to make a pictorial list that was intellectually complete. Other pictures of his drew up similar lists—Charles Lamb noted that 'his graphic representations are indeed books'. The reviewers saw that Thackeray collected together in the early writings, and later in *Vanity Fair*, as many examples as possible of self-seeking, sham, insincerity and hypocrisy—and, in the *Book of Snobs*, of the miserable ambition to rise higher in the social scale. Lewes noted that in his novels he 'shows us *everywhere* corruption underneath the mask' (No. 10). Deep in their Dickens, readers were puzzled at a method so different. Henry Kingsley, a born Thackerayan, was in his late teens when *Vanity Fair* began to appear, and we learn from him of the sense of puzzlement that was felt towards it even by well-wishers, even by those who were fascinated by what they could not fully feel at home with (No. 53).

As the reader of our book will see, Thackeray's choice of his 'design' —that is the term perceptively given to it on p. 85 below—was the principal item of discussion in the reviews. Right to the end some of the reviewers and readers felt that Thackeray had made a mistake in limiting his matter so strictly to one colour. They believed that exceptions were more numerous than his picture allowed. For such readers *Pendennis*, which followed next after *Vanity Fair*, was an improvement: on p. 109 below, Lewes judges its representation of life to be more proportional to the full range. And by the time *The Newcomes* was before them they all agreed that the rigour of choice had been much relaxed. Those who thought this an improvement might have thanked the critics. Forster, reviewing *Vanity Fair* (No. 13), gives Thackeray a friendly hint to expand and so mollify his philosophy, and fully expects the hint to be taken—he had some right to advise, having noted even in early work an occasional kindliness of tone among the more usual 'sneers'. (When in Chapter xiv of *The Newcomes* Thackeray insists, as we note on p. 54 below, that he is *not* sneering, we may be sure that he is pointedly answering the anonymous Forster—and also in the remarks on sneering in Chapter 1 of the same novel; in his correspondence, we may add, he seldom mentions reviews, standing aloof from them, calling them 'flummery' when they were pleasant and, when not, quickly putting them aside with a 'what I have written, I have written!' On p. 266 below, W. C. Roscoe discusses the whole matter and concludes that Thackeray can afford to smile at censure.)

Thackeray's novels puzzled his readers as they would not (except for their nineteenth century trappings) have puzzled Fielding's. Thackeray was a Rip Van Winkle author, a Fielding *redivivus*. He wrote at the prompting of his genius, but his genius did not prompt him to win the heart of the general public. In the end he did succeed in creating, or rather recreating the taste by which he was enjoyed by his tens of thousands. He well knew that he could never hope for the sweep of the Dickens audience.

What readers he had he always 'interested'. This is evinced by the reviewers, who paid him the highest compliment open to novelists and dramatists—that of making his picture of life an opportunity for discussion. His picture they did not dismiss as untrue (as we dismiss Bulwer-Lytton's), or as true but dull (as some contemporary reviewers dismissed Trollope's). They discussed the view of life pictured in *Vanity Fair* and the rest because it was worth discussing. And they discussed it at length and repeatedly because the real and teasing question was just how true it was. They felt that Thackeray demanded of them that they should write with their memories of life aroused. On the first page of our excerpts, the reviewer even of an early work, *The Yellowplush Papers*, found it 'searching'.

It is plain that Thackeray had a strong moral purpose in his fiction and indeed in some of his essays—those conspicuously that make up the *Book of Snobs*. He also had a strong literary purpose, particularly in *Catherine* and *Punch's Prize Novelists*, which held up to ridicule at least some of the characteristics of writers well known at the time. Other works of his, particularly his poem 'Daddy, I'm hungry', written during the great Irish famine, had a political purpose. And it is an indication of the disturbed times that at least one critic noted the absence from his novels of that violent sort—it seemed at the time to be the only purpose worth mentioning, and he bluntly called it 'purpose' without adjectival addition. It was Lewes who found the novels lacking in this desirable addition—Lewes, who was strongly aware of their *moral* purpose (No. 10). At the time when Dickens, Disraeli and Charles Kingsley were producing novels that were at least partly political the absence of politics from Thackeray's was felt to be a limitation. Thackeray, as we infer from his reviews of Disraeli's novels, was not unduly perturbed. He knew that the political purposes of any one time usually pertain to that time only. It would have been a more serious complaint if he had lacked a purpose of the moral sort.

IV

What truthfulness to life Thackeray did achieve he achieved against odds, according to his own way of reckoning, for he would have liked to take in more matter, matter of the sort that was in that age forbidden to writers. In the Preface to *Pendennis* (No. 20) he noted with envy that Fielding could give his readers a complete account of a man—he does not speak of woman—and that no later novelist had dared to. Coarseness had been allowed to all writers up to the late eighteenth century, and had proved especially useful for the comic and satiric writers. From the time of Smollett writers wishing to use it, could use it only in letters to close friends—part of the interest of the unexpurgated editions of the letters of the great nineteenth century writers is that they *are* unexpurgated, and in trying to form a complete picture of literary genius in the nineteenth century we must allow for the great number of brilliant but coarse letters that are still in MS. or that have been destroyed. When all the surviving letters of the great writers are in print we shall find nineteenth century literature more complete in its account of life than hitherto we could have known it to be. The official puritanism was a handicap at least to certain novelists. But having said that, we go on in fairness to say something more. In the first place we cannot but respect the proscription from print of what there had been too much of in actual life. The history of the nineteenth century is partly the history of an increase in personal privacy. There was less human dung seen among the rest in the public streets and pathways. And if there is less indecency in nineteenth century novels than in their predecessors, the diminution had an appropriateness that we must sympathize with. It is no idle claim that is tentatively advanced by J. R. Findlay: 'We would fain hope, indeed we cannot doubt, that there has been improvement, some of it we allow merely external, but certainly not a little real also' (No. 22). And in the second place, the novelists did not wholly ignore the indecency that they were not allowed to paint—they were able to suggest what they needed of it to their adult readers in ways that in themselves called for resource. Among the successes this way is Thackeray's description of Becky's doubtful life after her marriage—he sees her as a mermaid flashing about in dark waters. Not altogether surprisingly, Charlotte Brontë for one entered into this instance of his brilliance with something like relish (No. 12). That was in a letter. In the reviews it could no more be dwelt on than in the novels themselves.

V

One obvious interest of mid-nineteenth century reviews for critics of the contemporary novel is that they discuss what we ourselves are not yet wholly clear about—whether the method of their publication was altogether in the interests of their unity as works of art. It is plain that a novelist publishing in instalments had to bear in mind two sorts of reader—those who read the parts as they came out at monthly or weekly intervals, and those future readers who read the work as they read *Paradise Lost* or *Tom Jones* with the whole before them before they began. Our mid-twentieth century view—if it is clear enough to be called a view—is that the great novelists could satisfy both sorts of readers by moulding the part and arranging for it to fit into the whole. On the evidence here before us we have contemporary critics reaching a different decision. Those who comment on it think that the novelists are satisfying their first short-term public without due regard for their second. Rintoul found *Vanity Fair* rather loose in structure—he is prompted to use the word 'bits' (No. 14)—and he did not see why *Pendennis* should not have expanded into another twenty-four numbers (No. 23). This deficiency of plot he puts down as an inevitable 'defect of periodical publication'. Masson agreed: he saw periodical publication as one of the 'two literary devices or fashions' of the moment that detract from a novel's 'chance of having readers among posterity' (No. 25). And Samuel Phillips tells us that his hopes were raised when he heard that for *Esmond* Thackeray had 'resolved to eschew the serial form of publication and to make his next venture under the circumstances best calculated to display a writer's powers and to achieve permanent success', adding that 'month to month writing is but hand to mouth work, and satisfies neither author nor reader' (No. 32). Indeed Thackeray had adopted the new form of publication expressly to meet the complaint of casualness that the reviewers had brought up against him—not having enough faith in his discovery that a novel is not necessarily the better for having a defined rather than a loose shape. With *Bleak House* before us, not to mention *Vanity Fair* and Thackeray's other big novels, we think nowadays that the contemporary critics were hasty in their judgement. It is true that Henry James described mid-nineteenth century novels as 'large loose baggy monsters' but that was because he was trying to write novels that were more like racehorses—racehorses, we must add, that are given to browsing and an aversion from racing. If a novel is rightly called a monster that means that it is a live organism, and if it has bagginess it is as part of its organism. James saw this, as of course he would. Among his instances of monsters is *The Newcomes*, but, as he gladly concedes, it 'has life'.[1] There is one sort of organism for *The Awkward Age* and *The Golden Bowl*, and another sort for the novels of Dickens and Thackeray.

One further point about the constraints put on novelists by the

[1] Preface to *The Tragic Muse*.

methods imposed by the book trade. When Masson referred to the contemporary 'literary devices and fashions' he said they were two in number. The second of them was the novel in three volumes. We now know that this form of publication was not so much a rigid thing for the author as for the printer. Since that excellent statistical article by C. E. and E. S. Lauterbach in the *Papers of the Bibliographical Society of America* of 1957, 'The Nineteenth Century three-volume Novel', we have become aware that a far from very long novel could have its type so arranged by the printer as to fill out the three volumes demanded by the trade. Not all nineteenth century novels were of the length to demand three volumes inevitably, and this means that for the authors the demands of the trade were so much the less rigid.

From the items we have selected, it will be seen that *Barry Lyndon* was praised in the nineteenth century, as in the mid-twentieth century, for its well-constructed plot. In other words Aristotle with his liking for plot of that sort was still powerful as a theorist. Already, however, a new conception of plot was arising, in the forming of which Thackeray was a pioneer and 'powerful contributor' (No. 46). It was seen that a novel might achieve unity without having an action constructed as patently and methodically as a complicated diagram in Euclid. It was even seen that an action that was constructed loosely had something precious to commend it, which a well worked-out Chinese puzzle lacked. Robert Bell hit the nail on the head: 'The whole business of the fiction [of *Vanity Fair*] moves on before us, with as little reference to the beginning, middle, or end [he is using Aristotle's criterion], as the progress of one's own life' (No. 15). It was seen that a loose progressiveness represented life more faithfully than did the elaborate diagram of interlocking events, especially when too many of those events fell, at the behest of the diagram, into the doubtful class of coincidences. A plot was too often an imposition on life rather than an imitation of it. Elizabeth Rigby may not have seen how damaging to the older idea of plot were her remarks on the action of *Vanity Fair*:

It is not a novel, in the common acceptation of the word, with a plot purposely contrived to bring about certain scenes . . . but simply a history of those average sufferings, pleasures, penalties, and rewards to which various classes of mankind gravitate as naturally and certainly in this world as the sparks fly upward. (No. 18.)

Not a plot, not a purposeful contrivance, but a history, and 'simply' so. And though there were still critics who looked for purposeful contrivance, Goldwin Smith considered that the time had come to allow that there is room for both the tight and the loose construction, both being good of their kind (No. 45). We all like the evolutions of a cat's cradle, and we all like the way the length of string falls into curling lines when dropped on the carpet. Meanwhile there had been the contribution to the topic made by Roscoe in the review that is one of the high-lights of our anthology (No. 44). With his remark that Thackeray cuts 'a square out of life', he almost stumbles on the phrase that was to become standard for critics—the 'slice of life'. No doubt one of the reasons for the loosening of the plot was an increased interest in persons—in their character and in what significantly was coming to be called their 'personality'. We saw above that Masson thought that it was on the 'originality and interest of its characters that a novel is chiefly judged'—on its characters, not, as Aristotle said, on its plot. More than any other mid-nineteenth century novelist, Thackeray was working on these new lines, and that is one reason why he was some-times compared to Sterne, as by Bagehot (No. 55). *Tristram Shandy*, which had looked freakish beside *Tom Jones*, looked less so beside *Vanity Fair*.

VI

One thing the critics were agreed about from the start was the quality of the English Thackeray wrote, and it is a mark of their competence to handle great literature that they see the importance of the way language is used in it. When Thackeray reviewed Carlyle's *French Revolution* in 1837 he saw it as a work of genius, but was clearly reluctant to praise the genius shown in its noisy use of language. Accordingly it is not surprising to find Lewes responding to the language of Thackeray as that of 'the quietest perhaps of all contempo-rary writers', the writer least given to 'emphasis' (No. 10). His critics vie with each other in describing his style. From the first it earns such epithets as 'easy, masculine, felicitous, humorous and pleasant' (from Lewes) (No. 10), 'easy, close, pregnant' (from Rintoul) (No. 14), 'fresh' and 'fluent' (from Bell) (No. 15), 'clear and wholesome' (from the *Athenæum*) (No. 20), and so on. Lewes enlarged on it (No. 24), and Masson institutes a comparison of Thackeray's style with Dickens's (No. 25). One of the best compliments paid him is Bell's: 'No writer is less of a mannerist' (No. 15).

George Brimley discerned moral principle behind Thackeray's achievement as a writer expressing thought as well as the more concrete matter demanded by a novel. In his criticism of *Esmond*, he gives two reasons for finding the English 'manly, clear, terse, and vigorous', the first of which is that Thackeray 'does not give the public thoughts half-worked-out'. (Perhaps, we may interpose, Thackeray did sometimes err this way—even if his discussion on rogues at the close of *Catherine* goes deep (No. 4), it does not go as deep as his other novels must have brought him to see: brilliant and clear as the discussion is, it could have gone deeper, and still remained brilliant and clear—for Becky herself is a rogue and yet has her own range of virtues, as Nassau Senior noted (No. 36).) Brimley's second reason is that Thackeray avoids 'thoughts on matters where clear thinking is impossible'. In the nineteenth century there were many inducements to vaporize about the hundred new intellectual puzzles that were coming into view, and many mid-nineteenth century authors wrote in the mere hope that what they said about them would turn out to be true. Meanwhile their writing lacked clarity. Thackeray is given due credit for what Matthew Arnold saw as a process of staking posts on the frontiers of knowledge as far as light stretched. For Brimley this was a moral merit of Thackeray's.

Brimley spoke of 'thoughts'. A novelist, even a nineteenth century novelist, is not usually concerned with them. If Thackeray is clear as a novelist, his clarity is usually that of one who is narrating and describing. He achieves clarity of this sort by allowing his personages space to breathe and turn round in. Elizabeth Rigby, and others elsewhere, saw that the texture of the narration is closely matted (No. 18). That is true, but, as was also seen, the moving pictures are not crowded any more than a well-filled dance hall is when the dancers are expert. Abraham Hayward noted 'the apparent ease with which such a number and variety of characters are brought upon the stage without crossing or jostling' (No. 9). And there is similar but even stronger praise from Bell (No. 15).

Brimley's mentioning of 'thoughts' reminds us that one of the main characteristics of Thackeray's novels is the amount of authorial thinking in them—indeed the amount of it might be said to have led to his creating a new form for the novel, one which greatly benefited Charles Reade and Henry Kingsley. The reviewers do not say as much about this commentary as we might expect. Nassau Senior objected to it (No. 36), though surely the right comment is that of Elwin, who thinks that it cannot be spared on æsthetic grounds: 'These disquisitions would be blemishes if they were not signal beauties ... As it is, there is nothing which could so little be spared' (No. 41).

VII

It was during the progress of his commentary that Thackeray mainly constructed his authorial personality. Not all critics have been pleased with the result. Bell's praise is perhaps ambiguous: 'He dissects his victims with a smile; and performs the cruellest of operations on their self-love with a pleasantry which looks provokingly very like good-nature' (No. 15). But it is clear that Forster does not like it—he saw Thackeray as adopting too superior an attitude towards his personages, and therefore towards mankind (No. 30). What Forster was objecting to was in part something that was rarer in nineteenth century literature than in eighteenth century, something that can truly be called by that much misused term 'classical'. The great and perhaps final difference between the romantic and the classical is that between writing in which the writer is felt to be palpitating with earnestness and writing done with seeming coolness, at arm's length, as it were, distanced, and so enclosed in calm. We remember that Thackeray advised Charlotte Brontë not to be in a passion with her personages (which would do as an instance of his joint clearness and profundity), and we also remember that the young and greatly earnest Meredith envied the calm way Thackeray dealt with his own in *The Virginians*. There is something to be said for the godlike, as there is something to be said for the earnestly participant. Thackeray supplied both sorts. If as a narrator he proceeded as if a withdrawn onlooker, he spoke 'earnestly' when interspersing his commentary.

That earnestness was of the friendly sort. In her *Autobiography* Harriet Martineau noted the 'vigilance' he exercised over his person-ages, and also his 'sympathy' for them, describing both as 'paternal'. And Findlay quietly noted (No. 22) that Thackeray's voice when he is speaking of them is that of 'a brother not a judge', countering in advance the charge that Forster was to bring (No. 30). Another word for the same sort of thing is 'gentlemanly'. How often the reviewers noted that Thackeray's authorial personality was 'gentlemanly'! In the mid-nineteenth century to be so described was counted a compli-ment, as it would be an insult or something like it if used of an author

14

today. But the thing itself existed then in Thackeray as it exists in people and writers of today, even if that particular word for it is now out of favour. Another tarnished critical term of the nineteenth century is 'charm'. The reviewers applied it to Thackeray's authorial personality as Carlyle applied it to Elizabethan and seventeenth century prose, and Arnold to writings as various as those of Chaucer, Milton, Voltaire and Shelley, and Henry James to those of Scott. By 'charm' they meant power to attract, to be found likeable, and it therefore largely replaced the endearing eighteenth century critical term 'elegant'. Honouring the historical sense as the first requisite of a good critic, we can only say that anybody who cannot respect the term for what it meant in the nineteenth century is no fit critic of the critics using it. Thackeray described Dickens's writing as 'charming', and added 'that answers everything'. He glossed charm as 'wonderful sweetness and freshness' (No. 26).

There is one further word to say of the personality that was assumed by Thackeray in his novels. He conveys the impression that literature is a part of life and only a part, that there are seasons when it fades into the background. How touched he would have been by what we record on p. 189 below—that Nassau Senior's daughter apologized for her dying father because he would have regretted what was disapproving in the tone of his criticism, now that Thackeray had just died.

VIII

We have had little but praise for these reviewers, and the reader of our book will see that that course is the just one. But they had their defects, according to the Thackerayan law that so many of them shrank from. To begin with they are a little unsure in their judgement of a writer's rank on the permanent scale of greatness. Even the excellent Masson could speak in the same breath of 'Dickens, Thackeray and Jerrold', just as the great Matthew Arnold could include Campbell and Moore in a list of the great poets of the early nineteenth century. And in the mid-nineteenth century it was so often assumed, as by Mrs. Oliphant in a long review of Thackeray's works to date, which appeared anonymously in *Blackwood's Magazine*, that the greatest novelist of the nineteenth century was Bulwer-Lytton (No. 37). We recall that Matthew Arnold declined to write of his contemporaries (and almost completely lived up to the proscription) on the very ground that contemporary taste was unstable. Perhaps also we miss from the critics we have reprinted a power or at least a taste for analysis. They can well describe Thackeray's style, for instance, but they do not pause to note and describe what we might call its orchestration. Nor do they describe the means by which the commentary becomes part of the narrative. On the other hand, their reviews, now that some of the best are available here, may help to right a wrong. In the nineteenth century there was less neglect of Thackeray's early and minor writings than there is now. An anonymous reviewer described them as 'sparkling' (No. 3), which they precisely are.

We may leave the reviewers, remembering a phrase from one of them that includes as much of Thackeray as any phrase only two words long could do—Nassau Senior (No. 36) speaks of his 'exquisite truth'.

THE YELLOWPLUSH PAPERS

in *Fraser's Magazine*, November 1837–August 1838
January 1840

1. Unsigned review, the *Spectator*

4 January 1840, xiii, 17. Part of a notice of *Fraser's Magazine* for
January 1840.

... the story of *Catherine*, with its strong, coarse, literal painting of
men and manners in the profligate classes of the profligate times of
Queen ANNE, advances to its close. The gem of the number is a letter
from the illustrious flunky [sic] Charles Yellowplush to his brother
littérateur the 'Honrabble Barnet' Sir E. L. Bulwer, on the '*Sea Capting*'
and the 'preface to the fourth edition!'.[1] As a piece of criticism it is
sound and searching; and the playful, yet cutting ridicule, is so adroitly
applied that one would think MAGINN himself had donned the
masquerade livery of Yellowplush and held the pen of his pantry
friend the 'sellebrated Mr. Smith'.[2] It is also distinguished by a great
deal of sense, and 'the Honrabble Barnet' might do worse than follow
Yellowplush's advice.

[1] Bulwer's *The Sea Captain; or, the Birth-Right*, was first performed at the Haymarket
Theatre on 31 October 1839, and was published in the same year.
[2] William Maginn (1794–1842), who helped to found *Fraser's Magazine* in 1830, was
notorious for his 'slashing', ebullient writing in that periodical and others. Thackeray
knew him well, and depicted him as Captain Shandon in *Pendennis*.

2. Thackeray, from a letter to his mother

18 January 1840 (*Letters*, i, 412)

A new Yellowplush addressed to Bulwer has made a great noise and has hit the Baronet pretty smartly. It is very good-natured however: but you won't like that either: and it is better that ladies should not relish such grotesque humour: Rabelais, Fielding & so forth (apart the indecencies) are not good reading for women, & only for a small race of men—I don't mean to compare myself to one or the other mind—but the style of humour is the same.

3. The *Atlas*. Unsigned review of *Comic Tales and Sketches* (1841), 'Edited and Illustrated by Mr. Michael Angelo Titmarsh'

19 June 1841, 399

This collection in two volumes contained *The Yellowplush Papers*, *The Tremendous Adventures of Major Gahagan*, *The Professor*, *The Bedford Row Conspiracy* and *Stubbs's Calendar*.

There is some good sense very roughly delivered in these volumes. The author is a humourist, but, unhappily, his humour lies on the ill-natured side of things, and he can hardly ever say a funny thing without blending it with a sarcasm. We need not describe the inevitable consequences of this original defect of taste. It lowers the tone of his pleasantry, changes the sparkling relish to a bitter flavour, infuses an essential vulgarity into the whole work, and deprives it not only of the applause to which the writer's merits under more auspicious circumstances would entitle him, but of all chance of being generally read.

The personalities of this work are not merely gross in themselves, but they are gratuitous. *Mr. Yellowplush*, who thinks as well as writes like a footman, goes out of his way to fling dirt at people he happens to dislike; but it is a thousand to one whether he does not offend the bulk of his readers by such proceedings, even more than the objects of his gutter abuse.

MR. TITMARSH ought to seek subjects better suited to his talents than such topics as these. He has a vein of vigorous whim in him that will not fail him, if he tries a higher flight. Mere personalities—or, still worse, naked and shallow national prejudices—are beneath contempt. The utmost they can achieve for a writer, is to surround him for a moment with a little notoriety, which dies out as fast as a flash of fireworks, and leaves him in his former darkness. It is the business of a philosophical satirist to abandon the paths of personal malice, and generalize the attributes of society. If he cannot do this, but is still compelled from narrowness of intellect, or poverty of heart to hang upon the skirts of scandal, then there is no hope for him. This is not so with MICHAEL ANGELO TITMARSH. Why then does he not do something worthy of himself?

CATHERINE

in *Fraser's Magazine*, May–August, November 1839
January–February 1840

4. Thackeray, *Catherine*, the end of the novel

(*Works*, iii, 183–7)

Ring, ding, ding! the gloomy green curtain drops, the *dramatis personae* are duly disposed of, the nimble candle-snuffers put out the lights, and the audience goeth pondering home. If the critic take the pains to ask why the author, who hath been so diffuse in describing the early and fabulous acts of Mrs. Catherine's existence, should so hurry off the catastrophe where a deal of the very finest writing might have been employed, Solomons[1] replies that the 'ordinary' narrative as above condensed by him, is far more emphatic than any composition of his own could be, with all the rhetorical graces which he might employ. Mr. Aram's trial, as taken by the penny-a-liners of those days, hath always interested him more than the lengthened and poetical report which an eminent novelist (who hath lately, in compliment to his writings, been gratified by a permission to wear a bloody hand) has given of the same. Mr. Turpin's adventures are more instructive and agreeable to him in the account of the Newgate Plutarch, than in the learned Ainsworth's *Biographical Dictionary*;[2] and as he believes that the professional gentlemen who are employed to invest such heroes with the rewards that their great actions merit, will go through the ceremony of the grand cordon with much more accuracy and dispatch than can be shown by the most distinguished amateur; in like manner he thinks that the history of such investitures should be written by people directly concerned, and not by admiring persons without, who must be ignorant of many of the secrets of ketchcraft. We very much

---

[1] Thackeray wrote *Catherine* under the pseudonym of 'Ikey Solomons, Esq. Junior'.

[2] Thackeray alludes to *Eugene Aram* (1832) by Bulwer, who had been made a baronet in 1837, and to *Rookwood* (1834) by Ainsworth.

doubt if Milton himself could make a description of an execution half so horrible as yonder simple lines from the *Daily Post* of a hundred and ten years since, that now lies before us, 'herrlich wie am ersten tag,'—as bright and clean as on the day of publication. Think of it! it has been read by Belinda at her toilet, scanned at Button's and Will's, sneered at by wits, talked of in palaces and cottages by a busy race in wigs, red heels, hoops, patches, and rags of all variety—a busy race that hath long since plunged and vanished in the unfathomable gulf, towards which we march so briskly.

Where are they? 'Afflavit Deus,'—and they are gone! Hark! is not the same wind roaring still that shall sweep us down? and yonder stands the compositor at his types who shall put up a pretty paragraph some day to say how, '*Yesterday*, at his house in Grosvenor Square;' or, 'At Botany Bay, universally regretted,' died So-and-so. Into what profound moralities is the paragraph concerning Mrs. Catherine's burning leading us!

Aye, truly, and to that very point have we wished to come; for, having finished our delectable meal, it behoves us to say a word or two by way of grace at its conclusion, and be heartily thankful that it is over. It has been the writer's object carefully to exclude from his drama (except in two very insignificant instances—mere walking gentlemen parts), any characters but those of scoundrels of the very highest degree. That he has not altogether failed in the object he had in view, is evident from some newspaper critiques which he has had the good fortune to see; and which abuse the tale of *Catherine* as one of the dullest, most vulgar and immoral works extant. It is highly gratifying to the author to find that such opinions are abroad, as they convince him that the taste for Newgate literature is on the wane, and that when the public critic has right down undisguised immorality set before him, the honest creature is shocked at it, as he should be, and can declare his indignation in good round terms of abuse. The characters of the tale *are* immoral, and no doubt of it; but the writer humbly hopes the end is not so. The public was, in our notion, dosed and poisoned by the prevailing style of literary practice, and it was necessary to administer some medicine that would produce a wholesome nausea, and afterwards bring about a more healthy habit.

And, thank Heaven, this effect *has* been produced in very many instances, and that the *Catherine* cathartic has acted most efficaciously. The author has been pleased, sir, at the disgust which his work has excited, and has watched with benevolent carefulness the wry faces that have been made by many of the patients who have swallowed the dose. Solomons remembers, at the establishment in Birchin Lane, where he had the honour of receiving his education, there used to be administered to the boys a certain cough-medicine, which was so excessively agreeable that all the lads longed to have colds in order to partake of the remedy. Sir, some of our popular novelists have compounded their drugs in a similar way, and made them so palatable, that a public, once healthy and honest, has been wellnigh poisoned by their wares. Solomons defies anyone to say the like of himself—that his doses have been as pleasant as champagne, and his pills as sweet as barley-sugar;—it has been his attempt to make vice to appear entirely vicious; and in those instances where he hath occasionally introduced something like virtue, to make the sham as evident as possible, and not allow the meanest capacity a single chance to mistake it.

And what has been the consequence? That wholesome nausea which it has been his good fortune to create wherever he has been allowed to practise in his humble circle.

Has anyone thrown away a halfpenny-worth of sympathy upon any person mentioned in this history? Surely no. But abler and more famous men than Solomons have taken a different plan; and it becomes every man in his vocation to cry out against such, and expose their errors as best he may.

To begin with Mr. Dickens. No one has read that remarkable tale of *Oliver Twist* without being interested in poor Nancy and her murderer; and especially amused and tickled by the gambols of the Artful Dodger and his companions. The power of the writer is so amazing, that the reader at once becomes his captive, and must follow him withersoever he leads; and to what are we led? Breathless to watch all the crimes of Fagin, tenderly to deplore the errors of Nancy, to have for Bill Sikes a kind of pity and admiration, and an absolute love for the society of the Dodger. All these heroes stepped from the novel on to the stage; and the whole London public, from peers to chimney-sweeps, were interested about a set of ruffians whose occupations are thievery, murder, and prostitution. A most agreeable set of rascals, indeed, who have their virtues, too, but not good company for any man. We had better pass them by in decent silence; for, as no writer can or dare tell the *whole* truth concerning them, and faithfully explain their vices, there is no need to give *ex-parte* statements of their virtues.

And what came of *Oliver Twist?* The public wanted something more extravagant still, more sympathy for thieves, and so *Jack Sheppard* makes his appearance.[1] Jack and his two wives, and his faithful Blueskin, and his gin-drinking mother, that sweet Magdalen!—with what a wonderful gravity are all their adventures related, with what an honest simplicity and vigour does Jack's biographer record his actions and virtues! We are taught to hate Wild, to be sure; but then it is because he betrays thieves, the rogue! And yet bad, ludicrous, monstrous as the idea of this book is, we read, and read, and are interested, too. The author has a wondrous faith, and a most respectable notion, of the vastness of his subject. There is not one particle of banter in his composition; good and bad ideas, he hatches all with the same great gravity; and is just as earnest in his fine description of the storm on the Thames, and his admirable account of the escape from Newgate; as in the scenes in Whitefriars, and the conversation at Wild's, than which nothing was ever written more curiously unnatural. We are not, however, here criticizing the novels, but simply have to speak of the Newgate part of them, which gives birth to something a great deal worse than bad taste, and familiarizes the public with notions of crime. In the dreadful satire of *Jonathan Wild*, no reader is so dull as to make the mistake of admiring, and can overlook the grand and hearty contempt of the author for the character he has described; the bitter wit of the *Beggar's Opera*, too, hits the great, by showing their similarity with the wretches that figure in the play; and though the latter piece is so brilliant in its mask of gaiety and wit, that a very dull person may not see the dismal reality thus disguised, moral, at least, there is in the satire, for those who will take the trouble to find it. But in the sorrows of Nancy and the exploits of Sheppard, there is no such lurking moral, as far as we have been able to discover; we are asked for downright sympathy in the one case, and are called on in the second to admire the gallantry of a thief. The street-walker may be a very virtuous person, and the robber as brave as Wellington; but it is better to leave them alone, and their qualities, good and bad. The pathos of the workhouse scenes in *Oliver Twist*, of the Fleet Prison descriptions in *Pickwick*, *is* genuine and pure—as much of this as you please; as tender a hand to the poor, as kindly a word to the unhappy, as you will; but, in the name of common-sense, let us not expend our sympathies on cutthroats, and other such prodigies of evil!

---

[1] Ainsworth's novel, published January 1839–February 1840 in *Bentley's Miscellany*. The serialization of this, one of the most popular of the Newgate novels, was the immediate reason for Thackeray's writing *Catherine*.

Labouring under such ideas, Mr. Isaac Solomons, junior, produced the romance of Mrs. Cat, and confesses himself completely happy to have brought it to a conclusion. His poem may be dull—aye, and probably is. The great Blackmore, the great Dennis, the great Sprat, the great Pomfret,[1] not to mention great men of our own time—have they not also been dull, and had pretty reputations, too? Be it granted Solomons *is* dull, but don't attack his morality; he humbly submits that, in his poem, no man shall mistake virtue for vice, no man shall allow a single sentiment of pity or admiration to enter his bosom for any character of the piece; it being, from beginning to end, a scene of unmixed rascality performed by persons who never deviate into good feeling; and, although he doth not pretend to equal the great modern authors whom he hath mentioned, in wit or descriptive power, yet, in the point of moral, he meekly believes that he has been their superior; feeling the greatest disgust for the characters he describes, and using his humble endeavour to cause the public also to hate them.

5. Thackeray, from letters to his mother

February and March 1840 (*Letters*, i, 421, 432–3)

The Judges stand [up] for me: Carlyle says Catherine is wonderful, and many more laud it highly, b[ut it is] a disgusting subject & no mistake. I wish I had taken a pleasanter one & am [now] and have been for a fortnight in the pains of labor: horrible they are: and dreadfully cross to my poor little wife in consequence.

. . . it is very ingenious in you to find such beauties in Catherine wh. was a mistake all through—it was not made disgusting enough that is the fact, and the triumph of it would have been to make readers so horribly horrified as to cause them to give up or rather throw up the book and all of it's [*sic*] kind, whereas you see the author had a sneaking kindness for his heroine, and did not like to make her utterly worthless.

---

[1] Sir Richard Blackmore (1653–1729), Thomas Sprat (1635–1713) and John Pomfret (1667–1702) are included in Johnson's *Lives of the English Poets;* John Dennis (1657–1734), critic and playwright, is perhaps still best known for his inclusion in *The Dunciad.*

THE PARIS SKETCH BOOK

1840

6. Unsigned review, the *Spectator*

18 July 1840, xiii, 689

A collection of clever and smart papers, of the better kind of light magazine articles, and half of which have already appeared in periodicals; consisting of sketches and stories descriptive of Parisian life and character, with discursive remarks on French novels, dramas, and pictures. The flippant touch-and-go style of magazine-writing, where commonplace labours to appear dashing and brilliant, is not fit, however, for continuous reading: hence it may be that the sarcastic humour of this writer appears occasionally forced, and his descriptions exaggerated. This broad caricature style is suitable to the characteristics of demireps and gamblers, amongst whom he is most at home. His vein of humour is essentially satirical; it is too severe and biting to be pleasant. His etchings are masterly, and distinguished by grotesque drollery, of a caustic kind, that is shown to advantage in hitting off the expression of villains and their dupes.

BARRY LYNDON

in *Fraser's Magazine*, January–September, November–December
1844; revised, in *Miscellanies: Prose and Verse*, iii, 1856

---

7. [James Fitzjames Stephen], from a review in the *Saturday Review*

27 December 1856, ii, 783–5

Stephen (1829–94), brother of Leslie Stephen, barrister and
judge, and author of books on law, wrote prolifically for several
periodicals, contributing over three hundred articles to the
Saturday Review between 1855 and 1868.

Whatever we may think of the policy of republishing some parts of
Mr. Thackeray's *Miscellanies*, there can be no doubt that English
literature would have sustained a serious loss if *Barry Lyndon* had still
been buried in the pages of a magazine. In some respects, it appears to
us the most characteristic and best executed of Mr. Thackeray's novels,
though it is far less known, and is likely, we think, to be less popular
than the rest. *Barry Lyndon* is the history of a scoundrel from his own
point of view, and combines the habitual freshness of Fielding with a
large measure of the grave irony of *Jonathan Wild*. To be able, with
perfect decency and propriety, to take up his abode in the very heart
of a most unmitigated blackguard and scoundrel, and to show how,
as a matter of course, and without any kind of denial or concealment,
he *bonâ fide* considers himself one of the best and greatest of men, is
surely one of the hardest tasks which could be imposed on an author;
yet Mr. Thackeray has undertaken and executed it with perfect
success. . . .

[Summary of the story.]

Such is Mr. Barry's career—a riotous and miserable youth, a manhood of infamy, and an old age of ruin and beggary. Yet the genius

of the novelist not only makes us feel that his hero would naturally look upon himself as a wronged and virtuous man—'the victim,' as he is made to say on his title-page, 'of many cruel persecutions, conspiracies, and slanders,'—but also that even in this wretched kind of existence all was not bad—that wheat as well as tares grow in the most unkindly and ill-cultivated soil. The ability with which this is managed is quite wonderful. The whole book is founded on the great principle, that if a man only lies hardily enough and long enough, nothing is easier for him than to impose upon himself. In nine cases out of ten, hypocrisy is nothing else than self-deception. Describe the transactions in which you are engaged, not as your neighbours would describe them, but as you yourself would wish them to be, and it is surprising how soon they will appear to be capable of no other construction. Barry Lyndon's fundamental and universal postulate is, that he is a good and gallant man, that he is a model of manly virtue, and that, therefore, though he may be occasionally subject to human infirmities, his actions must always be, on the whole, in accordance with his character. . . .

The parenthesis which marks the point at which Mr. Barry has succeeded in convincing himself that his profession is, on the whole, highly honourable and noble, though a few mean interlopers may disgrace it, is inconceivably ludicrous, and shows a depth of humour almost sublime. It is a sort of typical specimen of the spirit which makes a free negro talk with contempt of 'black fellows,' or the vulgarest dandies who disgrace our name and nation on the Continent sneer at 'those English.' To show how Mr. Barry contrives to look upon himself as an ill-used man through the whole of his eventful life, would require little less than an abstract of the entire book. We may mention more particularly, however, his wonderful account of his relations to his wife, in which, after detailing with a high moral tone the measures which he thought necessary to bring her to a sense of her conjugal duties—consisting in a long series of the most brutal acts of tyranny and violence—he describes with a sort of contemptuous pity her low spirits, nervousness, bad health, and general dulness, and concludes by the quiet remark—'My company from this fancied I was a tyrant over her; whereas I was only a severe and careful guardian over a silly, bad-tempered, and weak-minded lady.' [Ch. xvii.] We have not the slightest doubt that such a man would seriously and *bonâ fide* take exactly that view of such conduct. Indeed, why should he not? It is much pleasanter to consider oneself a man of sense and honour than a low-minded villain; and to one who wishes to do so, and knows how to set about it, it is quite as easy.

The conception of Barry Lyndon's character involves, however, some grains of good. Indeed, their absence in any man whatever would have been conclusive evidence that the book in which he was depicted was not written by Mr. Thackeray. His courage is genuine courage. He really is a very brave man; and although he knows it, and is inordinately vain of it, we think the picture is true to nature. Sydney Smith long ago pointed out that where there is a great deal of vanity, there is generally some talent; and Mr. Thackeray seems to us to have shown his unusual acuteness in exposing the fallacy of the common notion that a bully and a braggart is generally a coward. We should agree with him in thinking such faults some evidence of courage—though of a courage lower both in kind and degree than that which such a person would claim. There is great beauty also in the parental affection which Mr. Thackeray ventures to attribute to this utter scoundrel. He has a son by his second wife, and loves him tenderly, wildly, passionately, with a sort of fierce instinct such as any other brute might show. He is almost heartbroken at his death, and, in his lowest degradation, wears a lock of his hair round his neck. There is something not only touching, but deeply true, in such a representation. It recognises the fact that a strong, unbridled character, full of fierce appetites and ungoverned passions, is not utterly devilish—that it sometimes gives birth to virtues, rough and animal, if you please, but still genuine. The character of old Mrs. Barry, the hero's mother, is a further illustration of the same thing. She is a greedy, proud, unprincipled woman, capable by turns of meanness, haughtiness, fanaticism, and gross cruelty; yet she loves her son dearly through all. There is something wonderfully true in the unity with which the character is drawn. During her son's absence in Prussia, the fanatical side of her character comes out, and she falls under the dominion of a hypocritical scoundrel, called Jowls, who wants to marry her. Her son visits Ireland, fights a duel, and comes to his mother for refuge. Mr. Jowls is scandalized and frightened, and wants to turn out the fugitive, saying 'he would have had the gentleman avoid the drink, and the quarrel, and the wicked duel altogether.' Whereupon 'my mother cut him short by saying "that such sort of conduct might be very well in a person of his cloth and his birth, but it neither became a Barry nor a Brady." In fact she was quite delighted with the thought that I had pinked an English marquis's son in a duel; and so, to console her, I told her of a score more in which I had been engaged . . .' [Ch. xv.] The curtain ultimately falls upon the tough old lady, supporting her blackguard broken-down offspring in his captivity by the labour of her own hands, and on the wrecks of her property.

Artistically considered, we should almost be inclined to place *Barry Lyndon* at the head of the list of Mr. Thackeray's books. It has an immense advantage over his better known works in being far shorter—for which reason the plot is clearer, simpler, and more connected that it is in *Vanity Fair, Pendennis,* or the *Newcomes.* Every page carries the story on, and with the exception of Barry's meeting with his uncle at Berlin, and of a rather melodramatic episode which takes place at a small German court, the story is as natural and easy as if it were true. We have attempted to show that the book has a moral, if the reader knows how to look for it; but it is kept in its proper place, and is suggested by the facts, instead of suggesting them. In most of Mr. Thackeray's more elaborate performances, his own views of the world appear to us to be insisted on too openly and too often; but there is nothing of this in *Barry Lyndon.* It is neither a melancholy nor a cheerful book, but a fair and wonderfully skilful portrait of a man whom we feel as if we had known personally. The accessories are described in as life-like and vigorous a manner as the main subject. We do not think that Mr. Thackeray's extraordinary power of description was ever more strongly illustrated than in the sketches which this volume contains of the wild, mad Irish life of Dublin and the provinces in the last century—of the horrible mechanism of man-stealing and espionage by which Frederick II. maintained his power—of the strange career (half-highwayman, half-*grand seigneur*) of a professional gambler—or of the petty Courts in which, before the French Revolution, so many sham sovereigns played at kings and queens, with human beings for their counters. All these, and many other subjects of the same kind, are sketched off rapidly, easily, and with a life and distinctness altogether marvellous in a volume which will not last an active reader through a very long railway journey. . . .

8. Anthony Trollope, *Thackeray*

1879, 70–76

In imagination, language, construction, and general literary capacity, Thackeray never did anything more remarkable than *Barry Lyndon*. I have quoted the words which he put into the mouth of Ikey Solomon, declaring that in the story which he has there told he has created nothing but disgust for the wicked characters he has produced, and that he has 'used his humble endeavours to cause the public also to hate them.'[1] Here, in *Barry Lyndon*, he has, probably unconsciously, acted in direct opposition to his own principles. Barry Lyndon is as great a scoundrel as the mind of man ever conceived. He is one who might have taken as his motto Satan's words; 'Evil, be thou my good.' And yet his story is so written that it is almost impossible not to entertain something of a friendly feeling for him. He tells his own adventures as a card-sharper, bully, and liar; as a heartless wretch, who had neither love nor gratitude in his composition; who had no sense even of loyalty; who regarded gambling as the highest occupation to which a man could devote himself, and fraud as always justified by success; a man possessed by all meannesses except cowardice. And the reader is so carried away by his frankness and energy as almost to rejoice when he succeeds, and to grieve with him when he is brought to the ground.

The man is perfectly satisfied as to the reasonableness,—I might almost say, as to the rectitude,—of his own conduct throughout. He is one of a decayed Irish family, that could boast of good blood. His father had obtained possession of the remnants of the property by turning Protestant, thus ousting the elder brother, who later on becomes his nephew's confederate in gambling. The elder brother is true to the old religion, and as the law stood in the last century, the younger brother, by changing his religion, was able to turn him out. Barry, when a boy, learns the slang and the gait of the debauched gentlemen of the day. He is specially proud of being a gentleman by birth and manners. He had been kidnapped, and made to serve as a

---

[1] See above, p. 24.

common soldier, but boasts that he was at once fit for the occasion when enabled to show as a court gentleman. 'I came to it at once,' he says, 'and as if I had never done anything else all my life. I had a gentleman to wait upon me, a French *friseur* to dress my hair of a morning. I knew the taste of chocolate as by intuition almost, and could distinguish between the right Spanish and the French before I had been a week in my new position. I had rings on all my fingers, watches in both my fobs, canes, trinkets, and snuffboxes of all sorts . . . I had the finest natural taste for lace and china of any man I ever knew.' (Ch. ix.)

To dress well, to wear a sword with a grace, to carry away his plunder with affected indifference, and to appear to be equally easy when he loses his last ducat, to be agreeable to women, and to look like a gentleman,—these are his accomplishments. In one place he rises to the height of a grand professor in the art of gambling, and gives his lessons with almost a noble air. 'Play grandly, honourably. Be not of course cast down at losing; but above all, be not eager at winning, as mean souls are.' And he boasts of his accomplishments with so much eloquence as to make the reader sure that he believes in them. He is quite pathetic over himself, and can describe with heartrending words the evils that befall him when others use against him successfully any of the arts which he practises himself.

The marvel of the book is not so much that the hero should evidently think well of himself, as that the author should so tell his story as to appear to be altogether on the hero's side. In *Catherine*, the horrors described are most truly disgusting,—so much that the story, though very clever, is not pleasant reading. The *Memoirs of Barry Lyndon* are very pleasant to read. There is nothing to shock or disgust. The style of narrative is exactly that which might be used as to the exploits of a man whom the author intended to represent as deserving of sympathy and praise,—so that the reader is almost brought to sympathise. But I should be doing an injustice to Thackeray if I were to leave an impression that he had taught lessons tending to evil practice, such as he supposed to have been left by *Jack Sheppard* or *Eugene Aram*. No one will be tempted to undertake the life of a *chevalier d'industrie* by reading the book, or be made to think that cheating at cards is either an agreeable or a profitable profession. The following is excellent as a tirade in favour of gambling, coming from Redmond de Balibari, as he came to be called during his adventures abroad, but it will hardly persuade anyone to be a gambler. [Quotation from Ch. ix; *Works*, vi, 128–130.]

This is very grand, and is put as an eloquent man would put it who really wished to defend gambling.

The rascal, of course, comes to a miserable end, but the tone of the narrative is continued throughout. He is brought to live at last with his old mother in the Fleet prison, on a wretched annuity of fifty pounds per annum, which she has saved out of the general wreck, and there he dies of delirium tremens. For an assumed tone of continued irony, maintained through the long memoir of a life, never becoming tedious, never unnatural, astounding us rather by its naturalness, I know nothing equal to *Barry Lyndon*.

As one reads, one sometimes is struck by a conviction that this or the other writer has thoroughly liked the work on which he is engaged. There is a gusto about his passages, a liveliness in the language, a spring in the motion of the words, an eagerness of description, a lilt, if I may so call it, in the progress of the narrative, which makes the reader feel that the author has himself greatly enjoyed what he has written. He has evidently gone on with his work without any sense of weariness, or doubt; and the words have come readily to him. So it has been with *Barry Lyndon*. 'My mind was filled full with those blackguards,' Thackeray once said to a friend. It is easy enough to see that it was so. In the passage which I have above quoted, his mind was running over with the idea that a rascal might be so far gone in rascality as to be in love with his own trade.

ESTIMATES OF THACKERAY'S EARLY WORK

9. [Abraham Hayward], from 'Thackeray's Writings', *Edinburgh Review*

January 1848, lxxxviii, 46–67

Hayward (1801–84), a barrister, translated French and German works and wrote books and articles on everything from politics to gastronomy. According to James Hannay in *A Brief Memoir of the late Mr. Thackeray* (1864; see below, No. 49), 'good judges said that a necessary impulse was given to [the] appreciation [of *Vanity Fair*], by an article during its progress, in the *Edinburgh Review*' (*A Brief Memoir*, 16). See also *Letters*, ii, 312 ff.

Fame, like wealth, is very unfairly and unequally distributed in this world. The remark, though hackneyed, ever and anon comes back upon us with a force and vividness affording, to our minds, unanswerable evidence of its truth. It has just been suggested to us anew, on observing within how small a circle the personal reputation of a highly influential writer may be confined, unless he puts forth a regular succession of quartos and octavos, and placards his real name on his title-pages. It may be right and natural that this should be so: anonymous writers have no reason to complain that their names are not familiar in men's mouths; and yet let us not be accused of an undue partiality towards the claims of our own calling when we say, that most of the great battles between truth and prejudice have been decided—most of the great steps in taste, criticism, correct feeling, and social improvement, have been made,—not by 'authors' in the grand dignified sense of the word, but by periodical essayists, pamphleteers, reviewers, and the calumniated tribe who fall under the large and generic description of 'gentlemen of the press.' Yet invaluable as their services have been and are, these only arrive at celebrity in rare instances,—when their writings are collected towards the end of their career, or when the grave has closed upon them and some admiring friend is looking round for a monument. The political tracts of Swift and the moral essays of Addison have long taken rank among the classics of our tongue; but at the time of their publication men speculated upon them much as they now speculate on an article that attracts attention in a newspaper or a review; the authorship was by turns the subject of bold assertion, rash conjecture, and confidential communication; and it may be doubted whether even the inner circle were aware that the tracts and essays in question were forming a new epoch in literature.

The periodical writers and journalists of France have of late years enjoyed a degree of consideration more commensurate with their real influence and importance, but it is curious to see how French pamphleteers were regarded at no distant period. Paul Louis Courier, who probably had done more for the language than any ten of the existing forty, was rejected with scorn by the Academy, and prosecuted as a *vile pamphleteer* by the government.[1]

'*Vile pamphleteer.*' This word raising against me the judges, the witnesss, the jury, the audience (my very advocate appeared shaken by it), this word decided all. I was condemned in the minds of these gentlemen from the moment that the king's man had called me *pamphleteer*, to which I knew of no reply. For in my innermost soul it appeared to me that I had produced what is called a pamphlet; I dared not deny it. I was then a pamphleteer according to my own estimate, and seeing the horror which such a name inspired in the whole auditory, I stood confounded.

Somewhat of the same horror is still inspired in the minds of a large class of English gentlemen by the bare mention of a newspaper writer; and we have known honourable and sensible men (at least, men commonly deemed sensible) act, and avow that they acted, differently from what they intended, because the line of conduct they really considered right had been too warmly advocated in the columns of a leading journal; imitating in this respect that sagacious animal the Irish pig, who, to manifest his perfect independence, makes a point of moving on all occasions in a diametrically opposite direction to the one indicated. When, therefore, we mention the late Mr. Barnes and the gentleman who lately edited the *Examiner* as illustrations of our

---

[1] Courier (1772–1825) satirized the restored Bourbon monarchy in a number of pamphlets.

theory,—as men whose general reputation is very far below their real claims and merits, we shall be met probably with vehement protests from many quarters.[1] Few or none, however, will deny that a widespread and lasting influence has been exercised through the pages of this review and those of our great Southern contemporary;[2] yet it is only within the last five or six years, and after most of the contributors with whom we started had retired from the arena or sunk full of years and honours to the grave, that the public have become familiar with the names and individual performances of those by whom they had been so long guided, instructed, and amused.

Our honoured and lamented friend, the late Sydney Smith, was fond of telling in detail the story (mentioned in his published letter to Mr. Mackintosh) of his being mistaken at a dinner party at Sir James Mackintosh's for his gallant synonyme the hero of Acre; but we well remember the time,—long after he had become the delight of the most polished and intellectual circles of London and Edinburgh, when it was necessary, among the uninitiated or in the provinces, to preface the repetition of one of his *bons mots* by a sort of biographical notice, and as it were establish the existence of a Rev. Sydney Smith in contradistinction to the Admiral.[3] Yet let any one, capable of estimating such matters, lay his hand upon his heart and declare whether any man living had done more to explode error, discredit bigotry, reform abuses, and diffuse intelligence.

That he has left no standard work of permanent interest and authority (for *Peter Plymley* has fulfilled its vocation) is little to the point; for it is not by standard works that the results we speak of are best or most frequently brought about. In an unpublished letter from a distinguished prelate of the Irish church (which we are quite sure he will excuse our quoting) it is said: 'There is a large proportion of the public with whom repetition does more than anything else; who require to have an argument obtruded on their notice many times before they can be brought to attend to it, and made familiar to them before they fully comprehend it. It is only from the intelligent, candid, and attentive, that an error can be at once pulled up by the roots; with the generality, the process must be like that of the backwoodsman in extirpating trees,

[1] Thomas Barnes (1785–1841) edited *The Times*, 1817–41; Albany Fonblanque (1793–1872) edited the *Examiner*, 1830–47.

[2] i.e. the *Quarterly Review*.

[3] Admiral Sir Sidney Smith (1764–1840), famous for his triumph at the Siege of Acre, 1799. Sir James Mackintosh (1765–1832), writer on law, history and philosophy, frequently entertained writers at his house.

which he first fells, and then, year by year, pulls off the shoots as they spring up, till the stump dies and decays; after which he pulls it up.' The excellent writer in question performed this backwoodsman's service to admiration; and many a time within the last year or two, stunned or wearied by Currency nonsense and Maynooth absurdity, have we exclaimed, 'Oh, for one hour of blind old *Dandolo*! oh, for one hour of *Peter Plymley*,' with his searching clenching ridicule, and masculine good sense.[1]

There is another mode in which periodical writers often benefit mankind, not only without having their services acknowledged, but without even being themselves aware of them. 'It is not always necessary' (says Goethe) 'for truth to embody itself; enough if it float spiritually about and induce agreement, if, like the deep, friendly sound of a bell, it undulates through the air.' Full many a valuable truth has been sent undulating through the air by men who have lived and died unknown: at this moment the rising generation are supplied with the best part of their mental aliment by writers whose names are a dead letter to the mass; and among the most remarkable of these is Michael Angelo Titmarsh, alias William Makepeace Thackeray, author of *The Irish Sketch Book*, of *A Journey from Cornhill to Grand Cairo*, of *Jeames' Diary*, of the 'Snob Papers' in *Punch*, of *Vanity Fair*, &c. &c.

Mr. Thackeray is now about thirty-seven years of age, of a good family, and originally intended for the bar. He kept seven or eight terms at Cambridge, but left the University, without taking a degree, with the view of becoming an artist; and we well remember, ten or twelve years ago, finding him day after day engaged in copying pictures in the Louvre in order to qualify himself for his intended profession. It may be doubted, however, whether any degree of assiduity would have enabled him to excel in the money-making branches, for his talent was altogether of the Hogarth kind, and was principally remarkable in the pen and ink sketches of character and situation which he dashed off for the amusement of his friends. At the end of two or three years of desultory application, he gave up the notion of becoming a painter and took to literature. He set up and edited with marked ability a weekly journal, on the plan of the *Athenæum* and *Literary*

---

[1] Smith's *Letters of Peter Plymley* came out in 1807 and 1808. The financial crisis of 1847 was largely due to excessive imports and the aftermath of 'railway mania'. The 'Maynooth absurdity' was Peel's grant in 1845 of an increased subsidy to the Roman Catholic priests' seminary there.

Gazette, but was unable to compete successfully with such long-established rivals.[1] He then became a regular man of letters; that is, he wrote for respectable magazines and newspapers, until the attention attracted to his contributions in *Fraser's Magazine* and *Punch* emboldened him to start on his own account, and risk an independent publication.

These biographical details will be found highly useful in forming a just estimate of Mr. Thackeray's merits and capacity; for much that is most characteristic in his style of expression and mode of looking at things and people, may be traced directly to his life, and to the peculiar society into which he has naturally and necessarily been thrown by it.

In forming our general estimate of this writer, we wish to be understood as referring principally, if not exclusively, to *Vanity Fair* (a novel in monthly parts), though still unfinished; so immeasurably superior, in our opinion, is this to every other known production of his pen. The great charm of this work is its entire freedom from mannerism and affectation both in style and sentiment,—the confiding frankness with which the reader is addressed,—the thoroughbred carelessness with which the author permits the thoughts and feelings suggested by the situations to flow in their natural channel, as if conscious that nothing mean or unworthy, nothing requiring to be shaded, gilded, or dressed up in company attire, could fall from him. In a word, the book is the work of a gentleman, which is one great merit; and not the work of a fine (or would-be fine) gentleman, which is another. Then, again, he never exhausts, elaborates, or insists too much upon anything; he drops his finest remarks and happiest illustrations as Buckingham dropped his pearls, and leaves them to be picked up and appreciated as chance may bring a discriminating observer to the spot. His effects are uniformly the effects of sound wholesome legitimate art; and we need hardly add that we are never harrowed up with physical horrors of the Eugène Sue school[2] in his writings, or that there are no melodramatic villains to be found in them. One touch of nature makes the whole world kin, and here are touches of nature by the dozen. His pathos (though not so deep as Mr. Dickens') is exquisite; the more so, perhaps, because he seems to struggle against it, and to be half ashamed of being caught in the melting mood: but the attempt to be caustic,

[1] The *National Standard*, which Thackeray bought from F. W. N. Bayley in the spring of 1833 but which he had to close in February 1834 because it lost money.
[2] The most popular novel by Eugène Sue (1804–59) was *Les Mystères de Paris*, which was frequently translated, dramatized and imitated in England in the eighteen-forties.

satirical, ironical, or philosophical, on such occasions, is uniformly vain; and again and again have we found reason to admire how an originally fine and kind nature remains essentially free from worldliness, and, in the highest pride of intellect, pays homage to the heart.

Vanity Fair was certainly meant for a satire: the follies, foibles and weaknesses (if not vices) of the world we live in, were to be shown up in it, and we can hardly be expected to learn philanthropy from the contemplation of them. Yet the author's real creed is evidently expressed in these few short sentences:

The world is a looking-glass, and gives forth to every man the reflection of his own face. Frown at it, and it will turn look sourly upon you; laugh at it and with it, and it is a jolly, kind companion; and so let all young persons take their choice. [*Vanity Fair*, ch. ii.]

But this theory of life does not lead Mr. Thackeray to the conclusion that virtue is invariably its own reward, nor prevent him from thinking that the relative positions held by great and small, prosperous and unprosperous, in social estimation, might sometimes be advantageously reversed. M. Emile Souvestre, the author of the very remarkable novel entitled *Riche et pauvre*, has written another novel of striking merit in its way, entitled *Les Réprouvés*.[1] The intended moral is indicated in a prefatory chapter, where the respectable people and the reprobates (*les réprouvés*) are supposed to be drawn up in the presence of an all-seeing judge;—the respectables, 'all honourable men,' but including the mean, the cold, the unsympathising, the ungenerous, the envious, the hard-hearted, the true self-seekers of this world, who always side with the strongest, get out of the way of a falling friend as eagerly as of a falling house, and define gratitude in their inmost souls as 'a lively sense of favours to come;'[2] the reprobates, reckless, thoughtless, improvident, bankrupt in estate and character, but including many who had become so through the dishonesty or injustice of others, the victims of misplaced confidence or ill-requited affection. The judge makes a sign; the breasts of both classes are laid bare; and in the hearts of a large proportion of the respectables is a serpent, in the hearts of a large proportion of the reprobates a star. Take self-sacrifice as the test of virtue, and the moral (though a dangerous one) will not be found so entirely fallacious as it may probably be thought at first. Mr.

---

[1] Souvestre (1806–54), *Riche et pauvre* (1836) and *Les Réprouvés et les élus* (1845).

[2] Hazlitt, in 'On Wit and Humour' (*Lectures on the English Comic Writers*, 1818), refers to 'Sir Robert Walpole's definition of the gratitude of place-expectants, that "it is a lively sense of *future* favours".'

Thackeray does not altogether adopt it, but he has a hard hit or two at the inequalities of our social order. [Quotes the description of Sir Pitt Crawley from *Vanity Fair*, ch. ix; *Works*, xi, 101–3.]

Still the balance is fairly held. There are good people of quality as well as bad in his pages,—pretty much as we find them in the world; and the work is certainly not written with the view of proving the want of re-organisation in society, nor indeed of proving any thing else, which to us is a great relief.

Mrs. Opie and Miss Edgeworth went quite far enough, when they made the illustration of some one particular rule or precept the main object of their stories, as in 'White Lies,' 'Murad the Unlucky,' &c. &c. Miss Martineau went a great deal too far when she made the inculcation of a doubtful (or at least disputed) doctrine in political economy the main object of *hers*;[1] for in all such cases the question must be begged, and it is obviously just as easy to sketch a ploughman's family thrown out of employ through the abolition of the corn laws, as a weaver's or cotton-spinner's reduced to the verge of starvation by the enactment of them. In fact, the mixture spoils two good things, as Charles Lamb (Elia) used to say of brandy and water; and we heartily rejoice that Mr. Thackeray has kept his science and political economy (if he has any) for some other emergency, and given us a plain old-fashioned love-story, which any genuine novel reader of the old school may honestly, plentifully, and conscientiously cry over.

We fear a novel reader must be literally of the old school to enter fully into the humour of the work; for the scene is laid when George the Fourth was (not king, but) regent; the most stirring period is the Waterloo year, 1815; and the dress, manner, modes of thought, amusements, &c. &c. are supposed to be in keeping. The war fever was at its height: Napoleon was regarded as an actual monster: the belief that one Englishman could beat two Frenchmen, and ought to do it whenever he had an opportunity, was universal, (perhaps beneficially so, for 'those can conquer who believe they can'): the stage coach was the only mode of travelling for the commonalty: gentlemen occasionally attended prize-fights: top-boots and hessians were the common wear: black neckcloths were confined to the military; and tight integuments for the nether man were held indispensable; so much so, indeed, that when some rash innovators attempted to introduce

---

[1] 'White Lies' is one of Mrs. Opie's *New Tales* (1818), and 'Murad the Unlucky' one of Maria Edgeworth's *Popular Tales* (1804). Harriet Martineau's stories about political economy include *The Rioters* (1827) and *The Turn-out* (1829).

trousers at Almack's, the indignant patronesses instantly posted up a notification, that, 'in future, no gentleman would on any account be admitted without breeches.'[1]

The *dramatis personæ* are not so easily described or enumerated; and the plot is less an object of attention than the episodes. We fear, however, that we cannot calculate on general familiarity with the story, and must attempt an outline of it. . . .

When the first part of *Clarissa* appeared, the winding up of the plot was left in doubt, and letter after letter poured in upon Richardson, imploring him to avert the worst portion of the catastrophe. Nor did the heroine monopolise the entire sympathies of the enlightened public of those days, for we find one female correspondent eager for the conversion of Lovelace, and intreating Richardson to 'save his soul;' as if (adds Sir Walter Scott) there had been actually a living sinner in the case, and his future state had literally depended on the decision to be pronounced by her admired author. We will not ask Mr. Thackeray to save Rawdon Crawley's soul, but we should be glad if he could save his body from the bailiffs, and appoint him to a consulship on the coast of Africa or South America; where Mrs. Rawdon would be sufficiently punished, by having no elderly generals or profligate peers to flirt with and no tradesmen or hotel-keepers to cheat. As regards Mrs. George Osborne, no intercession is needed; the precise lot we should have selected being obviously in store for her. She is to marry Major (or it may be Lieutenant-general, Sir William,) Dobbin; and we are happy to see, from the concluding sentences of the November Number that she is not likely to prove insensible to the happiness in store for her. [Quotes the end of ch. xxxviii; *Works*, xi, 497–8.]

The interest, however, is too much divided to be deep; and what strikes us most in the conduct of the narrative is, the apparent ease with which such a number and variety of characters are brought upon the stage without crossing or jostling. Numerous, too, and varied as they are, almost every one of them is obviously a copy from the life; whether it be the merchant indorsing his son's letters from school; the

---

[1] 'The fair ladies [including Lady Cowper, the Princess de Lieven and Lady Londonderry] who ruled supreme over this little dancing and gossiping world, issued a solemn proclamation that no gentleman should appear at the assemblies without being dressed in knee-breeches, white cravat, and *chapeau bras*' (*Reminiscences of Captain Gronow* (1st series, 1862), p. 44). Hayward points out in a footnote that 'This fact, curiously enough, is forgotten in the woodcuts [after drawings by Thackeray], old Sedley, Mr. Chopper, Rawdon Crawley, &c. &c., being represented in trousers' (p. 53 of his review). Almack's Assembly Rooms, built in 1765, were in King Street, Mayfair.

old military fribble penning a *poulet*[1] to the opera dancer; the jolly sporting parson receiving a curtain lecture from his wife; Mrs. Major O'Dowd packing her husband's best épaulettes in the tea-canister; or 'the Tutbury Pet and the Rottingdean Fibber, with three other gentlemen of their acquaintance,' who suddenly appeared on the cliff at Brighton to the confusion of poor James Crawley, 'in a taxcart, drawn by a bang-up pony, dressed in white flannel coats with mother-of-pearl buttons.' Mr. Thackeray's familiarity with foreign manners and modes of thinking, adds greatly to the reader's confidence; and we believe lady readers are pretty generally agreed that he has penetrated farther below the surface of their hearts than any other male writer; with perhaps the exception of Balzac, whose knowledge is confined to French women. Yet, though uniformly disposed to exalt the good qualities, he never glosses over the weaknesses, of the sex. . . .

It is hardly a reflection on a writer whose originality is indisputable, to say that two or three of his characters bear a partial resemblance to two or three master pieces of his greatest predecessors; and we cannot help thinking that Amelia, the wife of the careless vain spendthrift Captain Osborne, must be a near relation, first cousin at the farthest, of Amelia, the wife of our old acquaintance, the equally careless though not quite so vain spendthrift, Captain Booth; while Dobbin, though already a major and in a fair way to become a general and G. C. B., bears (as already intimated) some affinity to the ex-schoolmaster Partridge, and a very close one to the ex-barber Strap. The unconscious imitation into which the author has dropped in these instances, has in no respect impaired the truth of his delineations; for Amelias and Dobbins, Partridges and Straps, belong to all ages and are completely independent of conventionalities; but much of Sir Pitt Crawley's language is far better fitted for Squire Western and Parson Trulliber, who suggested it, than for a Baronet of ancient lineage, who had sat in parliament for a family borough during the first fifteen years of the present century.[2]

We have said, with reference to *Vanity Fair*, that Mr. Thackeray never exhausts, elaborates, or insists too much upon anything; but we cannot repeat the compliment with reference to 'The Snob Papers,' in *Punch*. The original notion of these was not a bad one, but it is

---

[1] A love-letter. *OED* records Thackeray as the first English writer to use the word, in *Vanity Fair*, ch. xxiv.

[2] Amelia and Booth are in Fielding's *Amelia* (1751); Partridge and Squire Western in his *Tom Jones* (1749); Trulliber in his *Joseph Andrews* (1742); Strap in Smollett's *Roderick Random* (1748).

literally worked thread-bare; and the author appears at last to have lost sight entirely of the true meaning of the term. According to him, every man who does a mean or dirty action (for example, an earl who haggles with or cheats a tradesman) is a *snob*. To give a precise definition of the word would puzzle the best of living etymologists; but we may safely say, that, in popular acceptation—the *jus et norma loquendi*—it implies both pretension and vulgarity. We include, of course, vulgarity of sentiment; and we admit that a loud, insolent, blustering, overbearing leader of fashion, or a cringing, mean-spirited follower, though rich, well-born, well-dressed and titled, may be a snob. But in speculating on the mixed and singularly constituted society of London, especial care should be taken not to confound in one common censure the legitimate success of cultivation and refinement, and the spurious triumphs of sycophancy. There really is no denying that the best society is emphatically the best: it is a laudable object of ambition to be received on a footing of equality in circles comprising most of the leading statesmen, artists and men of letters, as well as the beauties and fine gentlemen of the day: and if Miss B. or Lady C. sends Mr. D. a card for her evening parties, we submit, with all due deference to Mr. Thackeray, that he is not at once to be set down as a snob for accepting it, nor even for talking a little the day after of the distinguished persons whose acquaintance he may have made. In the 'Snob Papers' it seems taken for granted that any association between persons of unequal rank, or any mention of a man or woman of rank by a plebeian, implies degradation or meanness of some sort. It was the sagacious remark of Swift, that very nice persons must have very nasty ideas;[1] and (if Mr. Thackeray had not amply redeemed himself from the suspicion by the uniform tone of *Vanity Fair*) we should be apt to suspect, upon the same principle, that those who are so extremely anxious to bring in others guilty of snobbishness must be snobs.

We have another fault to find with his minor works, particularly discernible in that clever and amusing production of his entitled *Mrs. Perkins' Ball*. Why are the middle classes to be satirised if they venture to give parties without the means and appliances of wealth? Why are young ladies and gentlemen to be prevented dancing except to Weippert's music, or supping except under Mr. Gunter's presidency?[2]

[1] 'A nice man is a man of nasty ideas' (*Thoughts on Various Subjects*).
[2] Weippert was a fashionable conductor who, for instance, was in command of a band and singers to serenade Princess Victoria on her coming of age at Kensington Palace in 1837. Gunter's catering firm is still famous today.

Or what is there laughable in the necessity under which a ball-giver, in a house of limited dimensions, finds herself of taking down a bed to form a card-room, or making a passage or closet do duty as a *boudoir*?

> Nil habet infelix paupertas durius in se
> Quam quod *ridiculos* homines facit.[1]

This is only too true; but we fairly own it is a kind of fun we could never relish. When Balzac describes the poor student, unable to raise a franc for a cab, picking his way along the pavement towards the house where he is to meet his lady-love, till his visit is rendered impossible, and all his hopes are blighted for ever, by a splash,—we sympathise with him, instead of laughing at him; and the petty miseries entailed on the Perkins' family by their hospitality and good-nature, were fraught, to us, with more melancholy than mirth. The worst of setting up for a satirist is, that when food for satire is no longer to be found in sufficient quantity, it must be manufactured, or discovered by dint of a minute scrutiny into the allowable shifts and pardonable weaknesses of mankind or womankind.

A sturdy, untravelled friend of ours once startled a circle composed principally of Oriental travellers, who had been taking the lion's share of the conversation, by suddenly exclaiming, in a tone of deep conviction, that the East was a humbug. Mr. Thackeray's *Journey from Cornhill to Cairo in the steamers of the Peninsular and Oriental Company*, must have been written for the express purpose of establishing this great fact; *e.g.*:

The palace of the seraglio, the cloister with marble pillars, the hall of the ambassadors, the impenetrable gate guarded by eunuchs and ichoglans, has a romantic look in print; but not so in reality. Most of the marble is wood, almost all the gilding is faded, the guards are shabby, the foolish perspectives painted on the walls are half cracked off. *The place looks like Vauxhall in the day time.* [Ch. vii; Hayward's italics.]

He tells us that he actually saw a Turkish lady drive up to Sultan Achmet's mosque in a *Brougham*, and felt, on seeing her, that the schoolmaster was really abroad. . . .[2]

This is a dangerous kind of observer for the Celts of the Green

---

[1] Juvenal, *Satires*, iii, 152-3. 'Poverty, bitter though it be, has no sharper pang than this, that it makes men ridiculous.'

[2] In a speech made in 1825 Lord Brougham is supposed to have said, 'Look out, gentlemen, the schoolmaster is abroad!'

Island; and *The Irish Sketch-Book* is not a whit inferior to *Paddiana*,[1] in sketches, anecdotes, and traits of character, illustrative of the peculiarities of the race. . . .

A writer with such a pen and pencil as Mr. Thackeray's is an acquisition of real and high value to our literature, and we have not the slightest fear that he will either fall off, or write himself out; for, we repeat, he is not a mannerist, and his range of subjects is not limited to a class. High life, middle life, and low life, are (or very soon will be) pretty nearly the same to him: he has fancy as well as feeling; he can either laugh or cry without grimacing; he can skim the surface, and he can penetrate to the core. Let the public give him encouragement, and let him give himself time, and we fearlessly prophesy that he will soon become one of the acknowledged heads of his own peculiar walk of literature.

10. [George Henry Lewes], article in the *Morning Chronicle*

6 March 1848, 3

Lewes (1817–78), still well known for his happy association with George Eliot, was the best dramatic critic of his time, and wrote a great biography (of Goethe) and much on philosophy, psychology and biology. The present article was suggested by the publication in book form of *The Book of Snobs* (1848). For Thackeray's comments, see below, No. 11.

Thackeray is one of the foremost writers of the day; and considering the eminence to which he has risen of late, has very few detractors. In truth, his style of writing is so singularly winning, so easy, masculine, felicitous, humourous and pleasant, that unless to very obtuse perceptions, one sees not how he could fail of being attractive. He has no asperities; he presents no rough points against which the reader's mind

---

[1] *Paddiana; or, Scraps and Sketches of Irish Life, present and past* (1847), published anonymously, and variously attributed to Sir William Henry Gregory and Dr. Adam Blenkinsop.

is thrust with pain; his manner is unobtrusive, his mannerism is not obvious. He offends no one by the vehemence of his opinions, nor by dogmatism of manner. His wit is delicate, his pathos simple, and rather indicated than dwelt upon. He indulges in no false sentiment; disturbs you by no ambitious bursts of rhetoric. There is no fustian in him, no glare from the footlights is thrown upon exaggerated distortions of human nature. Trusting to truth and humour, he is the quietest perhaps of all contemporary writers.

Thackeray is not a man to create partizans. He espouses no 'cause;' has no party. The applause he seeks is the legitimate applause bestowed on an artist: and he excites, therefore, admiration rather than passionate attachment. The absence of any strong 'purpose' is in some sense a drawback to his popularity, but in another sense it is an additional aid. He does not please a party, but he does not offend the opponents of that party. His popularity thus gains in extent what it loses in intensity.

We, for our own part, cannot but applaud this. The artist, unfettered by political or social theories, is better enabled to represent human nature in its truth, and his works thus leave a more permanent and satisfactory impression. *Ridentem dicere verum quid vetat?*[1] But many humourists, taking advantage of the cap and bells, seem to have adopted as their motto—'Ridentem dicere *falsum* quid vetat?' Because laughter is not serious, and what is laughingly spoken is not critically accepted, they have sacrificed the truth (as well as their friends) to the joke. Perhaps no advocate of a cause should be more scrupulously watched than he who laughing teaches. Against the dogmas of the politician, philosopher, or theologian we prepare ourselves. He comes in such a questionable shape that we *must* examine him. His seriousness alarms us. We scrutinize his proofs, we combat his conclusions. Not so with the jester. He is privileged. He throws us off our guard, and storms conviction by enveloping it in laughter. A semblance of truth has more effect in a jest, because we do not look for it there, than a demonstration in a serious essay. The laughter passes, but the idea remains: it has gained admittance in our unsuspecting minds, and is left there unsuspected.

Although, therefore, we by no means wish to restrict the sphere of the jester, and are willing enough to take ridicule in some cases as the test of truth, we think it is the duty of critics to watch very narrowly the doctrines which the jester desires to disseminate. With regard to

[1] Horace, *Satires*, i, 1, 24. 'What is to prevent a person from telling the truth and laughing as well?'

ridicule as the test of truth, one simple rule will suffice to limit its efficiency: Whenever the ridicule is developed *ab intra*, and not cast upon the argument *ab extra*, then it is a test, and then only.

We are getting very serious; but it is surely no paradox to say that writers of Thackeray's stamp incline one to seriousness as much as to mirth? And while in this vein, while applauding him for his admirable judgment in steering clear of party questions, and didactic purposes, we must not let slip the occasion of remonstrance on two points—the only two—in which he seems to us reprehensible.

As a satirist, it is his business to tear away the mask from life, but as an artist and a teacher he grievously errs when he shows us *everywhere* corruption underneath the mask. His scepticism is pushed too far. While trampling on cant, while exposing what is base and mean, and despicable, he is not attentive enough to honour, and to paint what is high, and generous, and noble in human nature. Let us not be understood to say that he *fails* to honour the finer portion of our nature; but he does not honour it enough. He uses the good more as a condiment to relieve the exhausted palate. Touches here and there, exquisite though brief, show us that his heart responds to what is noble, and that his soul conceives it distinctly. But he almost seems ashamed of it, as if it were an unmanly weakness; and he turns it off with a laugh, like a man caught in tears at the theatre. In *Vanity Fair*, his greatest work, how little is there to love! The people are all scamps, scoundrels, or humbugs. The only persons who show paternal affection are Rawdon Crawley and old Osborne. Beautifully is it done, with exquisite truth and feeling; but by what bitter irony are this foolish blackleg[1] and this coarse brutal old wretch selected as the sole exhibitors of such an affection! Dobbin, whose heart is so noble—the only one in the book—is made ridiculous. We are perfectly aware of the *truth* of these portraits; we admit the use of contrasts in art; but we still think that in thus making the exception stand for the rule he has erred both against art and nature. Dickens has beautifully shown us the union of the noble and the ridiculous; but in his writings this union is by no means the rule. He has painted so many loveable people that people love him for it.

Thackeray laughs all round; his impartiality has something terrible in it; so complete is the irony that he turns it even upon himself. 'O brother wearers of motley!' he exclaims, 'are there not moments

---

[1] A late eighteenth century term for a dishonest gambler, often used by reviewers to describe Rawdon Crawley. See below, pp. 81, 84, 194.

when one grows sick of grinning and tumbling and the jingling of cap and bells?' He feels that there is something sad in that perpetual laughter; sad indeed, for it is blasphemy against the divine beauty which is in life. Yet what is his object? He has told us—if for once we are to take even him at his word—'This, dear friends and companions, is my amiable object—to walk with you through the Fair, to examine the shops and shows there, and that we should all come home after the flare, and the noise, and the gaiety, and be *perfectly miserable in private!*' [Ch. xix. Lewes's italics.] Said in jest, or said in earnest, that unhappily is the sentence which characterizes his writings. Whether carelessness or scepticism we know not, but the moral of his books is that every one—reader and author included—is no more than a puny, miserable pretender; that most of our virtues are pretences, and when not pretences are only kept up because removed from temptation.

And this brings us by a natural transition to the second count in our charge against him. We refer to a detestable passage in *Vanity Fair*, wherein, after allowing Becky, with dramatic propriety, to sophisticate with herself, to the effect that it is only her poverty which makes her vicious, he adds from himself this remark:—'And who knows but Rebecca was right in her speculations, and that it was only a question of money and fortune which made the difference between her and an honest woman? If you take temptations into account, who is to say that he is better than his neighbour? A comfortable career of prosperity, if it does not make men honest, at least keeps them so. An alderman coming from a turtle feast, will not step out of his carriage to steal a leg of mutton; *but put him to starve, and see if he will not purloin a loaf.*' [Ch. xli. Lewes's italics.] Was it carelessness, or deep misanthropy, distorting that otherwise clear judgment, which allowed such a remark to fall? What, in the face of starving thousands, men who literally die for want of bread, yet who prefer death to stealing, shall it be said that honesty is only the virtue of abundance!

There are many criminals in our vast population, and the majority are doubtless urged by poverty. But on the one hand, how many of the poor are heroically honest—honest while starving with temptation horribly besetting them; and on the other hand, how many of the comparatively wealthy stand in the prisoner's dock! Of all falsehoods, that about honesty being a question of money is the most glaring and the most insidious. Blot it out, Thackeray; let it no longer deface your delightful pages!

To quit this tone of serious remonstrance for one of more congenial admiration, let us notice how peculiarly his own is Thackeray's humour. It steals upon you in the quietest unpretending way, so that you seem to co-operate with him in producing the joke. He never frames and glazes his ideas. He never calls upon you to admire them by any trick of phrase or oddity of language. He does not insist upon your admiration—he wins it. The simplest words, and in the simplest manner, are used to bring out his meaning; and wit of the finest quality, as well as hearty humour, seem to spring from him without an effort. The ease of his writing is little less than marvellous; and to judge from the carelessness of his style in its idiomatic flow, we should suppose that it is really written with a facile, current pen.

Another peculiarity in Thackeray, which he has in common with all the great writers, and which distinguishes him from almost all his contemporaries, is the strong sense of reality pervading his writing— a reality never lost sight of even in his most extravagant bursts of humour. He has had experience; and he has done more—he has reflected on it, so as to be able to reflect in turn. Life, not the phantas-magoria of the stage and circulating library, is the storehouse from whence he draws. We said before that there was nothing theatrical in his manner; the same must be said of his people; they are all individuals (in the right sense of that word, and not in the loose sense which Archdeacon Hare so admirably ridicules, as current in modern writ-ing),[1] having the unmistakeable characteristics of men, and not being abstract ideas nor traditional conceptions of character. While reading Thackeray you feel that he is painting 'after nature;' not that he is inventing figments, nor drawing from the *repertoire* of a worthless stage.

In the book before us, what a variety of characters, and how un-mistakeable! *Snobs* perhaps they are not all; but are they not all real? And yet what a tempting subject to seduce a writer into farcical impossibilities—mere fancy pieces humorously drawn!

The impartiality with which he has laid on the lash, is one of the most amusing things in the book; he does not content himself with sneering at the rich and titled snobs, but turns round with equal severity upon the poor and envious snob. Grub-street writing diatribes against Belgravia, yet overwhelmed with delighted pride if Belgravia should happen to notice its existence, is happily shown up. The reader

---

[1] In *Guesses at Truth* (1st series, 1827), by Archdeacon Hare (1795–1855) and his brother Augustus (1792–1834), the use of 'individual' to mean 'man, woman or child' is condemned as 'a strange piece of pompous inanity'.

laughing at some ludicrous picture of sycophantic snobbishness, is suddenly turned upon by this terrible satirist, and made to confess that he, the laughing reader, in spite of his scorn of all this snobbishness, would do the very same thing were he in the same place.[1] We believe Thackeray stands alone in the art with which he achieves this. Other satirists flatter their readers, by implication at least,—but he ruthlessly arrests the complacent chuckle, and turns the laugh against the laugher.

There never was a humourist of high excellence without an accompanying power of pathos. In Thackeray we find repeated touches as exquisite as Sterne or Jean Paul;[2] but they are seldom more than touches. He seems averse to grief, and dwells not on the 'luxury of woe.' There is one passage, however, in *Vanity Fair*, where he seems to have lingered with a mournful pen that would not quit the subject; we allude to the affecting parting between Amelia and her boy, whom she is forced to give up to his grandfather: one bit we must copy, though it is difficult to read it, our eyes are not dry enough. [Quotes from ch. l; *Works*, xi, 625, the description of Amelia's making George read to her from the story of Samuel.]

And what a profound—almost savage—touch is that of the childlike selfishness with which Georgy receives the announcement of the approaching separation:—

The widow broke the matter to Georgy with great caution; she looked to see him very much affected by the intelligence. He was rather elated than otherwise, and the poor woman turned sadly away. He bragged about the news that day to the boys at school. [Ch. l.]

But if we venture into details we shall never conclude. To use the consecrated phrase—'Thackeray's writings will repay perusal'—and reperusal!

[1] Cf. Baudelaire's 'Hypocrite lecteur,—mon semblable,—mon frere!' ('Au Lecteur', *Les Fleurs du Mal*, 1857).
[2] i.e. Johann Paul Friedrich Richter (1763–1825), who adopted the pen-name of Jean Paul.

11. Thackeray, letter to G. H. Lewes

6 March 1848 (*Letters*, ii, 353–4)

My dear Sir

I have just read your notice in the Chronicle (I conclude it is a friend who has penned it) and am much affected by the friendliness of the sympathy, and by the kindness of the reproof of the critic.

That passage wʰ you quote bears very hardly upon the poor alderman certainly: but I don't mean that the man deprived of turtle would as a consequence steal bread: only that he in the possession of luxuries and riding through life respectably in a gig, should be very chary of despising poor Lazarus on foot, & look very humbly and leniently upon the faults of his less fortunate brethren—If Becky had had 5000 a year I have no doubt in my mind that she would have been respectable; increased her fortune advanced her family in the world: laid up treasures for herself in the shape of 3 per cents, social position, reputation &c—like Louis Philippe let us say, or like many a person highly & comfortably placed in the world not guilty of many wrongs of commission, satisfied with himself, never doubting of his merit, and decorously angry at the errors of less lucky men. What satire is so awful as Lead us not into temptation? What is the gospel and life of our Lord (excuse me for mentioning it) but a tremendous Protest against pride and self-righteousness? God forgive us all, I pray, and deliver us from evil.

I am quite aware of the dismal roguery wʰ goes all through the Vanity Fair story—and God forbid that the world should be like it altogether: though I fear it is more like it than we like to own. But my object is to make every body engaged, engaged in the pursuit of Vanity and I must carry my story through in this dreary minor key, with only occasional hints here & there of better things—of better things wʰ it does not become me to preach.

I never scarcely write letters to critics and beg you to excuse me for sending you this. It is only because I have just laid down the paper, and am much moved by the sincere goodwill of my critic.

very faithfully yours
W M Thackeray.

12. Charlotte Brontë, from letters to W. S. Williams

29 March 1848 and 14 August 1848 (*The Shakespeare Head Brontë, The Life and Letters* (1932), ii, 201, 244)

Charlotte Brontë dedicated the second edition of *Jane Eyre* to Thackeray and praised him at the end of her Preface (21 December 1847) to that edition. (See the beginning of No. 35 below).

... You mention Thackeray and the last number of 'Vanity Fair.' The more I read Thackeray's works the more certain I am that he stands alone—alone in his sagacity, alone in his truth, alone in his feeling (his feeling, though he makes no noise about it, is about the most genuine that ever lived on a printed page), alone in his power, alone in his simplicity, alone in his self-control. Thackeray is a Titan, so strong that he can afford to perform with calm the most herculean feats; there is the charm and majesty of repose in his greatest efforts; *he* borrows nothing from fever, his is never the energy of delirium—his energy is sane energy, deliberate energy, thoughtful energy. The last number of 'Vanity Fair' proves this peculiarly.[1] Forcible, exciting in its force, still more impressive than exciting, carrying on the interest of the narrative in a flow, deep, full, resistless, it is still quiet—as quiet as reflection, as quiet as memory; and to me there are parts of it that sound as solemn as an oracle. Thackeray is never borne away by his own ardour—he has it under control. His genius obeys him—it is his servant, it works no fantastic changes at its own wild will, it must still achieve the task which reason and sense assign it, and none other. Thackeray is unique. I *can* say no more, I *will* say no less. ...

[1] The 'last number' was the fifteenth (chs. li–liii), published at the beginning of March 1848.

I have already told you, I believe, that I regard Mr Thackeray as the first of modern masters, and as the legitimate high priest of Truth; I study him accordingly with reverence. He, I see, keeps the mermaid's tail below water, and only hints at the dead men's bones and noxious slime amidst which it wriggles;[1] *but,* his hint is more vivid than other men's elaborate explanations, and never is his satire whetted to so keen an edge as when with quiet mocking irony he modestly recommends to the approbation of the public his own exemplary discretion and forbearance. The world begins to know Thackeray rather better than it did two years or even a year ago, but as yet it only half knows him. His mind seems to me a fabric as simple and unpretending as it is deep-founded and enduring—there is no meretricious ornament to attract or fix a superficial glance; his great distinction of the genuine is one that can only be fully appreciated with time. There is something, a sort of 'still profound,' revealed in the concluding part of *Vanity Fair* which the discernment of one generation will not suffice to fathom. A hundred years hence, if he only lives to do justice to himself, he will be better known than he is now. A hundred years hence, some thoughtful critic, standing and looking down on the deep waters, will see shining through them the pearl without price of a purely original mind—such a mind as the Bulwers, etc., his contemporaries have *not,*— not acquirements gained from study, but the thing that came into the world with him—his inherent genius: the thing that made him, I doubt not, different as a child from other children, that caused him, perhaps, peculiar griefs and struggles in life, and that now makes him as a writer unlike other writers. Excuse me for recurring to this theme, I do not wish to bore you. . . .

[1] See *Vanity Fair*, ch. lxiv. Other places where Thackeray used a mermaid as a symbol of evil seductiveness include his design for the initial letter of ch. xviii in *Pendennis*, and *The Newcomes*, ch. xxxvi.

13. [John Forster], from a review in the *Examiner*

22 July 1848, 468–70

Forster (1812–76), the friend, mentor and biographer of Dickens, was also a friend of Thackeray's in the eighteen-forties. He wrote much journalism (he was on the staff of the *Examiner* from 1833 to 1856, first as a critic and then as editor) and biographies of Goldsmith and Landor. In No. 16, Thackeray comments on one of Forster's points (p. 57).

Laughing at the minute and interminable details, despising the conventional decencies and real indecorums, wearied by the want of all manly passion in Richardson's *Pamela*, that novel of the pattern morality of its day, Fielding at last revenged himself by a burlesque, which was meant to show how compatible the specious virtue of Mrs Pamela might be, with the absence of every virtue except the one by which she gained for a husband the man who had done his best to ruin her. But Fielding had too great an imagination to allow of his filling up one book with a mere parody of another. From Richardson his satire extended to the fashionable world: and there was in him that genial cordiality which made him soon forget, or sink into secondary importance, the joke he at first had contemplated. The manly character of his hero, the sublime *bonhomie* of Parson Adams, the ripe beauty and exquisite goodness of Fanny, became a thousand times more congenial to him than mere burlesque or sneering ever could; and the prominent subjects of his novel, which fetter attention and dwell for ever in the memory, are those true and living beauties in it which perhaps he had never dreamed of, when he sate down to revenge himself on Richardson's emasculated fiction by turning its wit 'the seamy side without'.

Put the fashionable-life manners of our day for the manners in Richardson's novels, and Mr Thackeray's position in the book before us in some respect resembles Fielding's. The task he first set himself, in

Vanity Fair, would seem to have been to portray or expose, with witty malice, their ideal of fine life in its various grades. But his better genius forced him beyond the narrow limits of a mere ill-natured joke or burlesque, and informed his pages with characters and incidents full of life and reality. If Mr Thackeray falls short of Fielding, much of whose peculiar power and more of whose manner he has inherited or studiously acquired, it is because an equal amount of large cordiality has not raised him entirely above the region of the sneering, into that of simple uncontaminated human affection.[1] His satiric pencil is dipped in deeper colours than that of his prototype. Not Vanity Fair so properly as Rascality Fair is the scene he lays open to our view; and he never wholly escapes from its equivocal associations, scarcely ever lays aside for a whole page his accustomed sneer. His is a less comfortable, and on the whole therefore, let us add, a less true view of society than Fielding's.

Vanity Fair is the work of a mind, at once accomplished and subtle, which has enjoyed opportunities of observing many and varied circles of society. Its author is endowed with penetrating discrimination and just appreciation of character, and with a rare power of graphic delineation. His *genteel* characters (we dislike the word as much as Dr Johnson did *cleverness*,[2] but we have no better at hand) have a reality about them which we do not remember to have met with in any recent work of fiction except *Pelham*.[3] They are drawn from actual life, not from books and fancy; and they are presented by means of brief, decisive, yet always most discriminative, touches. It never is necessary to have recourse to supplementary reflections and associations, to make amends for dimness and indistinctness in the portraiture. This, for the most part, holds true of all Mr Thackeray's characteristic sketches. But there is a tendency to caricature, to select in preference grotesque and unpleasing lineaments even where no exaggeration is indulged, that detracts considerably from the pleasure such high artistic abilities might otherwise afford; and we are seldom permitted to enjoy the appreciation of all gentle and kind things which we continually meet with in the book, without some neighbouring quip or sneer that would seem to show the author ashamed of what he yet cannot help giving way to.

[1] Thackeray seems to be meeting this objection in *The Newcomes*, ch. xiv.

[2] In his Dictionary, Johnson thought 'clever' 'a low word,' when used as a general epithet of satisfaction or liking. See *OED*, s.v. 'clever.'

[3] Bulwer's novel, published 1828.

It would be tasking the reader's patience too severely to inflict upon him a dry analysis of a story already familiar to a wide public, and daily attracting more attention. But a brief review of its elements is necessary to a just estimate of its character and value. If the novel is without a hero, it has two heroines. We are introduced to them as they leave their boarding-school, described in a very few pages, but with inimitable humour; and we follow their adventures, conjointly or alternately, till we leave the one in the secure haven of a second and comfortable marriage, and the other in an incipient old age of missionary and philanthropic societies, cognac, and stalls at fancy fairs. In tracing the fortunes of the artistically accomplished, clever, sensible, daring, selfish, and unprincipled Becky, we are led through beggarly scenes tenanted by adventurers, through avowedly rakish and more splendid circles, through those where a conventional tone of decorum prevails; thence, into the squalid resorts of tattered finery and habitual vice which lie beyond; and thence again, into that withered, sapless, and flowerless region where sham penitents find a refuge, who have returned to external decency without reawakening to virtue. In tracing, on the one hand, the fortunes of the good and amiable but somewhat selfish and insipid Amelia, we are led from the vulgar comfort and splendour of the *bourgeoisie* of Vanity Fair, through sudden reverses of bankruptcy; allowed again to emerge into commonplace affluence; and after a short excursion through the stately haunts of poor German princes, are conducted finally to a home of worth and virtue. The relations of the heroines afford a connecting link between those dissimilar routes and the passengers who crowd them. The scene shifts from England to the continent, and the time of action extends from before the battle of Waterloo to the year of grace in which we write. The heroes and heroines of high life and low life, of town life and country life, and of that amphibious life which is neither, pass in succession before us; and all, whether we like and admire them or the contrary, are presented with a startling reality of effect.

It must not be imagined, because we have hinted at Mr Thackeray's inferior power of escaping from the mere satirical and burlesque when compared with Fielding, that there are not many finely-conceived characters in his book,—characters which win upon us by their intrinsic worth, and are all the more dear from the dash of the ridiculous that mingles with their better qualities. The hero (for after all there is a hero in the novel), Dobbin, though perhaps elaborated here and there in too minute detail, is a noble portrait of awkward devoted affection, of unobtrusive talents, and of uncompromising integrity. We love him from the first page to the last; from his gawky beginnings at school, through his inadequate rewards during life, to his doubtful happiness at the close. He is always kind, loving, truthful, heroical-hearted; a gentleman. The ineffable Peggy O'Dowd, too, is always welcome; whether brushing her husband's accoutrements and preparing his cup of coffee while he takes his natural rest before the battle of Waterloo, or plotting and planning to marry the major with Glorvina, or watching tenderly over the sick bed of the desolate Amelia, or breaking off the intrigue between the lieutenant and the surgeon's wife, or quarrelling with all the other ladies of the regiment, or dancing down an interminable succession of military men and civilians in an Irish jig. Nor less is her quiet, submissive, gallant, and good-natured husband worthy of her. The poor curate at Brompton, Miss Clapp, Miss Swartz, Jemima, Miss Briggs, Lady Jane, and others, are also people we can take to our heart, and in whose society we edify. Perhaps the noblest conception of all, however, is the manner in which the good qualities of the manly but battered old *roué*, Rawdon, ignorant and uneducated except by vice, are developed under the combined influence of paternal affection, adversity, and occasional association with the good.

Still it cannot be denied that it is in those characters where great natural talents and energy are combined with unredeemed depravity that the author puts forth his full powers, and that in the management and contemplation of them he seems absolutely to revel. The Marquis of Steyne is a magnificent picture; his fiendish sagacity, energy, absorbing self-indulgences, and contemptuous tramplings upon everything human and divine, fascinate while they revolt. It is in like manner impossible to escape being charmed with the indomitable buoyancy, self-possession, and *aplomb* of the little adventuress, Becky, even while we are conscious of her utter depravity. She commits every conceivable wickedness; dishonours her husband, betrays her friend, degrades and embrutes herself, and finally commits a murder; without in the least losing those smart, good-tempered, sensible manners and ways, which ingratiate her with the reader in spite of all their atrocities. In this we may think the art questionably employed, but it is not to be denied that it is very extraordinary art; and it is due to Mr Thackeray to add that he has been careful to explain the blended good and evil in this woman by very curious and impressive early details of the circumstances of her birth and bringing up. Nor is it so much with respect to these exceptional characters that we feel inclined to complain of the taunting, cynical, sarcastic tone that too much pervades the work, as with respect to a preponderance of unredeemed selfishness in the more common-place as well as the leading characters, such as the Bullocks, Mrs Clapp, the Miss Dobbinses even, and Amelia's mother. We can relish the shrewd egoism of Miss Crawley; can admire, while we tremble at, the terrible intentness of Mrs Bute Crawley, who writes her husband's sermons, drills her daughters, and persecutes with selfish sycophancy till everybody flies from her; we can bow with awe and veneration before Lady Southdown, that miraculous compound of Lady Bountiful and Lady Macbeth; we can triumph completely over such fribblers as Sir Pitt Crawley the second, and Tapeworm; we see what power there is in making young Osborne so heartless, old Osborne so hateful, old Sedley so contemptible; but we feel that the atmosphere of the work is overloaded with these exhalations of human folly and wickedness. We gasp for a more liberal alternation of refreshing breezes of unsophisticated honesty. Fielding, after he has administered a sufficient dose of Blifil's choke-damp, purifies the air by a hearty laugh from Tom Jones. But the stifling ingredients are administered by Mr Thackeray to excess, without the necessary relief.

It is exclusively in an artistical point of view that we offer this criticism. It would be unjust in the extreme to impute an immoral tendency to *Vanity Fair*. Vice and folly are never made alluring in it, though all justice is done to their superficial meretricious charms. Mr Thackeray's moral is true and just. It is the victims of such adventurers as Becky who are made so mainly by their own faults and follies. Unsuspicious virtue and innocence—as in the case of Dobbin and Amelia—have a charm in their own simple integrity that unconsciously baffles her spells. It is the vices of her victims that subject them to her power—whether their vices be inherent, gross, and revolting, as in the case of Sir Pitt Crawley; or superinduced on a naturally better, but ignorant and uneducated nature, as in the case of poor Rawdon; or feeble and degrading, as in that compound of silly vanity and selfishness, Joseph Sedley; or merely insipidly heartless and unthinking, as with young Osborne. But this moral is insisted upon with a pertinacity, and illustrations of it are heaped upon us with a redundant profusion, unalleviated by a sufficient amount of more gratifying images, that seems to us to go beyond the limits of the pleasurable, and consequently of true art.

Notwithstanding this defect, *Vanity Fair* must be admitted to be one of the most original works of real genius that has of late been given to the world. The author contemplates many phases of society from a point of view entirely his own. The very novelty of tone in the book impeded its first success; but it will be daily more justly appreciated, and will take a lasting place in our literature. If we have not scrupled to dwell with force upon what we conceive to be its grave defect, it is because we are convinced that the author is capable of avoiding it in his future works, and of producing characteristic tales less alloyed in their enjoyment, and equal, if not superior, in racy power.

14. [Robert Stephen Rintoul], from a review in the *Spectator*

22 July 1848, xxi, 709–10

Rintoul (1787–1858) worked as a journalist in Dundee, Edinburgh and London. He edited the *Spectator* from its founding in 1828 almost up to his death.

The completion of Mr. Thackeray's novel of *Vanity Fair* enables us to take a more entire view of the production, and to form a more complete judgment of it as a work of art, than was possible in the course of piecemeal publication in monthly numbers. Our impression from that review is, that the novel is distinguished by the more remarkable qualities which have created the reputation of the author,—his keen perception of the weaknesses, vanities, and humbug of society, the felicitous point with which he displays or the pungent though goodnatured satire with which he exposes them, and the easy, close, and pregnant diction in which he clothes his perceptions; though, possibly, happier specimens of his peculiar excellencies may be found in some of his other works. *Vanity Fair* displays a depth and at times a pathos which we do not remember to have met with in Mr. Thackeray's previous writings; but, considered as a whole, it is rather a succession of connected scenes and characters than a well-constructed story. Both incidents and persons belong more to the sketch than the finished picture. Either from natural bias or long habits of composition, Mr. Thackeray seems to have looked at life by bits rather than as a whole. A half-length here, a whole-length there, a group in another place, a character or a clique with single actions or incidents belonging to them, have been studied, and transferred to paper with a humour, truth, and spirit, that have rarely been equalled. But something more than this is needed for a finished picture of human life. Such things, indeed, are scarcely its entire elements, for they are little more than parts; and so remain till very many such have been compared by the artist—their general laws evolved by this comparison, and the whole animated and fused by the imagination, so as to present the type of a class without loss of individuality. Mr. Thackeray has rarely accomplished this in *Vanity Fair*. There is, indeed, plenty of individuality; the work is full of it. However exceptional, outré, distasteful, or even farcical the characters may be, they have strong particular traits, well supported in the main, and their delineation is always capital: but this peculiarity attaches to the principal characters—that no useful deduction, no available rule of life, can be drawn from their conduct; except in that of the elder Osborne, who points the moral of sordid vanity and a grovelling love of distinction, and points it with effect, as his vices are made the means of his punishment.

It may be said that this largeness is of no consequence, if there be particular or even exceptional nature: which is true as regards sketches, that exhibit a character on one or two occasions and then drop it. Such sketches of passing phases of society do not, however, suffice to form the materials of a fiction: it requires a whole career—the before and after as well as the present. When the characters have no types in nature, or have that obvious weakness or low vice about them that their example conduces to nothing, they tire in a lengthened exhibition, because we have little sympathy with them. *Vanity Fair* is said by its author to be a novel without a hero: which is undoubtedly a truth; but the heroines do not make up for this omission, since one is without a heart, and the other without a head. The author evidently has his misgivings about Amelia Osborne, (née Sedley,) for although she is clearly a favourite, he deems it necessary occasionally to appeal to the reader in favour of her weakness. But there is rarely weakness without vice; and though the extreme attachment of Amelia to a selfish, worthless, neglectful young man, may be forgiven as *so* natural, yet the manner in which she yields to it, and nurses her sentiment to the neglect of her duties, as well as her subsequent shilly-shally conduct to her obsequious admirer Major Dobbin, is rather mawkish than interesting.

Rebecca Crawley (formerly Sharp) is the principal person of the book, with whom nearly all the others are more or less connected: and a very wonderfully-drawn picture she is, as a woman scheming for self-advancement, without either heart or principle, yet with a constitutional vivacity and a readiness to please, that save her from the contempt or disgust she deserves. As a creation or *character*, we know not where Rebecca can be matched in prose fiction: but she is too deficient in morale to excite interest. The want of entirety we have spoken of is visible in Rebecca's finale. The discredit of a separation from her husband, when not followed by public proceedings, might be surmounted; but a demirep who gambles, consorts with blacklegs and all kinds of disreputables, and raises the wind by advertising concerts that she never gives after getting the money for the tickets, could hardly have regained a place in reputable society, although backed by religious hypocrisy. This conclusion, which was quite needless, is not only wrong as wanting in poetical justice, but untrue as a picture of society even in *Vanity Fair*.

A similar want of attractive sympathy runs through the male characters, either from grossness, weakness, sordidness, or vice. It may be urged that these defects of *Vanity Fair* are owing to its periodical publication. That has probably induced an occasional but strong sacrifice of consistency in the characters, to produce an immediate effect; and the same necessity of making parts tell may have given rise to some exaggerations that would otherwise have been avoided. There are also obvious drawbacks to continuous perusal, such as direct addresses to the reader, and a little of *writing* for the million, which would have been omitted in another mode of publication. But we think all the peculiarities arising from the mode of publication could be got rid of by revision: the defects we speak of lie deeper, and are owing, we think, to a want of imagination and large comprehension of life.

But if, putting *Vanity Fair* aside as a fiction of high art, we look at it as a series of bits from life, it is entitled to the first rank as a set of sketches lifelike and natural. Sir Pitt Crawley—the selfish, low-minded baronet, the coarsest of the coarse old school, who cannot spell, and who living meanly, acting harshly and cruelly, and exercising great shrewdness in money matters, is notwithstanding always a loser—is a capital portrait; and, though exceptional even in his day, (which was the early part of the century,) still might be found in life. His brother, the jovial, fox-hunting, port-drinking rector, is equal to him as a real piece of flesh and blood. The Marquis of Steyne—the roué whom everybody censures, (except the serious,) but all visit when they get an invitation—revives some reminiscences of a similar personage in *Coningsby*[1]: though Thackeray penetrates the pomps and strips off the conventions that rather imposed upon Disraeli. There are numerous other characters, which, if not quite so powerfully painted as these, are quite as truthful individually; but, always excepting Rebecca, the most large and vigorous delineation in the book is old Mr. Osborne. He is a type of a class; he points a moral; and, though sordid, selfish, sullen, half-savage, and meanly subservient to greatness, he obtains a hold on the reader by the force of his will, at least till he turns to a sort of goodness towards the conclusion.

These characters are frequently engaged in scenes that create amusement or exhibit society; and the sketches are intermingled with lively descriptions or shrewd remarks on life. Read as a series of sketches connected with persons whose fortunes serve to introduce them, *Vanity Fair* will furnish a lively and agreeable entertainment. Read as a continuous story, it will perhaps be felt to lack the interest which a story requires, except in the scenes connected with Rawdon Crawley's arrest, release, and subsequent discovery of his wife's liaison with the Marquis of Steyne. . . .

As is usual with works of fiction published periodically, *Vanity Fair* is profusely illustrated with wood-cuts and etchings representing the persons and incidents of the text, by Mr. Thackeray himself. If only of passable or average merit, they would be creditable, as arguing the possession of a double art; but they strike us as exhibiting powers akin to the literary abilities of the author, besides possessing this further quality: the spirit of the scene and the character—the idiosyncracy of the persons—is more thoroughly entered into and presented to the reader than is common with professional artists.

[1] i.e. Lord Monmouth, who—like Lord Steyne—was modelled on the third Marquis of Hertford.

15. [Robert Bell], from a review in *Fraser's Magazine*

September 1848, xxxviii, 320–33

Bell (1800–67), miscellaneous writer and journalist, edited the *Atlas* for a time. His well-known edition of the English Poets was never completed. For Thackeray's comments on the present review, see below, No. 16.

Every periodical has its white days and ambrosial memories. We have ours, and the great indigo book before us reminds us of one of them. *Fraser's Magazine* was the nursery-bed in which Michael Angelo Titmarsh quickened. Out of the *Yellow-Plush Correspondence* grew the Jameses and the Perkinses, the Crawleys, Dobbins, and Sharps. Transplanted into more open ground, Michael Angelo expanded with increased luxuriance; more salt was laid at the roots of his humour, which fattened and flourished accordingly.

But he is the same Michael Angelo still. The same characteristics may be traced throughout; the same quality of subtle observation, penetrating rarely below the epidermis, but taking up all the small vessels with microscopic vision; the same grotesque exaggeration, with truth at the bottom; the same constitutional instinct for seizing on the ridiculous aspect of things, for turning the 'seamy side' of society outwards, and for exposing false pretensions and the genteel ambition of *parvenus*. The task to which the natural bent of Michael Angelo's genius leads him is a disagreeable one, and often distressingly painful; but he never seems to be aware of that fact. He dissects his victims with a smile; and performs the cruellest of operations on their self-love with a pleasantry which looks provokingly very like good-nature. The peculiarities and eccentricities of matter and manner with which he started are here as trenchant as ever. No author ever advanced so far in reputation without advancing further in novelty of enterprise. He has never gone out of himself from the beginning, or out of the subjects over which he possesses so complete a mastery. He has never broken new pastures, but only taken a wider and more thoughtful survey of the old. Yet such are the inexhaustible resources of the soil, and such the skill with which he works them, that we are never conscious of the slightest sense of monotony. All is fresh, versatile, and original.

The follies, vices, and meannesses of society are the game hunted down by Mr. Thackeray. He keeps almost exclusively amongst the middle-classes; not the fashionable circles, but the people who ape them. The distinction is important, since it gives him a larger scope with less restriction. It is by this standard he must be tested. We must always keep in mind that his *Vanity Fair* is not the Vanity Fair of the upper ranks, where a certain equanimity of breeding absorbs all crudenesses and angularities of character, but the Vanity Fair of the vulgar great, who have no breeding at all. Into this picture all sorts of portraits are freely admissible. There is nothing too base or too low to be huddled up in a corner of the canvas. The most improbable combinations, the most absurd contrasts, are not out of place in this miscellaneous *mélange*. The life that is here painted is not that of high comedy, but of satiric farce; and it is the business of the artist to shew you all its deformities, its cringing affectations, its paltry pride, its despicable finery, its lying, treachery, and penury of soul in the broadest light. Starting from this point, and with this clear understanding, we shall be the better able to comprehend and estimate the nature of the entertainment prepared for us.

The people who fill up the motley scenes of *Vanity Fair*, with two or three exceptions, are as vicious and odious as a clever condensation of the vilest qualities can make them. The women are especially detestable. Cunning, low pride, selfishness, envy, malice, and all uncharitableness, are scattered amongst them with impartial liberality. It does not enter into the design of *Vanity Fair* to qualify these bitter ingredients with a little sweetness now and then; to shew the close neighbourhood of the vices and the virtues as it lies on the map of the human heart, that mixture of good and evil, of weakness and strength, which, in infinitely varied proportions, constitutes the compound individual. The parts here are all patented for set functions, and no lapse into their opposites ever compromises the integrity of the *rôle*. There is some reason in this. The special section of society painted in this book resembles, in more particulars than mere debauchery of life, the conduct of a masquerade where a character is put on as a disguise, and played out with the best skill of the actor, until drunkenness or the death-bed betrays his secret. It is a lie from first to last; and no class of people in the world stand in such need of consistency as liars. We must not quarrel with Mr. Thackeray, then, for not giving Rebecca Sharp an occasional touch of remorse or tenderness, for not suffering paternal Osborne to undergo a twitch of misgiving, and for bringing together a company of fools and rogues who cannot muster up amongst them a single grain of sincerity or good feeling. He knows his sitters well, and has drawn them to the life. *Vanity Fair* is a movable wardrobe, without hearts or understandings beneath.[1] But there still remains the question—important to all Art that addresses itself to the laudable business of scourging the foibles and criminalities of mankind—Is there any den of vice so utterly depraved, any round of intercourse so utterly hollow and deceitful, that there is not some redeeming feature lurking somewhere, under rags or tinsel?

This revolting reflex of society is literally true enough. But it does not shew us the whole truth. Are there not women, even in *Vanity Fair*, capable of nobler things than are here set down for them? Are they all schemers or *intrigantes*, worldwise, shuffling, perfidious, empty-headed? With the exception of poor Amelia, whose pale lustre shines out so gently in the midst of these harpies, there is scarcely a woman in *Vanity Fair* from whom we should not shrink in private life as from a contagion. And poor Amelia goes but a short way to purify the foul atmosphere. The author has given her a heart, but no understanding. If he has made her patient and good, loving, trusting, enduring, he has also made her a fool. Her meekness under suffering, her innocent faith in the evils which she lacks sagacity to penetrate, constantly excite our pity; but the helpless weakness of her character forces the sentiment to the verge of that feeling to which pity is said to be akin.

We touch upon this obvious defect in this remarkable work because it lies upon the surface, and must not only challenge general observation, but is not unlikely to draw down in some quarters indiscriminating censure. Over-good people will be apt to shudder at a story so full of petty vices and grovelling passions. They will be afraid to trust it in the hands of young ladies and gentlemen, lest the unredeemed wickedness of its pictures should corrupt their morals, and send them into the world shut up in a crust of selfishness and suspicion. But this sort of apprehension, natural enough in its way, is manifestly founded upon a false and superficial estimate of the tendency

[1] Cf. Pope's 'They shift the moving toyshop of their heart' (*The Rape of the Lock* (1712–14), i, 100).

of the work. Beneath the sneers and cynicism of *Vanity Fair* there is an important moral, which the large population of novel-readers, who skim hastily over the pages of a book, are almost sure to miss, although they are the very people of all the world to whom practically it ought to be most useful. The vices painted in this book lie about us as 'thick as leaves in Vallambrosa.' We tread amongst them every day of our lives. Mr. Thackeray exposes them for the benefit of mankind. He shews them plainly in all their hideousness. He warns us off the infected spots. It is not enough to say that he never makes them tempting or successful, although he exhibits the attractions by which they sometimes prosper, and even goes so far as to give us a glimpse of the uneasy triumphs they sometimes achieve (more repulsive than the most ignominious failures); but that he produces upon the whole such a view of the egotism, faithlessness, and low depravities of the society he depicts, as to force us to look into the depths of a loathsome truth which the best of us are willing enough to evade, if we can. No doubt we pant for a little clear air in this pestiferous region; we feel oppressed by the weight of these loaded vapours, this stifling malaria. But who objects to Hogarth's 'Gin Lane' that it discloses a scene which offends his taste and shocks his sensibility? The moralist often effects the largest amount of good when he assails the nerves and faltering judgment of people who want the courage to follow out his labours to their final issues.

The defect is not in the moral of *Vanity Fair*, but in the artistical management of the subject. More light and air would have rendered it more agreeable and more healthy. The author's genius takes him off too much in the direction of satire. He has so quick an instinct for the ridiculous, that he finds it out even in the most pathetic passages. He cannot call up a tear without dashing it off with a sarcasm. Yet his power of creating emotion is equal to his wit, although he seems to have less confidence in it, or to have an inferior relish for the use of it. Hence the book, with a great capacity for tenderer and graver things, excels in keen ridicule, and grotesque caricature, and irresistible exaggerations of all sorts of social follies and delinquencies. The universal traits and general truths which he scatters about are accidental, not elementary; his men and women are expressly denizens of Russell Square and Park Lane; he keeps close to his text throughout; his heads are portraits, not passions; he describes less the philosophy of human action than the contrasts and collisions of a conventional world; and he seizes upon the small details which make up the whole business of the kind of life he paints with a minuteness, precision, and certainty, and throws them out with a sharpness of outline and depth of colour rarely if ever equalled. The sustaining power with which these influential trivialities are carried through a narrative of extraordinary length, and the tact with which they are selected and accumulated, display a knowledge of the 'frets and stops' of familiar experience, and an artistical faculty which will present as salient attractions to future readers as to ourselves. Alas! there will always be a Vanity Fair in this world, of which this crafty book will be recognized as the faithful image. . . .

Looking back upon this story, we are struck more than ever by the simplicity of its conduct. It is not constructed upon a legitimate principle, or upon any principle at all. It is a novel without a plan, as without a hero. There are two distinct narratives running through it, which not only never interfere with each other, but frequently help each other on. Shoals of characters are drafted through its pages, but they never crowd or jostle each other, or produce the slightest confusion of action or obscurity of incident. The whole business of the fiction moves on before us, with as little reference to a beginning, middle, or end, as the progress of one's own life. The established usages of novels are entirely set aside. Instead of winding up with the merry marriage bells, as if all human interest in the personages of a story terminated in Doctors' Commons, the real interest does not fairly begin until the marriage bells have done their office. Nor is this interest kept up by factitious means. There are no extraneous sources opened as we go along—no episodes to relieve the route—no superfluous characters to strew it with variety. The interest is progressive and complete to the end.

There is another merit in this story. It is free from over-refinement or elaboration. All is direct, palpable, and close. The touches exhibit the decisive hand of a true artist. There is never any necessity to repeat them, or to go back to clear up knots or mysteries in the narrative: there is nothing to clear up; it is all onward and straightforward.

'A great book', says the proverb, 'is a great evil'; and although we should be unwilling to lose a page of *Vanity Fair*, we may advise the author to keep within narrower limits in future. It is a gigantic undertaking to get through this massive volume, and in this age the consumption of time is a consideration. Inordinate length, however ably maintained, is an obstruction to enjoyment; and an author may be said to stand in his own light who produces a book that makes an unreasonable demand on the leisure of his readers. The attraction must be of a remarkable kind which can hold us in suspense over so huge an octavo; yet, large as this octavo is, we put it down with reluctance. The originality of the treatment, the freshness and fluency of the style, and the absence of peculiarities in the diction or terms of expression, inspire it with the charm of perpetual variety. No writer was ever less of a mannerist, and few writers have displayed within the compass of a single story more fertility of invention, or a more accurate knowledge of life. . . .

16. Thackeray, letter to Robert Bell

3 September 1848 (*Letters*, ii, 423–5)

My dear Bell
　　Although I have made a rule to myself never to thank critics yet I like to break it continually, and especially in the present instance for what I hope is the excellent article in Fraser. It seems to me very just in most points as regards the author: some he questions as usual— If I had put in more fresh air as you call it my object would have been defeated—It is to indicate, in cheerful terms, that we are for the most part an abominably foolish and selfish people 'desperately wicked' and all eager after vanities. Everybody is you see in that book,—for instance if I had made Amelia a higher order of woman there would have been no vanity in Dobbins falling in love with her, whereas the impression at present is that he is a fool for his pains that he has married a silly little thing and in fact has found out his error rather a sweet and tender one however, *quia multum amavit* I want to leave everybody dissatisfied and unhappy at the end of the story—we ought all to be with out own and all other stories. Good God don't I see (in that may-be cracked and warped looking glass in which I am always looking) my own weaknesses wickednesses lusts follies shortcomings? in company let us hope with better qualities about which we will pretermit discourse. We must lift up our voices about these and howl to a congregation of fools: so much at least has been my endeavour. You have all of you taken my misanthropy to task—I wish I could myself: but take the world by a certain standard (you know what I mean) and who dares talk of having any virtue at all? For instance Forster says After a scene with Blifil, the air is cleared by a laugh of

Tom Jones[1]—Why Tom Jones in my holding is as big a rogue as Blifil. Before God he is—I mean the man is selfish according to his nature as Blifil according to his. In fact I've a strong impression that we are most of us not fit for—never mind.

Pathos I hold should be very occasional indeed in humorous works and indicated rather than expressed or expressed very rarely. In the passage where Amelia is represented as trying to separate herself from the boy—She goes upstairs and leaves him with his aunt 'as that poor Lady Jane Grey tried the axe that was to separate her slender life' [Ch. l]. I say that is a fine image whoever wrote it (& I came on it quite by surprize in a review the other day) that is greatly pathetic I think: it leaves you to make your own sad pictures—We shouldn't do much more than that I think in comic books—In a story written in the pathetic key it would be different & then the comedy perhaps should be occasional. Some day—but a truce to egotistical twaddle. It seems to me such a time ago that V F was written that one may talk of it as of some body elses performance. My dear Bell I am very thankful for your friendliness & pleased to have your good opinion.

Faithfully yours

W. M. Thackeray.

17. [Charles Astor Bristed], from 'Vanity Fair', the *American Review*

New York, October 1848, viii, 421–31

Bristed (1820–74), a grandson of John Jacob Astor II, was educated at Yale and Trinity College, Cambridge. He was a miscellaneous writer, critic, translator and classical scholar.

An Anglo-Saxon can appreciate, although he may not altogether admire Gallic wit; but a Gaul is hopelessly incompetent to understand Saxon humor. It is to him what the Teutonic humor is to both Saxon and Gaul, who suppose it must be humorous to the Teuton because he vastly delights in it, but find it, so far as themselves are concerned,

[1] See No. 13, p. 36.

dreary in the extreme, and utterly valueless for purposes of amusement. Here is a book which has a brilliant run in England, where its author is acknowledged as one of the first periodical writers; we doubt if any Frenchman could go through it without falling asleep in spite of the pictures. In our own country, where the original Saxon character has become partially Gallicized, the public opinion (setting aside that class of readers, unfortunately too large, who are the willing slaves of the publishers, and feel bound to read and talk about a book because it is advertised by a big house, in big letters, as 'Thackeray's Masterpiece,') is about equally divided, some much enjoying *Vanity Fair*, others voting it a great bore.

French wit and English humor! We do not mean to expatiate on this often-discussed theme, tempting though it be, affording copious opportunity for antitheses more or less false, and distinctions without differences, but shall merely hint at what seems the most natural way to explain this national diversity of taste and appreciation in respect of the two faculties. Wit consists in the expression more than in the matter—it depends very considerably on the words employed—and hence the wittiest French sayings are, if not inexpressible, at least *inexpressive* in English. Under the homely Saxon garb they generally become very stupid or very wicked remarks—not unfrequently both. But an Englishman with a respectable knowledge of French can understand and be amused by French wit, though he will probably not enter into it very heartily. Humor, on the other hand, depends on a particular habit of mind; so that, to enjoy English humor, a Frenchman must not only understand English, but become intellectually Anglicized to a degree that is unnatural to him. In proof of this, it may be noticed that French-educated or *French-minded* Americans find Thackeray tedious, and (to take a stronger case, where no national prejudice but a favorable one can be at work,) yawn over Washington Irving.

And yet, if we wished to give an idea of Thackeray's writings to a person who had never read them, we should go to France for our first illustration; but it would be to French art, not French literature. No one who has ever been familiar with the pictured representations of Parisian life which embellish that repository of wicked wit, the *Charivari*—no one who knows *Les Lorettes, Les Enfants Terribles*, &c., would think of applying to the designs of Gavarni and his brother artists the term *caricatures*.[1] He would say, 'There is no caricature

[1] Paul Gavarni (1804–66) drew for *Le Charivari*, the comic and satirical magazine founded by Charles Philipon in 1832.

about them; they are life itself.' And so it is with Thackeray's writings; they present you with humorous sketches of real life—literal comic pictures—never rising to the ideal or diverging into the grotesque. Thus, while his stories are excellent as a collection of separate sketches, they have but moderate merit *as stories*, nor are his single characters great as single characters. Becky Sharp is the only one that can be called a first-rate hit; for 'Chawls Yellowplush' is characterized chiefly by his ludicrous spelling, and his mantle fits 'Jeemes' just as well. And just as Gavarni differs from and is inferior to Hogarth, should we say Thackeray differs from and is inferior to Dickens, a writer with whom he is sometimes compared, and to whom he undoubtedly has some points of resemblance, though he cannot with any propriety be called 'of the Dickens school,' or 'an imitator of Dickens,' any more than Gavarni could be called an imitator of Hogarth.

Thackeray has his points of contact, also, with another great humorous writer, Washington Irving. Very gracefully and prettily does Mr. Titmarsh write at times; there is many a little bit, here and there, in the *Journey from Cornhill to Cairo*, that would not disgrace Geoffrey Crayon in his best mood.[1] But his geniality is not so genuine, or so continuous. Not that there is anything affected about his mirth—he is one of the most natural of modern English writers: Cobbett or Sidney Smith could hardly be more so; but it is dashed with stronger ingredients. Instead of welling up with perennial jollity, like our most good-humored of humorous authors, he is evidently a little *blasé*, and somewhat disposed to be cynical.

To compare Thackeray with Dickens and Irving, most of our readers will think paying him a high compliment, but we are not at all sure that his set would be particularly obliged to us; for it is the fortune—good in some respects, evil in others—of Mr. Titmarsh to be one of a set. But wherever there are literary men there will be sets; and those who have been bored and disgusted by the impertinence and nonsense of stupid cliques will be charitable to the occasional conceits of clever ones. Having had some happy experience of that literary society which is carried to greater perfection in England than in any other country, we can pardon the amiable cockneyism with which Michael Angelo's thoughts revert to his Club even amid the finest scenery of other lands, and the semi-ludicrous earnestness with which he dwells on the circumstance of your name being posted among the 'members deceased,' as if that were the most awful and striking circum-

[1] Geoffrey Crayon was a pseudonym of Irving's.

stance attendant on dissolution. And, inasmuch as all his books are really books to be read, we can excuse the quiet way in which he assumes that you *have* read them all, and alludes, as a matter of course, to the Hon. Algernon Deuceace and the Earl of Crabs, and such ideal personages, much after the manner of that precious Balzac who interweaves the same characters throughout the half-hundred or more volumes which compose his panorama of Parisian society—a society in which, as Macaulay says of another school, 'the women are like very bad men, and the men too bad for anything.'

This mention of Balzac brings to mind a more serious charge than that of occasional conceit or affectation which we have more than once heard urged against our author; namely, that his sketches contain too many disagreeable characters. A queer charge this to come from a reading generation which swallows copious illustrated editions of *Les Mystères* and *Le Juif*, and is lenient to the loathsome vulgarities of Wuthering Heights and Wildfell Hall.[1] But let us draw a distinction or 'discriminate a difference,' as a transcendentalist acquaintance of ours used to say. If a story is written for mere purposes of amusement, there certainly ought not to be more disagreeable characters introduced than are absolutely necessary for relief and contrast. But the moral and end of a story may often compel the author to bring before us a great number of unpleasant people. In a former volume of this Review the opinion was pretty broadly stated that no eminent novelist writes merely for amusement without some ulterior aim; most decidedly Thackeray does not at any rate. We shall have occasion to refer to this more than once, for it is doing vast injustice to Mr. T. to regard him merely as a provider of temporary fun. He does introduce us to many scamps, and profligates, and hypocrites, but it is to show them up and put us on our guard against them. His bad people are evidently and unmistakably bad; we hate them, and he hates them, too, and doesn't try to make us fall in love with them, like the philosophers of the 'Centre of Civilization,' who dish you up seraphic poisoners and chaste adulteresses in a way that perplexes and confounds all established ideas of morality.[2] And if he ever does bestow attractive traits on his rogues, it is to expose the worthlessness and emptiness of some things which are to the world attractive—to show that the good things of

---

[1] *Les Mystères de Paris* (1842–3) and *Le Juif errant* (1844–5) were by Eugène Sue (see above, p. 37). *Wuthering Heights* and *The Tenant of Wildfell Hall* were published in 1847 and 1848 respectively.

[2] Similar objections to French novels were frequently made in British periodicals of the time.

Vanity Fair are not good *per se*, but may be coincident with much depravity.

Thus Becky Sharp, as portrayed by his graphic pen, is an object of envy and admiration for her cleverness and accomplishments to many a fine lady. There are plenty of the 'upper ten' who would like to be as 'smart' as Rebecca.[1] She speaks French like a French woman, and gets up beautiful dresses out of nothing, and makes all the men admire her, and always has a repartee ready, and insinuates herself everywhere with an irresistible nonchalance. Then comes in the sage moralist, and shows us that a woman may do all these fine things, and yet be ready to lie right and left to every one, and ruin any amount of confiding tradesmen; to sell one man and poison another; to betray her husband and neglect her child. (That last touch is the most hateful one: in our simplicity we hope it is an exaggeration. That a woman should be utterly regardless of her offspring seems an impossibility— in this country, we are proud to say, it *is* an impossibility.) Or if any of his doubtful personages command our temporary respect and sympathy, it is because they are for the time in the right. Rawdon Crawley is not a very lofty character; he frequently comes before us in a position not even respectable; but when he is defending his honor against the old sybarite Lord Steyne, he rises with the occasion: even the guilty wife is forced to admire her husband, as he stands 'strong, brave, and victorious.' Nor though he finds it sometimes necessary to expose hypocrites, does Thackeray delight in the existence of hypocrisy, and love to seek out bad motives for apparently good actions. His charity rather leads him to attribute with a most humane irony pretended wickedness to weakness. Your French writer brings an upright gentleman before the footlights, and grudges you the pleasure of admiring him; he is impatient to carry him off behind the scenes, strip off his Christian garments, and show him to you in private a very fiend. But Thackeray, when he has put into a youth's mouth an atrociously piratical song, is overjoyed to add quietly that he 'remembers seeing him awfully sick on board a Greenwich steamer'.

Thus far our description has been one of negatives. It is time to say something of the positive peculiarities of Mr. T., two of which are strikingly observable,—the one in his serious, the other in his comic vein. We shall begin by the latter, for though to us he is greater as a

[1] The 'upper ten' or 'upper ten thousand' refers to American families of the highest social status. Bristed himself wrote *The Upper Ten Thousand: Sketches of American Society* (New York, 1852), which first appeared in *Fraser's Magazine* in 1850.

moralist than as a humorist, we are well aware that the general opinion is the other way, and that he is most generally valued for his fun. Many of the present English comic writers excel to an almost Aristophanic degree in parody and travestie, but in the latter Thackeray is unrivalled. Now he derides in the most ludicrous jargon, the absurd fopperies of the Court Circulars: 'Head dress of knockers and bell-pulls, stomacher a muffin;' now he audaciously burlesques the most classic allusions 'about Mademoiselle Arianne of the French Opera, and who had left her, and how she was consoled by Panther Carr.' Some men have that felicity in story-telling that they will make you laugh at the veriest Joe Miller as if it had been just invented, and similarly there is nothing so old or so dry, but it becomes a subject for mirth under Titmarsh's ready pen or pencil, (for Michael Angelo is an artist himself, and a right clever one, and needs no Cruikshank or Leech to illustrate him). Every one has heard the story of the Eastern monarch, who used to impose upon travelling poets by means of his astonishing memory, and how a Dervish finally outwitted him. Thousands had read it without dreaming of its capabilities. In one of the early volumes of *Punch* you will find it Thackerayized into something very rich. Living poets and poetasters are brought in under Oriental disguises; the mischievous king learns a whole poem of 'Buhl-ware Khan' by dint of memory, 'without understanding one word of it'; the Dervish is a 'Syncretic' poet, 'Jam Jawbrahim Heraudee,' (Heraud), who puts the king to sleep by discharging an epic at him.[1] But Thackeray never sets about a story of any length without having a will and a purpose. And this indeed is a noticeable difference generally existing between the wit and the humorist, that while the former sparkles away without any object beyond his own momentary amusement, the latter has a definite aim, some abuse to attack, some moral to hint. Thackeray attacks abuses, and it is with an honest indignation and simple earnestness that form the distinguishing features of his serious writings. He assaults all manner of social sham, humbug and flunkeyism, and gives it to them in a way that does you good to hear. Against toadyism, affectation and mobbery, he preaches a crusade in the sturdiest Anglo-Saxon. The charge began in the *Snobs of England*; it is now followed up in *Vanity Fair*. Any one, therefore, who reads the latter book should read the 'Snob Papers' in *Punch*, by way of introduction to it. Tin-worship and title-worship, and that 'praise of men'

---

[1] 'The Legend of Jawbrahim-Heraudee' was Thackeray's first authenticated contribution to *Punch* (18 June 1842); it is in *Works*, vii, 239–50.

which your fashionables love more than the 'praise of God'—Titmarsh is sworn foe to all these, and wages unrelenting war on them—but with none of that cant which runs all through Jerrold and half through Dickens: he does not make all his poor people angels, nor all his rich people devils, because they are rich. Nor has he any marked prejudice against Christianity in general, or the Christianity of his own church in particular—which we are weak enough to think rather to his credit. Moreover his sledge-hammer invective against fashionable fooleries, is not engendered of or alloyed with any rusticity or inability to appreciate the refinements of civilized life, as a backwoodsman or Down-easter might abuse things he did not comprehend; for Titmarsh has a soul for art and poetry, and good living, and all that is æsthetic and elegant. . . .

[Summary, with extracts, of the plot and chief characters.]

Some notice should be taken of the Osbornes and Sedleys who make up the underplot of the story. We have some suspicion that Thackeray finished up old Osborne, the purse-proud merchant, more carefully than he had intended at first, in opposition to Mr. Dombey, to show *his* view of such a character in opposition to that of Dickens. If such a comparison is challenged, there can be no doubt that so far as verisimilitude and nature are concerned, Mr. Osborne, Sr., has it by long odds. There never was such a merchant or man of business at all as Mr. Dombey. His calm, icy pride is not the pride of a merchant at all; it would be in character for a nobleman or a gentleman of old family. We wonder Dickens did not make him one or the other. There was nothing in the exigencies of the story to forbid it. Noblemen are ruined easily enough now-a-days—witness the Duke of Bucking-ham, who has just been sold out as completely as the veriest Wall-street speculator, to the great joy of all radicals.[1] Nor is Mr. D. let down and made to relent in a natural, gradual and plausible way, as Mr. O. is; but taken off the stage as melo-dramatically as he was brought on.

The loves and fortunes of young Osborne and Amelia Sedley, are designed to carry out still further the attack on what formed one of the strongest topics of denunciation in the 'Snob Papers,'—that heartless system (flourishing to perfection in France, but deep-rooted enough in England) which considers matrimony as the union, not of a young

---

[1] The second Duke of Buckingham (1797–1861) came to financial ruin in 1847; most of his estates and possessions were sold in 1848.

man to a young woman, but of *so much to so much*. A splendid theme for indignant declamation, and one in which the satirist is sure to meet with much sympathy from the young of both sexes. But we must remember that the principle of union for love has, like all principles, its limitations. That two young people, long and fondly attached to each other, should be afraid to marry because they would be obliged to drop a little in the social scale, and deny themselves some of the outward luxuries they enjoy separately; that they should sacrifice their hearts to those abominable dictates of fashion which Titmarsh has summed up in his Snob Commandment, 'Thou shalt not marry unless thou hast a Brougham and a man-servant;' this is truly matter of indignation and mourning, against which it is not possible to say too much. But we must also protest against the opposite extreme—the inference drawn from an extension of our principle—that love ought to overcome and exclude *all* objections, want of principles and character in the man for instance; or utter want of means on both sides to support a family; or even—what is generally the first thing to be disregarded in such cases—incompatibility of relations and friends. Sentimentalists talk as if love were to be the substitute for, or at least the equal of religion, (it *is* the only religion of the French writers), whereas, in truth, it is no more infallible in its decisions or imperative in its claims than ambition, or courage, or benevolence, or various other passions, which, either indifferent or positively laudable in themselves, are liable to sad perversion and exaggeration. The lover makes great sacrifices for his mistress; so does the ambitious man for his ambition; the covetous man for his fortune; and, to take a passion wholly and unmitigatedly bad, the vindictive man for his revenge. In all these cases the sacrifices are made for the same end—the securing of a desired object for self; but because, in the first case, the object of desire is not the possession of a mere abstraction like fame, or of a mere material like money, but of another human being, therefore love has the *appearance* of being the most disinterested and self-sacrificing of the passions, while it is, in reality, generally the most selfish. Is this view a soulless and worldly one? We appeal to your own experience, reader. Of all the *pur sang* love-matches you have known—matches where one or more of the impediments we have mentioned existed—how many have turned out happily? Nay, we appeal to Titmarsh himself and *his own characters in this very book*. Would it not have been a thousand times better for Amelia if she had married Dobbin in the first place? And might not George as well have taken Miss Swartz as wed Amelia one month and been ready to run away with another woman the next?*

We must take leave of Titmarsh; for he is carrying us off into all sorts of digressions. We never were so long filling the same number of pages as we have been on the present occasion, for whenever we opened the book to make an extract we were tempted to read on, on, on—the same things which we had read a dozen times—but there was no resisting. And when we resolutely turned our back to his people, it was only to think, and reason, and argue about them. How many of the hundreds of novels, published every year, leave any impression in your mind or give you one afterthought about any character in them? It is easy to take exceptions to the book—we have taken our share; we might go on to pick out little slips, instances of forgetfulness, as where we are told first that Amelia Sedley is not the heroine, and two or three pages after that she is; or when the climate of Coventry Island is so bad that no office will insure Rawdon's life there, yet in the very same number it is mentioned how much his life-insurance cost him. But, say what you will, the book draws you back to it, over and over again. Farewell then, O Titmarsh! Truly, thou deservest better treatment than we can give thee. Thy book should be written about in a natural, even, continuous, flowing style like thine own, not in our lumbering paragraphs, that blunder out only half of what we mean to say. And do thou, O reader, buy this book if thou has not bought it; if thou hast, throw it not away into the chiffonier-basket as thou dost many brown-paper-covered volumes; but put it into a good binding and lay it by—not among the works 'that no gentleman's library should be without'—but somewhere easy of access; for it is a book to keep and read, and there are many sermons in it.

* This is an element that never enters into the sentimentalist's calculation—if sentimentalists ever make calculations—the inconstancy of love. Could the continuance of a first passion be insured, there would be more excuse for putting it above prudence, and duty, and filial affection; but alas! it often vanishes in what D'Israeli not unfelicitously calls 'a crash of iconoclastic surfeit,' and then, when that, for which everything was given up, becomes itself nothing, the reaction is awful [Bristed's note].

18. [Elizabeth Rigby (later, Lady Eastlake)], from 'Vanity Fair—and Jane Eyre', Quarterly Review

December 1848, lxxxiv, 153–85

Besides her many articles in the *Quarterly*, Lady Eastlake (1809–93) wrote books on art—her husband, Sir Charles, was P.R.A. from 1850 to 1865. The present article is perhaps most famous for its objections to the unchristian tone of *Jane Eyre* in a passage here omitted.

A remarkable novel is a great event for English society. It is a kind of common friend, about whom people can speak the truth without fear of being compromised, and confess their emotions without being ashamed. We are a particularly shy and reserved people, and set about nothing so awkwardly as the simple art of getting really acquainted with each other. We meet over and over again in what is conventionally called 'easy society,' with the tacit understanding to go so far and no farther; to be as polite as we ought to be, and as intellectual as we can; but mutually and honourably to forbear lifting those veils which each spreads over his inner sentiments and sympathies. For this purpose a host of devices have been contrived by which all the forms of friendship may be gone through, without committing ourselves to one spark of the spirit. We fly with eagerness to some common ground in which each can take the liveliest interest, without taking the slightest in the world in his companion. Our various fashionable manias, for charity one season, for science the next, are only so many clever contrivances for keeping our neighbour at arm's length. We can attend committees, and canvass for subscribers, and archæologise, and geologise, and take ether with our fellow Christians for a twelvemonth, as we might sit cross-legged and smoke the pipe of fraternity with a Turk for the same period—and know at the end of the time as little of the real feelings of the one as we should about the domestic relations of the other. But there are ways and means for lifting the veil which equally favour our national idiosyncrasy; and a new and

77

remarkable novel is one of them—especially the nearer it comes to real life. We invite our neighbour to a walk with the deliberate and malicious object of getting thoroughly acquainted with him. We ask no impertinent questions—we proffer no indiscreet confidences—we do not even sound him, ever so delicately, as to his opinion of a common friend, for he would be sure not to say, lest we should go and tell; but we simply discuss Becky Sharp, or Jane Eyre, and our object is answered at once.

There is something about these two new and noticeable characters which especially compels everybody to speak out. They are not to be dismissed with a few commonplace moralities and sentimentalities. They do not fit any ready-made criticism. They give the most stupid something to think of, and the most reserved something to say; the most charitable too are betrayed into home comparisons which they usually condemn, and the most ingenious stumble into paradoxes which they can hardly defend. Becky and Jane also stand well side by side both in their analogies and their contrasts. Both the ladies are governesses, and both make the same move in society; the one, in Jane Eyre phraseology, marrying her 'master,' and the other her master's son. Neither starts in life with more than a moderate capital of good looks—Jane Eyre with hardly that—for it is the fashion now-a-days with novelists to give no encouragement to the insolence of mere beauty, but rather to prove to all whom it may concern how little a sensible woman requires to get on with in the world. Both have also an elfish kind of nature, with which they divine the secrets of other hearts, and conceal those of their own; and both rejoice in that peculiarity of feature which Mademoiselle de Luzy[1] has not contributed to render popular, viz., green eyes. Beyond this, however, there is no similarity either in the minds, manners, or fortunes of the two heroines. They think and act upon diametrically opposite principles—at least so the author of *Jane Eyre* intends us to believe—and each, were they to meet, which we should of all things enjoy to see them do, would cordially despise and abominate the other. Which of the two, however, would most successfully *dupe* the other is a different question, and one not so easy to decide; though we have our own ideas upon the subject.

We must discuss *Vanity Fair* first, which, much as we were entitled to expect from its author's pen, has fairly taken us by surprise. We were perfectly aware that Mr. Thackeray had of old assumed the

[1] Reference not traced.

jester's habit, in order the more unrestrainedly to indulge the privilege of speaking the truth;—we had traced his clever progress through *Fraser's Magazine* and the ever-improving pages of *Punch*—which wonder of the time has been infinitely obliged to him[1]—but still we were little prepared for the keen observation, the deep wisdom, and the consummate art which he has interwoven in the slight texture and whimsical pattern of *Vanity Fair*. Everybody, it is to be supposed, has read the volume by this time; and even for those who have not, it is not necessary to describe the order of the story. It is not a novel, in the common acceptation of the word, with a plot purposely contrived to bring about certain scenes, and develop certain characters, but simply a history of those average sufferings, pleasures, penalties, and rewards to which various classes of mankind gravitate as naturally and certainly in this world as the sparks fly upward. It is only the same game of life which every player sooner or later makes for himself—were he to have a hundred chances, and shuffle the cards of circumstance every time. It is only the same busy, involved drama which may be seen at any time by any one, who is not engrossed with the magnified minutiæ of his own petty part, but with composed curiosity looks on to the stage where his fellow men and women are the actors; and that not even heightened by the conventional colouring which Madame de Staël philosophically declares that fiction always wants in order to make up for its not being truth.[2] Indeed, so far from taking any advantage of this novelist's licence, Mr. Thackeray has hardly availed himself of the natural average of remarkable events that really do occur in this life. The battle of Waterloo, it is true, is introduced; but, as far as regards the story, it brings about only one death and one bankruptcy, which might either of them have happened in a hundred other ways. Otherwise the tale runs on, with little exception, in that humdrum course of daily monotony, out of which some people coin materials to act, and others excuses to doze, just as their dispositions may be.

It is this reality which is at once the charm and the misery here. With all these unpretending materials it is one of the most amusing, but also one of the most distressing books we have read for many a long year. We almost long for a little exaggeration and improbability

---

[1] *Punch*, which began on 17 July 1841, was not outstandingly successful at first, but by 1848 had become prosperous and popular, thanks to such features as Leech's drawings, Hood's 'The Song of the Shirt,' Jerrold's 'Mrs. Caudle's Curtain Lectures,' and Thackeray's 'The Snobs of England'.

[2] See the third section of her 'Essai sur les fictions' (1795), prefixed to her volume of three stories, *Mirza*, *Adelaide et Théodore*, and *Pauline*.

to relieve us of that sense of dead truthfulness which weighs down our hearts, not for the Amelias and Georges of the story, but for poor kindred human nature. In one light this truthfulness is even an objection. With few exceptions the personages are too like our every-day selves and neighbours to draw any distinct moral from. We cannot see our way clearly. Palliations of the bad and disappointments in the good are perpetually obstructing our judgment, by bringing what should decide it too close to that common standard of experience in which our only rule of opinion is charity. For it is only in fictitious characters which are highly coloured for one definite object, or in notorious personages viewed from a distance, that the course of the true moral can be seen to run straight—once bring the individual with his life and circumstances closely before you, and it is lost to the mental eye in the thousand pleas and witnesses, unseen and unheard before, which rise up to overshadow it. And what are all these personages in *Vanity Fair* but feigned names for our own beloved friends and acquaintances, seen under such a puzzling cross-light of good in evil, and evil in good, of sins and sinnings against, of little to be praised virtues, and much to be excused vices, that we cannot presume to moralise upon them—not even to judge them,—content to exclaim sorrowfully with the old prophet, 'Alas! my brother!' Every actor on the crowded stage of *Vanity Fair* represents some type of that perverse mixture of humanity in which there is ever something not wholly to approve or to condemn. There is the desperate devotion of a fond heart to a false object, which we cannot respect; there is the vain, weak man, half good and half bad, who is more despicable in our eyes than the decided villain. There are the irretrievably wretched education, and the unquenchably manly instincts, both contending in the confirmed *roué*, which melt us to the tenderest pity. There is the selfishness and self-will which the possessor of great wealth and fawning relations can hardly avoid. There is the vanity and fear of the world, which assist mysteriously with pious principles in keeping a man respectable; there are combinations of this kind of every imaginable human form and colour, redeemed but feebly by the steady excellence of an awkward man, and the genuine heart of a vulgar woman, till we feel inclined to tax Mr. Thackeray with an under estimate of our nature, forgetting that Madame de Staël is right after all, and that without a little conventional rouge no human complexion can stand the stage-lights of fiction.

But if these performers give us pain, we are not ashamed to own, as we are speaking openly, that the chief actress herself gives us none at all. For there is of course a principal pilgrim in *Vanity Fair*, as much as in its emblematical original, Bunyan's *Progress*;[1] only unfortunately this one is travelling the wrong way. And we say 'unfortunately' merely by way of courtesy, for in reality we care little about the matter. No, Becky—our hearts neither bleed for you, nor cry out against you. You are wonderfully clever, and amusing, and accomplished, and intelligent, and the Soho *ateliers* were not the best nurseries for a moral training; and you were married early in life to a regular blackleg, and you have had to live upon your wits ever since, which is not an improving sort of maintenance; and there is much to be said for and against; but still you are not one of us, and there is an end to our sympathies and censures. People who allow their feelings to be lacerated by such a character and career as yours, are doing both you and themselves great injustice. No author could have openly introduced a near connexion of Satan's into the best London society, nor would the moral end intended have been answered by it; but really and honestly, considering Becky in her human character, we know of none which so thoroughly satisfies our highest *beau idéal* of feminine wickedness, with so slight a shock to our feelings and proprieties. It is very dreadful, doubtless, that Becky neither loved the husband who loved her, nor the child of her own flesh and blood, nor indeed any body but herself; but, as far as she is concerned, we cannot pretend to be scandalized—for how could she without a heart? It is very shocking of course that she committed all sorts of dirty tricks, and jockeyed her neighbours, and never cared what she trampled under foot if it happened to obstruct her step; but how could she be expected to do otherwise without a conscience? The poor little woman was most tryingly placed; she came into the world without the customary letters of credit upon those two great bankers of humanity, 'Heart and Conscience,' and it was no fault of hers if they dishonoured all her bills. All she could do in this dilemma was to establish the firmest connexion with the inferior commercial branches of 'Sense and Tact,' who secretly do much business in the name of the head concern, and with whom her 'fine frontal development' gave her unlimited credit.[2] She saw that selfishness was the metal which the stamp of heart was suborned to pass; that hypocrisy was the homage that vice rendered to virtue; that honesty was, at all events, acted, because it was the best

---

[1] Thackeray took his title, *Vanity Fair*, from *The Pilgrim's Progress*.

[2] Widespread interest in phrenology began in England in the eighteen-thirties.

policy; and so she practised the arts of selfishness and hypocrisy like anybody else in Vanity Fair, only with this difference, that she brought them to their highest possible pitch of perfection. For why is it that, looking round in this world, we find plenty of characters to compare with her up to a certain pitch, but none which reach her actual standard? Why is it that, speaking of this friend or that, we say in the tender mercies of our hearts, 'No, she is not *quite* so bad as Becky?' We fear not only because she has more heart and conscience, but also because she has less cleverness.

No; let us give Becky her due. There is enough in this world of ours, as we all know, to provoke a saint, far more a poor little devil like her. She had none of those fellow-feelings which make us wondrous kind. She saw people around her cowards in vice, and simpletons in virtue, and she had no patience with either, for she was as little the one as the other herself. She saw women who loved their husbands and yet teazed them, and ruining their children although they doated upon them, and she sneered at their utter inconsistency. Wickedness or goodness, unless coupled with strength, were alike worthless to her. That weakness which is the blessed pledge of our humanity, was to her only the despicable badge of our imperfection. She thought, it might be, of her master's words, 'Fallen cherub! to be weak is to be miserable!' and wondered how we could be such fools as first to sin and then to be sorry. Becky's light was defective, but she acted up to it. Her goodness goes as far as good temper, and her principles as far as shrewd sense, and we may thank her consistency for showing us what they are both worth.

It is another thing to pretend to settle whether such a character be *primâ facie* impossible, though devotion to the better sex might well demand the assertion. There are mysteries of iniquity, under the semblance of man and woman, read of in history, or met with in the unchronicled sufferings of private life, which would almost make us believe that the powers of Darkness occasionally made use of this earth for a Foundling Hospital, and sent their imps to us, already provided with a return-ticket. We shall not decide on the lawfulness or otherwise of any attempt to depict such importations; we can only rest perfectly satisfied that, granting the author's premises, it is impossible to imagine them carried out with more felicitous skill and more exquisite consistency than in the heroine of *Vanity Fair*. At all events, the infernal regions have no reason to be ashamed of little Becky, nor the ladies either: she has, at least, all the cleverness of the sex.

The great charm, therefore, and comfort of Becky is, that we may study her without any compunctions. The misery of this life is not the evil that we see, but the good and the evil which are so inextricably twisted together. It is that perpetual memento ever meeting one—

> How in this vile world below
> Noblest things find vilest using,[1]

that is so very distressing to those who have hearts as well as eyes. But Becky relieves them of all this pain—at least in her own person. Pity would be thrown away upon one who has not heart enough for it to ache even for herself. Becky is perfectly happy, as all must be who excel in what they love best. Her life is one exertion of successful power. Shame never visits her, for ''Tis conscience that makes cowards of us all'—and she has none. She realizes that *ne plus ultra* of sublunary comfort which it was reserved for a Frenchman to define—the blessed combination of '*le bon estomac et le mauvais cœur:*' for Becky adds to her other good qualities that of an excellent digestion.

Upon the whole, we are not afraid to own that we rather enjoy her *ignis fatuus* course, dragging the weak and the vain and the selfish, through mud and mire, after her, and acting all parts, from the modest rushlight to the gracious star, just as it suits her. Clever little imp that she is! What exquisite tact she shows!—what unflagging good humour!—what ready self-possession! Becky never disappoints us; she never even makes us tremble. We know that her answer will come exactly suiting her one particular object, and frequently three or four more in prospect. What respect, too, she has for those decencies which more virtuous, but more stupid humanity, often disdains! What detection of all that is false and mean! What instinct for all that is true and great! She is her master's true pupil in that: she knows what is really divine as well as he, and bows before it. She honours Dobbin in spite of his big feet; she respects her husband more than ever she did before, perhaps for the first time, at the very moment when he is stripping not only her jewels, but name, honour, and comfort off her.

We are not so sure either whether we are justified in calling hers '*le mauvais cœur.*' Becky does not pursue any one vindictively; she never does gratuitous mischief. The fountain is more dry than poisoned. She is even generous—when she can afford it. Witness that burst of plain speaking in Dobbin's favour to the little dolt Amelia, for which

---

[1] A misquotation from John Keble's 'Palm Sunday' (*The Christian Year*, 1827).

we forgive her many a sin. 'Tis true she wanted to get rid of her; but let that pass. Becky was a thrifty dame, and liked to despatch two birds with one stone. And she was honest, too, after a fashion. The part of wife she acts at first as well, and better than most; but as for that of mother, there she fails from the beginning. She knew that maternal love was no business of hers—that a fine frontal development could give her no help there—and puts so little spirit into her imitation that no one could be taken in for a moment. She felt that that bill, of all others, would be sure to be dishonoured, and it went against her conscience—we mean her sense—to send it in.

In short, the only respect in which Becky's course gives us pain is when it locks itself into that of another, and more genuine child of this earth. No one can regret those being entangled in her nets whose vanity and meanness of spirit alone led them into its meshes—such are rightly served; but we do grudge her that real sacred thing called *love*, even of a Rawdon Crawley, who has more of that self-forgetting, all-purifying feeling for his little evil spirit than many a better man has for a good woman. We do grudge Becky *a heart*, though it belong only to a swindler. Poor, sinned against, vile, degraded, but still true-hearted Rawdon!—you stand next in our affections and sympathies to honest Dobbin himself. It was the instinct of a good nature which made the Major feel that the stamp of the Evil One was upon Becky; and it was the stupidity of a good nature which made the Colonel never suspect it. He was a cheat, a black-leg, an unprincipled dog; but still 'Rawdon *is* a man, and be hanged to him,' as the Rector says. We follow him through the illustrations, which are, in many instances, a delightful enhancement to the text—as he stands there, with his gentle eyelid, coarse moustache, and foolish chin, bringing up Becky's coffee-cup with a kind of dumb fidelity; or looking down at little Rawdon with a more than paternal tenderness. All Amelia's philoprogenitive idolatries do not touch us like one fond instinct of 'stupid Rawdon.'

Dobbin sheds a halo over all the long-necked, loose-jointed, Scotch-looking gentlemen of our acquaintance. Flat feet and flap ears seem henceforth incompatible with evil. He reminds us of one of the sweetest creations that have appeared from any modern pen—that plain, awkward, loveable 'Long Walter,' in Lady Georgiana Fullerton's beautiful novel of *Grantley Manor*.[1] Like him, too, in his proper self-respect; for Dobbin—lumbering, heavy, shy, and absurdly over modest as the ugly fellow is—is yet true to himself. At one time he seems to be

---

[1] Lady Georgiana Fullerton (1812–85), *Grantley Manor* (1847).

sinking into the mere abject dangler after Amelia; but he breaks his chains like a man, and resumes them again like a man, too, although half disenchanted of his amiable delusion.

But to return for a moment to Becky. The only criticism we would offer is one which the author has almost disarmed by making her mother a Frenchwoman. The construction of this little clever monster is diabolically French. Such a *lusus naturæ* as a woman without a heart and conscience would, in England, be a mere brutal savage, and poison half a village. France is the land for the real Syren, with the woman's face and the dragon's claws. The genus of Pigeon and Laffarge claims her for its own—only that our heroine takes a far higher class by not requiring the vulgar matter of fact of crime to develop her full powers.[1] It is an affront to Becky's tactics to believe that she could ever be reduced to so low a resource, or, that if she were, anybody would find it out. We, therefore, cannot sufficiently applaud the extreme discretion with which Mr. Thackeray has hinted at the possibly assistant circumstances of Joseph Sedley's dissolution. A less delicacy of handling would have marred the harmony of the whole design. Such a casualty as that suggested to our imagination was not intended for the light net of *Vanity Fair* to draw on shore; it would have torn it to pieces. Besides it is not wanted. Poor little Becky is bad enough to satisfy the most ardent student of 'good books.' Wickedness, beyond a certain pitch, gives no increase of gratification even to the sternest moralist; and one of Mr. Thackeray's excellences is the sparing quantity he consumes. The whole *use*, too, of the work—that of generously measuring one another by this standard—is lost, the moment you convict Becky of a capital crime. Who can, with any face, liken a dear friend to a murderess? Whereas now there are no little symptoms of fascinating ruthlessness, graceful ingratitude, or ladylike selfishness, observable among our charming acquaintance, that we may not immediately detect to an inch, and more effectually intimidate by the simple application of the Becky gauge than by the most vehement use of all ten commandments. Thanks to Mr. Thackeray, the world is now provided with an *idea*, which, if we mistake not, will be the skeleton in the corner of every ball-room and boudoir for a long time to come. Let us leave it intact in its unique point and freshness—a Becky, and nothing more. We should, therefore, advise our readers to cut out that picture of our heroine's 'Second Appearance as Clytemnestra,' which casts so

[1] Marie Lafarge was imprisoned in 1840 for poisoning her husband but was pardoned by Napoleon III. We have not traced the identity of Pigeon.

uncomfortable a glare over the latter part of the volume, and, disregarding all hints and innuendoes, simply to let the changes and chances of this mortal life have due weight in their minds. Jos had been much in India. His was a bad life; he ate and drank most imprudently, and his digestion was not to be compared with Becky's. No respectable office would have ensured 'Waterloo Sedley.'

Vanity Fair is pre-eminently a novel of the day—not in the vulgar sense, of which there are too many, but as a literal photograph of the manners and habits of the nineteenth century, thrown on to paper by the light of a powerful mind; and one also of the most artistic effect. Mr. Thackeray has a peculiar adroitness in leading on the fancy, or rather memory of his reader from one set of circumstances to another by the seeming chances and coincidences of common life, as an artist leads the spectator's eye through the subject of his picture by a skilful repetition of colour. This is why it is impossible to quote from his book with any justice to it. The whole growth of the narrative is so matted and interwoven together with tendril-like links and bindings, that there is no detaching a flower with sufficient length of stalk to exhibit it to advantage. There is that mutual dependence in his characters which is the first requisite in painting every-day life: no one is stuck on a separate pedestal—no one is sitting for his portrait. There may be one exception—we mean Sir Pitt Crawley, senior: it is possible, nay, we hardly doubt, that this baronet was closer drawn from individual life than anybody else in the book; but granting that fact, the animal was so unique an exception, that we wonder so shrewd an artist could stick him into a gallery so full of our familiars. The scenes in Germany, we can believe, will seem to many readers of an English book hardly less extravagantly absurd—grossly and gratuitously overdrawn; but the initiated will value them as containing some of the keenest strokes of truth and humour that *Vanity Fair* exhibits, and not enjoy them the less for being at our neighbour's expense. For the thorough appreciation of the chief character they are quite indispensable too. The whole course of the work may be viewed as the *Wander-Jahre* of a far cleverer female *Wilhelm Meister*. We have watched her in the ups-and-downs of life—among the humble, the fashionable, the great, and the pious—and found her ever new, yet ever the same; but still Becky among the students was requisite to complete the full measure of our admiration. . . .

19. John Ruskin, two comments, (a) from a MS. note to *Modern Painters*, iii (1856), Part IV, ch. xii, and (b) from *The Storm-Cloud of the Nineteenth Century* (1884)

See *The Works of John Ruskin*, ed. Cook, E. T. and Wedderburn, Alexander, 1903–12, v. 212–13, 213n; xxvii, 562

(a) Compare [with a passage from the *Iliad*, iii, 243] the hammer-stroke at the close of the [thirty-second] chapter of *Vanity Fair*—'Darkness came down on the field and city; and Amelia was praying for George, who was lying on his face, dead, with a bullet through his heart.' A great deal might have been said about it. The writer is very sorry for Amelia, neither does he want faith in prayer. He knows as well as any of us that prayer must be answered in some sort; but those are the facts. The man and the woman sixteen miles apart—one on her knees on the floor, the other on his face in the clay. So much love in her heart, so much lead in his. Make what you can of it.

(b) 'Blasphemy.'—If the reader can refer to my papers on Fiction in the *Nineteenth Century*, he will find this word carefully defined in its Scriptural, and evermore necessary, meaning,—'Harmful speaking'—not against God only, but against man, and against all the good works and purposes of Nature. The word is accurately opposed to 'Euphemy', the right or well-speaking of God and His world; and the two modes of speech are those which, going out of the mouth, sanctify or defile the man.

Going out of the mouth, that is to say, deliberately and of purpose. A French postillion's 'Sacr-r-ré'—loud, with the low 'Nom de Dieu' following between his teeth, is not blasphemy, unless against his horse; but Mr. Thackeray's close of his Waterloo chapter in *Vanity Fair*, 'And all the night long Amelia was praying for George, who was lying on his face, dead, with a bullet through his heart' [*sic*], is blasphemy of the most fatal and subtle kind.

PENDENNIS

1848–50

20. Thackeray, Preface to *Pendennis*

26 November 1850

If this kind of composition, of which the two years' product is now laid before the public, fail in art, as it constantly does and must, it at least has the advantage of a certain truth and honesty, which a work more elaborate might lose. In his constant communication with the reader, the writer is forced into frankness of expression, and to speak out his own mind and feelings as they urge him. Many a slip of the pen and the printer, many a word spoken in haste, he sees and would recall as he looks over his volume. It is a sort of confidential talk between writer and reader, which must often be dull, must often flag. In the course of his volubility, the perpetual speaker must of necessity lay bare his own weaknesses, vanities, peculiarities. And as we judge of a man's character, after long frequenting his society, not by one speech, or by one mood or opinion, or by one day's talk, but by the tenor of his general bearing and conversation; so of a writer, who delivers himself up to you perforce unreservedly, you say, Is he honest? Does he tell the truth in the main? Does he seem actuated by a desire to find out and speak it? Is he a quack, who shams sentiment, or mouths for effect? Does he seek popularity by claptraps or other arts? I can no more ignore good fortune than any other chance which has befallen me. I have found many thousands more readers than I ever looked for. I have no right to say to these, You shall not find fault with my art, or fall asleep over my pages; but I ask you to believe that this person writing strives to tell the truth. If there is not that, there is nothing.

Perhaps the lovers of 'excitement' may care to know that this book began with a very precise plan, which was entirely put aside. Ladies and gentlemen, you were to have been treated, and the writer's and the publishers' pocket benefited, by the recital of the most active horrors.

What more exciting than a ruffian (with many admirable virtues) in St. Giles's, visited constantly by a young lady from Belgravia? What more stirring than the contrasts of society? the mixture of slang and fashionable language? the escapes, the battles, the murders? Nay, up to nine o'clock this very morning, my poor friend, Colonel Altamont, was doomed to execution, and the author only relented when his victim was actually at the window.

The 'exciting' plan was laid aside (with a very honourable forbearance on the part of the publishers) because, on attempting it, I found that I failed from want of experience of my subject; and never having been intimate with any convict in my life, and the manners of ruffians and jail-birds being quite unfamiliar to me, the idea of entering into competition with M. Eugène Sue was abandoned. To describe a real rascal, you must make him so horrible that he would be too hideous to show; and unless the painter paints him fairly, I hold he has no right to show him at all.

Even the gentlemen of our age—this is an attempt to describe one of them, no better nor worse than most educated men—even these we cannot show as they are, with the notorious foibles and selfishness of their lives and their education. Since the author of *Tom Jones* was buried, no writer of fiction among us has been permitted to depict to his utmost power a MAN. We must drape him, and give him a certain conventional simper. Society will not tolerate the Natural in our Art. Many ladies have remonstrated and subscribers left me because, in the course of the story, I described a young man resisting and affected by temptation. My object was to say that he had the passions to feel, and the manliness and generosity to overcome them. You will not hear—it is best to know it—what moves in the real world, what passes in society, in the clubs, colleges, mess-rooms,—what is the life and talk of your sons. A little more frankness than is customary has been attempted in this story; with no bad desire on the writer's part, it is hoped, and with no ill consequence to any reader. If truth is not always pleasant, at any rate truth is best, from whatever chair—from those whence graver writers or thinkers argue, as from that at which the story-teller sits as he concludes his labour, and bids his kind reader farewell.

Though *Pendennis* is full of true, brilliant, deep things,—though it contains many passages of clear and wholesome English such as must rejoice all who are weary of the spasmodic and superb styles of narration,—it cannot be described as an advance on *Vanity Fair*. It is rather like a pair of volumes added to that story,—containing the results of a second ramble among the booths, the wild-beast shows, and the merry-go-rounds of that chaos of folly, vice, and charlatanry. Why must Mr. Thackeray be always 'going to the fair'?—is a question which will occur to many besides ourselves. His authorship seems in some danger of becoming a performance on one string: an execution of a long *fantasia*, with several variations, but all in the same key and all on the same theme of 'Humbug everywhere.' In his Preface he claims the character of a plain speaker. Such a one must also be a candid hearer. Thus, as critics who would fain be of use, we must to the utmost urge our objections to such a monotonous crusade against an enemy whose existence every one admits,—to such a ruthless insistence on the blemishes, incompletenesses, and disappointments which canker every human good and happiness.—This is not overstated. If we are looking at a *Venus*, straight does our anatomist lay his pen point on the ill-modelled corner of the forehead over which the Goddess has drawn her curls. If we are listening to a *Vates*, 'Got-up enthusiasm and eloquence!' whispers the satirist close at our ear. If we are weeping over the sorrows of a heroine, our *Momus* shows us the half-discussed leg of mutton, which like the *Lady Cherubina de Willoughby*, she pushed under the sofa just before we entered and just before she placed herself in that Niobe-like attitude.[1] Now, such being the humour, if not the drift, of this tale, how are we to believe Mr. Thackeray implicitly when he does his best to disclaim effect in his Preface?—how are we to acquit him of being 'a man and a brother,' like every one of those whom he dissects; a creature of mixed motives, into whose authorship a certain professional causticity may have come to be kneaded, from

---

[1] Reference to Lady Cherubina untraced, but cf. *Vanity Fair*, ch. lxv.

its having been found on former occasions appetizing rather than unpleasant?—There seems to us great need that an alarm should be rung pretty loudly in the ears of one of our most shrewd, vigorous, accomplished, and kindly writers,—bidding him beware of his own tendencies lest they become organic defects. The denouncer of nuisances, the omnipresent and omniloquent accuser, who cries 'Death in the pot!'[1] over every morsel that we put into our mouths, becomes himself of nuisances the worst: a perpetual skeleton at the banquet; in its influences nearly as deadly as the vitriols and the sulphates and the rancid particles upon which he is for ever pouncing. The observer who is always watching the follies and pretensions of the second table,— who can hardly get to the end of his monthly part without gossip gathered from the valets' club, or a fling against powdered-head and shoulder-knot, canes and plush breeches,—lies open to the charge, not of despising such 'conventionalisms,' but of being tormented by an irritating sense of their authority. Among all the characters who figure in *Pendennis*, we can name only four depicted as amiable. One is Helen, the hero's mother; and she is often sadly silly. The second is Laura, his Mentor and his reward,—whose womanly pettiness towards poor little Fanny Bolton is exposed with a gratuitous ungraciousness of manner not to be excused by these subsequent revelations, which show little Fanny to be coarse in putting up with young Huxter as a husband, and coquettish in trying to fascinate all her husband's fellow medical students. Foker is number three,—who is nothing when not talking slang. George Warrington is the fourth; and capital as is the sketch, the saturnine and cynical points of his manner and personal habits are as much insisted on as the brave and tender heart over which they are the husk. We are led into the world of literary enterprise to be shown a domain which is only a better sort of literary Back Kitchen. We are introduced into the realm of Art in order that we may have it dinned into our ears that the *Cordelia*, *Lady Macbeth*, *Rosalind* in whom we delight is merely a stupid, soulless puppet, who can move us without being herself moved to a tear, a smile, or a thought by her commerce with the greatest 'beings of the mind' ever evoked by magician. It is true that in this particular province our author has relented over his labours of morbid anatomy. With many of Mr. Thackeray's readers Bows—who some will think might have been added to our list of the amiables—will be a favourite character, precisely because he supplies the element of poetry to that artist life which the

[1] See I *Kings*, xxii, 40.

ruthless author of *Pendennis* has tried so hard to unpoetize. That such an element, by the way, is a constant quality in the theatrical world, all whose imagination is outraged by the picture of such a stupid, pie-making, puppet player-Queen as Miss Fotheringay may take comfort in reflecting. In *Violet, the Danseuse*, there was one of the Bows tribe:—and he it is (taking the name of *Michonnet*) who gives its artless and real pathos to the *Adrienne Lecouvreur* of M. Scribe.[1]

While we protest against the soundness, the sense, nay, we must add, the sincerity of this universal-demolition principle of making dismal effects everywhere in a work professing to give pictures from the world around us,—we willingly do honour to the power and acuteness of the painter. There is one character in *Pendennis* whom Mr. Thackeray has surpassed only in his own *Becky:*—we mean, of course, the Major. On him the author has lavished all his resources. A perfect gentleman of the world he is—expert in detaching the boy from the Costigan nets—heroic in braving the threatening insolence of his valet—pathetic when begging his nephew not to pull down the card-castle built with false cards for the said nephew's benefit. But even in this character Mr. Thackeray, under the desire of sparing no foible, has outraged average nature. The Major Pendennis described to us would not have stooped to an intrigue so sullying as the one by which he tries to secure the Clavering seat and the Begum's fortune for his nephew. To suppress all knowledge of the existence of a felon father with the purpose of grasping a fortune and extorting a settlement—is a villanous meanness, too near kennel-practice for the average club man, be he ever so selfish, to stoop to.

The story in *Pendennis* goes for little:—our author trying to account for its level character by telling us, in his Preface, that he had at first intended to be as strong and murderous as the Sues of novel writing, but gave up the matter in despair from never having lived in the necessary bad company. We are aware, too,—and were at the time, with cordial sympathy—of the serious and all but fatal interruption which this story sustained in its writer's severe illness:—but why need Mr. Thackeray have wound it up with such a helter-skelter indifference? The way in which Pendennis was delivered of Miss Blanche (who, by the way, is capital, as a sort of picaroon sentimentalist) we had foreseen,—and we can swallow Sir Henry Foker's emancipation

[1] The novel *Violet; or, the Danseuse* (1836) was published anonymously and is variously attributed to Lady Malet and one Beasley. Scribe's play was first performed and published in 1849.

from the same *Cleopatra's* toils; but the relief provided for the Begum, which at once relieves all concerned and loads them with a deeper ignominy, is Minerva Press[1] every grain of it.

These objections made,—we may recur to our praise of Mr. Thackeray as an admirable writer of clear, succinct, vigorous English.

22. [John Ritchie Findlay], review in the *Scotsman*

18 December 1850

Findlay (1824–98) joined the *Scotsman* in 1842 and through inheritance became its owner in 1870. In 1886 he published his recollections of De Quincey.

Pendennis is ended; a supply of pleasure and wisdom, anticipated from month to month by many eager votaries, has ceased to flow; the last two bottles of this double dozen of fine-flavoured well-matured wine, have been sent in and drunk, and we must now patiently wait for a renewal of the stock. The readers of periodical novels contract a certain habit of exaction towards the authors who serve up their works in courses of two or three chapters at a time; they come to fancy that the feast should be perpetually renewed. When three volumes of fiction are devoured together, a certain time is felt to be necessary for the repose of both writer and reader, but when the former doles out the portions slowly, the latter is willing that they should be 'continued.' We wonder whether a clever romancist might not profitably take advantage of this feeling, and carry on a work for a series of years, either by spinning it out into seven or eight volumes, after Richardson, or by continually grafting one story to another, and interlacing the threads of interest in the fashion of the *Arabian Nights*.

We only know the value of a thing when it is lost; we can estimate the enjoyment derived from *Pendennis* by its cessation. Pen and his friends have been so long familiar to us that we have regarded them and talked of them as if they were actual men and women, and are only convinced of the truth that they are, in no merely metaphorical sense, 'of such stuff as dreams are made of,' by their little lives being

---

[1] Noted for its sentimental novels.

all so abruptly rounded with a sleep. Let us look back a little, then, on their two years' existence—not merely on the closing events recorded in the double number before us.

In taking such a general survey, it appears to us that this latter novel of Mr Thackeray's is quite worthy of his first. His manner and views do not, of course, seem so fresh, because every man involuntarily repeats himself, and the closeness with which Mr Thackeray follows his own idiosyncrasies prevents him assuming those disguises or affectations of style and thought that others delight in; but there are here greater variety both of character and sentiment, and a less constant indulgence in that cynical philosophy to which our author is prone, and which he is sometimes inclined to carry to an unhealthy and even untrue extent. The interest in *Pendennis* is not so much concentrated upon a single figure as in *Vanity Fair*, the picture is sketched upon a larger canvas, and while the principal characters all attract a fair share of attention, the accessories are yet quite as carefully managed, and the available space filled with quite as many and as cleverly drawn subordinate groups. Nor is the one string of vanity, vanity, so unceasingly harped upon; strains more cheerful and not less true are sometimes heard. We are not of those who condemn Mr Thackeray as one who, having seated himself presumptuously in the chair of the censor, has, in exposing follies, sneering at weaknesses, and castigating cowardice, pretence, and pride, forgotten that he is himself of like nature and subject to similar failings. Such objections, as it seems to us, if not born of affectation, result from a total misapprehension of our author's spirit and tone. It is one of his best peculiarities that he remonstrates as a brother, rather than reproves as a judge, and speaks the bitterest home-truths in a tone generally as full of charity as of contempt. It would be difficult to find any writer dealing so largely in close and special satire who displays so little of personal acerbity. Even where the strokes are thickest and sharpest, one may see that it is a kindly heart and relenting hand that guides the rod. We do not, then, object to the manner of the moralising, but rather to its frequency. We wish for a little more sunshine and less of the shadow on the page. There is, in truth, no good reason why we should always persist in gazing so closely on the picture as to see the roughnesses and false lines in the fair face, or the dark, slovenly corners in the smiling landscape that it represents. Though it be true that the evening cloud that 'turns its silver lining to the light' is nothing better than suspended moisture, it is not less true that it is full of beauty and splendour, which

It is pleasant with a heart at ease,
Just after sunset, or by moonlight skies,[1]

to contemplate, transient though it be; and not less pleasant is it to think also that it probably bears within its bosom showers of fertility and blessing. There is much real goodness and beauty, moral and physical, in the world, and it is better sometimes to ignore the fact that such excellence is never altogether pure and perfect—to forget the flaw in the jewel, the fly in the ointment, the Mordecai sitting at the gate. And the lesson of the worthlessness of human life is one that must be carefully preached on and turned to the best uses, for as it is one that comes in different ways alike to the exhausted votary of pleasure and the self-denying sage, he who inculcates it must take care that he directs his lesson to the production not of misanthropic ennui and disgust, but of the most exalted views and feelings. In *Vanity Fair* the darker shades of life were out of proportion to the lighter and more cheering, and the book consequently leaves a feeling of dissatisfaction and oppressive melancholy on the mind. In *Pendennis* the ingredients are better mixed and balanced, and the impression it produces is much more agreeable and salutary.

It is not the province of the novelist to present us with the cold, naked truth—the 'truth severe' must be 'in fairy fiction dressed,'[2] so as to be presentable and tolerable. In the capital preface in his last number Mr Thackeray candidly admits that 'this kind of composition constantly does and must fail in art,' but claims consideration and credit for 'truth and honesty,' 'frankness of expression,' and avoidance of sham sentiment, quackery, and clap-traps, all of which we most cordially and gratefully grant him to the utmost extent. We do not ask him to shirk telling the truth because 'it is not always pleasant,' but to tell us unpleasant truths only when it is absolutely necessary for us, himself, and his book, and to allow the proportion of the pleasant to the unpleasant to be such that the whole mixture shall not leave a taste in the mouth like that of a dose of bitters—disagreeable though wholesome—but rather of an enlivening, strengthening draught of good liquor. We the rather press this point because our author gently complains that he is not permitted even to speak out so boldly as he would wish to do, and that he has modified his book merely in deference to popular prejudice. [Quotes part of the last paragraph of the

---

[1] Coleridge, 'Fancy in Nubibus' (1818), 1–2.
[2] 'And truth severe, by fairy fiction drest' (Gray, 'The Bard' (1757), iii, 3. 3.)

Preface to *Pendennis*.] Mr Thackeray's 'frankness' in the instance alluded to has not been too great, neither has he constrained himself too much. The fact is, that his very excellence as a delineator of modern life and manners, imposes on him peculiar limitations. He paints so closely, and deals so little in the vague and general, that some subjects which can only be treated in a vague and general style, are in a manner to him forbidden. Thus, though Mr Dickens introduced, in his last novel, a seduction of the worst character, aggravated by every accessary, and episodical and needless as regards the main current of his tale, we should very much question if with him 'ladies remonstrated and subscribers left,' and we doubt it simply because he enveloped the whole in a cloud of sentiment, fancy, and fine writing.[1] Mr Thackeray's bent and genius is towards the actual and elaborately detailed, he would do ill to thwart it, he would perhaps do worse to indulge it in certain cases. Poor Pen was carried far enough towards the verge, no wonder that ladies trembled for him, when Laura and his mother dreaded, almost suspected, him guilty. The degree of difference between the freedom of speech and the amount of strict fidelity allowed to Fielding, and to his successors in our generation, corresponds to the degree of difference between his time and ours, in manners and morals. We would fain hope, indeed we cannot doubt, that there has been improvement, some of it we allow merely external, but certainly not a little real also.

After the frank acknowledgment of a deficiency in art, and the further avowal in the preface of an entire change of the plan, it is perhaps unfair to say much of the failings of the story as a story. Few readers there are that will not be found willing to forgive disproportion of parts, extraneousness of matter and character, breaks and diversions of interest, and a little hurry and staleness of expedient in the winding-up, when they recollect, after all, how much satisfaction they have had in the perusal of almost every page of these two well-filled volumes. On the same plea, they will excuse the bulk of the book, which will however, it is to be feared, prove rather detrimental to its author's future interests, for new readers may be apt to start back affrighted from encountering some eight hundred closely printed pages, though they did not look formidable when spread through a couple of years. It is difficult for us, too, to *praise Pendennis*; we should have so much to say when we began, and should be so sure to repeat much that we have already said from time to time throughout its periodical publica-

---

[1] Steerforth's seduction of Emily (*David Copperfield* (1849–50), chs. xxxi, xlvi, l).

tion.[1] It is full of genius and penetration; calm humour, and tenderest touches of pathos; satire as delicate as it is pungent, and knowledge of life and character generally unpretentious as it is profound. As a sort of moral anatomist Mr Thackeray is altogether without a peer, he discovers and points out with a skill that is marvellous the mixed motives and springs of human action. In this respect he is among novelists what Dr Thomas Brown is among metaphysicians, and possesses, as Thomas Campbell said of the latter, 'an understanding of a mysterious and almost miraculous subtlety.'[2] And what a portrait gallery *Pendennis* is! Our old favourite the Major, dandy and diplomatist to the last, full of bodily infirmity and military resolution, good-natured and hard-hearted, cool, worldly, and clever, clear-sighted within his own range, and with purely conventional notions of virtue and honour; that irreclaimable tippler and innocent braggart, 'the brave ould *General*' Costigan; the generous, rough, noble-hearted, semi-cynic Warrington; the foolish, *gentish*, and dull but well-meaning Foker; these (with, of course, Pen himself) are all highly-finished full-lengths. So on the female side are Helen Pendennis, so soft, feminine, and feeble of mind; 'the Fotheringay,' with her superficial genius and real stolidity; the crafty would-be-sentimental flirt and husband-hunter Blanche (who is as perfect in her own way, and as masterly a creation as the never-to-be-forgotten Becky herself); and, last and best, Laura. We are glad that Mr Thackeray has given us Laura, a woman so perfectly womanly; amiable and gentle, yet with plenty of sense and spirit; not a mere heroine, but a good-looking, lady-like, sensible girl. By-the-by, talking of Laura, does not Mr Thackeray make a little too much of the sisterly and fraternal element in the relations between her and Pen, if he all along meant to arrange matters as they are finally? On subordinate sketches, we should fail in any attempt at characteristic enumeration. But with the Begum, Altamont, Sir Francis, Dr Portman, Smirke, Morgan, Fanny, Huxter, Bows, and a host of others, we advise all readers who are not already so, to become immediately acquainted. They will find them a very entertaining company.

Mr Thackeray is his own illustrator, and his quaint and finely characteristic etchings abound in Hogarth-like touches. They convey an impression of their being scraps and pencillings from the portfolio

[1] Periodicals customarily reviewed monthly parts of novels.
[2] Thomas Brown (1778–1820), Professor of Moral Philosophy at the University of Edinburgh from 1810 until his death.

of an eminent and able artist, as without doubt they are, though the artist works with the pen rather than the brush.

23. [R. S. Rintoul], from 'Thackeray's *Pendennis*', the *Spectator*

21 December 1850, xxiii, 1213–15

As it is a wise rule in social life, not to be always calling to mind little singularities of character or habit in a man who is upon the whole more than usually worthy and agreeable, we are disposed to extend its application just now to our critical practice.[1] It is an established fact that Mr. Thackeray cannot or will not frame a coherent story, of which all the incidents flow naturally one from another, and are so necessarily connected with each other as to form a whole, whose completeness would be marred equally by taking away or by adding to it. It is also certain that he does not write his books to illustrate any speculative theory of life, in which facts and characters, apparently having no connexion with each other, are made to cohere into a real unity by serving as the agencies through which the growth of an individual mind is effected. Still less has he shown a disposition to embody in his fictions the great social questions of the day, and to administer to an unsuspecting public religious or political polemic in the disguise of a novel. All these ends have been pursued by different authors with more or less success; and honour is due to high aims in art, even when the execution falls short. But Mr. Thackeray had already, when he wrote *Vanity Fair*, arrived at a mature age and an adequate estimate of his own powers; and we had no reason to expect that he would profit by criticism and write his next novel upon a different plan. We do not doubt that he knew as well as his critics the faults that could not fail to be noticed in the construction of his work; and that he knew better than they did the sort of book which it suited his pocket, his indolence, or his peculiar talents, to present to an audience very busy, but very well inclined to give both money and fame to one who would amuse their snatches of leisure by sketches of themselves in all the attitudes of real life, drawn with a vigour and a truth seldom equalled, and marked

---

[1] These remarks were probably suggested by Thackeray's Preface (No. 20).

with a tone of sarcastic cynicism which lends emphatic value to the exceptional traits of goodness and worth.

Premising, then, that *Pendennis* is just as incomplete, just as fragmentary as its predecessor, and therefore no more entitling its author to take rank with our greatest novel-writers than it did, we are quite prepared to agree with the praise which we have heard generally bestowed upon the numbers as they successively appeared. The canvass is marvellously crowded with characters, most of them well and strikingly drawn; the incidents are upon the whole probable, though occasionally of too melodramatic a cast to harmonize with the everyday life and people depicted; the dialogue is appropriate to the speakers and the occasions—smart, grave, sarcastic, or pathetic, by turns, and always, except where slang, fashionable or otherwise, is demanded by dramatic propriety, phrased in pure, terse, idiomatic English. Nor must we omit to mention those passages of reflection in which the author speaks more undisguisedly in his own person: frequent as they are, and greatly as they would mar the effect of a more artistic work, they seem not out of place in this, and are both in style and matter admirable specimens of Mr. Thackeray's genius.

If we were asked to tell the story of *Pendennis*, we could only answer with the Knife-grinder of classic memory, 'Story! God bless you, I have none to tell, Sir!'[1] Such continuity and connection as the book has, it derives from the fact that it narrates certain adventures which befall Mr. Arthur Pendennis between the periods of his birth and marriage. . . .

Slender as this thread is, the author has managed, by portraying a variety of characters with whom his hero is brought into contact, many of them much more interesting than himself, and by a profuse embroidery of by-plots and episodes and reflections by the way, to spin it out through twenty-four numbers, scarcely ever flagging in interest; which at least have kept the idle part of the public, and many busy people too, on the qui vive for as many months. And we know no reason why, by pursuing the same course, and continually introducing such new characters as the mere onward course of life brings a man into temporary relation of friendship or hostility with, he may not carry on the married life of Mr. Arthur Pendennis through twenty-four more numbers, all equally lively and equally profitable and entertaining. At least till within a few pages of the close of the last number, there seemed no particular reason, beyond the length to which the book had already attained, why it should be brought to an end; and

[1] In Canning's poem, 'The Friend of Humanity and the Knife-Grinder' (1797).

we are sure that the indulgent public will accord to such a favourite as Mr. Thackeray the permission to reconsider his denouement, and so save himself the trouble of inventing an entirely new set of names and circumstances,—which to a man of his established singularity must be a terrible hardship.

We do not, however, suppose that Mr. Thackeray was absolutely without any purpose in writing this book beyond amusing his readers and swelling his own purse and fame. There are proofs in this work, as in its predecessor, of a high morality, and an earnest desire to make his fellow men better than they are, which forbid us to entertain so harsh a thought. The preface, moreover, lets us know that it is an attempt to show, as far as conventional decency will allow them to be shown, the notorious foibles and selfishness of the lives and education of our gentlemen. The limitation implies not obscurely that it is in relation to women that their foibles and selfishness have most impressed Mr. Thackeray: and every man who knows English society will acknowledge that the women are purer and less selfish than the men, not only in those classes which Mr. Thackeray chiefly depicts, but in all classes—and may we not add, in all countries and in all ages. Something of this may be owing to sexual constitution—something to the circumstances of life, the necessity that is imposed upon the man to enter upon the exciting and hardening struggles for bread and social position—something to old-world traditions and time-honoured customs; but the question must sometimes recur to one who thinks what an all-important relation that between man and woman is, either as son and mother, brother and sister, husband and wife, whether this difference of character need be so wide as it generally is; whether, in fact, if men were but nearer to women in purity and self-sacrificing affection, society would not be reinvigorated with a new life, and much of the weariness and satiety and disappointment that now hang over us like a November fog pass away, and let in upon us again the pure blue heaven, the soft air of vernal hope and happiness.

A strong sense that the English upper classes are far from what is good and right in this respect, and that generally selfishness under one form or other, a love of money, of pleasure, or of power, is substituted for true social principles of action among them,—and that, pervading and poisoning all the relations of life, it gives rise to a hard materialism in the practice of most, and even in the theory of some,—is the root of Mr. Thackeray's cynicism, and of that melancholy which at once charms and startles us often in his writings. Even the education of the boy, and still more the common experiences of life for the man, only seem to him to draw out and strengthen this propensity to make the gratification of self the end of existence. We regard *Pendennis*, no less than *Vanity Fair*, as a protest against this corruption of the individual by society; as a lesson to each one of us against that sin which is the root of all bitterness; as a timely warning to society to draw back from the gulph which it is approaching. The nineteenth century is quite self-complacent enough, or we might hint that the protest and the warning would be more effective if accompanied by a recognition of the forces which are undeniably at work in our country to counteract the anti-social tendency—may we not say, finally to triumph over it. To us, at least, Mr. Thackeray seems sometimes to adopt the merest heathen cynicism, and to have reached that last state, so finely dramatized in Tennyson's 'Vision of Sin,' in which a man abandons all hope of himself and his kind, and takes a savage delight in anatomizing all pretensions to goodness and exploding all motives to action.

That this mood is only occasional—that society has not fallen over the gulph, even in Mr. Thackeray's opinion—is evidenced by such characters in his picture of life as Mrs. Pendennis, Laura Bell, and George Warrington. Even *Vanity Fair* could show such exceptions as Amelia Sedley and Major Dobbin; though the latter annoyed us by a gaucherie which seldom accompanies genuine goodness and simplicity, and the former went far to forfeit our sympathy by extreme silliness and an insensibility to real manly worth. No such drawbacks mar our interest in the three exceptional characters, above mentioned, of the work we are reviewing. Mrs. Pendennis is a true English lady, and, with all the reserve and undemonstrativeness of her class to ordinary acquaintance, completely embodies in her relation to her son that idea of self-sacrificing affection which is Thackeray's normal type of good women; just as the opposite character, shown forth in Becky Sharpe and Blanche Amory, serves, in spite of admirable qualities in the one and great attractions in the other, for the type of those women from whom their own sex instinctively shrink, and whom men amuse themselves with, abuse, and despise. George Warrington, we have no doubt, will be the favourite by universal assent both with men and women. His surface coating of roughness is but a pleasant humour, and is seen through at a glance, revealing beneath it the finest humanity. A 'healthy animalism' is still a prominent characteristic of our better class of young men; and in spite of much dissipation, much dandyism, and much pseudo-philosophy, it is no very rare thing among that class to find the best scholars and the truest gentlemen neither too fine to drink beer and smoke short pipes, nor too delicate to have both the will and the power to thrash bargemen when occasion demands. In England, where to rise by one's own exertion requires such a combination of physical and mental power, and where the national ideal leans rather to strength than subtilty, to sense than to learning, to rank plainness of manners and of speech and kindness of heart than to stately courtesy and elaborate polish, many a dignitary of church and law, and many a man eminent for social and political success, might have supplied the oddest as well as the noblest traits of Warrington's character. And over the whole is thrown such a softening influence from the mysterious sadness which tinges alike his joyous and sarcastic moods, and gives depth and earnestness to his serious conversation, that, while one of the most literal, he is at the same time one of the most delightful of Thackeray's portraits. His kindness to Pendennis, his appreciation of the talents and good qualities which lie half-hidden in him, his development and encouragement of all that is manly and upright in him, win our affection and esteem, even before his display of profound tenderness and his capacity for passion take our sympathies by storm. There is one conversation of his with Pendennis (No. 20) that we long to quote, both because it is very noble in itself, and because it seems to us the author's most earnest utterance on the most solemn things—somewhat of a confession of faith, which goes far to soften and modify the harsh occasional cynicism we have noticed. [Ch. lxi.] It sounds like an echo from *In Memoriam*, which appeared shortly before the number where it occurs. But our space forbids, and we hasten to usher in Miss Laura Bell, an especial favourite, and Miss Blanche Amory, an especial abomination of ours. The passage we have selected to illustrate the character of the former needs no preface, except that Lady Rockminster has taken Laura to live with her after the death of Mrs. Pendennis, her mother by adoption.

[Quotes the description of Laura's 'cheerful' acceptance of her loneliness after Helen's death, ch. lxvi; *Works*, xii, 855-6.]

With the spirit of unrepining sacrifice of ease and inclination for the good or even the comfort of those with whom her circumstances associate her, (a spirit which made Amelia a favourite in spite of her weakness, and which is the true household virtue,) Laura combines all that goes to make up a good and charming woman,—tenderness, high spirit, (witness her first rejection of Arthur,) clear sense, and self-respect; and these characteristics, united with unfailing good-humour and a delicate appreciation of the ridiculous, form a portrait that completely rescues Mr. Thackeray from the reproach of not being able to draw a good woman without making her silly and uninteresting. Even Laura's temporary outbreak of jealousy and cruelty to poor Fanny Bolton only makes her more thoroughly a flesh-and-blood woman; a creature whom, in our present mundane imperfection, we prefer to an angel.

Miss Amory, 'the muse, the mystery, the femme incomprise,' otherwise called La Sylphide, is a portrait full of vigour, painted by one whom no weakness escapes, who allows no meanness to lurk undetected and unlashed. We cannot sum her up more concisely than by saying that she is Becky without Becky's cleverness, tact, and good-nature. These are replaced by accomplishments in abundance, and that kind of sensibility which is nurtured by an early and assiduous perusal of French romances. Madame Sand and Eugène Sue supplied her with friends in the spirit world, in comparison with whose trans-cendant qualities the people she lived with were contemptible and uninteresting. And so, while she snubbed her goodnatured mother, sneered at her odious father-in-law, hated and bullied her small brother, worried almost to death her poor maid, and in short displayed a surprising knack of making everybody miserable in her own family circle, she confided to her album, which was inscribed 'Mes Larmes,' a constant overflow of tenderness and sentiment, sufficient, if worked out in action, for the happiness of a whole village. We shall quote a scene in which this young lady, who presents us with the real-life side of the ordinary sentimental-novel heroine, appears to more advantage than usual; her mere heartlessness and frivolity and sham sentiment giving way when brought face to face with the terrible reality of worldliness in a worn, disappointed, and hardened man. The conversa-tion is between Miss Amory and Arthur Pendennis, after their engage-ment; and the allusion at the commencement is to the fate of Fanny Bolton, who, after the supreme felicity of attracting the momentary notice of the speaker, has the bad taste and misfortune to marry a respectable though somewhat snobbish surgeon, and to be content with her lot.

[Quotation from ch. lxiv; *Works*, xii, 835–8.]

The character of the hero himself offers no salient points for criti-cism. Slightly reminding us in his worst features—his conceit and unconscious selfishness—of George Osborne, he wins upon us by frequent impulses of generosity and good feeling, to which that quintessence of all that is mean and stupid, veiled under a dashing recklessness and a showy exterior, was quite unused. Especially after he comes under the influence of Warrington does he rapidly grow in manliness and worth; and in spite of his airs and his affectedly cynical tone, we really like and admire him for his considerate treatment of Fanny Bolton, and his honourable behaviour to Blanche Amory. Taking him from first to last, he is, we think, a favourable specimen of his class both in talent and character; and probably the author thought, that such lessons as are to be learned from his experience and growth are of more extensive application from the ordinary nature of the elements that enter into his composition. A far more carefully-finished and noteworthy portrait is that of Major Pendennis, his uncle; a perfectly well-bred gentleman, who, though with little more than his half-pay, has the entrée of the best houses in town and country. It would perhaps be too hard to say that he quite realizes the Frenchman's beau idéal of a happy man, in having 'un mauvais cœur et un bon estomac'; he is a little too old for the latter happiness, and Englishmen seldom attain the perfection of the former. Still he is far gone in the theory and practice of the art of which Chesterfield is popularly considered the master; and belongs indeed, especially in the elaborate polish of his manner, and the conscious avowal of his selfish and worldly ends, rather to a generation that has passed away.[1]

We have spoken of only three or four characters, and there are twenty so drawn as to be worth speaking of. Strong is a man whose hearty animation raises our spirits like a clear October day; Bows is a queer old sentimental man of genius, who would not disgrace the page of Sterne; Foker, a thoroughly goodnatured sketch of a 'fast' young English gentleman, with sound heart and good practical sense, though led away by a bad education and the follies of his class. But for the rest, the reader must (as most doubtless have done) buy or borrow or steal the book itself; and he can scarcely fail to be beguiled of many an hour in amusement, and we venture to think not altogether unprofitably.

[1] The fourth Earl of Chesterfield (1694–1773) gave worldly-wise advice to his natural son in a series of letters, published posthumously (1774).

24. [G. H. Lewes], review in the *Leader*

21 December 1850, i, 929–30

'No age,' says Carlyle, 'is romantic to itself,' and no age thinks its writers equal to those who have gone before—

> 'Tis distance lends enchantment to the view;[1]

and we turn from the 'superficial trash' of our age to the grander thews and sinews of those who wrote the 'superficial trash' of their time. The history of Literature is full of such complaints. Old Nestor, speaking to the illustrious host before Troy could see nothing in Achilles, Ajax, Diomed, and the King of Men, equal to the heroes who had flourished in *his* youth. Tacitus, in the opening of his *Dialogue on the Orators* (if it be is) speaks of the sterile epoch when the name of orator could not be applied to any living man, 'for *our* men are dissertators, gabblers, lawyers, everything, in short, but orators—*horum autem temporum diserti causidici et advocati, et patroni et quidvis potius quam oratores vocantur.*'

That the men of our day should think slightingly of their contemporaries in comparison with the writers of former times, is no more than natural, and we are prepared for uplifted eyebrows when we gravely assert that England has at no time produced a writer of fiction with whom Thackeray may not stand in honourable comparison. Others have surpassed him in particular qualities, but taking the sum total of his powers, as the only fair means of comparison, we are prepared to maintain our position. But will he live as they have lived? That is another question, and one which no amount of present popularity can affect; for popularity, as Victor Hugo admirably says, is the vulgarization of fame—

> La popularité? C'est la gloire en gros sous.[2]

He has the two great qualities which embalm a reputation—truth and style. But he is to be separated from the great writers of other days

---

[1] Thomas Campbell, *The Pleasures of Hope* (1799), i, 7.
[2] *Ruy Blas* (1838), iii, 4.

by one peculiarity of our own, and one that endangers the durability of his renown—we mean a want of respect for his art, a want of respect for his public. In the care with which former writers, however, pressed by poverty, planned and executed their works, we see something wholly different from that nonchalance and easy confidence in his own powers, which makes Thackeray (nor is he alone in this) sacrifice the artist to the improvisatore. How greatly his writings suffer from this it is impossible to calculate; our marvel is that they are so remarkable in spite of it. To gossip with the reader, to wander from the path into pleasant digressions and sketches of society, is a facile method of discharging his monthly task; and with knowledge so abundant and a style so graceful and winning, the success is great enough to foster the temptation. But that which is written for the hour is apt to perish with the hour; and he is capable of enduring works.

Pendennis has, perhaps, even more of this fault than *Vanity Fair*, and it flags occasionally in consequence. But it is, nevertheless, a great, a masterly work, weighty with knowledge, luminous with beautiful thoughts, caustic, subtle, pathetic, varied with unrivalled pictures of human life and character, and incomparable in style. A loving spirit moves throughout the book, taking from its satire all the bitterness of misanthropy, making human nature loveable amidst all its infirmities. As everyone must have read or will read it, we need occupy no space by an exposition of its contents; a few remarks on his general characteristics, as therein exhibited, will suffice.

First let us mention the beauty of his style. For clearness, strength, idiomatic ease, delicacy, and variety, there is no one since Goldsmith to compare with him. It is not a style in the vulgar sense of the word; that is to say, it is not a *trick*. It is the flowing garment which robes his thoughts, and moves with every movement of his mind into different and appropriate shapes, simple in narrative, terse and glittering in epigram, playful in conversation or digression, rising into rhythmic periods when the mood is of more sustained seriousness, and becoming indescribably affecting in its simplicity when it utters pathetic or solemn thoughts. It is devoid of trick though not devoid of art. Somebody said of it that it was essentially the style of a gentleman. We wish gentlemen would write so.

Then as to knowledge. The endless charm of his writing for men and women who have experience cannot be divined by those who as yet know nothing (though their hairs be grey). It is the same with Horace. No schoolboy, no young poet cares a straw for Horace. Men who have lived like him better as they grow older. In Thackeray we see many resemblances to Horace: both have outlived their illusions, and yet look back with fondness on them, so that their laughter is rather sad than bitter. It seems as if most of the various scenes of the drama of life had been acted in Thackeray's breast, and he laughs as we laugh at our youthful follies, with a certain regret that those follies are past, and a respect for the ingenuousness which committed them. It is a great mistake to suppose Thackeray's experience to lie only on the surface, and that the life he depicts is merely the movement of society. Although he knows that better, and depicts it more truly than any one else, he is separated from the fashionable novelists by the power they have little claim to—the power of representing human life. Take Disraeli for example, and compare any sketch of fashionable life by him with one by Thackeray, and the difference is at once apparent. Disraeli sees society—not very clearly, but he sees it; Thackeray sees it, and sees through it, sees all the human feelings, all the motives, high and low, simple and complicated, which make it what it is. Observe Major Pendennis, Warrington, Laura, Blanche Amory, Old Costigan, or even one of the minor persons, and on examination you will find that he seizes *characters* where other writers seize only *characteristics;* he does not give you a peculiarity for the man, he places the man himself, that 'bundle of motives,' before you. To test how true this is, you have only to ask yourself 'Can I describe one of his characters truly in a phrase?' Or you may test it thus: In Becky Sharp and in Blanche Amory he has drawn the same class of woman; did that ever strike you? did you ever think he was repeating himself? Is Blanche more like Becky than Iago is like Edmund? Yet the two women belong to one type, and so marvellously true to nature, so minutely and profoundly true, that we who know one who might have sat for the portraits (but did not) are puzzled to say which of the two is most like her. Blanche does not play the same important part in *Pendennis* that Becky does in *Vanity Fair*, but the Artist's power is equally apparent to a connoisseur. By knowledge then we mean not merely the familiarity with the modes of life from Gaunt House to the Back Kitchen, but familiarity also with the realities of life as they move in human breasts.

Another peculiarity he has, and one which makes critics remonstrant, viz., that of mercilessly pointing out the skeleton which is in every closet. He passes among illusions only to show them to be follies; he turns round upon you while the tears are standing in your eyes, only to laugh at your emotion; he stands at the feast only to declare its vanity; he recites a noble sentiment only to connect it with some ignoble motive. A mocking Mephistopheles, he will not suffer you to be deceived; he laughs at you, at everybody, at himself.

There is some truth in this; but, as respects *Pendennis*, it is overstated, and the cause, we take it, does not lie in his mocking spirit, but elsewhere. It lies—if we have read his nature aright—in a predominating tendency to *antithesis*. Other writers have this tendency; but in him it acquires peculiar force. He does not, as others do, manifest it in antitheses of diction. His writing, one may say, is remarkably free from that. Nor does he proceed with the false systematic method of Victor Hugo, in whom the love of antithesis amounts to a disease (to be sure, Hugo excuses himself on the plea that God is greater in that department than himself, God being *le plus grand faiseur d'antithèses*!— a modest and satisfactory exculpation!), but, nevertheless, the law of Thackeray's mind seems to be a conception of opposites, which makes him a perfect Janus Bifrons. No sooner does he think of poetic aspirations than his mind suddenly swerves to the other side to contemplate the foolish sentimentalism which apes those aspirations. If he were drawing Cæsar, he would lift up the laurel wreath to expose his baldness. His own Warrington is seen 'drinking beer like a coalheaver, and yet you couldn't but perceive that he was a gentleman.' Miss Fotheringay is a splendid actress and as ignorant as a horse. Foker is a blackguard in his tastes, but a gentleman in feeling. We might run through the volumes and point out this constant antithesis, but the reader must know very well how characteristic it is. Enough if we have indicated the reason for its constant presence.

That it does not arise from a mocking spirit, may easily be shown by reference to the examples, in which he shows a soul of goodness in things evil, as well as the spot of evil in things good. Look at Old Costigan, the Major, Strong, Altamont, and see how characters which in ordinary hands would be simply contemptible or hateful from their selfishness and scoundrelism, are preserved from corruption by the salt of human virtues, and your very scorn is modified, human sympathy appealed to, and Charity made to own a brother in the sinner. The same tendency of his mind which makes him see that a hero has the gout, makes him perceive that a scamp is not all vice. The antithesis in the one case *may* proceed from a mocking spirit: it cannot in the latter; unless we are to suppose him destitute of all reverence for human worth, and wishing to revile even goodness by locating it in vile places: a supposition contradicted, we venture to say, by the whole temper of his writings. Thackeray is a man who loves all worth, and reverences whatever is true, though his scorn of pretence is uncomprising enough. It seemed to us while reading this work, as if he had drawn himself in Warrington—a sad, thoughtful, kindly, yet sarcastic man, whose very scorn proceeds from love of what is high and noble; whose dislike of pretence is so great, that he is afraid of being suspected of pretence if he adopt a more serious manner.

Not a mocking spirit but a loving spirit has he; not a Mephisto but a Goethe sits at his elbow. Goethe, too, is often reproached for the same thing, and is pronounced 'cold' because he was not one-sided. Moreover, Thackeray's antitheses differ from those of Sue and Victor Hugo in arising out of the actual truth of nature, and not out of a systematic desire for contrast. You do not catch him selecting his type of Chastity from among young ladies at the *tapis franc;* in depicting the paternal and maternal sentiment he does not seek a Triboulet or a Lucrèce Borgia;[1] to show the venerableness of age he does not exhibit a brutal bandit; to show the power of love he does not choose a courtezan. He takes the Contradictions offered him daily by Nature— such as they are in us and in those around us; and the difference between him and other novelists is that he sees these Contradictions, they do not.

In *Vanity Fair* we felt the scoundrelism and pretence oppressive. In *Pendennis* this is no longer the case. It abounds of course, for Thackeray is above all things a satirist; but in *Pendennis* we note a very decided advance upon *Vanity Fair* with respect to a broader and more generous view of humanity, a larger admixture of goodness with what is evil, and a more loving mellowed tone throughout. It brought the tears into our eyes at several passages of manly pathos, and revealed to us capabilities for more serious writing than is to be found in *Vanity Fair*. Nevertheless, it is not so popular; partly because it is not so new, but mostly because it wants the leading interest of a story: Pen is not so strong a thread to hang pearls on as Becky. Yet *Vanity Fair* has no such charming woman as Laura, no such noble fellow as Warrington. Old Bows, too, is very touching: his hopeless love for the Fotheringay, and then for Fanny, and the way he educates these two only to see others carry them off, are in the best manner of poor Balzac.

Miss Fotheringay has been pronounced a caricature—by those not very familiar with theatrical life. But it was a bold and a successful stroke thus to paint the truth and to show the public that success in

---

[1] In Hugo's *Le Roi s'amuse* (1832) and *Lucrèce Borgia* (1833) respectively.

acting implies no commensurate intelligence, or even sympathy with the passions depicted. There are exceptions, but, speaking generally, actors are certainly *below* par rather than above it in intellect. So much of acting is factitious, so much tradition, that a very mediocre person, with tolerable physique and mimetic powers, may 'take the town by storm.' You might as reasonably suppose the leading trage-dians endowed with all the heroism of the parts they play, as capable of intellectual sympathy with them. If any one doubts this, let him listen to a greenroom conversation for half an hour![1]

We find that we have said little or nothing of the faults of *Pendennis;* but, although we could have indulged in that *antithesis* without much expenditure of ingenuity through some columns, yet in truth we thought little of the faults while reading, and care not to be critical just now; they seem to us all resolvable into natural defects which no criticism can cure, or into that carelessness which, at the outset, we declared to constitute his one inferiority to the great writers of other days. But this we will say, that we do *not* count it as a fault when we see him holding up an unflattering picture to society; nor do we think the truth immoral, 'It must be bad, indeed,' says Goethe, 'if a book *has a more demoralizing effect than life itself,* which daily displays the most scandalous scenes in abundance, if not before our eyes, at least before our ears.'

[1] This reminds us that Lewes was a dramatic critic.

Masson (1822–1907) was Professor at University College,
London, and later at Edinburgh. He edited *Macmillan's Magazine*
from its beginning in 1859 to 1867. He used some of the material
from the present article in his *British Novelists and their Styles*
(1859), 233–53. *David Copperfield* was issued in monthly parts
from May 1849 to November 1850 and thus for much of its
course ran parallel with *Pendennis* (November 1848–September
1849; January 1850–December 1850). For Thackeray's comments, see below, No. 26.

. . . Both [Dickens and Thackeray] seem to be easy penmen, and to
have language very readily at their command; both also seem to
convey their meaning as simply as they can, and to be careful, according to their notions of verbal accuracy; but in Mr. Dickens's sentences
there is a leafiness, a tendency to words and images, for their own sake;
whereas in Mr. Thackeray's one sees the stem and outline of the
thought better. We have no great respect for that canon of style which
demands in English writers the use of Saxon in preference to Latin
words, thinking that a rule to which there are natural limitations, vari-
able with the writer's aim and with the subject he treats; but we should
suppose that critics who do regard the rule would find Mr. Thackeray's
style the more accordant with it. On the whole, if we had to choose
passages at random, to be set before young scholars as examples of
easy and vigorous English composition, we would take them rather
from Thackeray than from Dickens. There is a Horatian strictness, a
racy strength, in Mr. Thackeray's expressions, even in his more level
and tame passages, which we miss in the corresponding passages in
Mr. Dickens's writings, and in which we seem to recognise the effect
of those classical studies through which an accurate and determinate,

though somewhat bald, use of words becomes a fixed habit. In the ease, and, at the same time, thorough polish and propriety with which Mr. Thackeray can use slang words, we seem especially to detect the University man. Snob, swell, buck, gent, fellow, fogy—these, and many more such expressive appellatives, not yet sanctioned by the Dictionary, Mr. Thackeray employs more frequently, we believe, than any other living writer, and yet always with unexceptionable taste. In so doing he is conscious, no doubt, of the same kind of security that permits Oxford and Cambridge men, and even, as we can testify, Oxford and Cambridge clergymen, to season their conversation with similar words—namely, the evident air of educated manliness with which they can be introduced, and which, however rough the guise, no one can mistake. In the use of the words genteel, vulgar, female, and the like—words which men diffident of their own breeding are observed not to risk; as well as in the art of alternating gracefully between the noun lady and the noun woman, the Scylla and Charybdis, if we may so say, of shy talkers—Mr. Thackeray is also a perfect master, commanding his language in such cases with an unconscious ease, not unlike that which enables the true English gentleman he is so fond of portraying, either to name titled personages of his acquaintance without seeming a tuft-hunter, or to refrain from naming them without the affectation of Radicalism. In Mr. Dickens, of course, we have the same perfect taste and propriety; but in him the result appears to arise, if we may so express ourselves, rather from the keen and feminine sensibility of a fine genius, whose instinct is always for the pure and beautiful, than from the self-possession of a mind correct under any circumstances, by discipline and sure habit. Where Mr. Dickens is not exerting himself, that is, in passages of mere equable narrative or description, where there is nothing to move or excite him, his style, as we have already said, seems to us more careless and languid than that of Mr. Thackeray; sometimes, indeed, a whole page is only redeemed from weakness by those little touches of wit and those humorous terms of conception which he knows so well how to sprinkle over it. It is due to Mr. Dickens to state, however, that in this respect his *Copperfield* is one of his most pleasing productions, and a decided improvement on its predecessor *Dombey*. Not only is the spirit of the book more gentle and mellow, but the style is more continuous and careful, with fewer of those recurring tricks of expression, the dead remnants of former felicities, which constituted what was called his mannerism. Nor must we omit to remark also, that in passages where higher feeling is called into play, Mr. Dickens's style always rises into greater purity and vigour, the weakness and the superfluity disappearing before the concentrating force of passion, and the language often pouring itself forth in a clear and flowing song. This, in fact, is according to the nature of the luxuriant or poetical genius, which never expresses itself in its best or most concise manner unless the mood be high as well as the meaning clear;—for maintaining the excellence of the style of a terse and highly reflective writer, such as Thackeray, on the other hand, the presence of a clear meaning is at all times sufficient, though, of course, here also the pitch and melody will depend on the mood. . . .

Mr. Thackeray, though more competent, according to our view of him, to appear in the character of a general critic or essayist, seems far more of a *pococurante* than Mr. Dickens. Whether it is that he is naturally disposed to take the world as he finds it, or that, having at some time or other had very unsatisfactory experience of the trade of trying to mend it, he has taken up *pococurantism* as a theory, we have no means of saying; but certain it is, that in the writings he has given forth since he became known as one of our most distinguished literary men, he has meddled far less with the external arrangements of society than Mr. Dickens, and made far fewer appearances as a controversialist or reformer. An exception might, indeed, be taken to this remark with reference to certain essays in *Punch*, and particularly certain recent satirical sketches there of Jesuits and Jesuitism, which bear the stamp of Thackeray's manner. But generally, and even with regard to these particular papers, it will be found that it is not of the social arrangements and conventions amid which men and women move, so much as of men and women themselves, that Mr. Thackeray is the satirist. The foibles and vices of individual human beings; the ugly things that are transacted and the commotions that go on in that little world, twenty-three inches or thereby in circumference, which each man carries under his own hat[1]—these, and not the storms and discussions of the big world without, are the stuff out of which Mr. Thackeray weaves his fictions. His care is not about the conditions, political or social, to which this conceited young dandy, that old debauchee, that sentimental little minx, and all the rest of us, must submit during our little bit of life; what he delights to do is to follow these various personages as they get on amid these conditions—to watch, with an interest half humorous, half sad, the dandy as he struts along Pall Mall;

---

[1] A favourite expression of Carlyle's.

to trace the old wretch to his haunts; to detect the young minx boxing her brother's ears in private. And here, certainly, he is fierce and pitiless enough. What he likes in men and women, what he hates, what he will tolerate, and what moves his indignation and contempt, are indicated with too great clearness to be mistaken. But he does not carry his polemics into the field of exterior circumstances. The 'snob,' as such, is his quarry, and as he hovers aloft on the watch for him, it matters nothing whether he descries him in Crim Tartary or in England—on this side or on that side of any political frontier; the snob, and not his environment, is the object of his attention; hawk-like he gives chase and pins the victim. 'Let us cease to be snobs; till then, whether we are in Crim Tartary or in England, whether we have liberal institutions or live under a despot, is of very secondary consequence;' such is virtually the rule according to which he writes. How in his more private and unprofessional character he may think it right to act; whether or not he would make a busy vestryman if elected, or whether he regards all partizanship in public politics as a mere Hoolan and Doolan[1] affair, to be left to the editors of newspapers, we have no means of knowing; the impression made by his writings, however, is that, in these matters, like many more of our best men, he is far gone in a kind of grim, courteous pococurantism. . . .

In the real style of art, the aim is to produce pictures that shall impress by their close and truthful resemblance to something or other in real nature or life. It would be false to say that there may not be a genuine exercise of the poetic or imaginative faculty in this walk of art. Even in the humblest specimen of imitative painting, if it is to rise at all above the character of a mere copy, the artist must contribute some special conception or intention of his own, according to which the objects may be arranged, and which shall give them their effect as a whole. Still, in the higher sense in which the word imagination is often used, as implying a rarer exercise of inventive power, it cannot be said that the real style of painting is so imaginative as that which we have called the ideal. In this style of art the conception or intention supplied by the painter bears a larger proportion to the matter outwardly given than in the other. A picture executed in this style strikes, not by recalling real scenes and occurrences, but by taking the mind out of itself into a region of higher possibilities, wherein objects shall be more glorious, and modes of action more transcendent, than any we

[1] In *Pendennis* (chs. xxx, xxxiv), they are Irish journalists who are friends but work for rival papers.

see, and yet all shall seem in nature. When the aspiration of the artist in this style is greater than his powers of harmonious conception, the result is the extravagant or the unnatural; perfect art is attained only when the objects as represented are elevated above objects as they appear, precisely to that degree in which a world constructed expressly in the mood of the artist's intention might be expected to exceed the common world. It is observed, too, that artists who favour the ideal theory, usually work in the more ambitious departments of landscape or figure painting; and hence probably it is that the real style is sometimes, though perhaps not very happily, called Low Art, and the ideal style, High Art.

All this may be transferred with ease to the occupation of the literary artist, or writer of fiction. Thus, applying it to the particular case in view, it may be said, in the first place, with respect to our two novelists, that the artistic faculty of Dickens is more comprehensive, goes over a wider range of the whole field of art, than that of Thackeray. Take Dickens, for example, in the landscape or background department. Here he is capable of great variety. He can give you a landscape proper —a piece of the rural English earth in its summer or in its winter dress, with a bit of water, and a pretty village spire, in it; he can give you, what painters seldom attempt, a great patch of flat country by night, with the red trail of a railway train traversing the darkness; he can even succeed in a sea-piece; he can describe the crowded quarter of a city, or the main street of a country town, by night or by day; he can paint a garden, sketch the interior of a cathedral, or daguerreotype the interior of a hut or drawing-room with equal ease; he can even be minute in his delineations of single articles of dress or furniture. Take him, again, in the figure department. Here he can be an animal-painter with Landseer when he likes, as witness his dogs, ponies, and ravens; he can be a historical painter, as witness his description of the Gordon riots;[1] he can be a portrait-painter or a caricaturist like Leech; he can give you a bit of village or country life, like Wilkie; he can paint a haggard or squalid scene of low city-life, so as to remind one of some of the Dutch artists, Rembrandt included, or a pleasant family-scene, gay or sentimental, reminding one of Maclise or Frank Stone;[2] he can body forth romantic conceptions of terror or beauty,

[1] In *Barnaby Rudge* (1841).
[2] Sir Edwin Landseer (1802–73), the animal-painter, was at the height of his fame; John Leech (1817–64) was the principal cartoonist in *Punch*; Sir David Wilkie (1785–1841) was noted for his *genre* paintings; Daniel Maclise (1806–70) was an historical painter and book-illustrator; Frank Stone (1800–59) was a popular painter of family scenes. Leech, Maclise and Stone all illustrated books by Dickens.

that have risen in his own imagination; he can compose a fantastic fairy piece, he can even succeed in a powerful dream or allegory, where the figures are hardly human. The range of Thackeray, on the other hand, is more restricted. In the landscape department he can give you a quiet little bit of background, such as a park, a clump of trees, or the vicinity of a country-house, with a village seen in the sunset; a London street, also, by night or by day, is familiar to his eye; but, upon the whole, his scenes are laid in those more habitual places of resort, where the business or pleasure of aristocratic or middle-class society goes on—a pillared club-house in Pall Mall, the box or pit of a theatre, a brilliant *salon* in Mayfair, a public dancing-room, a newspaper office, a shop in Paternoster Row, the deck of a steamer, the interior of a married man's house, or a bachelor's chambers in the Temple. And his choice of subjects from the life corresponds with this. Men and women as they are, and as they behave daily, especially in the charmed circles of rank, literature, and fashion, are the subjects of Mr. Thackeray's pencil; and in his delineations of them he seems to unite the strong and fierce characteristics of Hogarth, with a touch both of Wilkie and Maclise, and not a little of that regular grace and fine sense of colour which charm us in the groups of Watteau. . . .

On the whole it may be said that, while there are few things that Mr. Thackeray can do in the way of description which Mr. Dickens could not also do, there is a large region of objects and appearances familiar to the artistic activity of Mr. Dickens, where Mr. Thackeray would not find himself at home. And as Mr. Dickens's artistic range is thus wider than that of Mr. Thackeray, so also his style of art is the more elevated. Thackeray is essentially an artist of the real school; he belongs to what, in painting, would be called the school of low art. All that he portrays—scenes as well as characters—is within the limits, and rigidly true to the features, of real existence. In this lies his particular merit; and, like Wilkie, he would probably fail, if, hankering after a reputation in high art, he were to prove untrue to his special faculty as a delineator of actual life. Dickens, on the other hand, works more in the ideal. It is nonsense to say of his characters generally, intending the observation for praise, that they are life-like. They are nothing of the kind. Not only are his serious or tragic creations—his Old Humphreys, his Maypole Hughs, his little Nells, &c.—persons of romance; but even his comic or satiric portraitures do not come within the strict bounds of the real. There never was a real Mr. Pickwick, a real Sam Weller, a real Mrs. Nickleby, a real Quilp, a real Micawber, a real

Uriah Heep, or a real Toots, in the same accurate sense that there has been or might be a real Major Pendennis, a real Captain Costigan, a real Becky, a real Sir Pitt Crawley, and a real Mr. Foker. Nature may, indeed, have furnished hints of Wellers and Pickwicks, may have scattered the germs or indications of such odd fishes abroad; and, having once added such characters to our gallery of fictitious portraits, we cannot move a step in actual life without stumbling upon individuals to whom they will apply most aptly as nicknames—good-humoured bald-headed old gentleman, who remind us of Pickwick; careless, easy spendthrifts of the Micawber type; fawning rascals of the Heep species; or bashful young gentlemen like Toots. But, at most, those characters are real only thus far, that they are transcendental renderings of certain hints furnished by nature. Seizing the notion of some oddity as seen in the real world, Mr. Dickens has run away with it into a kind of outer or ideal region, there to play with it and work it out at leisure as extravagantly as he might choose, without the least impediment from any facts except those of his own story. One result of this method is, that his characters do not present the mixture of good and bad in the same proportions as we find in nature. Some of his characters are thoroughly and ideally perfect; others are thoroughly and ideally detestable; and even in those where he has intended a mingled impression, vice and virtue are blended in a purely ideal manner. It is different with Mr. Thackeray. The last words of his *Pendennis* are a petition for the charity of his readers in behalf of the principal personage of the story, on the ground that not having meant to represent him as a hero, but 'only as a man and a brother,' he has exposed his foibles rather too freely. So, also, in almost all his other characters his study seems to be to give the good and the bad together, in very nearly the same proportions that the cunning apothecary, Nature herself, uses. Now, while, according to Mr. Thackeray's style of art, this is perfectly proper, it does not follow that Mr. Dickens's method is wrong. The characters of Shakespeare are not, in any common sense, life-like. They are not portraits of existing men and women, though doubtless there are splendid specimens even of this kind of art among them; they are grand hyperbolic beings created by the breath of the poet himself out of hints taken from all that is most sublime in nature; they are humanity caught, as it were, and kept permanent in its highest and extremest mood, nay carried forth and compelled to think, speak, and act in conditions superior to that mood. As in Greek tragedy, the character that an artist of the higher or poetical school is expected to bring before us, is not, and never was meant to be, a puny 'man and brother,' resembling ourselves in his virtues and his foibles, but an ancestor and a demigod, large, superb, and unapproachable. Art is called Art, says Goethe, precisely because it is *not* Nature; and even such a department of art as the modern novel is entitled to the benefit of this maxim. While, therefore, in Mr. Thackeray's style of delineation, the just ground of praise is, as he claims it to be, the verisimilitude of the fictions, it would be no fair ground of blame against Mr. Dickens, in *his* style of delineation, to say that his fictions are hyperbolic. A truer accusation against him, in this respect, would be that, in the exercise of the right of hyperbole, he does not always preserve harmony; that, in his romantic creations, he sometimes falls into the extravagant, and, in his comic creations, sometimes into the grotesque.

But, while Mr. Dickens is both more extensive in the range, and more poetic in the style of his art than Mr. Thackeray, the latter is, perhaps, within his own range and in his own style, the more careful artist. His stroke is truer and surer, and his attention to finish greater. This may be, in part, owing to the fact that Mr. Thackeray can handle the pencil as well as the pen. Being the illustrator of his own works, and accustomed, therefore, to reduce his fancies to visible form and outline, he attains, in the result, greater clearness and precision, than one who works only in language, or who has to get his fancies made visible to himself by the pencil of another. Apart, however, from the real talent with which Mr. Thackeray illustrates his pages, it may be cited as a proof of the distinctness with which he conceives what he writes, that the names of his characters are almost always excellent. Mr. Dickens has always been thought particularly happy in this respect; we are not sure, however, that Mr. Thackeray does not sometimes surpass him. Dr. Slocum, Miss Mactoddy, the Scotch surgeon Glowry, Jeames the footman—these and such-like names, which Mr. Thackeray seems to throw off with such ease, that he lavishes them even on his incidental and minor characters—are, in themselves, positive bits of humour.

It is by the originality and interest of its characters that a novel is chiefly judged. And certainly it is a high privilege, that which the novelist possesses, of calling into existence new imaginary beings; of adding, as it were, to that population of aerial men and women, the offspring of past genius, which hovers over the heads of the actual population of the world. Into this respectable company of invisibles, the eldest and most august members of which are the Achilleses, the Theseuses, the Helens, and the Œdipuses of ancient mythus; the middle-aged and now most influential members of which are the Hamlets, the Falstaffs, the Panurges, the Fausts, and the Manfreds of later European invention; and the youngest and least serious members of which (the Scotch element here predominating) are the Meg Merrilieses, the Nicol Jarvies, the Cuddie Headriggs, and the Sandy Mackayes of the modern tale-writers[1]—two flights of new creatures take wing from the volumes before us. In a Pantheon already so multitudinous, the new comers run no small risk of being soon lost in the throng; for a while, however, they will be remembered at our firesides, and invoked as ministers of harmless enjoyment. First, with the gentle and dreamy David Copperfield at its head, comes a train of figures such as Dickens loves to draw—Steerforth, the handsome, the brave, the selfish, whose awful end is told with such tragic terror; Mr. Peggotty the elder, who appears in the beginning of the story only as a hearty Yarmouth fisherman, but becomes absolutely heroic ere the close; the three other Peggotty's, honest inarticulate Ham, poor lost little Em'ly, and Peggotty of the buttons; the affectionate broken-spirited Mrs. Copperfield, with her tormentors, the Murdstones; the active aunt, Betsy Trotwood, with her ward, Mr. Dick; the inimitable Micawber family; the good, absurd Traddles; the dying child-wife Dora, and her successor Agnes; Rosa Dartle, the fierce, the fiendish, with the scar on her lip; the 'willin'' Barkis, the 'lone lorn' Mrs. Gummidge, the ''umble' Heep, the 'respectable' Littimer, and very many more. Surrounding the vain and clever Mr. Arthur Pendennis, on the other hand, comes a group quite different, and quite Thackeristic—the fine, firm, worldly old Major; the pious, fond Mrs. Pendennis, and the high-spirited Laura; the Fotheringay, stupid, yet a glorious actress; her father, the maudlin, tipsy reprobate, Captain Costigan; the Clavering family, with that repetition of Becky, the syren Blanche Amory; the all-accomplished Chevalier Strong; Monsieur Mirobolant, the French cook; Pen's friend and Mentor, the manly, rough, cynical George Warrington, who was found 'drinking beer like a coal-heaver, and yet you could see he was a gentleman;' shrewd, likeable, little Harry Foker; poor, lonely Bows, the musician; Captain Shandon, the reckless dissolute man of genius, with his literary

---

[1] Meg Merrilies is in Scott's *Guy Mannering* (1815); Nicol Jarvie in his *Rob Roy* (1817); Cuddie Headrigg in his *Old Mortality* (1816); Saunders Mackaye in Charles Kingsley's *Alton Locke* (1850).

attendants, the Finucanes, the Doolans, the Bludyers, and the rest; Bungay, the publisher, and Mrs. Bungay; Morgan, the major's man; Fanny Bolton and Mr. Huxter; Madame Fribsby, the milliner, and minor characters innumerable. A glance even at these mere lists of *dramatis personæ*, will, we think, verify our preceding remarks, and recognise Mr. Dickens as being decidedly the more poetical and ideal, and Mr. Thackeray as being decidedly the more world-like and real in the style and tendency of his conceptions. For our own part, liking both styles well, we would point out as our favourite characters in the one group, Steerforth, the elder Mr. Peggotty, Mr. Micawber, and the child-wife Dora; and as our favourites in the other, the Major, Captain Costigan, Blanche Amory, and George Warrington. Were we required to say which single character is, to our taste, artistically the best in each, we should hesitate, in the one case, between Mr. Peggotty and the child-wife, in the other, between Major Pendennis and George Warrington; but, in the end, allowing ourselves to be swayed by sentimental liking, we should probably decide for the child-wife and Warrington. The former is an exquisite and most touching conception, such as Mr. Dickens has hardly equalled before; the latter is a perfectly original addition to our gallery of fictitious portraits, and is especially interesting as being a nearer approach than Mr. Thackeray had before favoured us with, to an exhibition of his serious *beau idéal* of a man. We are great admirers of 'the stunning Warrington.' . . . Why is Mr. Dickens, on the whole, genial, kindly, and romantic, and Mr. Thackeray, on the whole, caustic, shrewd, and satirical in his fictions? Clearly, the difference must arise from some radical difference in their ways of looking at the world, and in their conclusions as to the business and destinies of men in it.

Kindliness is the first principle of Mr. Dickens's philosophy, the sum and substance of his moral system. He does not, of course, exclude such things as pain and indignation from his catalogue of legitimate existences; indeed, as we have seen, few writers are capable of more honest bursts of indignation against what is glaringly wrong; still, in what may be called his speculative ethics, kindliness has the foremost place. His purely doctrinal protests in favour of this virtue, would, if collected, fill a little volume. His Christmas Books have been, one and all, fine fantastic sermons on this text; and, in his larger works, passages abound enforcing it. Not being able to lay our hands at this moment on any passage of this kind in *Copperfield*, short, and at the same time characteristic, we avail ourselves of the following from *Barnaby Rudge*.

Mr. Dickens's Apology for Mirth.—It is something even to look upon enjoy-ment, so that it be free and wild, and in the face of nature, though it is but the enjoyment of an idiot. It is something to know that Heaven has left the capacity of gladness in such a creature's breast; it is something to be assured, that how-ever lightly men may crush that faculty in their fellows, the Great Creator of mankind imparts it even to his despised and slighted work. Who would not rather see a poor idiot happy in the sunlight, than a wise man pining in a darkened jail? Ye men of gloom and austerity, who paint the face of Infinite Benevolence with an eternal frown, read in the everlasting book, wide open to your view, the lesson it would teach. Its pictures are not in black and sombre hues, but bright and glowing tints; its music, save when ye drown it, is not in sighs and groans, but songs and cheerful sounds. Listen to the million voices in the summer air, and find one dismal as your own. Remember, if ye can, the sense of hope and pleasure which every glad return of day awakens in the breast of all your kind, who have not changed their nature; and learn some wisdom even from the witless, when their hearts are lifted up, they know not why, by all the mirth and happiness it brings. [Ch. xxv.]

This doctrine, we repeat, is diffused through all Mr. Dickens's writings, and is affirmed again and again in express and very eloquent passages. Now, certainly, there is a fine and loveable spirit in the doctrine; and a man may be borne up by it in his airy imaginings, as Mr. Dickens is, (we might add the name of Mr. Leigh Hunt,) so cheerily and beautifully, that it were a barbarity to demur to it at the moment without serious provocation. Who can fail to see that only a benevolent heart, overflowing with faith in this doctrine, could have written the *Christmas Chimes*, or conceived those exquisite reminis-cences of childhood which delight us in the early pages of *Copperfield?* But when Mr. Dickens becomes aggressive in behalf of his doctrine, as he does in the foregoing, and in fifty other passages; when, as Mr. Cobden[1] is pugnacious for peace, and as some men are said to be bigots for toleration, so Mr. Dickens is harsh in behalf of kindliness— then a word of remonstrance seems really necessary. Is the foregoing doctrine, then, so axiomatic and absolute that no one may, without moral ugliness of soul, impugn or limit it? For our part, we do not think so. We know men, and very noble men, too, who would *not* rather see a poor idiot happy in the sunlight than a wise man pining in a darkened jail; we know men, and very cheerful men, too, who do *not* find the pictures of the book of nature to be all in bright and glowing tints, nor the sounds of nature to be all pleasant songs. In

---

[1] Richard Cobden (1804–65), the statesman, advocated international arbitration and disarmament.

short, in his antipathy to Puritanism, Mr. Dickens seems to have adopted a principle closely resembling that which pervades the ethical part of Unitarianism, the essence of which is, that it places a facile disposition at the centre of the universe. Now, without here offering any speculative or spiritual discussion, which might be deemed inappropriate, we may venture to say, that any man or artist who shall enter upon his sphere of activity, without in some way or other realizing and holding fast those truths which Puritanism sets such store by, and which it has embodied, according to its own grand phraseology, in the words sin, wrath, and justice, must necessarily take but half the facts of the world along with him, and go through his task too lightly and nimbly. To express our meaning in one word, such a man will miss out that great and noble element in all that is human—the element of *difficulty*. And though Mr. Dickens's happy poetic genius suggests to him much that his main ethical doctrine, if it were practically supreme in his mind, would certainly leave out, yet we think we can trace in the peculiar character of his romantic and most merry phantasies something of the want of this element.

Mr. Thackeray being, as we have already hinted, less dogmatic in his habits of writing than Mr. Dickens, less given to state and argue maxims in a propositional form, it is not so easy to obtain passages from his writings explaining his general views in the first person. On the whole, however, judging from little indications, from the general tone of his writings, and from literary analogy, we should say that he differs from Mr. Dickens in this, that, instead of clinging to any positive doctrine, from the neighbourhood of which he might survey nature and life, he holds his mind in a general state of negation and scepticism. There is in *Pendennis* a very interesting chapter, entitled 'The Way of the World,' written after that severe illness which interrupted the author in the progress of his work, and threatened to do more, and in which Mr. Thackeray falls into a more serious strain than usual. A long, and almost religious, dialogue takes place between Pen, then in a low moral state, and professing himself a sceptic and *pococurante*, and his elder friend Warrington, who retorts his arguments, denounces his conclusions, and tries to rekindle in him faith and enthusiasm. The dialogue is thus wound up.

[Quotation from end of ch. lxi; *Works*, xii, 800–2]

After Mr. Thackeray's protest that he is not to be held responsible for Pen's opinions, as delivered in the foregoing extract, and in the dialogue which precedes it, we may not, of course, seek his philosophy in these opinions alone. Indeed, we are too thankful to Mr. Thackeray for having had the boldness to introduce so serious a passage at all into a work of popular fiction, to wish to take any unfair advantage of it. But, it will be observed, Mr. Thackeray does not only report Pen's opinions, he also comments on these opinions very gravely in his own name, and he combats them through the medium of Warrington. When, however, a writer is at the pains to represent dramatically both the *pro* and the *con* of any question, we may be pretty sure that he has distributed nearly the entire bulk of his own sentiments on it between the two speakers to whom he assigns the task of conducting the argument. Accordingly, it seems to us, that in this antinomy between Pen and Warrington, we may, without any injustice, discern the main features of the author's own philosophy of life. In other words, it seems to us that there are many parts of Mr. Thackeray's writings in which the spirit of the Pendennis theory may be assumed to predominate; but that, ever and anon, traces of the Warrington spirit are also to be found in them.

Pen, in the passage before us, appears as a *pococurante* and a sceptic. Still honest and kindly, and above any positive meanness, he has sunk, for the time, into a general lowness of the spiritual faculty, the visible form of which is 'a sneering acquiescence with the world as it is,' or rather 'a belief, qualified with scorn, in all things extant.' But precisely here lies the point. To a man in this state of mind, all the things that do exist are not *extant*. As his eye sweeps through the universe, it rests by an internal necessity only on the meaner, minuter, and more terrestrial phenomena, which strike by their intense nearness; while the facts of the higher physics fade away into an invisibility, which, like that of the stars by day, passes for non-existence. Beings like Raphael, Gabriel, and Michael, may, as the poet sublimely teaches, sing of God's mightier works—of the sun hymning in chorus with his kindred stars, of the fair earth wheeling on her axis, of the storms that rage between land and sea. *They* may speak of these things, for these things are extant to their vision. But let Mephistopheles enter, and how the note is changed! *He* cannot talk fine; *he* cannot gabble of suns and worlds, and all that sort of thing! What *he* sees and can report upon, is a far more matter-of-fact concern—how men are daily growing more foolish and miserable; how the little god of earth is still as odd in his ways as ever, and is continually getting into some new mess or other! Precisely such, though with less profundity and more principle, is the spirit of Pen. He is, like Mephistopheles, a *pococurante*. The higher things of the world not being extant for him, he qualifies his belief in all he does see with a sneer. Suppose, now, this spirit transferred into literature; how will it show itself there? In a general tone of scoffing; in a disbelief in enthusiasm, or any species of mental exaltation; in a tendency to avoid in one's self, and to turn into ridicule in others, all words or phrases that recognise the diviner truths of existence or the higher developments of mind; in a fondness for scandal and vile social investigations, and in a distaste for the magnificent and the beautiful. What, for example, is Mephistopheles's speech in the presence of the angels, but another version of that of which our modern literature is full—a perpetual tirade against such entities and expressions as (to enumerate a few in different departments,) spiritual-mindedness, fervid affection, a Christian life, the transcendental metaphysics, noble aspiration, high art? It would be unjust to say that, even in the least earnest portion of Mr. Thackeray's writings, he exhibits the spirit of scorn to anything like this extent. An admirer of Tennyson—the poet who, most of all men living, represents, and would woo back among us, the rare, the religious, and the exquisite—could hardly do this. Still, Mr. Thackeray is not altogether blameless in this respect; and, probably, whatever amount of truth there is in the general complaint against him, as a writer who delights in the contemplation of human weaknesses and absurdities, may be resolved into the cause under notice.

But there are moments in Mr. Thackeray's writings when Warrington breaks in. Believing many things that Pen believes; sympathizing with him in many of his feelings, and probably without any much more definite creed of his own, that he could state in words—Warrington is yet a nobler being than Pen. Higher things are extant to him; and though his hatred of cant, and his rough cynical habit, would probably lead him to show his sense of these things in any other way rather than that of seasoning his talk with references to them, and might even prompt him to kick the words art, the ideal, transcendentalism, &c., to death, if ever they came too provokingly across his path, (a murder in which, but that the words still do serve a kind of useful purpose, we know many that would assist him); yet in his own soul he cherishes a fund of finer emotion, which will betray itself in bursts and flashes. Something of this we remark in Thackeray himself. It is seen in the general conception of some of his characters, such as Laura and Mrs. Pendennis, as well as Warrington; it is seen in occasional passages of serious reflection, of which perhaps the most remarkable is the one from which we have made an extract; and it is seen also in a frequent touch of real pathos, such as no mere affectation of the sorrowful could enable a writer to assume. On the whole, we should say that Mr. Thackeray has nowhere exhibited this serious spirit so conspicuously as in the second volume of his *Pendennis;* and remarking this, and how good the effect is, we must admit, without any prejudice to our previous observation regarding the necessity of Mr. Thackeray's keeping obstinately to his own style of art, that we should like to see him in future diminish the Pen a little and develop the Warrington.

There is one piece of positive doctrine, however, in which both Pen and Warrington agree, and of which Mr. Thackeray's writings are as decidedly the exponents in the present day, as Mr. Dickens's are of the doctrine of kindliness. This doctrine may be called the doctrine of *Anti-snobbism.* Singular fact! in the great city of London, where higher and more ancient faiths seem to have all but perished, and where men bustle in myriads, scarce restrained by any spiritual law, there has arisen of late years, as there arose in Mecca of old, a native form of ethical belief, by which its inhabitants are tried and try each other. 'Thou shalt not be a snob,' such is the first principle at present of Cockney ethics. And observe how much real sincerity there is in this principle, how it really addresses itself to facts, and only to facts, known and admitted. It is not the major morals of human nature, but what are called the minor morals of society, and these chiefly in their æsthetic aspect, as modes of pleasant breeding, that the Cockney system of ethics recognises. Its maxims and commands are not 'Thou shalt do no wrong,' 'Thou shalt have no other Gods before me,' 'Thou shalt not covet,'—but 'Thou shalt pronounce thy H's,' 'Thou shalt not abuse waiters as if they were dogs,' 'Thou shalt not falsely make a boast of dining with peers and Members of Parliament.' He who offends in these respects is a snob. Thus, at least, the Cockney moralist professes no more than he really believes. The real species of moral evil recognised in London, the real kind of offence which the moral sentiment there punishes, and cannot away with, is snobbism. The very name, it will be observed, is characteristic and unpretentious— curt, London-born, irreverent. When you say that a man is a snob, it does not mean that you detest and abhor him, but only that you must cut him, or make fun of him. Such is *Anti-snobbism,* the doctrine of which Mr. Thackeray, among his other merits, has the merit of being the chief literary expounder and apostle! Now it is not a very awful doctrine, certainly; it is not, as our friend Warrington would be the first to admit, the doctrine in the strength of which one would like to guide his own soul, or to face the future and the everlasting; still it has its use, and by all means let it have, yes, let it have its scribes and preachers!

We had thought, after this more grave investigation, to indulge in some remarks illustrative more especially of the humours of the two writers, as compared with each other, of the forms of the comic in which they respectively excel and show their mastery. Here also we should have seen the difference of their ultimate method and spirit; and should have found Dickens to be the more kindly, genial, and fantastic, and Thackeray to be the more tart, satirical, and truculent humorist. Forbearing any such process of contrast, however, the scope and results of which we have already indicated, we must close with a general remark, applicable to both writers.

Although the aim of all fictitious literature is primarily to interest the reader; and although, in a certain deep sense, it may be maintained that no kind of literary composition whatever is valuable that is not interesting, it would yet seem as if recently the determination to achieve that special kind of interest which consists in mere amusement, had prevailed too largely among our writers of tales and novels. We do not often see now that effort at artistic perfection, that calm resolution to infuse into a performance the concentrated thought and observation of the writer, and to give it final roundness and finish, which did exist in old times, and which supreme authorities have always recommended. The spirit of craft and money-making has crept into our artistic literature; and, even in our best writers, we have but a compromise between the inner desire and the outer necessity. Nor is this to be very harshly condemned, or very gravely wondered at. Our writers of fiction, for the most part, candidly own that they write to make money and amuse people. Their merit is therefore the greater, when, like the two eminent writers whose works we have been discussing, they do more than this. Should we suggest that their functions would be intrinsically higher, and more satisfactory to their own better judgment, did they work less according to the external demand, and more accord-ing to the internal wish and form, they will admit the suggestion to the full, but say that on the whole they are not strong enough to follow it. Should we farther adduce the old consideration of fame, and the opinion of posterity, as an argument on the right side, they may even turn the laugh against us. 'Posterity!' they may say, with Mr. Merry-man in the Prelude to *Faust*:—

> Would of posterity I heard less mention!
> Suppose posterity had *my* attention,
> Who'd make contemporary fun?

Besides, in the present and still increasing multitudinousness of books and authors, the chance of having readers among posterity is, even for the best, a very sorry hope. Still, we would adhere to our wish; and that very multitudinousness of books and authors may bring us right again one day. There are two literary devices or fashions to which at present one may trace much of the particular evil now under view. The one is the fashion or device of the three-volume novel; the other the fashion of publishing novels in serial numbers. The first, which we are happy to see is losing ground, is a wretched piece of publisher's despotism in literature, redeemed from absolute vileness only by that mystical artistic value which there is, and always will be, in the number three. The other, which is still gaining ground, operates deleteriously, by compelling an author to supply the parts of his story before he has thoroughly conceived the whole, and also by compelling him to spice each separate part, so that it may please alone. These conditions exist, and it is not given to any man, in any time, to be independent of conditions that will thwart him, and compel him to deviate from his ideal of excellence. Still, if such writers as Dickens, Thackeray, and Jerrold, who have already earned a reputation, who have as much talent as any of those past novelists of whom our literature is proud, and who may even venture now to lead the public against its own prejudices, were to set the example, by each doing his best, in the style each in his inner heart believes to be best, the good that would be effected might be very great.

26. Thackeray, letter to David Masson

6(?) May 1851 (*Letters*, ii, 771–3)

My dear sir,

I received the *NB Review* and am very glad to know the name of the critic who has spoken so kindly in my favor. Did I not once before see your handwriting, in a note w^h pointed out to me a friendly notice of Vanity Fair[1]—then not very well known or much cared for, and struggling to get a place in the world? If you were the author of the article to w^h I allude, let me thank you for that too; I remember it as gratefully, as a boy remembers his 'tips' at school, when sovereigns were rare & precious to him. I don't know what to say respecting your present paper comparisons being difficult, & no two minds in the least alike. I think Mr. Dickens has in many things quite a divine genius so to speak, and certain notes in his song are so delightful and admirable, that I should never think of trying to imitate him, only hold my tongue and admire him. I quarrel with his Art in many respects: w^h I don't think represents Nature duly; for instance Micawber appears to me an exaggeration of a man, as his name is of a name. It is delightful and makes me laugh: but it is no more a real man than my friend Punch is: and in so far I protest against him— and against the doctrine quoted by my Reviewer from Goethe too— holding that the Art of Novels *is* to represent Nature: to convey as strongly as possible the sentiment of reality—in a tragedy or a poem or a lofty drama you aim at producing different emotions; the figures moving, and their words sounding, heroically: but in a drawing-room drama a coat is a coat and a poker a poker; and must be nothing else according to my ethics, not an embroidered tunic, nor a great red-hot instrument like the Pantomime weapon. But let what defects you (or rather I), will, be in Dickens's theory—there is no doubt according to my notion that his writing has one admirable quality— it is charming—that answers everything. Another may write the most perfect English have the greatest fund of wit learning & so forth— but I doubt if any novel-writer has that quality, that wonderful sweetness & freshness w^h belongs to Dickens—And now I have carried my note out of all bounds and remain dear Sir

Yours very faithfully,

W. M. Thackeray.

---

[1] The first three numbers of *Vanity Fair* were briefly reviewed in 'Popular Serial Literature,' *North British Review* (May 1847), vii, 112–36.

27. [Samuel Phillips], from 'David Copperfield and Arthur Pendennis', *The Times*

11 June 1851, 8. Reprinted in Phillips's *Essays from 'The Times'* (1871), ii, 320–38

Phillips (1814–54) settled down as a journalist, and worked on *The Times* from about 1845. Gordon Ray, in his biography of Thackeray, calls Phillips Thackeray's 'old enemy', and it is thought that he wrote the criticism in *The Times* of *The Kickleburys on the Rhine*—an article which angered Thackeray, who retaliated in 'An Essay on Thunder and Small Beer', prefixed to the second edition (*Works*, x, 219–27).

What an epic was to the old world—a continuous narration of stirring events, with linked sweetness long drawn out—that is the romance to the modern world. With the change of matter there has been a change of form; it is no longer the story of 'physical force' that absorbs and delights mankind, it is the battle of life,—not the encounter of flesh and blood, but the clash of principles and the conflict of passion. The decease of the three volume fiction has often been foretold, but has never come to pass, because it exists as the supply of a want, and a very complex want. All men want amusement; but, more than this, mankind, however civilized, require some stimulus of the simpler emotions; overlaid as these may be by habit, perverted by selfishness or dilapidated by overwear, they are still the chief source of pleasure. That, therefore, must be welcome which awakes them. The novel has, for the unimaginative, incidents,—for the student of human nature, character,—for the critical ear, vigour or beauty of language,—for the theorist, an ample store of cobwebs. It offers love and children to the spinster, red coats and glory to the legal or the literary drudge; and, if it does harm by exhausting the sympathies of some, it does good by exalting and keeping them fresh in sluggish and mechanical natures. The Romance, we say, occupies the place of the epic; it is more various, because the forms of society are more manifold, and men's knowledge and their requirements alike more diverse.

It is not long since two of our best-known epopœists, or, to use the more common term, of our novel-writers, have concluded each a work published by instalments, and sent them forth in their perfect form from the presses of Bradbury and Evans. Little matter to us whether it was the lust of scribbling, the desire of fame, or the appetite for what university statutes still term 'solids' which prompted them to utterance. We need not, with Mr. Wickfield, decipher the motives which induced Mr. Dickens and Mr. Thackeray to compile respectively the lives of David Copperfield and Arthur Pendennis;[1] enough for us that each of them has produced something neither devoid of interest nor unworthy of his fame. . . .

[Mr. Thackeray's story] is intended to represent simply the way of the world, and it does so. Its merits consist in the truth of that representation. The interest given to Mr. Dickens's work by its biographical form was here impossible, for the centre figure is not meant to be a hero at all, and Laura only a heroine in the sense in which all good young women are such. Carrying out the proposition which he announced in *Vanity Fair*, Mr. Thackeray has once more depicted the average features of the people one meets, neither ascending to any great heights nor descending to any extraordinary depths. The whole story is consistent with this intention. We have drawing-rooms before us, never cottages; fashion rather than nature; in other words, that second nature which custom creates. We have a style which harmonizes with the topics, and a philosophy which, whether intended to do so or not, never rises above the obvious and the commonplace. Perhaps no greater distinction can be drawn between the two works than this, that the one confines itself to the artificial phase of society, the other to the real. Allowing this, the wider scope of Mr. Dickens's novel is at once explained. There is room for more range of character—for more diversity of adventure—for a more thoughtful and suggestive tone. Mr. Thackeray tells us in his preface that he could willingly have treated us to squalor and crime—St. Giles's and a gallows' scene, but that he mistrusted his powers. The resolve was judicious, for what he has done he has done well, catching not a little of the force and spirit with which his favourite models, Smollett, Fielding, and Sterne, illustrated the realities of a century ago. Pendennis is not exactly a Tom Jones, but he is conceived from the same point of view. The only question is whether Mr. Thackeray has done wisely in applying the doctrine of limits to character so unvaryingly, and we are inclined to

[1] In *David Copperfield*, Mr. Wickfield is always 'fishing for motives' (e.g. in ch. xv).

believe that, while he has observed keenly enough the peculiarities of the world which he depicts, he has not gauged universal humanity so skilfully as Mr. Dickens. In *David Copperfield* there are more contrasts of character, more varieties of intellect, a more diverse scenery, and more picturesqueness of detail. It is the whole world rather than a bit of it which you see before you. There is first the childhood, vividly painted, happy and unsuspicious, with its ideas and feelings not at all overdone; in *Pendennis*, on the contrary, you have rather the fact that he was once a child than childhood described. There are, secondly,— and it is an artifice of which Mr. Dickens is somewhat too fond, —some people without wits in his tale. With Mr. Batley we find no fault, for he is a pendant to Miss Trotwood, who could ill be spared; but Dora is an infliction. The effect, however, of these portraits is to throw the intellect of others into relief, and also to give a colouring such as the harmless enjoyments and simple affection of crazed people alone can give. There is no satire in the description of their extravagances; on the contrary, there is something at once joyous and tender, something mysterious and impressive, in the history of a lunatic, which makes the Swiss and the Oriental revere him, and which made Wordsworth put him into verse. As he goes lower in the scale of intellect and manners, so also Mr. Dickens rises higher than Mr. Thackeray—his hero is greater than Pendennis, and his heroine than Laura, while 'my Aunt' might alike, on the score of eccentricities and kindliness, take the shine out of Lady Rockminster. The Yarmouth group, again, is no exaggeration, and, while introducing another of Mr. Dickens's merits, the power of description gives at once the effect of a general contrast running through the tale, and absorbs as much interest as the central figures by the force and dignity of the delineation; the depth of feeling revealed in Mr. Peggotty and in Ham, the energetic patience of one, the passive endurance of the other, not less than Mrs. Gummidge's sudden conversion from querulousness to activity and self-forgetfulness, are the evidence at once of knowledge and of imagination. Nor is the mute Mr. Barkis's expressive gesture, or the leg-rubbing and strong vernacular of the boatman, less true to the life. What we cannot allow to Mr. Dickens is the invariable fidelity which accompanies Mr. Thackeray's characters. There are cases where his facts are not so true as his ideas. It might be quite true, for instance, that Miss Dartle would hate Steerforth's victim with all the rancour of jealousy; but it is very unlikely that she should seek her out in order to reproach her with her shame, and gloat over her misery with the fiendish violence ascribed to her. The thing is alto-gether overstrained. We have already said that Dora is not a fact, and we must extend the censure to a frequent want of truth in language, not that the dialect of Mr. Peggotty is less racy than the brogue of Captain Costigan, but that in any passage of sentiment Mr. Dickens lets the sentiment run away with him. Who ever heard of one young man saying gravely to another, 'You are always equally loved and cherished in my heart,' or of a bride who has just entered the travelling carriage coming out with so Tennysonian a decasyllabic as—

'It grows out of the night when Dora died'?

—a fault this, which grows out of the over-poetical tendencies of the author, tendencies discoverable enough in all his works, and evidenced as much, perhaps, in the characters of Barnaby Rudge and Paul Dombey as in any discursiveness of mere expression. It is Mr. Thacke-ray's merit that his prose is downright prose; he does not seem, indeed, to have the faculty of committing such mistakes as these; but compare the fidelity of the greeting between Pendennis and Warrington, and the remarks thereon, with the conversation of David and Steerforth; or compare the rage of Miss Dartle with anything said or accomplished by Becky, in *Vanity Fair*, and you will not hesitate to say which way the balance inclines. It may be said, however, that Mr. Thackeray was preserved in some degree from such faults by casting all his characters within a narrow sphere, and that sphere one in which language is easily caught, and all of one pattern. Yet we are inclined to take exception against the profusion of 'egads' and 'begads,' with which that most gentlemanly old man the Major interlards his discourse, even if not against their Irish first cousin 'bedad,' which emphasizes the rich brogue of 'the *pore* old man who was dthriven to dthrinking by ingratitude.' As in language so in exterior and manners, Mr. Thackeray's people are less marked. He does not wish to individualize. Mr. Dickens has a perfect passion for being particular, as if the portrait might be wanted in the *Hue and Cry*. We must suppose either that people in the best society have not their little tricks—tricks of the body, that is—or else that Mr. Dickens has an unnatural faculty of detecting them. All the accessory characters in his books gesticulate. They have a hundred little ways of identifying themselves. Like the gentleman in *Lavengro* who must for the life of him touch something, they are always popping out with some peculiarity, which might make us think that Mr. Dickens, with the doctor quoted the other day by

Lord Campbell, believed in universal monomania.[1] Uriah Heep, for instance, is first introduced to us as trying to put a spell upon the pony —his sinuous contortions and shadowless eyes are for ever before us as illustrative of his wily wickedness. Mrs. Steerforth is to be the quintessence of pride, Miss Trotwood of firmness and eccentric good nature, the Murdstones of firmness and ill nature. Mrs. Steerforth, therefore, is tall and rigid, Miss Trotwood rigid and tall. So is Mr. Murdstone, so is Miss Murdstone, so was Mr. Dombey. Mr. Spenlow's sisters are to be like a pair of canaries, neat, dapper, twittering sort of females; accordingly they have a curious appetite for lumps of sugar and seedcake. Again, Mr. Dickens is as deep in nasology as the learned Slawkenbergius;[2] his people are perpetually wagging their noses, or flattening them against windows, or rubbing them, or evincing some restlessness or other in connexion with them. He is not much less scientific in eyes, and ought by this time to have a regular classification of them. The effect of all this is that you trace something genuine in Mr. Thackeray's figures more easily than you do in Mr. Dickens's. You have not such a series of peculiarities to separate before you can regard the nature by itself. Fokers, Pendennises, Helens, and Lauras abound everywhere. You can't go out without meeting them, nor do they, the first especially, deny the portraiture; if there is any desire to deny it, that arises, not from Mr. Thackeray's allowing them too little goodness, but from his not allowing them enough wits. The ladies, however, ought to be propitiated by something of additional beauty and force assigned to them in *Pendennis*. Compare the tone of the two books, and one will be found, as a whole, light-hearted and hopeful, the other dolorous and depressing. Both books are comic in much of their expression, for both writers are humourists, but the humour of one is more gloomy than that of the other, as if from a shadow fallen upon a life. While in *David Copperfield* the tragedy is consummated in a single chapter, in *Pendennis* it is spread over the whole surface of the story. In the former case a man is slain; in the latter case human aspirations and complacencies are demolished. Rising from the perusal of Mr. Dickens's work, you forget that there is evil in the world, and remember only the good. The distinction

---

[1] See George Borrow's *Lavengro* (1851), ch. lxiv. Lord Campbell (1799–1861) was the famous judge.

[2] 'The great and learned Hafen Slawkenbergius', whose Latin treatise on noses is treasured by Tristram Shandy's father (*Tristram Shandy* (1760–67), vol. iii, chs. xxxv–xlii; beginning of vol. iv).

drawn between the bad and good is a broad one. Rising from Mr. Thackeray's, you are doubtful of yourself and of humanity at large, for nobody is very bad or very good, and everybody seems pretty well contented. The *morale* might almost be summed up into the American's creed, 'There's nothing new, there's nothing true, and it don't signify.' One might almost fancy that Mr. Thackeray had reduced his own theory of life to that average which he strikes from the practice of all around him. We are brought into a mess and left there, woman's love and purity being the only light upon our path. Mr. Dickens touches a higher key; his villains, Heep and Littimer, stand out as villains; his women—and we may take My Aunt and Agnes as equally faithful pictures,—hold an eminence which women may and do reach in this world, and which mere purity and love do not suffice to attain.

We do not wish, however, to be hard on Mr. Thackeray's selection of his scene. As forms of sensual existence, varied only by circumstance and taste, his characters are as true as the velvet of Mr. Hunt's Mariana, so lately a topic of discussion,[1] or the topers of Teniers—only do not let the picture be taken as expressing the whole truth of the matter; there is a large suppression. We must grant, by way of counterpoise, that Mr. Dickens frequently sins in excess. He contemplates human nature in its strength, and on its unsophisticated side;—Mr. Thackeray in its weakness and on its most artificial basis. The consequence is, that the former verges on the sentimental, the latter on the cynical, one being the reaction of the other; only while the first is no unmanly weapon in Mr. Dickens's hand, the last is a sufficiently temperate one in the hand of Mr. Thackeray. As to actual influence, we should, for the reasons aforesaid, assign the higher place to Mr. Dickens, partly because the expressed morality comes forth as something definite, the fruit of personal experience, yet conveyed through a personage of the tale, partly because the highest lessons inculcated, such as those of faith in Mr. Peggotty and resignation in Ham, are some of the highest that can be inculcated, and partly, also, because the world which Mr. Thackeray experiments on is a world of salamanders, fireproof, inclined to disbelieve that the lesson they can criticise may possibly increase their condemnation. Each rejoices to be what he is. Foker and Major Pendennis rejoice in their portraits, save that the latter don't think he is so 'doosedly' made-up, after all. You may as

---

[1] Phillips has presumably confused Holman Hunt with his fellow-pre-Raphaelite, John Millais, whose painting, 'Mariana of the Moated Grange', was exhibited in 1851.

well write at them as preach at them; and did not the Major go to church? Perfect as *Pendennis* is, then, in execution, we are bound, when weighing it with *Copperfield*, to adjudge the chief merit where the most universal interest is conciliated and the most exalted teaching hidden beneath the tale. The epic is greater than the satire.

HENRY ESMOND

1852

---

28. [G. H. Lewes], from 'Thackeray's New Novel', the *Leader*

6 November 1852, iii, 1071–3

The opening paragraph of this history is not only characteristic of its author, but of the work. [Quotation from the beginning of Book I; *Works*, xiii, 13–14.]

It is to show us some reflected image of the time that this book is written; and therefore, unless duly warned, the reader may feel some disappointment when he finds that 'Thackeray's new novel' is not a comic novel, scarcely a novel at all, and in no sense a satire. It is a beautiful book, not one sentence of which may be skipped; but it is as unlike *Vanity Fair* and *Pendennis* as a book written by Thackeray can be.

To those who look beyond the passing hour, and see something more in literature than the occupation of a languid leisure, *Esmond* will have many sources of interest. One of these may be the purely biographical one of representing a new phase in Thackeray's growth. Tracing the evolution of his genius from the wild and random sketches which preceded *Vanity Fair*, we perceive an advancing growth, both as a moralist and as an artist. In *Vanity Fair* the mocking mephistophelic spirit was painfully obtrusive; to laugh at the world—to tear away its many masks—to raise the crown even from Cæsar's head, that we might note the baldness which the laurels covered—to make love and devotion themselves ridiculous, seemed his dominant purpose; and had it not been for the unmistakeable kindliness, the love of generosity, and the sympathy with truth which brightened those mocking pages, all that has been ignorantly or maliciously said of Thackeray's 'heart-lessness' would have had its evidence.

In *Pendennis* there was a decided change. The serious and nobler element, before subordinate, there rose to supremacy; the mockery withdrew into the second place. A kinder and a juster appreciation of life gave increased charm to the work. Although, perhaps, not on the whole so amusing, because less novel, and, in some respects, a repetition of *Vanity Fair*, it was, nevertheless, an advance in art, was written with more care, and, as before hinted, was less sarcastic and sceptical.

That vein of seriousness which ran like a small silver thread through the tapestry of *Vanity Fair*, has become the woof of *Esmond;* the mocking spirit has fled; such sarcasm as remains is of another sort—a kind of sad smile, that speaks of pity, not of scorn. Nor is this the only change. That careless disrespect, which on a former occasion we charged him with [See No. 24], is nowhere visible in *Esmond*. If as a work of art *Esmond* has defects, they are not the defects of carelessness. What he has set himself to do, he has done seriously, after due preparation.

Seeing, as we do, such evidences of growth, and of growth *upwards*, and remembering that he is only now in his forty-second year, may we not form the highest hopes of such a mind? Considered as a landmark on his career, *Esmond* is of peculiar significance. But we have here to consider it in another light; the reader impatiently asks, 'What am I to think of it?'

Little Sir, you are to think *this* of it: An autobiography, written in the autumn light of a calm and noble life, sets before you much of the private and domestic, no less than of the public and historic activity of the reigns of William and Anne. The thread which holds these together is a simple and a touching one—the history of *two* devotions. All who have *lived* will feel here the pulse of real suffering, so different from 'romantic woe;' all who have loved will trace a real affection here, more touching because it has a quiet reserve in its expression; but we shall not be in the least surprised to hear even 'highly intelligent persons' pronounce it 'rather a falling off.' But you, good sir, who follow your *Leader*, will honestly declare that it touched and delighted you; that from the first page to the last you loved the book and its author.

Without pretending to that minute knowledge of the period which could alone justify an authoritative opinion, we may say that this book has so much the air and accent of the time, it would impose on us if presented as a veritable History of Colonel Esmond; and this verisimilitude is nowhere obtruded; the art has concealed the art.

In structure and purpose it reminds us of Leigh Hunt's *Sir Ralph*

Esher,[1] to which justice has not been done, because it has been read for a novel. The men of those days, no less than the events, move across the scene, and we get hasty yet vivid glimpses of Addison, Steele, Swift, Bolingbroke, Marlborough, Atterbury, Lord Mohun, and the Pretender. True to that opening passage we have quoted, these historic persons have none of the 'dignity of history'—they walk before us 'in their habit as they lived.'

The characters are numerous, but are rather 'sketched in,' as one would find them in memoirs, than elaborately developed, as in a fiction. Lady Castlewood and Beatrix are, indeed, full-length portraits; both charmingly drawn, from the same originals, we suspect, as Mrs. Pendennis and Blanche Amory. The attentive reader will note, however, that in the portrait of the coquette, Beatrix, he has thrown so much real impulsive goodness, that she becomes a new creation—and, let us add, a *true* one. She is not bad—she is vain; and her fascination is made very intelligible.

What novel readers will say to Lady Castlewood's love, and to Esmond's love for the woman who calls him 'son,' we will not prophecy; for ourselves we feel, that although *vrai*, it is not always *vraisemblable*. Novel readers will be more unanimous about the dramatic interest of the scenes at the close of the first and third volumes. . . .

29. [George Brimley], from 'Thackeray's Esmond', the *Spectator*

6 November 1852, xxv, 1066–7. Reprinted in *Essays by the late George Brimley, M.A.*, ed. Clark, W. G., (1860), 252–62

Brimley (1819–57) was librarian of Trinity College, Cambridge, and wrote literary criticism for *Fraser's Magazine* and the *Spectator*.

Esmond is an autobiographical memoir of the first five-and-thirty years of the life of an English gentleman of family, written in his old age after his retirement to Virginia; and edited with an introduction by

1 Published 1830.

his daughter, for the instruction and amusement of her children and descendants, and to give them a lively portrait of the noble gentleman her father. It is historical, inasmuch as political events enter both as motives to the actors and as facts influencing their fortunes, and because historical personages are brought upon the scene: both are necessary elements in the career of a gentleman and a soldier, but neither forms the staple or the main object of the book,—which concerns itself with the characters and fortunes of the noble family of Castlewood, of which Henry Esmond is a member. The period embraced is from the accession of James the Second to the death of Queen Anne, and the manners depicted are those of the English aristocracy. Archæology is not a special object with the author; though both costume, in its more limited sense, and manners, are, we believe, accurately preserved. But Wardour Street and the Royal Academy need fear no competitor in Mr. Thackeray. His business lies mainly with men and women, not with high-heeled shoes and hoops and patches, and old china and carved high-backed chairs. Nor have Mr. Macaulay's forthcoming volumes[1] been anticipated, except in one instance, where the Chevalier St. George is brought to England, has an interview with his sister at Kensington just before her death, is absolutely present in London at the proclamation of George the First, and indeed only misses being James the Third, King of Great Britain and Ireland, by grace of his own exceeding baseness and folly. Scott, who had a reverence for the Stuarts impossible to Mr. Thackeray with his habit of looking at the actors in life from the side-scenes and in the green-room rather than from before the footlights, has not scrupled to take a similar liberty with his Chevalier in *Redgauntlet*, merely to arrange a striking tableau at the fall of the curtain. But these violations of received tradition with respect to such well-known historical personages, force upon the reader unnecessarily the fictitious character of the narrative, and are therefore better avoided.

There is abundance of incident in the book, but not much more plot than in one of Defoe's novels: neither is there, generally speaking, a plot in a man's life, though there may be and often is in sections of it. Unity is given not by a consecutive and self-developing story, but by the ordinary events of life blended with those peculiar to a stirring time acting on a family group, and bringing out and ripening their qualities; these again controlling the subsequent events, just as happens in life. The book has the great charm of reality. The framework is,

[1] The third and fourth volumes of Macaulay's *History of England* appeared in 1855.

as we have said, historical: men with well-known names, political, literary, military, pass and repass; their sayings and doings are interwoven with the sayings and doings of the fictitious characters; and all reads like a genuine memoir of the time. The rock ahead of historical novelists is the danger of reproducing too much of their raw material; making the art visible by which they construct their image of a bygone time; painting its manners and the outside of its life with the sense of contrast with which men of the present naturally view them, or looking at its parties and its politics in the light of modern questions: the rock ahead of Mr. Thackeray, in particular, was the temptation merely to dramatize his lectures: but he has triumphed over these difficulties, and Queen Anne's Colonel writes his life,—and a very interesting life it is,—just as such a Queen Anne's Colonel might be supposed to have written it. We shall give no epitome of the story, because the merit of the book does not lie there, and what story there is readers like to find out for themselves.

Mr. Thackeray's humour does not mainly consist in the creation of oddities of manner, habit, or feeling; but in so representing actual men and women as to excite a sense of incongruity in the reader's mind—a feeling that the follies and vices described are deviations from an ideal of humanity always present to the writer. The real is described vividly, with that perception of individuality which constitutes the artist; but the description implies and suggests a standard higher than itself, not by any direct assertion of such a standard, but by an unmistakeable irony. The moral antithesis of actual and ideal is the root from which springs the peculiar charm of Mr. Thackeray's writings; that mixture of gayety and seriousness, of sarcasm and tenderness, of enjoyment and cynicism, which reflects so well the contradictory consciousness of man as a being with senses and passions and limited knowledge, yet with a conscience and a reason speaking to him of eternal laws and a moral order of the universe. It is this that makes Mr. Thackeray a profound moralist, just as Hogarth showed his knowledge of perspective by drawing a landscape throughout in violation of its rules. So, in Mr. Thackeray's picture of society as it is, society as it ought to be is implied. He could not have painted Vanity Fair as he has, unless Eden had been shining brightly in his inner eyes. The historian of 'snobs' indicates in every touch his fine sense of a gentleman or a lady. No one could be simply amused with Mr. Thackeray's descriptions or his dialogues. A shame at one's own defects, at the defects of the world in which one was living, was irresistibly aroused along with the reception of the particular portraiture. But while he was dealing with his own age, his keen perceptive faculty prevailed, and the actual predominates in his pictures of modern society. His fine appreciation of high character has hitherto been chiefly shown (though with bright exceptions) by his definition of its contrary. But, getting quite out of the region of his personal experiences, he has shown his true nature without this mark of satire and irony. The ideal is no longer implied, but realized, in the two leading characters of *Esmond*. The medal is reversed, and what appeared as scorn of baseness is revealed as love of goodness and nobleness—what appeared as cynicism is presented as a heart-worship of what is pure, affectionate, and unselfish. He has selected for his hero a very noble type of the Cavalier softening into the man of the eighteenth century, and for his heroine one of the sweetest women that ever breathed from canvass or from book since Raffaelle painted Maries and Shakspere created a new and higher consciousness of woman in the mind of Germanic Europe. Colonel Esmond is indeed a fine gentleman,—the accomplished man, the gallant soldier, the loyal heart, and the passionate lover, whose richly contrasted but harmonious character Clarendon would have delighted to describe; while Falkland and Richard Lovelace would have worn him in their hearts' core. Lucy Hutchinson's husband might have stood for his model in all but politics, and his Toryism has in it more than a smack of English freedom very much akin to that noble patriot's Republicanism.[1] Especially does he recall Colonel Hutchinson in his lofty principle, his unswerving devotion to it, a certain sweet seriousness which comes in happily to temper a penetrating intellect, and a faculty of seeing things and persons as they are, to which we owe passage after passage in the book, that it requires no effort to imagine Thackeray uttering himself in those famous lectures of his, and looking up with his kind glance to catch the delighted smile of his audience at his best points.[2] Nor is there anything unartistic in this reminder of the author; for this quality of clear insight into men and things united with a kindly nature and a large capacity for loving is not limited to any particular time or age, and combines with Colonel Esmond's other qualities so as to give no impression of incongruity. But besides the harmonizing effect of this sweetly serious temperament, the record

---

[1] *The Memoirs of the Life of Colonel Hutchinson* by Lucy Hutchinson (b. 1620) were not printed until 1806.

[2] Thackeray's lectures on the English Humourists were delivered in London, May–July 1851, and published in book form in 1853.

of Colonel Esmond's life is throughout a record of his attachment to one woman, towards whom his childish gratitude for protection grows with his growth into a complex feeling, in which filial affection and an unconscious passion are curiously blended. So unconscious, indeed, is the passion, that, though the reader has no difficulty in interpreting it, Esmond himself is for years the avowed and persevering though hopeless lover of this very lady's daughter. The relation between Esmond and Rachel Viscountess Castlewood is of that sort that nothing short of consummate skill could have saved it from becoming ridiculous or offensive, or both. In Mr. Thackeray's hands, the difficulty has become a triumph, and has given rise to beauties which a safer ambition would have not dared to attempt. The triumph is attained by the conception of Lady Castlewood's character. She is one of those women who never grow old, because their lives are in the affections, and the suffering that comes upon such lives only brings out strength and beauty unperceived before. The graces of the girl never pass away, but maturer loveliness is added to them, and spring, summer, autumn, all bloom on their faces and in their hearts at once. A faint foreshadowing of this character we have had before in Helen Pendennis: but she had been depressed and crushed in early life, had married for a home, certainly without passion; and her nature was chilled and despondent. Lady Castlewood has the development that a happy girlhood, and a marriage with the man she devotedly loves, can give to a woman; and her high spirit has time to grow for her support when it is needed. Even the weaknesses of her character are but as dimples on a lovely face, and make us like her the better for them, because they give individuality to what might else be felt as too ideal. Nothing can be more true or touching than the way this lady demeans herself when she finds her husband's affection waning from her; and Mr. Thackeray is eminently Mr. Thackeray in his delineation of that waning love on the one side, and the strength and dignity which the neglected wife gradually draws from her own hitherto untried resources, when she ceases to lean on the arm that was withdrawn, and discovers that the heart she had worshipped was no worthy idol. But to those who would think the mother 'slow' we can have no hesitation in recommending the daughter. Miss Beatrix Esmond—familiarly and correctly termed 'Trix' by her friends—is one of those dangerous young ladies who fascinate every one, man or woman, that they choose to fascinate, but care for nobody but themselves; and their care for themselves simply extends to the continual gratification of a boundless love of admiration, and the kind of power which results from it. If Miss Rebecca Sharp had really been a Montmorency, and a matchless beauty, and a maid of honour to a Queen, she might have sublimated into a Beatrix Esmond. It is for this proud, capricious, and heartless beauty, that Henry Esmond sighs out many years of his life, and does not find out, till she is lost to him and to herself, how much he loves her 'little mamma,' as the saucy young lady is fond of calling Lady Castlewood. Beatrix belongs to the class of women who figure most in history, with eyes as bright and hearts as hard as diamonds, as Mary Stuart said of herself; and Mary Stuart and Miss Esmond have many points in common. Of her end we are almost disposed to say with Othello, 'Oh! the pity of it, Iago, oh! the pity of it.' Unlovely as she is because unloving, yet her graces are too fair to be so dragged through the dirt—that stream is too bright to end in a city sewer. But the tragedy is no less tragical for the tawdry comedy of its close. Life has no pity for the pitiless, no sentiment for those who trample on love as a weakness.

These three characters are the most prominent in the book. With one or the other of the two women Henry Esmond's thoughts are almost always engaged; and it is to win the reluctant love of the daughter that he seeks distinction as a soldier, a politician, and finally a conspirator in behalf of the son of King James. In this threefold career, he has intercourse with Addison, Steele, and the wits; serves under Marlborough at Blenheim and Ramillies; is on terms of intimacy with St. John and the Tory leaders. A succession of Viscounts Castlewood figure on the scene, all unmistakeable English noblemen of the Stuart period. A dowager Viscountess is a more faithful than flattering portrait of a class of ladies of rank of that time. The Chevalier St. George appears oftener than once. The great Duke of Hamilton is about to make Beatrix his Duchess, when he is basely murdered in that doubly fatal duel with the execrable Lord Mohun, who had twelve years before slain, also in a duel, my Lord Viscount Castlewood, the father of Beatrix. The book has certainly no lack of incident; the persons come and go as on the scene of real life; and all are clearly conceived, and sketched or painted in full with no uncertain aim or faltering hand. To draw character has been the predominant object of the author; and he has so done it as to sustain a lively interest and an agreeable alternation of emotions, through a form of composition particularly difficult to manage without becoming soon tedious, or breaking the true conditions of the form. Mr. Thackeray has overcome not only this self-imposed difficulty, but one greater still, which he could not avoid—his own reputation. *Esmond* will, we think, rank higher as a work of art than either *Vanity Fair* or *Pendennis;* because the characters are of a higher type, and drawn with greater finish, and the book is more of a complete whole: not that we anticipate for it anything like the popularity of the former of these two books, as it is altogether of a graver cast, the satire is not so pungent, the canvass is far less crowded, and the subject is distant and unfamiliar; and, may be, its excellences will not help it to a very large public. . . .

[The style] is manly, clear, terse, and vigorous, reflecting every mood—pathetic, grave, or sarcastic—of the writer: and the writing has these qualities because the writer knows what he means to say, and does not give the public thoughts half-worked-out, or thoughts on matters where clear thinking is impossible.

Mr. Thackeray has left this delightful book behind him to console London for his absence in America. In wishing him a prosperous enterprise and a safe return, may we not hope that his genial presence may add another to the many links which bind England to the United States, and that Americans may learn from him that our highest order of men of letters can find something in the great Transatlantic Saxon-dom beyond food for a flippant sneer or farcical description?[1]

30. [John Forster], from a review in the *Examiner*

13 November 1852, 723–6

Professing to be the autobiography of a gentleman who reached maturity under the reign of Queen Anne, this book is printed in old type, and writ in the manner of the time. A clever volume known as *Lady Willoughby's Diary*,[2] and other less happy attempts in the same vein, had familiarised English readers with the idea of giving piquancy to books by a recurrence to the more remote style of our forefathers;

---

[1] Probably a hit at Dickens's *American Notes* (1842) and parts of *Martin Chuzzlewit* (1843–4).

[2] A fictitious diary, set in the reign of Charles I, by Hannah Mary Rathbone (1844; further portions, 1848).

but no writer hath been so bold as to propose to himself a reproduction of the English prose style proper to a polished writer in the days of Addison and Fielding. It was meet that this dangerous and difficult adventure should be undertaken by one known to the town as a man of genius, himself in possession of an excellent style; and the result justifies the attempt, with all its hazard.

We have at once to express, in the warmest terms of praise, our appreciation of the skill and taste with which *Esmond* is written. Mr Thackeray has caught the true tone of the writers of Queen Anne's time, and has sprinkled with a duly sparing hand the few peculiarities of grammar proper to them, imitating at the same time their more numerous peculiarities of diction, and throwing in here and there little marks of an elegant, yet what we now should call somewhat of a pedantic, display of classical quotation, with consummate tact. There is no excess, no strain after effect. In his most habitual moods Mr Thackeray is a very easy, polished writer; he has lately been engaged in a close study of the authors upon whose style he founds his present manner; and the result displayed in the volumes before us is a novel of which the literary workmanship commands unstinted praise. We should remark, at the same time, that Mr Thackeray has not so much imitated any single writer, as he has carried his own pen back into Queen Anne's time; they are his own characteristic trains of thought with which his pages are informed, his own touches of humour with which they are enlivened. The story of the novel, too, is sufficiently ingenious, and although faulty in several respects, is very elegantly constructed, and carried onward through ingenious windings, gratifying constant curiosity until the end. The first volume has a catastrophe as well as the third, and that of the third is unfortunately the least connected with the hero; but great skill in working up an interest is shown in both. Whether by its style, or by the treatment of its subject, in short, the book thoroughly occupies our minds with a sense of strength on the part of the writer, of which the manifestation is made always gracefully. The way in which Mr. Thackeray causes his auto-biographer to write of himself modestly in the third person, and the effect which he then produces by an occasional well-timed 'we,' or the use of an 'I,' when personal feeling might have been supposed to rise above the common level, is an illustration of the elegance of form which marks the whole work. Certain passages also which might, but would not, have been written in Queen Anne's time, dexterously interpolated here and there, carry back the fancy of the reader to the period, and are to be regarded rather as excellencies than as faults.

Thus planned and written, *Esmond*, though by no means equal to *Vanity Fair* in interest, excels even that well-written work as a display of literary power; and we are glad also to see that many of its passages show a better and healthier tone of social feeling. We wish it were possible for us to say more than this, and to add that Mr Thackeray, before writing *Esmond*, had quite conquered what we hold to be the defect in his mind which obstructs the free development of his genius, and appears hitherto to have rendered it impossible for him to present pictures of life that we can regard as true copies. If Mr Thackeray could but have faith in the hidden spark of the divinity which few men or women lose out of their hearts, if he could see his neighbours really as they are and so describe them, if he could be brought to feel that there is fairer play in finding the good that is in evil things than in dragging out the evil that is in good things,—his hold upon a true fame, still for the present doubtful, would be assured and strong. As he now sees life, and paints it, he is wasting the genius and resources of an admirable colourist on pictures false in drawing and perspective.

Should this continue to be so? Is it matter of necessity that so radical a defect in the works of an author who abounds in ready wit, tact, and genius, should run uncorrected through his writings to the last? We cannot think it. It seems to us that Mr Thackeray has already suffered himself partially to correct his crude way of viewing human nature, and that to some such sense we are indebted for genial and graceful passages that occur not unfrequently in *Esmond*. But the old vice still remains; and the consequence of a false method of treatment founded upon it is, that, with all our admiration for the writing of *Esmond*, we read it from the first page to the last without receiving in our minds, from any character or scene depicted in it, a distinct impression of vitality. We cannot persuade ourselves that there is a single character described at any length in this history which could belong to any being made of flesh and blood. High as the standing will be which the book is entitled to take in modern literature, we cannot believe that it will add one to the number of fictitious persons whose reality of character has caused them to be talked about as types of living men, or positive additions to the population of the world.

The truth is that Mr Thackeray hangs over the fictitious people on his paper too much as their creator and their judge. He does not think his own way in among them, and talk of them as a man should talk of men. If they be men and women, he must be the God who judges them; if he be a man, they must be puppets. In every case they lie without him and beneath him. There is not a character in *Esmond*, not the most spotless, over which we do not constantly feel that Mr Thackeray is bending with a smile of pity; turning up now and then the prettiest coat, to show some dirt upon the lining; exhibiting to us something adorable, that he may aggravate our perception in it of something detestable; laying down for us such consolatory doctrine as that kindness and meanness are both manly; producing for his own satisfaction, in a word, mere distortions and unnatural defects,—all because the wires are held by him, and it is his sovereign will and pleasure to show the working of his men and women thoroughly.

Here is one of the passages to be found in *Esmond* apparently put forward as justificatory of the kind of treatment we describe.

As, according to the famous maxim of Monsieur de Rochefoucault, 'in our friends' misfortunes there's something secretly pleasant to us;' so, on the other hand, their good fortune is disagreeable. If 'tis hard for a man to bear his own good luck, 'tis harder still for his friends to bear it for him; and but few of them ordinarily can stand that trial: whereas one of the 'precious uses' of adversity is, that it is a great reconciler; that it brings back averted kindness, disarms animosity, and causes yesterday's enemy to fling his hatred aside, and hold out a hand to the fallen friend of old days. There's pity and love, as well as envy, in the same heart and towards the same person. The rivalry stops when the competitor tumbles; and, as I view it, we should look at these agreeable and disagreeable qualities of our humanity humbly alike. They are consequent and natural, and our kindness and meanness both manly. [Book II, ch. v.]

Not quite prepared to own, and perhaps as little disposed to deny, that there is good in everybody, Mr Thackeray falls back upon another fundamental principle which he is able to regard with greater satisfaction, and on the whole with less misgiving, namely, that in everybody there is some part bad, and that for truth's sake the bad portion must not be kept out of sight. Now, we are not of those who would have it to be kept out of sight. Faultless monsters never have been drawn by the best novelists; but he must observe the world generously, and with abundant sympathy, moving among the characters he notices not as their judge but their companion, who would acquire a delicate perception of those shades of opinion and feeling which are found most commonly in combination with each other. Though most surely it is true (and we wish much that Mr Thackeray would own it by his writings), that we fail to detect the good within our neighbour's heart ten times for every one time that we overlook his failings, we would not have any man described without anything of speck or blot upon his character. Still it is better to paint men too pleasantly, than to describe society as a gay fair in which every man puts forward what is best in him, and hides his raggedness. That view of life is true only in a very superficial sense. The heart of every man who is no better or worse than the mass of his neighbours, will tell him distinctly that the world knows nothing of, because he himself shrinks from telling to the world, the holiest and best part of his nature. Secret aspirations, untold sacrifices, hidden charities, thoughts of the warmest good-will and friendship between man and man which very rarely rise into expressions of equivalent intensity,—these things lie under the calm surface of a thousand faces; and such secrets are kept more wisely, and lie a thousand times more frequently unseen, than any vice or folly that we try to hide. Every man knows that his lips would stammer, and his cheeks would burn, if he attempted to abandon the reserve which keeps the brightest spark of the divine nature—not extinguished in the basest of us—deep in his heart, away from the eyes of the many, and safe from daily comment. But it is not for these secrets that the author of *Esmond* looks. Mr Thackeray prefers to search below the surface of a character only for those things which the hypocrisy of worldliness may have concealed; or for some blot which the world, in admiring a good character, might be goodnaturedly disposed to overlook.

We might not unfairly exhibit something of the falseness of the rule with which he thus sets out to take the measure of a character, by referring to his people taken from history. We have already seen it in his Lectures on the English Humourists, and we now again see it in the historical characters introduced into *Esmond*—that, data being given for the measuring of a real character, he can by no means, in our judgment, arrive at a correct result. In the present story by Mr Thackeray, Steele figures largely; and precisely in that proportion, we must say, suffers patronage severely at his hands.

[Quotation from Bk. II, ch. xv; *Works*, xiii, 305.]

Marlborough figures also largely in the book, and is painted in the most impossible way, without a shade between coal black and lily white. Over and over again traits recur, in this portraiture, which we cannot but regard as quite incompatible with any consistent theory of man's nature. But the fault may be exhibited with sufficient prominence in a single passage, which we are also pleased to quote as an excellent piece of writing.

[Quotation from Bk. II, ch. ix; *Works*, xiii, 236–7.]

In giving these extracts we touch in fact upon the most prominent result of Mr Thackeray's method of working out a character. Where there is anything good, he says, there must be something bad; that is the nature to which I must be true. But he does not, because from his point of view he cannot see what the faults and follies are which harmonize with any character of goodness. Tom Jones with his careless vices would no more have been capable of letting Sophia's pet bird escape, than Blifil with his prudent virtues could have fallen into doubtful relations with Lady Bellaston. Every real character is a consistent whole. There are faults that attend necessarily upon the unusual development of certain virtues; others that can, others that cannot, consist with certain forms of excellence; and the combinations, as they exist in each real character, produce a whole so complete, that no one ingredient can be put away without causing a change in the balance of the rest. When we read Fielding, we enter into the society of men and women all of whom we know as well as we know our own friends in flesh and blood. They stir before us; subject now to one emotion, now to another: each acting, on all occasions, upon impulses thoroughly consistent, and so displayed that the whole sum of them, when put together, make up a character with all its strong and its weak points properly proportioned. Such a fictitious person becomes real to us. If he did not live and breathe in the world, he lived and breathed in the works of Fielding, which were nothing but the world of his own time and country put into the form of writing. Compared with such creations we too often find in Mr Thackeray's works dream figures only, almost always brilliant or grotesque, almost always impossible. Even Becky Sharp, remembered as she is among the figures of English fiction likely to endure, too often verges on the unreal; and one of the leading characters in the present volumes, Beatrix,—a readjustment, with some change of the materials, of Becky Sharp,—is a being perfectly impossible. She is beautiful, vain, heartless; a coquette, losing a series of rich matches; yet she is represented as declaiming against her own worthlessness, not in a moment of compunction, under an hour's impulse towards better things, but in a way perfectly inconsistent with her nature. . . .

[The] mother of the proud Beatrix, whom Esmond calls his

'mistress,' is a golden-haired lady who was married at the age of fifteen, and at the age of twenty became Esmond's guardian; Esmond then being twelve years old. The boy played the part of tutor to his mistress and her children; and the lady having fallen in love with him on the occasion of his taking to himself, and giving to her, the small-pox, retains the passion during what remains of her husband's life, and nurses it in secret as a widow until her fortieth year. During all this time, Esmond styles her his mistress; adores her; believes in her; and yet, though he is represented as a person of much sense and gravity, and cannot fail to see and feel all the love lavished upon him by the angelic widow, bothers the poor lady with confidences of his passion for her heartless, frivolous daughter; dangles with impossible constancy, under quite hopeless circumstances, after Beatrix; and nevertheless still keeps on worshipping the saint her mother, whom finally, when she has reached the mature age of forty, he finds out that it is his mission in the world to marry. Many beautiful passages of emotion, much delicate writing, and here and there a subtle stroke of passionate nature, cannot induce us to accept or tolerate such a set of incidents as these. The thing is incredible, and there an end on't. . . . All educated readers, we are sure, will enjoy *Esmond* heartily; though how far the circulating libraries may approve of the shadowy impression left by it as a story of life, we cannot undertake to say. It is the work, in many respects, of a master's hand; yet it incurs the risk of perishing, because the genius and labour in it are spent upon ill-chosen material. Worse writing on a better ground would have the chance of lasting longer; and we cannot refrain from stating our belief that Mr Thackeray is to a great extent writing upon sand while he is founding books upon his present notions of society.

31. George Eliot, from a letter to Mr. and Mrs. Charles Bray

13 November 1852

(The George Eliot Letters, ed. Haight, Gordon S., (1954), ii, 67)

'Esmond' is the most uncomfortable book you can imagine. You remember, Cara, how you disliked 'François le Champi' (George Sand's). Well, the story of Esmond is just the same. The hero is in love with the daughter all through the book, and marries the mother at the end.

32. [Samuel Phillips], from 'Mr. Thackeray's New Novel', *The Times*

22 December 1852, 8

In a letter of 27 December 1858 to Captain Atkinson Thackeray recalled that the sale of *Henry Esmond* 'was absolutely stopped by a Times article' (*Letters*, iv, 125).

We are neither surprised nor disappointed by this first complete novel from the skilful pen of the author of *Vanity Fair*. We knew the level below which the genius of Mr. Thackeray would not fall, and above which its wings are not solicitous to soar. Every intelligent reader of *Pendennis* must have taken a tolerably fair gauge of the writer's powers and aspirations when he closed the last page of that volume. It had followed, with the accustomed celerity of popular serials, close upon the heels of *Vanity Fair*, and all the faults, as well as some of the good points of the first—in many respects most admirable—production were repeated. In both works we had that incomparably easy and un-forced style in which Mr. Thackeray has courage to narrate his story

and describe his incidents; in both we had the same partial and unpleasant view of men and things; in both there presented themselves to
our unquestionable annoyance and for our improper delight virtuous
characters as insipid as they were good, and wicked personages as
amusing as they were naughty.

If before the appearance of *Esmond* we had been asked to define the
limits of Mr. Thackeray's field of operations, we should have said
that it was bounded on the north by Baker-street, and on the south by
Pall-mall. Nowhere had this novelist seemed more at home than in the
drawing-rooms of the Baker-street district, and in the coffee-rooms of
the Pall-mall Clubhouse. The petty vices and disagreeable foibles of
the middle classes were as familiar to him as his own countenance, and,
to speak the truth, it would really seem that he loved to contemplate
them with as much enjoyment as a fond woman might her face. Life
drawn by the pencil of Mr. Thackeray was life without the bright
light of heaven upon it; it was life looked upon with a disbelieving, a
disappointed, and a jaundiced eye. It was real, but only as sickness is
real, or any other earthly visitation. Travel whithersoever we might
with our clever but too sceptical companion, it was impossible to feel
happy or at ease. We dared not believe in heroism, for he rebuked the
belief with a sneer; we could not talk of human perfectibility, for he
pooh-poohed the idea with a smile of contempt. If he introduced us
to a clever girl, it was simply that we might detect hideous selfishness
in its most delicate form. Did we note goodness in man or woman, it
was only to be reminded that we gazed upon fools. Generous impulses
crossed our path, but invariably allied with sottishness or worse.
Inquiring minds were pointed out to us, listening industriously at key-
holes, and ambition was deemed to have a fit illustration in the career
of an aspiring swindler. It was not easy to proceed for an hour with
Mr. Thackeray without being fascinated by the tranquil and self-
confident flow of his discourse, and without deriving instruction from
his words: but the most cheerful was doomed to lose all comfort in
his walk. Who can be comfortable in a hospital? Who can be comfortable spending his days with people not passionate enough for the
perpetration of great faults, and not sufficiently pure for the perfect
performance of the humblest virtues? Who is comfortable in a spong-
ing house, in a gambling booth, in any place on earth where the least
creditable of man's great faculties are in full play, and where the
highest and most ennobling are for the time annihilated and extinct?

Boswell tells us that Dr. Johnson used to quote with great approbation the saying of a novelist, 'that the virtues of Fielding's heroes were the vices of a truly good man.'[1] We could not say even that of Mr. Thackeray's heroes. Their virtues are rather the weaknesses of the truly stupid. We affirm that few things could be duller than Mr. Thackeray's pen engaged in the delineation of heroine or hero. We looked at the picture in the spirit of unconquerable incredulity. No matter how strongly the author insisted upon the genuineness of the article, we were unmoved by his pertinacity and proof against his assertion. Twenty times in the course of *Vanity Fair* he stops in order to look slyly into the reader's face, and to ascertain whether he is smiling at, or sympathising with, that very uninteresting widow, Mrs. Osborne. 'You think,' he vehemently exclaims, 'that this isn't a heroine. I assure you she is. You mayn't believe it; she doesn't look like one, but take my word you are mistaken.' The reader is not mistaken. Mr. Thackeray is not mistaken. Nobody is mistaken. In spite of his vehemence the author is quite as incredulous as everybody else. How shall he inspire faith when he is no believer? How shall he hope to persuade others when he has not the power, even if he had the desire, to persuade himself?

The temper and spirit with which the author of *Vanity Fair* is wont to approach our poor humanity are fraught with peril; for the undoubted genius and capability of the sceptic simply add to his power for mischief. It is a terrible thing to be taught by a master of his craft that in life there is little to excite admiration—nothing to inspire enthusiasm. It is fearful to have an insight into the human heart, and to detect in that holy of holies not even one solitary spark of the once pure flame. We live and are supported by the conviction that goodness still prevails in the earth, and that the soul of man is still susceptible of the noblest impulses. Guilt is among us—crime abounds—falsehood is around and about us; but, conscious as we are of these facts, we know and feel that man may yet trust to his fellow man, and that evil is not permitted to outweigh good. A series of novels, based upon the principle which Mr. Thackeray delights to illustrate, would utterly destroy this knowledge and render us a race of unbelievers—animals less happy than the brutes who, dumb and unreasoning as they are, can still consort together and derive some consolation from their companionship.

To the unreflecting, Thackeray and Dickens represent one school of fiction. But a greater mistake cannot be made. The two novelists have little or nothing in common. Their styles of composition are as opposed as their views of life. We have already spoken of the matchless

[1] A saying of Richardson's (Boswell's *Life of Johnson* (O.U.P. edition, 1933), i, 368).

and courageous ease with which Mr. Thackeray is content to tell his story. Too much praise cannot be awarded to him for this evidence of intellectual independence. His story may not be good, his philosophy may be tainted; but, whatever his subject matter, you have it before you with no factitious adornment in order to make it appear other than it is. Not so the inimitable author of *Pickwick*, whose style betrays effect and constant straining for effect. Again, Mr. Dickens sympathises deeply with his species, and is never so happy as when dealing with its better qualities. Mr. Thackeray never recognises such qualities, or when he finds them knows not what to do with them. Another and still more striking difference yet remains. It was said of Richardson, years ago, that the characters he drew were characters of nature, while those drawn by Fielding were characters of manners. At the present day we may have another opinion on this subject; but, undoubtedly, as regards Mr. Thackeray and Mr. Dickens, the distinction, to a great extent, holds good. The longer Mr. Dickens lives, and the more he writes, the more prone he becomes to leave the broad field of nature for the narrower path of art. The great Sam Weller, delightful as he is, after all is but a character of manners, one which, while it affords inexpressible amusement to the readers of the present day, may be utterly untranslateable to the readers of a century hence. But Sam Weller will be understood and appreciated years after the later grotesque creations of the same gifted author, who would seem in his more recent productions to prefer the strange, the wonderful, the abnormal, and the exaggerated, to the familiar, the natural, the obvious, and the easily understood. Now, whatever may be the faults of Mr. Thackeray, no one can accuse him of making his books vehicles for the exhibition of monstrosities. His characters are often disagreeable enough, but the stamp of nature and of truth is upon them. Our quarrel with him is not that he is unreal, but that what is exceptional in life becomes under his treatment the abiding rule: not that Captain Crawley, Mr. Foker, Mr. Costigan, and Colonel Altamont are creatures that do not occasionally jostle against us in the streets, but that he would have us believe that the world is peopled with few *but* Fokers, Costigans, Altamonts, and Crawleys.

We were gratified with the announcement which reached us about a twelvemonth since, that the author of *Vanity Fair* had resolved to eschew the serial form of publication and to make his next venture under the circumstances best calculated to display a writer's powers and to achieve permanent success. Month to month writing is but hand to mouth work, and satisfies neither author nor reader. But the announcement was accompanied by another not altogether so agreeable. Mr. Thackeray had entertained the town with some lively lectures upon the humourists of the days of Queen Anne, and had grown so familiar and fascinated with the period during the interesting process, that he resolved not only to write a Queen Anne novel, but positively to write it with a Queen Anne quill, held by a Queen Anne penman. In other words, the distinguished novelist, whose very breath of life is the atmosphere in which he lives, and whose most engaging quality is his own natural style, had suicidally determined to convey himself to a strange climate and to take absolute leave of his choicest characteristic. We confess that a more desperate venture we could hardly conceive it possible for a popular writer to make. We have a great respect for Queen Anne and for the writers of Her Majesty's augustan age, and when we read Addison and Swift we are charmed with the classic grace of the one, and made strong by the bold English of the other. But why lose our genuine Thackeray in order to get a spurious Steele or Budgell?[1] Having made up his mind to write a novel in monthly parts no more, and to do as Scott and Fielding did before him, why, Mr. Thackeray, in the name of all that is rational, why write in fetters? Why have your genius in leading strings? Why have the mind and hand crippled? Why pursue the muse under difficulties? Garrick must have been a great actor; so was John Kemble; but what would our fathers have said to Kemble had he undertaken to destroy for a season his own identity, in order to present a counterfeit of his great predecessor? We decline to judge Mr. Thackeray's powers from his present exhibition. He shall have justice from us, though he has none from himself. We reserve our opinion whether or not Mr. Thackeray is equal to a masterly and complete work of fiction until he attempts the labour with the energies of his spirit free.

We wanted no assurance of the imitative skill of the author of *Vanity Fair*. If imitation were the highest kind of art Mr. Thackeray would be the first of living artists. Who can have forgotten those piquant chapters in *Punch* in which Mr. James, Mr. Disraeli, and Sir Edward Bulwer Lytton looked rather more original and like themselves than in their own works?[2] Had the imitator thought proper to

[1] Eustace Budgell (1686–1737) contributed to the *Spectator*.

[2] 'Punch's Prize Novelists,' in which Thackeray burlesqued the novels of Bulwer, Disraeli, Mrs. Gore, G. P. R. James, Lever and Fenimore Cooper (*Punch*, April–October 1847; partly reprinted as 'Novels by Eminent Hands' in *Miscellanies*, ii (1856)).

continue the series, and to give us a specimen of every known author of eminence, we should have welcomed the samples, for we are sure they would have been perfect. But a sample of goods is not a bale. Horace Smith and his brother, though they did not hesitate in *The Rejected Addresses*[1] to amuse the public with a specimen of Wordsworth in the shape of *The Baby's Début*, would never have dared to approach them with a close copy of *The Excursion*. Surely the least imaginative among us can fancy the probable result of that experiment.

The inconvenience of the plan to which Mr. Thackeray has chained down his intellect is made manifest in every part of his work. It is no disparagement to say that his disguise is too cumbrous to be perfect. That it is maintained so well is marvellous. The patience and perse-verance of the writer must have been incessant, and infinite skill has been thrown away, which we feel with vexation and disappointment might have been devoted to the noblest uses. But in spite of all the cleverness and industry discrepancies and anomalies are inevitable; and one discrepancy in such a work is sufficient to take the veil from the reader's eyes and to put an end to the whole illusion. That Steele should be described as a private in the Guards in the year 1690, when he was only 15 years old and a schoolboy at the Charter-house, is, perhaps, no great offence in a work of fiction; but a fatal smile in-voluntarily crosses the reader's cheek, when he learns, in an early part of the story, that a nobleman is 'made to play at ball and billiards by sharpers, who take his money;' and is informed some time after-wards that the same lord has 'gotten a new game from London, a French game, called a billiard.' It is not surprising that for a moment Mr. Thackeray should forget that he is Mr. Esmond, and speak of 'rapid new coaches' that '*performed* the journey between London and the University in a single day,' when he means to say '*perform;*' neither is it astonishing that the writer of 1852 should announce it as a memor-able fact, that in the days of Queen Anne young fellows would 'make merry at their taverns and call toasts,' although it is quite out of place for the writer of 1742 to marvel at the same custom, seeing that Colonel Esmond must have known the fashion to be in vogue in the times of George the Second. A less pardonable oversight certainly occurs in the second volume, when [at the end of Bk. II, ch. ii], the reign of William III, and that of Queen Anne seem unaccountably jumbled together in the same paragraph; but were such faults as we have indicated to present themselves with tenfold frequency, it would

[1] A collection of parodies (1812) by James and Horace Smith.

be idle and unfair to insist upon imperfections inseparable from such an effort as that to which Mr. Thackeray has doomed himself for no better reason that we can discern than that of demonstrating how much more amusing, lively, and companionable he is in his own easy attire than when tricked out with the wig, buckles, and other accoutrements of our deceased and venerated ancestors.

The History of Henry Esmond, Esq., is not a very striking one. The most remarkable fact connected with it is, that it proves, beyond a doubt, that folks very like our contemporaries lived and prospered in the days of Queen Anne. All our friends that entertained us for so many months in *Vanity Fair* and *Pendennis* have their *facsimiles* in Mr. Esmond's volume. The colonel himself is just such another creature as Dobbin—as kind-hearted, as self-denying, as generous, as devoted, and, must we add? almost as weak and simple. Captain Crawley, the *roué,* belongs to the same family as Castlewood, for all the lords of that name indulge in his propensities. Miss Amory is the very embodiment of intrigue and selfishness; so is Beatrix Castlewood, who sets her cap at great people without caring a straw for them, precisely like the other lady. It must have been generally remarked that Mr. Thackeray is morbidly fond of reproducing his old creations upon the scene. The *dramatis personæ* of *Pendennis* bore not only a great resemblance to the characters of *Vanity Fair,* but some of them were actually reproduced in the second production, or referred to by name. In like manner, our old friends the Crawleys are familiarly spoken of in Colonel Esmond's history. It is well to have a natural affection for your offspring, but there may be occasions when to obtrude them upon the notice of your visitors is to betray want of tact, of breeding, and good sense.

Infinite pains are taken to beguile us into the notion that we are reading a book written and printed upwards of a century ago. Mr. Thackeray has done his part in the matter, and the printers and publishers have done theirs, but perfect contentment, after all, does not dwell upon the mind of the reader. The style is an admirable imitation, and would be charming if it were not tedious; the type is most delusive, even to the title-page, which acquaints us that the book is printed by 'Smith and Elder, over against St. Peter's Church, in Cornhill;' but the vital part of the work is no more a representation of the spirit and soul of the time than it is of the age that preceded or followed it. The depths of society are not probed, and the merest glimpses of its outward shape are vouchsafed. There are two great faults in the volumes, and this is one of them. Had the book really proceeded from the pen of an officer in the service of Queen Anne, he would unquestionably have written in the quaint fashion of this work, but he would have done a great deal more. He would not in the substance of his production have imitated Mr. Thackeray as Mr. Thackeray has imitated him in the form. He must have displayed in a domestic story something like a social picture of his time, and afforded his present readers infinite amusement from the comparison of two widely separated epochs. Even *Tom Jones* and *Pamela* are most instructive in this respect, for both reveal a condition of society very different indeed from that in which we play our part. How much more different and interesting the domestic proceedings of the loyal subjects of Queen Anne! If any one will take the trouble to translate Mr. Esmond's language into modern English, he will be surprised to find how much of the book applies with as much force to men and manners in 1852 as to men and manners in 1702. It is very true that Mr. Esmond tells us that he went to the theatre to witness the performance of Mrs. Bracegirdle; but he might have said that he went to listen to Mrs. Kean for anything that follows from his visit. Mr. Esmond proceeds to Cambridge University, and, to our astonishment, we discover that University life in the days of Queen Anne differed in no respect whatever from University life in the happier times of our gracious Queen Victoria. We learn, indeed, that Mr. Esmond's friends drink, fight, quarrel with their wives, intrigue, and are very selfish and good for nothing, or good for something and very stupid, but precisely this account reached us of the friends of Mr. Pendennis and of Mr. Osborne, so that, indeed, Mr. Esmond is quite as much indebted to the author of *Vanity Fair* as the author of *Vanity Fair* is to him. We say again Mr. Thackeray is not to be too harshly dealt with for not accomplishing a feat which a life-long and exclusive study of one peculiar period of his nation's history would hardly enable him to achieve with unqualified success. But he is to be remonstrated with for presenting us with a very questionable and cracked specimen of old China when he had it in his power to offer us sound and genuine British porcelain. Our foremost writers must not become the vendors of sham curiosities.

The second grave fault in Colonel Esmond's narrative is one for which Mr. Thackeray must be prepared to answer in his own proper person. He has inflicted a stain upon the good taste and feeling of the worthy colonel, of which that gentleman has every reason to complain. Nothing can be more amiable than Mr. Esmond's character as described in every incident of his story, yet the sentiment with which we take leave of him is one of unaffected disgust. No hero of any age ever finished his career less heroically than Mr. Esmond. . . .

We repeat, we will not accept the present novel as an evidence of Mr. Thackeray's powers as a writer of fiction. We desire to see a complete novel from his pen, but he must give himself an unencumbered field and allow the reader as well as himself fair play. That he is capable of greater efforts than any he has hitherto made, we believe; that he has a potent pen for description of character, is manifest from the very striking portraiture of Marlborough that appears in these volumes, and that he may make a permanent impression upon the literary character of his times, is quite possible if he will only trust to his better impulses and survey mankind in the spirit of trust, affection, and belief, rather than of doubt, incredulity, and contempt.

33. From an unsigned review, the *United States Review*

New York, March 1853, i, 247–54

Setting aside the foreign reputation of the author, this book is of more than ordinary interest for two reasons: first, because the concluding part of the drama takes place in this country; and secondly, and perhaps mainly, because Mr. Thackeray has lately been an object of personal attention in our lecture-rooms and household circles, and has received a share of deferential admiration such as we are accustomed to bestow on very few literary men. We do not say that Mr. Thackeray has been at all toadied during this visit to America, or nauseated by flattery, or bored by an excess of kindness. We have seen quite enough of such nonsense in times gone by, and we have shown but little disposition to repeat our past follies. But Mr. Thackeray has been most indubitably lionized. His lectures have been listened to by crowded audiences. The hospitality of our citizens has been largely tendered him. He has met with few unfriendly criticisms. His visit from first to last has been an undeniable personal and literary success.[1] . . .

Mr. Thackeray, in writing *Henry Esmond*, undertook a very difficult

[1] Thackeray had lectured in the U.S.A. in the winter of 1852–3.

task. To write a novel of the social and literary life of a past age is not Mr. Thackeray's *forte*, nor is it the *forte* of any other man. It does not come by nature. When honest Dogberry averred that reading and writing came by this easy process, he was not far wrong, and might have attributed the same origin to many other accomplishments. It is one of the most natural things in the world to write an account of what is going on about you, to dress it off with the graces and liberties of fiction, and—to publish your novel. How many pleasing and attractive books are thus produced! With what ease are they written, how freely are they read, with how little concern we cast them aside! They save us a world of observation, by giving us the results of observation ready to hand. When we have read about Bluff, the Major, and Prig, the Lawyer; when we have listened to the tea-talk of Mrs. So-and-so, and Miss This-and-that; when we have been introduced to the Collegian, and been lectured by the Divine; when we have heard the wise saws of the Doctor, and the commercial maxims of the Merchant—all through the medium of the novel—we feel quite well rewarded for investigations made with so little trouble. Do we read novels for any other purpose than to taste of the dish of human nature, without going through the labor and vexation of cooking it? It would require a great deal of time and expense, Madame, to get together Vanity Fair upon your carpet. It is much cheaper and more expeditious to recline on your sofa, and read the history of the personages who figure in that celebrated show.

But it is quite a different thing when we go back a century or two. The imitative faculties which prompt men to delineate the manners of present society, fail them as soon as they go back beyond the range of their memories. Our fathers and mothers can tell us nothing of the times of Charles, or Queen Anne, or Mary, or Elizabeth. Our grandfathers and grandmothers are equally ignorant. Of course we can only form our estimate of those times from books. But the reading of a book is very different from the observation of life. An author who reads a book for the purpose of writing another book, loses that assistance of the senses, that subtle intelligence communicated by the eyes, by hearing, by actual contact with living individuals and manners, which give vigor to the mind and vivacity and point to its productions. It is by no means an extraordinary feat to compose a romance in the style of Walter Scott, or of James; the main interest of the narration depends upon the actions of the characters and not upon what they say. The more tournaments, the more battles, the more single combats, the more acts of heroism and love, the better we like the story. To describe social life is quite another matter. It is impossible to give naturalness to a social conversation between personages who lived out of our memory. The genius of Satire shakes his swift wings when it is attempted. The assistance of Humor is invoked in vain. The figures called up are puppets. They will fight and run and make love, in pantomime, but they will not talk, and the author is obliged to talk for them. But if he be alone the sole supporter and spirit of the dialogue, will not the spectators very soon find him out?

Few men have yet succeeded in this kind of writing. *Tom Jones* is a picture of Fielding's own age. Le Sage makes Gil Blas a contemporary of himself. Can any man a hundred years hence delineate another Pickwick of the time of Dickens? How infinitely difficult to go back and attempt to mingle again with the shades of the departed wits and courtly ladies of ages long departed!

Would not Bulwer have cautioned Mr. Thackeray against writing such a book as *Esmond?* Does not the reader recollect *Devereux,*[1] and the stiff and awkward shadows of the very men whom Mr. Thackeray has endeavored to resuscitate, which glide through the scenes of that unsuccessful novel? Steele, Bolingbroke, Pope, Swift, Cibber—they are all in *Devereux*, and the reader will be very glad to get out of their company as soon as he can. We are introduced to Steele, who we are assured is a famous wit, and says such clever things that it is dangerous for one's ribs to remain long in his society. But we are somewhat surprised, having had our expectations raised by this description, and remembering some charming passages in the 'British Classics,' at not finding any of these wonderful *bon-mots*. Indeed, after a short conversation, enlivened by scarcely a gleam of fancy, we are suddenly bowed out of the great man's presence as follows:

'Devereux,' said Tarleton, yawning, 'what a d—d delightful thing it is to hear so much wit—pity that the atmosphere is so fine that no lungs unaccustomed to it can bear it long. Let us recover ourselves by a walk.' [Book 2, ch. iii.]

We are then shown to Swift, of whom we are perpetually told that he was constantly uttering brilliant sayings. Unfortunately, we hear none of them. We suspect, however, that *Devereux* does Swift more justice than the Dean receives at the hands of Mr. Thackeray.

[1] Published 1829. Thackeray read it soon afterwards (see *Letters*, i, 95).

That evening with Swift had in it more of broad and familiar mirth than any I have ever wasted in the company of the youngest and noisiest disciples of the bowl and its concomitants. Even amid all the coarse ore of Swift's conversation, the diamond perpetually broke out; his vulgarity was never that of a vulgar mind. Pity, that while he condemned Bolingbroke's over-affectation of the graces of life, he never perceived that his own affectation of the *grossièretés* of manner was to the full as unworthy of the simplicity of intellect.' [Book 2, ch. vii.]

And so we go the rounds of these famous personages. Their faces and figures are described to us; and we are told *about* their wonderful wit and genius, but we have not *Devereux* to thank for believing that they possessed such accomplishments. To judge by the novel alone, we should be perfectly satisfied to call them very dull companions.

Bulwer having failed in representing the social life of the Queen Anne wits, and having quite candidly acknowledged that his novel was no better than it should be, Mr. Thackeray now attempts the same *rôle*. As we have before intimated, we cannot compliment him on his success. He has done even worse than his illustrious rival. For while Bulwer alleviates the faults of these erratic men, and explains much which we might otherwise regard with a blind aversion, Mr. Thackeray exercises no such tact. All men, according to Mr. Thackeray, are either very good or very bad, and the good are few and the bad are many. This is the essence of his philosophy, which he is especially fond of applying to the characters of men who are unable to defend themselves. When Mr. Thackeray paints historical pictures, the world will not at all thank him for distorting his figures, for heightening their occasional deformities and exposing their sores.

When we say that *Esmond* is a very dull book, in spite of the reasons we gave at the outset of this article for its being of interest to American readers, we are only uttering what is very obviously true. It is, indeed, a difficult book to read. We shudder at the sufferings of unhappy Englishmen and Englishwomen who are obliged to read it from the old fashioned type of the Aldine Press, on which its author caused it to be printed. This double antiquation is really too much, and the American publishers did well in not imitating it.

It is hardly worth while to condense the story into our pages. Such abridgments are always tedious, and readers invariably skip them. The tale abounds in genealogical descriptions, for Mr. Thackeray never mentions any individual without also acquainting you with the history of his father and grandfather. Esmond is introduced in the character of a page in a nobleman's family, and on the death of the nobleman is informed that he is the rightful owner of the estates and title. He then falls in love with the nobleman's widow, then with her daughter, and finally returning to his first love, whom he is perpetually calling his 'dear mistress,' marries her, and settles in America for life. A marriage is a natural catastrophe in novels, but this is, to us, a very disagreeable marriage. His wife is very much older than himself, very much care-worn, and excessively melancholy. We submit that partners like this are not desirable, to say the least, for ambitious young men. As for the daughter, by whom Esmond was refused, her matrimonial specu-lations turn out badly, and she goes to Paris, where she becomes so naughty that Mr. Thackeray drops her entirely. All this is revolting and unnatural. Was there no other way of punishing the vanities and foibles of a high-spirited girl, Mr. Thackeray, than by turning her into the streets outright?

Various classic personages, as before stated, pass and repass among the scenes, and very stiff and disagreeable personages they are. In this style of representation Mr. Thackeray has really done very much worse than Bulwer, and the remarks made about *Devereux* on a preced-ing page, will apply with increased force to *Esmond*. We had marked several passages of their conversation for extract, but our readers will excuse us from quoting a succession of very dull commonplaces, such as could be achieved by the most inferior writers. . . .

Mr. Thackeray makes it his business to tell us of the faults of others, and he is therefore a popular writer. He is the great Scandal-Monger of the day, and each one of his readers is flattered directly in proportion to the magnitude of the follies and wickednesses of which the rest of the world are represented to be guilty. How much such a feeling tends to universal or individual reformation, may be questioned. We do not consider it a very safe prescription for the great moral maladies of mankind.

We should be willing, however, that Mr. Thackeray should enjoy this cheap popularity, did we not fear its influence upon other men—upon writers abroad, and writers at home. We remember a Byron mania, not many years ago, when it became the fashion for men to hate themselves; may there not come a Thackeray mania, when it shall become the fashion for men to hate their neighbors? We do not wish to be guilty of irrational alarm. Should such a disease appear, it will undoubtedly work out its own cure in due time. But it could not run its course without producing many injurious effects, without disturbing many weak minds, and causing a great deal of absurd and unhappy skepticism. Mr. Thackeray has been sufficiently imitated already to convince us that he will be imitated a great deal more. We know of nothing more despicable than imitated cynicism. Let us imagine a chattering fool in the tub of Diogenes, or a child attempting the maledictions of a practised scoffer. We can then estimate the Thackeray school of writers. We shall be much mistaken if our literary horizon is not darkened with a flight of obscene birds, following the greater vulture, and equally clamorous in voice, if not equally keen of scent.

We fear Mr. Thackeray's influence the more because he is essentially an anti-republican. We do not wish to be misunderstood. We would not have him a communist, or a leveller, or a regicide. But we would have him treat all classes well, which he has never yet done. Mr. Thackeray lives in a country where Rank and Trade were formerly kept very wide apart, one looking down upon the other. The two are very rapidly coming nearer, but Mr. Thackeray does not keep pace with the friendly movement. There cannot be found in all his works a single passage in which tradesmen are mentioned with respect. We are made to despise the bootmaker, the tailor, the oil merchant, the manufacturer. They are low, tipsy, silly fellows. They speak bad English and do not keep themselves clean. They are coarse and vulgar, and we cannot help disliking them. This is unjust and false. It does not become any man, in an age of industry like our own, to endeavor to prop the falling edifice of aristocratic pride. Let the building come down, if its foundation is no longer able to support it. There was a time for it, once; but we do not want it any more. You cannot delay its ruin at home, Mr. Thackeray;—do not put it into the heads of any of the American people to erect another such frame-work here.

We have wandered somewhat from Henry Esmond. We return to that gentleman only to take leave of him with sincere expressions of regret that we have had so little enjoyment in his society, and in that of his friends. When Mr. Thackeray again plays the Amphitryon, we hope to be introduced to a more attractive, and a better circle of guests.

34. Anthony Trollope, from *Thackeray*

1879, 122–6, 136

The novel with which we are now going to deal I regard as the greatest work that Thackeray did. Though I do not hesitate to compare himself with himself, I will make no comparison between him and others; I therefore abstain from assigning to *Esmond* any special niche among prose fictions in the English language, but I rank it so high as to justify me in placing him among the small number of the highest class of English novelists. Much as I think of *Barry Lyndon* and *Vanity Fair*, I cannot quite say this of them; but, as a chain is not stronger than its weakest link, so is a poet, or a dramatist, or a novelist to be placed in no lower level than that which he has attained by his highest sustained flight. The excellence which has been reached here Thackeray achieved, without doubt, by giving a greater amount of forethought to the work he had before him than had been his wont. When we were young we used to be told, in our house at home, that 'elbow-grease' was the one essential necessary to getting a tough piece of work well done. If a mahogany table was to be made to shine, it was elbow-grease that the operation needed. Forethought is the elbow-grease which a novelist,—or poet, or dramatist,—requires. It is not only his plot that has to be turned and re-turned in his mind, not his plot chiefly, but he has to make himself sure of his situations, of his characters, of his effects, so that when the time comes for hitting the nail he may know where to hit it on the head,—so that he may himself understand the passion, the calmness, the virtues, the vices, the rewards and punishments which he means to explain to others,—so that his proportions shall be correct, and he be saved from the absurdity of devoting two-thirds of his book to the beginning, or two-thirds to the completion of his task. It is from want of this special labour, more frequently than from intellectual deficiency, that the tellers of stories fail so often to hit their nails on the head. To think of a story is much harder work than to write it. The author can sit down with the pen in his hand for a given time, and produce a certain number of words. That is comparatively easy, and if he have a conscience in regard to his task, work

165

will be done regularly. But to think it over as you lie in bed, or walk about, or sit cosily over your fire, to turn it all in your thoughts, and make the things fit,—that requires elbow-grease of the mind. The arrangement of the words is as though you were walking simply along a road. The arrangement of your story is as though you were carrying a sack of flour while you walked. Fielding had carried his sack of flour before he wrote *Tom Jones*, and Scott his before he produced *Ivanhoe*. So had Thackeray done,—a very heavy sack of flour,—in creating *Esmond*. In *Vanity Fair*, in *Pendennis*, and in *The Newcomes*, there was more of that mere wandering in which no heavy burden was borne. The richness of the author's mind, the beauty of his language, his imagination and perception of character are all there. For that which was lovely he has shown his love, and for the hateful his hatred; but, nevertheless, they are comparatively idle books. His only work, as far as I can judge them, in which there is no touch of idleness, is *Esmond*. *Barry Lyndon* is consecutive, and has the well-sustained purpose of exhibiting a finished rascal; but *Barry Lyndon* is not quite the same from beginning to end. All his full-fledged novels, except *Esmond*, contain rather strings of incidents and memoirs of individuals, than a completed story. But *Esmond* is a whole from beginning to end, with its tale well told, its purpose developed, its moral brought home, —and its nail hit well on the head and driven in.

I told Thackeray once that it was not only his best work, but so much the best, that there was none second to it. 'That was what I intended,' he said, 'but I have failed. Nobody reads it. After all, what does it matter?' he went on after awhile. 'If they like anything, one ought to be satisfied. After all, Esmond was a prig.' Then he laughed and changed the subject, not caring to dwell on thoughts painful to him. The elbow-grease of thinking was always distasteful to him, and had no doubt been so when he conceived and carried out this work.

To the ordinary labour necessary for such a novel he added very much by his resolution to write it in a style different, not only from that which he had made his own, but from that also which belonged to the time. He had devoted himself to the reading of the literature of Queen Anne's reign, and having chosen to throw his story into that period, and to create in it personages who were to be peculiarly concerned with the period, he resolved to use as the vehicle for his story the forms of expression then prevalent. No one who has not tried it can understand how great is the difficulty of mastering a phase of one's own language other than that which habit has made familiar. To write in another language, if the language be sufficiently known, is a much less arduous undertaking. The lad who attempts to write his essay in Ciceronian Latin struggles to achieve a style which is not indeed common to him, but is more common than any other he has become acquainted with in that tongue. But Thackeray in his work had always to remember his Swift, his Steele, and his Addison, and to forget at the same time the modes of expression which the day had adopted. Whether he asked advice on the subject, I do not know. But I feel sure that if he did he must have been counselled against it. Let my reader think what advice he would give to any writer on such a subject. Probably he asked no advice, and would have taken none. No doubt he found himself, at first imperceptibly, gliding into a phraseology which had attractions for his ear, and then probably was so charmed with the peculiarly masculine forms of sentences which thus became familiar to him, that he thought it would be almost as difficult to drop them altogether as altogether to assume the use of them. And if he could do so successfully, how great would be the assistance given to the local colouring which is needed for a novel in prose, the scene of which is thrown far back from the writer's period! Were I to write a poem about Cœur de Lion I should not mar my poem by using the simple language of the day; but if I write a prose story of the time, I cannot altogether avoid some attempt at far-away quaintnesses in language. To call a purse a 'gypsire,' and to begin your little speeches with 'Marry come up,' or to finish them with 'Quotha,' are but poor attempts. But even they have had their effect. Scott did the best he could with his Cœur de Lion. When we look to it we find that it was but little; though in his hands it passed for much. 'By my troth,' said the knight, 'thou hast sung well and heartily, and in high praise of thine order.' We doubt whether he achieved any similarity to the language of the time; but still, even in the little which he attempted there was something of the picturesque. But how much more would be done if in very truth the whole language of a story could be thrown with correctness into the form of expression used at the time depicted?

It was this that Thackeray tried in his *Esmond*, and he has done it almost without a flaw. The time in question is near enough to us, and the literature sufficiently familiar to enable us to judge. Whether folk swore by their troth in the days of King Richard I we do not know, but when we read Swift's letters, and Addison's papers, or Defoe's novels we do catch the veritable sounds of Queen Anne's age, and can say for ourselves whether Thackeray has caught them correctly or not.

No reader can doubt that he has done so. Nor is the reader ever struck with the affectation of an assumed dialect. The words come as though they had been written naturally,—though not natural to the middle of the nineteenth century. It was a tour de force; and successful as such a tour de force so seldom is. But though Thackeray was successful in adopting the tone he wished to assume, he never quite succeeded, as far as my ear can judge, in altogether dropping it again. . . .

And yet there is not a page in the book over which a thoughtful reader cannot pause with delight. The nature in it is true nature. Given a story thus sad, and persons thus situated, and it is thus that the details would follow each other, and thus that the people would conduct themselves. It was the tone of Thackeray's mind to turn away from the prospect of things joyful, and to see,—or believe that he saw,—in all human affairs, the seed of something base, of something which would be antagonistic to true contentment. All his snobs, and all his fools, and all his knaves, come from the same conviction. Is it not the doctrine on which our religion is founded,—though the sadness of it there is alleviated by the doubtful promise of a heaven?

> Though thrice a thousand years are passed
> Since David's son, the sad and splendid,
> The weary king ecclesiast
> Upon his awful tablets penned it.
>
> [From Thackeray's 'Vanitas Vanitatum'.]

So it was that Thackeray preached his sermon. But melancholy though it be, the lesson taught in *Esmond* is salutary from beginning to end. The sermon truly preached is that glory can only come from that which is truly glorious, and that the results of meanness end always in the mean. No girl will be taught to wish to shine like Beatrix, nor will any youth be made to think that to gain the love of such a one it can be worth his while to expend his energy or his heart.

THREE GENERAL SURVEYS

35. [Theodore Martin], 'Thackeray's Works'
Westminster Review

April 1853, new series, iii, 363–88

Martin (1816–1909) collaborated with W. E. Aytoun in the *Bon Gaultier Ballads* (1845), contributed to various periodicals, translated works from German, Italian and Latin, and wrote a life of the Prince Consort (1875–80).

Five years ago, in dedicating the second edition of *Jane Eyre* to the author of *Vanity Fair*, Currer Bell spoke of him thus:—'Why have I alluded to this man? I have alluded to him, reader, because I think I see in him an intellect profounder and more unique than his contemporaries have yet recognised; because I regard him as the first social regenerator of the day—as the very master of that working corps who would restore to rectitude the warped system of things; because, I think no commentator on his writings has yet found the comparison that suits him, the terms which rightly characterize his talent. They say he is like Fielding; they talk of his wit, humour, comic powers. He resembles Fielding as an eagle does a vulture; Fielding could stoop on carrion, but Thackeray never does. His wit is bright, his humour attractive, but both bear the same relation to his serious genius, that the mere lambent sheet-lightning, playing under the edge of the summer-cloud, does to the electric death-spark hid in its womb.' When this was written, Mr. Thackeray was not the popular favourite he has since become. He counts readers now by hundreds, where then he only counted tens. In those days, Currer Bell's panegyric was pronounced extravagant by many who now, if they do not echo, will at least scarcely venture to dispute it; but it may be doubted whether, up to the present time, full justice has been done by any of Mr. Thackeray's critics to the peculiar genius of the man, or to the purpose with which the later books have been written. It is not, indeed, to the Press that he owes the appreciation which it is probable he values most. Its praise has generally been coupled with censure for what has occupied his most deliberate thought, and been conceived with the most earnest purpose. While it has extolled his wit, his keen eye, his graphic style, his trenchant sarcasm, his power of exposing cant and Pharisaism in all its phases, it has, at the same time, been loud in its outcry against the writer's cynicism and want of faith, the absence of heroism and elevation in his characters—the foibles of all his women, the vices of all his men. Enough, and more than enough, has been said and written upon these points; but among a large section of his readers it has long been felt, that it may not have been without a purpose that Mr. Thackeray has never endowed his characters with ostentatious heroic virtues, or dwelt much on the brighter aspects of humanity; that his most unsparing ridicule, and his most pungent delineations of human folly or vice, are not tinged by the sour humours of the cynic or misan- thrope, but that, through his harshest tones, there may be heard the sweet undernotes of a nature kindly and loving, and a heart warm and unspoiled, full of sympathy for goodness and all simple worth, and of reverence for all unaffected greatness.

Not many years ago, when reputations which are now effete were at their zenith, a pen was busy in our periodical literature, in which the presence of a power was felt by those who watched that literature, which seemed only to want happier circumstances to develop into forms worthy of a permanent place among English classics. Under many patronymics, its graphic sketches and original views were ushered into the world. The immortal Yellowplush, the James de-la- Pluche of a later date, the vivacious George Fitzboodle, the versatile Michael Angelo Titmarsh, were names well-known and prized within a limited circle. In Mr. Thackeray's lucubrations under all these pseudo- nyms, there was a freshness and force, a truthfulness of touch, a shrewdness of perception, and a freedom from conventionalism, whether in thought or expression, which argued in their originator something more akin to genius than to mere talent. Here was a man who looked below the surface of things, taking nothing for granted, and shrinking from no scrutiny of human motives, however painful; who saw clearly and felt deeply, and who spoke out his thought man- fully and well. In an age of pretence, he had the courage to be simple. To strip sentimentalism of its frippery, pretension of its tinsel, vanity of its masks, and humbug literary and social of its disguises, appeared to be the vocation of this graphic satirist. The time gave him work to do in abundance, and manifestly neither skill nor will were wanting in him for the task. Best of all, he did not look down upon his fellow-men from those heights of contempt and scorn, which make satirists commonly the most hateful as well as the most profitless of writers. The hand that was mailed to smite had an inward side soft to caress. He claimed no superiority, arrogated for himself no peculiar exemption from the vices and follies he satirized; he had his own mind to clear of cant as well as his neighbours', and professed to know their weak side only through a consciousness of his own. Just as he proclaimed himself as Mr. Snob, *par excellence,* when writing of the universal snobbishness of society at a later date, so in the 'Confessions of Fitzboodle,' or *The Yellowplush Papers,* he made no parade of being one whit wiser, purer, or more disinterested than other people. Relentless to foppery, falsehood, and rascality, however ingeniously smoothed over or concealed, he was not prone to sneer at frailty, where it laid no claim to strength, or folly where it made no pretence of wisdom. The vices of our modern social life were the standing marks for the shafts of his ridicule, but here and there, across his pages, there shot gleams of a more pleasing light, which showed how eagerly the lynx-eyed observer hailed the presence of goodness, and candour, and generosity, whenever they crossed his path.

That he may, in those days, have thought them rarer than his subsequent experience has proved, is more than probable; and, indeed, this circumstance gave to many of his earlier sketches a depth of shade, which leaves an impression on the mind all the more painful, from the terrible force with which the tints are dashed in. No man ever sketched the varieties of scoundrelism or folly with more force than Yellowplush or Fitzboodle, but we cannot move long among fools and scoundrels without disgust. In these sketches, the shadows of life are too little relieved for them to be either altogether true to nature, or tolerable as works of art. We use them as studies of character, but, this purpose served, are fain to put them aside for ever after. Hence, no doubt, it was that these vigorous sketches, at the time they appeared, missed the popularity which was being won by far inferior works; and hence, too, they will never become popular even among those whom Mr. Thackeray's subsequent writings have made his warmest admirers. Bring them to the touchstone whose test all delineations of life must bear, to be worthy of lasting repute,—the approval of a woman's mind and taste,—and they are at once found to fail. Men will read them, and smile or ponder as they read, and, it may be, reap lessons useful for after needs; but a woman lays down the book, feeling that it deals with characters and situations, real perhaps, but which she can gain nothing by contemplating. No word, image, or suggestion, indeed, is there to offend her modesty—for, in this respect, Mr. Thackeray in all his writings has shown that reverence for womanhood and youth, which satirists have not often maintained;—but just as there are many things in life which it is best not to know, so in these pictures of tainted humanity there is much to startle the faith, and to disquiet the fancy, without being atoned for by any commensurate advantage. With what admirable force, for example, are all the characters etched in Yellowplush's 'Amours of Mr. Deuceace'! The Hon. Algernon Percy Deuceace himself,—his amiable father, the Earl of Crabs,—Mr. Blewitt,—where in literature shall we find such a trio of scoundrels, so distinct in their outlines, so unmistakeably true in all their tints? How perfect, too, as portraits, are Dawkins, the pigeon, of whom Deuceace and Blewitt, well-trained hawks, make so summary a meal, and Lady Griffin, the young widow of Sir George Griffin, K.C.B., and her ugly step-daughter, Matilda! No one can question the probability of all the incidents of the story. Such things are happening every day. Young fools like Dawkins fall among thieves like Deuceace and Blewitt, and the same game of matrimonial speculation is being played daily, which is played with such notable results by Deuceace and Miss Matilda Griffin. The accomplished swindler is ever and anon caught like him, the fond silly woman as constantly awakened, like her, out of an insane dream, to find herself the slave of cowardice and brutality. Villany so cold, so polished, so armed at all points, as that of the Earl of Crabs, is more rare, but men learn by bitter experience, that there are in society rascals equally agreeable and equally unredeemed. There is no vulgar daubing in the portraiture of all these worthies;—the lines are all true as life itself, and bitten into the page as it were with vitriol. Every touch bears the traces of a master's hand, and yet what man ever cared to return to the book, what woman ever got through it without a sensation of humiliation and disgust? Both would wish to believe the writer untrue to nature, if they could; both would willingly forego the exhibition of what, under the aspect in which it is here shown, is truly 'that hideous sight, a naked human heart.'

Of all Mr. Thackeray's books this is, perhaps, the most open to the charge of sneering cynicism, and yet even here glimpses of that stern but deep pathos are to be found, of which Mr. Thackeray has since proved himself so great a master. We can even now remember the mingled sensation of shuddering pity and horror, with which the conclusion of this story years ago impressed us. Deuceace, expecting an immense fortune with Miss Matilda Griffin, who, on her part, believes him to be in possession of a fine income, marries her;—the marriage having been managed by his father, the Earl of Crabs, in order that he may secure Lady Griffin for himself, with all Miss Griffin's fortune, which falls to her ladyship, in the event of Matilda marrying without her consent. Lady Griffin has previously revenged herself for the Honourable Algernon's slight of her own attachment to him, by involving him in a duel with a Frenchman, in which he loses his right hand. The marriage once concluded, Deuceace and his wife find their mutual mistake, and the penniless pair, on appealing for aid to the Earl of Crabs and his new-made wife, are spurned with remorseless contempt. What ensues, let Mr. Yellowplush tell in his own peculiar style:—

'About three months after, when the season was beginning at Paris, and the autumn leafs was on the ground, my lord, my lady, me and Mortimer, were taking a stroal on the Boddy Balong, the carridge driving on slowly a head, and us as happy as posbill, admiring the pleasnt woods, and the golden sunset.

'My lord was expayshating to my lady upon the exquizet beauty of the sean, and pouring forth a host of butifle and virtuous sentament sootable to the hour. It was dalitefle to hear him. "Ah!" said he, "black must be the heart, my love, which does not feel the influence of a scene like this; gathering, as it were, from those sunlit skies a portion of their celestial gold, and gaining somewhat of heaven with each pure draught of this delicious air!"

'Lady Crabs did not speak, but prest his arm, and looked upwards. Mortimer and I, too, felt some of the infliwents of the sean, and lent on our goold sticks in silence. The carriage drew up close to us, and my lord and my lady sauntered slowly tords it.

'Jest at the place was a bench, and on the bench sate a poorly drest woman, and by her, leaning against a tree, was a man whom I thought I'd sean befor. He was drest in a shabby blew coat, with white seems and copper buttons; a torn hat was on his head, and great quantities of matted hair and whiskers disfiggared his countnints. He was not shaved and as pale as stone.

'My lord and lady didn take the slightest notice of him, but past on to the carridge. Me and Mortimer lickwise took *our* places. As we past, the man had got a grip of the woman's shoulder, who was holding down her head, sobbing bitterly.

'No sooner were my lord and lady seated, than they both, with igstrame dellixy and good natur, bust into a ror of lafter, peal upon peal, whooping and screaching, enough to frighten the evening silents.

'Deuceace turned round. I see his face now—the face of a devvle of hell! Fust, he lookt towards the carridge, and pointed to it with his maimed arm; then he raised the other, *and struck the woman by his side*. She fell, screaming.

'Poor thing! Poor thing!'

['Mr. Deuceace at Paris,' the end of the story.]

There is a frightful truthfulness in this picture that makes the heart sick. We turn from it, as we do from the hideous realities of an old Flemish painter, or from some dismal revelation in a police report. Still, the author's power burns into the memory the image of that miserable woman, and his simple exclamation at the close tells of a heart that has bled at the monstrous brutalities to the sex, of which the secret records are awfully prolific, but which the romance writer rarely ventures to approach. If we have smiled at the miserable vanity and weakness of poor Matilda Griffin before, we remember them no more after that woful scene.

The Luck of Barry Lyndon, which followed soon after the appearance of *The Yellowplush Papers*, was a little relieved by brighter aspects of humanity, but so little, that it can never be referred to with pleasure, despite the sparkling brilliancy of the narrative, and abundant traces of the most delightful humour. How completely, in a sentence, does Barry convey to us a picture of his mother!

Often and often has she talked to me and the neighbours regarding her own humility and piety, pointing them out in such a way, that I would defy the most obstinate to disbelieve her. [Ch. i.]

The same vein of delicate sarcasm runs throughout the tale, where every page is marked by that matchless expressiveness and ease of style for which Mr. Thackeray is the envy of his contemporaries. The hero is as worthless a scoundrel as ever swindled at *écarté*, or earthed his man in a duel. He narrates his own adventures and rascalities with the artless *naïveté* of a man troubled by no scruples of conscience or misgivings of the moral sense,—a conception as daring as the execution is admirable. For a time the reader is carried along, with a smiling admiration of the author's humour, and quiet way of bringing into view the seamy side of a number of respectable shams; but when he finds that he is passed along from rake to swindler, from gambler to ruffian, —that the men lie, cheat, and cog the dice, and that the women intrigue, or drink brandy in their tea, or are fatuous fools, the atmosphere becomes oppressive, and even the brilliancy of the wit begins to pall. Yet there are passages in this story, and sketches of character, which

Mr. Thackeray has never surpassed. Had these been only mingled with some pictures of people not either hateful for wickedness or despicable for weakness, and in whom we could have felt a cordial interest, the tale might have won for its author much of the popularity which he must have seen, with no small chagrin, carried off by men altogether unfit to cope with him in originality or power.

There is always apparent in Mr. Thackeray's works, so much natural kindliness, so true a sympathy with goodness, that only some bitter and unfortunate experiences can explain, as it seems to us, the tendency of his mind at this period to present human nature in its least ennobling aspects. Whenever the man himself speaks out in the first person, as in his pleasant books of travel,—his *Irish Sketch Book*, and his *Journey from Cornhill to Cairo*,—he shows so little of the cynic, or the melancholy Jaques—finds so hearty a delight in the contemplation of all simple pleasures, and so cordially recognises all social worth and all elevation of character, as to create surprise that he should have taken so little pains in his fictions to delineate good or lofty natures. That this arose from no want of love for his fellow-men, or of admiration for the power which, by depicting goodness, self-sacrifice, and greatness, inspires men with something of these qualities, is obvious,—for even at the time when he was writing those sketches to which we have adverted, Mr. Thackeray's pen was recording, with delightful cordiality, the praises of his great rival, Dickens, for these very excellences, the absence of which in his own writings is their greatest drawback. It is thus he wrote in February, 1844, of Dickens's *Christmas Carol*. We quote from *Fraser's Magazine*.

And now there is but one book left in the box, the smallest one, but oh! how much the best of all. It is the work of the master of all the English humourists now alive; the young man who came and took his place calmly at the head of the whole tribe, and who has kept it. Think of all we owe Mr. Dickens since those half dozen years, the store of happy hours that he has made us pass, the kindly and pleasant companions whom he has introduced to us; the harmless laughter, the generous wit, the frank, manly, human love which he has taught us to feel! Every month of those years has brought us some kind token from this delightful genius. His books may have lost in art, perhaps, but could we afford to wait? Since the days when the *Spectator* was produced by a man of kindred mind and temper, what books have appeared that have taken so affectionate a hold of the English public as these? They have made millions of rich and poor happy; they might have been locked up for nine years, doubtless, and pruned here and there, and improved (which I doubt), but where would have been the reader's benefit all this time, while the author was elaborating his performance? Would the communion between the writer and the public have been what it is now,—something continual, confidential, something like personal affection?. . . . .

Who can listen to objections regarding such a book as this? It seems to me a national benefit, and to every man or woman who reads it a personal kindness. The last two people I heard speak of it were women; neither knows the other or the author, and both said, by way of criticism, 'God bless him!' . . . . . As for TINY TIM, there is a certain passage in the book regarding that young gentleman about which a man should hardly venture to speak in print or in public, any more than he would of any other affections of his private heart. There is not a reader in England but that little creature will be a bond of union between the author and him; and he will say of Charles Dickens, as the woman just now, 'God bless him!' What a feeling is this for a writer to be able to inspire, and what a reward to reap!

[From 'A Box of Novels,' *Works*, vi, 386–416.]

In a writer who felt and wrote thus, it was most strange to find no effort made to link himself to the affections of his readers by some portraiture, calculated to take hold of their hearts, and to be remembered with a feeling of gratitude and love! Whatever Mr. Thackeray's previous experiences may have been, however his faith in human goodness may have been shaken, the very influences which he here recognises of such a writer as Dickens must have taught him how much there is in his fellow-men that is neither weak nor wicked, and how many sunny and hopeful aspects our common life presents to lighten even the saddest heart.

The salutary influence of Dickens's spirit may, indeed, be traced in the writings of Mr. Thackeray about this period, tempering the bitterness of his sarcasm, and suggesting more pleasing views of human nature. The genius of the men is, however, as diverse as can well be conceived. The mind of the one is as hopeful as it is loving. That of the other, not less loving, though less expansive in its love, is constitutionally unhopeful. We smile at folly with the one; the other makes us smile, indeed, but he makes us think too. The one sketches humours and eccentricities which are the casualties of character; the other paints characters in their essence, and with a living truth which will be recognized a hundred years hence as much as now. Dickens's serious characters, for the most part, relish of melodramatic extravagance; there is no mistake about Thackeray's being from the life. Dickens's sentiment, which, when good, is good in the first class, is frequently far-fetched and pitched in an unnatural key—his pathos elaborated by

the artifices of the practised writer. Thackeray's sentiment, rarely
indulged, is never otherwise than genuine; his pathos is unforced, and
goes to the roots of the heart. The style of Dickens, originally lucid,
and departing from directness and simplicity only to be amusingly
quaint, soon became vicious, affected, and obscure: that of Thackeray
has always been manly and transparent, presenting his idea in the very
fittest garb. Dickens's excellence springs from his heart, to whose
promptings he trusts himself with an unshrinking faith that kindles a
reciprocal enthusiasm in his readers: there is no want of heart in
Thackeray, but its utterances are timorous and few, and held in check
by the predominance of intellectual energy and the habit of reflection.
Thackeray keeps the realities of life always before his eyes: Dickens
wanders frequently into the realms of imagination, and, if at times he
only brings back, especially of late, fantastic and unnatural beings, we
must not forget, that he has added to literature some of its most
beautiful ideals. When he moves us to laughter, the laughter is broad
and joyous; when he bathes the cheek in tears, he leaves in the heart
the sunshine of a bright after-hope. The mirth which Thackeray moves
rarely passes beyond a smile, and his pathos, while it leaves the eye
unmoistened, too often makes the heart sad to the core, and leaves it so.
Both are satirists of the vices of the social system; but the one would
rally us into amendment, the other takes us straight up to the flaw,
and compels us to admit it. Our fancy merely is amused by Dickens,
and this often when he means to satirize some grave vice of character
or the defects of a tyrannous system. It is never so with Thackeray: he
forces the mind to acknowledge the truth of his picture, and to take
the lesson home. Dickens seeks to amend the heart by depicting virtue;
Thackeray seeks to achieve the same end by exposing vice. Both are
great moralists; but it is absurd to class them as belonging to one school.
In matter and in manner they are so thoroughly unlike, that when we
find this done, as by Sir Archibald Alison, in the review of the literature
of the present century in his *History of Europe*, we can only attribute
the mistake to a limited acquaintance with their works. Of Dickens,
Sir Archibald apparently knows something, but he can know little
of Mr. Thackeray's writings, to limit his merits, as he does, to 'talent
and graphic powers,' and the ridicule of ephemeral vices.[1] On the
contrary, the very qualities are to be found in them which in the same
paragraph he defines as essential to the writer for lasting fame—'profound insight into the human heart, condensed power of expression,'

[1] See Alison, *History of Europe* (1853–9), i, 482–4.

—the power of 'diving deep into the inmost recesses of the soul, and reaching failings universal in mankind,' like Juvenal, Cervantes, Le Sage, or Molière.

Sir Archibald comes nearer to the truth when he ascribes to Mr. Thackeray the want of imaginative power and elevation of thought. But what right have we to expect to find the qualities of a Raphael in a Hogarth, or of a Milton in a Fielding? If genius exercises its peculiar gifts to pure ends, we are surely not entitled to ask for more, or to measure it by an inapplicable standard. It cannot be denied that Mr. Thackeray's ideas of excellence, as they appear in his books, are low, and that there is little in them to elevate the imagination, or to fire the heart with noble impulses. His vocation does not lie peculiarly in this direction; and he would have been false to himself had he simulated an exaltation of sentiment which was foreign to his nature. It has always seemed to us, however, that he has scarcely done himself justice in this particular. Traces may be seen in his writings of a latent enthusiasm, and a fervent admiration for beauty and worth, overlaid by a crust of cold distrustfulness, which we hope to see give way before happier experiences, and a more extended range of observation. To find the good and true in life, one must believe heartily in both. Men who shut up their own hearts in scepticism are apt to freeze the fountains of human love and generosity in others. Mr. Thackeray must, ere now, have learned, by the most pleasing of all proofs, that there is a world of nobleness, loving-kindness, purity, and self-denial in daily exercise under the surface of that society whose distempers he has so skilfully probed. The best movements of his own nature, in his works, have brought back to him, we doubt not, many a cordial response, calculated to inspire him with a more cheerful hope, and a warmer faith in our common humanity. Indeed, his writings already bear the marks of this salutary influence; and it is not always in depicting wickedness or weakness that he has latterly shown his greatest power.

The unpretending character of Mr. Thackeray's fictions has no doubt arisen in a great degree from a desire to avoid the vices into which the great throng of recent novelists had fallen. While professing to depict the manners and events of every-day life, their works were, for the most part, essentially untrue to nature. The men and women were shadows, the motives wide of the springs of action by which life is actually governed, the sentiments false and exaggerated, the manners deficient in local colouring. Imaginative power was not wanting, but it revelled so wildly, that it merely stimulated the nerves, and left no permanent impression on the heart or understanding. Elevation of sentiment abounded in excess, but the conduct of the heroes and heroines was frequently hard to square with the rules of morality, or the precepts of religion. Bulwer's genius had run wild in pseudo-philosophy and spurious sentimentalism. James was reeling off interminable yarns of florid verbiage.[1] Mrs. Gore's facile pen was reiterating the sickening conventionalisms of so-called fashionable life; and Ainsworth had exalted the scum of Newgate and Hounslow into heroic beings of generous impulses and passionate souls. Things had ceased to be called by their right names; the principles of right and wrong were becoming more and more confounded; sham sentiment, sham morality, sham heroism, were everywhere rampant; and romance-writers every day wandering farther and farther from nature and truth. Their characters were either paragons of excellence, or monsters of iniquity—grotesque caricatures, or impossible contradictions; and the laws of nature, and the courses of heaven, were turned aside to enable the authors to round off their tales according to their own low standard of morality or ambition, and narrow conceptions of the working of God's providence. In criticism and in parody, Mr. Thackeray did his utmost to demolish this vicious state of things. The main object of his *Luck of Barry Lyndon*, and his *Catherine Hayes*, was to show in their true colours the class of rogues, ruffians, and demireps, towards whom the sympathies of the public had been directed by Bulwer, Ainsworth, and Dickens. Mr. Thackeray felt deeply the injury to public morals, and the disgrace to literature, inflicted by the perverted exercise of these writers' powers upon subjects which had hitherto been wisely confined to such recondite chronicles as *The Terrific Register*, and the *Newgate Calendar*. Never was antidote more required; and the instinct of truth, which uniformly guides Mr. Thackeray's pen, stamped his pictures with the hues of a ghastly reality. Public taste, however, rejected the genuine article, and rejoiced in the counterfeit. The philosophical cut-throat, or the sentimental Magdalene, were more piquant than the low-browed ruffian of the condemned cell, or the vulgar Circe of Shire-lane; and until the mad fit had spent itself in the exhaustion of a false excitement, the public ear was deaf to the remonstrances of its caustic monitor.

Nor was it only in the literature of Newgate, as it was well named, that he found matter for reproof and reformation. He had looked too earnestly and closely at life, and its issues, not to see that the old and

[1] i.e. G. P. R. James (1799-1860).

easy manner of the novelist in distributing what is called poetical justice, and lodging his favourites in a haven of common-place comfort at the close of some improbable game of cross-purposes, had little in common with the actual course of things in the world, and could convey little either to instruct the understanding, to school the affections, or to strengthen the will. At the close of his *Barry Lyndon*, we find his views on this matter expressed in the following words:—

There is something *naïve* and simple in that time-honoured style of novel writing, by which Prince Prettyman, at the end of his adventures, is put in possession of every wordly prosperity, as he has been endowed with every mental and bodily excellence previously. The novelist thinks that he can do no more for his darling hero than make him a lord. Is it not a poor standard that, of the *summum bonum?* The greatest good in life is not to be a lord, *perhaps not even to be happy.* Poverty, illness, a humpback, may be rewards and conditions of good, as well as that bodily prosperity which all of us unconsciously set up for worship. [From a footnote in ch. xvii, sometimes omitted; *Works*, vi, 245. Martin's italics.]

With these views, it was natural that in his first work of magnitude, *Vanity Fair*, Mr. Thackeray should strike out a course which might well startle those who had been accustomed to the old routine of caterers for the circulating libraries. The press had already teemed with so many heroes of unexceptionable attractions, personal and mental,— so many heroines, in whom the existence of human frailty had been altogether ignored; we had been so drenched with fine writing and poetical sensibility, that he probably thought a little wholesome abstinence in all these respects might not be unprofitable. He plainly had no ambition to go on feeding the public complacency with pictures of life, from which nothing was to be learned,—which merely amused the fancy, or inflated the mind with windy aspirations, and false conceptions of human destiny and duty. To place before us the men and women who compose the sum of that life in the midst of which we are moving,—to show them to us in such situations as we might see them in any day of our lives,—to probe the principles upon which the framework of society in the nineteenth century is based,—to bring his characters to the test of trial and temptation, such as all may experience,—to force us to recognize goodness and worth, however unattractive the guise in which they may appear,—in a word, to paint life as it is, coloured as little as may be with the hues of the imagination, and to teach wholesome truths for every-day necessities, was the higher task to which Mr. Thackeray now addressed himself. He could not carry out this purpose without disappointing those who think a novel flat which does not centre its interest on a handsome and faultless hero, with a comfortable balance at his banker's, or a heroine of good family and high imaginative qualities. Life does not abound in such. Its greatest virtues are most frequently hid in the humblest and least attractive shapes; its greatest vices most commonly veiled under a fascinating exterior, and a carriage of unquestionable respectability. It would have cost a writer of Mr. Thackeray's practised skill little effort to have thrown into his picture figures which would have satisfied the demands of those who insist upon delineations of ideal excellence in works of fiction; but, we apprehend, these would not have been consistent with his design of holding up, as in a mirror, the strange chaos of that *Vanity Fair*, on which his own meditative eye had so earnestly rested.

That Mr. Thackeray may have pushed his views to excess, we do not deny. He might, we think, have accomplished his object quite as effectually by letting in a little more sunshine on his picture, and by lightening the shadows in some of his characters. Without any compromise of truth, he might have given us somebody to admire and esteem, without qualifications or humiliating reserves. That no human being is exempt from frailties, we need not be reminded. The 'divine Imogen' herself, we daresay, had her faults, if the whole truth were told; and we will not undertake to say, that Juliet may not have cost old Capulet a good deal of excusable anxiety. But why dash our admiration by needlessly reminding us of such facts? There is a wantonness in fixing the eye upon some merely casual flaw, after you have filled the heart and imagination with a beautiful image. It is a sorry morality which evermore places the death's-head among the flowers and garlands of the banquet. In *Vanity Fair*, Mr. Thackeray has frequently fallen into this error; and he has further marred it by wilfully injuring our interest in the only characters which he puts forward for our regard. Anxious to avoid the propensity of novelists to make Apollos of their heroes, and paragons of their heroines, he has run into the opposite extreme and made Dobbin,—the only thoroughly excellent and loveable character in the book,—so ungainly as to be all but objectionable, and his pet heroine, Amelia, so foolishly weak as to wear out our patience.

This is all the more vexatious, seeing that the love of Dobbin for Amelia is the finest delineation of pure and unselfish devotion within the whole range of fiction. Such love in woman has often been depicted, but Mr. Thackeray is the first who has had the courage to essay, and the delicacy of touch to perfect, a portraiture of this lifelong devotion in the opposite sex. It is a favourite theory of his, that men who love best are prone to be most mistaken in their choice. We doubt the truth of the position; and we question the accuracy of the illustration in Dobbin. He would have got off his knees, we think, and gone away long before he did; at all events, having once gone, the very strength of character which attached him to Amelia so long would have kept him away. Why come back to mate with one whom he had proved unable to reach to the height of the attachment which he bore her? Admirable as are the concluding scenes between Amelia and the Major, we wish Mr. Thackeray could have wound up his story in some other way, for nothing is, to our minds, sadder among the grave impressions left by this saddening book, than the thought that even Dobbin has found his ennobling dream of devotion to be a weariness and a vanity. It is as though one had ruthlessly trodden down some single solitary flower in a desert place.

Mr. Thackeray has inflicted a similar shock upon his readers' feelings in handing over Laura Bell, with her fresh, frank heart, and fine understanding, to Arthur Pendennis, that aged youth, who is just as unworthy of her as Amelia is of Dobbin. If such things do occur in life—and who has been so fortunate in his experiences as to say they do not!—is the novelist, whose vocation it is to cheer as well as to instruct, only to give us the unhappy issues of feelings the highest and purest, and never to gladden us with the hope that all is not disappointment, and our utmost bliss not merely a putting up with something which might have been worse? With all the latitude of life to choose from, why be evermore reminding us of the limitations of our happiness,—the compromise of our fairest hopes? It was a poor and false conception of human happiness which placed it always in worldly prosperity; but is it not also wide of truth, to make the good and noble always suffer, and to teach that all high desires are vain—that they must either be baffled, or, if achieved, dissolve in disappointment? This is a cheerless creed, and false as cheerless; and it is by bringing it too prominently forward, that Mr. Thackeray has exposed himself to a charge of cynicism and want of heart.

Of these defects, however, no thoughtful reader will accuse him. His writings abound in passages of tenderness, which bespeak a heart gentle as a woman's, a sensitiveness only less fine;—a depth of pity and charity, which writers of more pretence to these qualities never approach. 'The still, sad music of humanity' reverberates through all his writings. He has painted so much of the bad qualities of mankind, and painted them so well, that this power has been very generally mistaken for that delight in the contemplation of wickedness or frailty, and that distrust of human goodness, which constitute the cynic. But this is to judge him unfairly. If his pen be most graphic in such characters as Becky Sharp, the Marquis of Steyne, Miss Crawley, or Major Pendennis, it is so because such characters present stronger lines than the quiet charities or homely chivalry in which alone it is possible for excellence to express itself in the kind of life with which his writings deal. Such men and women strike the eye more than the Dobbins, the Helen Pendennises, and Warringtons of society. These must be followed with a loving heart and open understanding, before their worth will blossom into view; and it is, to our mind, one of Mr. Thackeray's finest characteristics, that he makes personages of this class so subordinate as he does to the wickedly amusing and amusingly wicked characters which crowd his pages. This, indeed, is one of those features which help to give to his pictures the air of reality in which lies their peculiar charm, and make us feel while we read them as though we were moving among the experiences of our own very life. Here and there amid the struggle, and swagger, and hypocrisy, and time-serving, and vanity, and falsehood of the world, we come upon some true soul, some trait of shrinking goodness, of brave endurance, of noble sacrifice. So is it in Mr. Thackeray's books. In the midst of his most brilliant satire, or his most crowded scenes, some simple suggestion of love and goodness occurs, some sweet touch of pathos, that reveals to us how kind is the nature, how loving and simple the soul, from which they spring.

It is not cynicism, we believe, but a constitutional proneness to a melancholy view of life, which gives that unpleasing colour to many of Mr. Thackeray's books which most readers resent. He will not let his eye rest upon a fair face, without thinking of the ugly skull beneath, and reminding himself and us 'that beauty cannot keep her lustrous eyes.' In his heartiest mirth he seems to have in view the headache, or the labours of tomorrow. Because all humanity is frail, and all joys are fleeting, he will not hope the best of the one, nor permit us to taste heartily of the other. He insists on dashing his brightest fancies with needless shadows, and will not let us be comfortable, after he has done his best to make us so. There is a perversity in this, which Mr. Thackeray, in justice to himself and kindness to his readers, should subdue. Let him not diminish his efforts to make them honester, and simpler, and wiser; but let him feed them more with cheerful images, and the contemplation of beauty without its flaws and worth without its drawbacks. No writer of the day has the same power of doing this, if he pleases. We could cite many passages in proof of this, but can it be doubted by any one who reads the following essay, from the series which appeared in *Punch* some years ago, as from the pen of Dr. Solomon Pacifico?

[Quotes 'On a Good-Looking Young Lady', *Punch*, 8 June 1850; *Works*, viii, 362–6.]

Why should not Mr. Thackeray give us another Erminia in his next novel, and confute his detractors? Addison never wrote anything finer in substance or in manner than this sketch. Indeed, a selection of Mr. Thackeray's best essays would, in our opinion, eclipse the united splendour of the whole British Essayists, both for absolute value in thought, and for purity and force of style. Had he never written anything of this kind but *The Book of Snobs*, he would have taken first honours. What a book is this, so teeming with humour, character, and wisdom! How, like Jaques, does he 'pierce through the body of the country, city, court!' Not, however, like him 'invectively,' but with a genial raillery which soothes while it strikes. The kindly playfulness of Horace is his model. It is only in dealing with utter worthlessness, as in his portrait of Lieutenant-General the Honourable Sir George Granby Tufto, K.C.B., K.T.S., K.H., K.S.W., &c. &c., that he wields the merciless lash of Juvenal. How every word tells!

[Quotation from ch. ix, 'On Some Military Snobs'; *Works*, ix, 302–3.]

If this book were read in every household, especially in every household where the British Peerage is studied, what a world of weariness and vexation of spirit, of hypocrisy and meanness, of triviality and foolish extravagance, would be saved! We would prescribe it as a manual for the British youth of both sexes; containing more suggestions for useful thought, more considerations for practical exercise, in reference to the common duties of life, than any lay volume we know. Never was satire more wholesomely applied, more genially administered. We have read it again and again with increasing admiration of the sagacity, the knowledge of the human heart, the humour, and the graphic brilliancy which it displays. Every page furnishes illustrations of some or all of these qualities. Take as an example of its lighter merits this exquisite sketch of suffering humanity at that most inane of all fashionable inanities—a London conversazione . . .

[Quotation from ch. xxv, 'Party-Giving Snobs'; *Works*, ix, 363–6.]

What wonder Mr. Thackeray should be so often condemned, when the foibles and vices which he paints are just those which, more or less, infect the whole body of society. Some way or other, he hits the weakness or sore point of us all. Nothing escapes his eye; and with an instinct almost Shakspearian he probes the secrets of a character at one venture. Like all honest teachers, he inevitably inflicts pain; and hence the soreness of wounded vanity is often at the root of the unfavourable criticism of which he is the subject. It requires both generosity and candour to accept such severe lessons thankfully, and to love the master who schools us with his bitter, if salutary, wisdom. But Mr. Thackeray has wisely trusted to the ultimate justice of public opinion; and he now stands better in it for never having stooped to flatter its prejudices, nor modified the rigorous conclusions of his observant spirit for the sake of a speedier popularity. Despite the carping of critics, his teaching has found its way to men's hearts and minds, and helped to make them more simple, more humble, more sincere, and altogether more genuine than they would have been but for *Vanity Fair, Pendennis*, and *The Book of Snobs*.

The strength of Mr. Thackeray's genius seemed to lie so peculiarly in describing contemporary life and manners, that we looked with some anxiety for the appearance of his *Esmond*, which was to revive for us the period of Queen Anne. We did not expect in it any great improvement upon his former works, in point of art, for we confess we have never felt the deficiencies in this respect, which are commonly urged against them. Minor incongruities and anachronisms are unquestionably to be found; but the characters are never inconsistent, and the events follow in easy succession to a natural close. The canvas is unusually crowded, still there is no confusion in the grouping, nor want of proportion in the figures. As they are in substance unlike the novels of any other writer, so do they seem, in point of construction, to be entirely in harmony with their purpose. We therefore feared that in a novel removed both in subject and in style from our own times, we should miss something of the living reality of Mr. Thackeray's former works, and of their delightful frankness of expression, without gaining anything more artistic in form. The result has, we think, confirmed these fears.

Esmond is admirable as a literary feat. In point of style, it is equal to anything in English literature; and it will be read for this quality when the interest of its story is disregarded. The imitation of the manner of the writers of the period is as nearly as possible perfect, except that while not less racy, the language is perhaps more grammatically correct. Never did any man write with more ease under self-imposed fetters than Mr. Thackeray has done; but while we admire his skill, the question constantly recurs, why impose them upon himself at all? He has not the power—who has?—of reviving the tone as well as the manner of the time; and, disguise his characters as he will, in wigs, ruffles, hair powder, and sacs, we cannot help feeling it is but a disguise, and that the forms of passion and of thought are essentially modern— the judgments those of the historian, not the contemporary.

It is, moreover, a great mistake for a novelist to introduce into his story, as Mr. Thackeray has done, personages of either literary or political eminence, for he thereby needlessly hampers his own imagination, and places his readers in an attitude of criticism unfavourable to the success of his story. Every educated reader has formed, for example, certain ideas, more or less vivid, according to the extent of his reading or the vigour of his imagination, of Marlborough, Swift, Bolingbroke, Addison, or Steele; and what chance has the novelist of hitting in any one feature the ideal which his reader has so worked out for himself? The novelist cannot, moreover, keep within the limits of the biographer, but must heighten or tone down features of character for the purposes of his story. This he cannot do without violating that rigorous truth which ought uniformly to be preserved, wherever the character or conduct of eminent men is concerned. It would be easy to convict Mr. Thackeray not only of serious offences against this wholesome law, but also of anachronisms far more serious than any in his former works, and of inaccuracies in regard to well-known facts, which are fatal to the verisimilitude of the book as an autobiography. One of these latter is so gross as to be altogether inexcusable,—the betrothal of the Duke of Hamilton, just before his duel with Lord Mohun, to Beatrix Castlewood, whereas it is notorious that the Duchess of Hamilton was alive at the time. We can scarcely suppose Mr. Thackeray ignorant of a circumstance which is elaborately recorded in Swift's *Journal*, but in any case his perversion of the facts transcends all lawful licence in matters of the kind. A still graver transgression has been committed in his portraiture of Marlborough, which is so masterly as a piece of writing that its deviation from historical truth is the more to be deprecated. When he has branded him for posterity in words that imbed themselves in the memory, it is idle to attempt to neutralize the impression by making Esmond admit that, but for certain personal slights from the hero of Blenheim, he might have formed a very different estimate of his character. This admission is a trait true to life, but it is one which is not allowable in a novelist where the reputation of a historical personage is at stake. History is full enough of perversions without our romancers being allowed to add to them. Such defects as we have adverted to are probably inseparable from any attempt to place a fictitious character among historical incidents, but if this be the case, it only proves that the attempt should never be made.

These defects are the more to be regretted in a work distinguished by so much fine thought and subtle delineation of character. It has been alleged against it that Mr. Thackeray repeats himself,—that *Esmond* has his prototype in Dobbin, Lord Castlewood in Rawdon Crawley, and Beatrix Castlewood in Blanche Amory. We cannot think so. It is surely but a superficial eye which is unable to see how widely removed a little hypocritical affected coquette like Blanche Amory is from the woman of high breeding and fiery impulse—'the weed of glorious feature,'—who is presented for our admiration and surprise in Beatrix Castlewood. It were easy to point out in detail the differences between the prominent characters in this and Mr. Thackeray's other books, but such criticism is of little avail to those who cannot perceive such differences for themselves. The only feature which it owns in common with *Vanity Fair* is the insane attachment of Esmond to Beatrix. This pertinacity of devotion bears some analogy to Dobbin's for Amelia. But there was nothing humiliating in Dobbin's love: in Esmond's there is much. He is content to go on besieging with his addresses a woman, who not only rejects them, but has passed from the hands of one accepted suitor to another, till the whole bloom is worn off her nature. It is taxing our credulity too far to ask us to reconcile this with the other characteristics of Esmond. We never lose our respect for Dobbin: Esmond has wearied it out long before he shakes off his fetters, and weds the lady's mother, who has been wasting her heart upon him for years. Lady Castlewood is a portrait so exquisitely made out in all the details, so thoroughly loveable, and adorned by so many gracious characteristics, that we cannot but regret Mr. Thackeray should have placed her in a situation so repugnant to common feeling, as that of being the enamoured consoler of her own daughter's lover.

Could we but forget this blemish, how much is there to admire in the delicacy with which the progress of her love for Esmond is traced,—the long martyrdom of feeling which she suffers so gently and unobtrusively,—the yearning fondness which hovered about him like a holy influence! Mr. Thackeray's worship for the sex is loyal, devout, and pure; and when he paints their love, a feeling of reverence and holiness infinitely sweet and noble pervades his pictures. Many instances may be cited from this book; but as an illustration we would merely point to the chapter where Esmond returns to England, after his first campaign, and meets Lady Castlewood at the cathedral.

[Quotation from Book II, ch. vi; *Works*, xiii, 212–4.]

How cruel must be the necessities of novel writing, which drove Mr. Thackeray to spoil our interest in the actors in this exquisite scene by placing them afterwards in circumstances so incongruous! Mr. Thackeray is, we believe, no favourite with women generally. Yet he ought to be so; for, despite his sarcasms on their foibles, no writer has enforced their virtues more earnestly, or represented with equal energy the wrongs they suffer daily and hourly in their hearts and homes from the selfishness and sensualism of men. There are passages in this book for which they may well say of him, as that woman said of Dickens for his *Christmas Carol*, 'God bless him!' They do not forgive him, however, for the unnatural relation in which he has placed his hero and Lady Castlewood, and he is too wise an observer not to regard this as conclusive against his own judgment in the matter.

Mr. Thackeray will write better books than this, for his powers are ripening with every fresh emanation from his pen; his wisdom is more searching, his pathos sweeter, his humour of a more delicate flavour. He fills a large space now in the world's eye, and his reputation has become a matter of pride to his country. He is not a man to be insensible to the high regard in which he is so widely held, or to trifle with a fame which has been slowly but surely won. Kind wishes followed him to America from many an unknown friend, and kinder greetings await the return of the only satirist who mingles loving-kindness with his sarcasm, and charity and humility with his gravest rebuke.

36. [Nassau Senior], from 'Thackeray's Works'
Edinburgh Review

January 1854, xliv, 196–243. Reprinted in Senior's *Essays on Fiction* (1864), 321–96

Senior (1790–1864) wrote mostly on political economy, was a Master in Chancery from 1836 to 1855, and a member of several royal commissions. His articles on literature include an essay on Scott's novels. In a prefatory note to *Essays on Fiction*, his daughter writes that her father, who was too ill in 1864 to revise his work, 'would have felt that to send forth the notice on the greatest novelist of our own day, William Makepeace Thackeray, without one word of explanation or regret, into a world still smarting from his loss, would have been treason to the friendship which united both author and reviewer. To ears in which the sound of the last strokes of the funeral knell still lingers, this criticism will probably seem severe; but when the article first appeared, Mr. Thackeray, with the generous cordiality for which he was so remarkable, expressed his entire approval. No doubt he thought that the impartial judgment and diligent study which it evinced were a more precious tribute to his temper and genius than the indiscriminate flattery too often lavished upon authors by their friends' (pp. vi–vii).

. . . The reader will have inferred, from the attention which we have paid to the character of Amelia, that we think it a creation of extraordinary skill. We do so. It appears to us to unite the two greatest merits that a fictitious character can possess,—originality and nature. And yet it is the source of one of the greatest blemishes of the work. Mr. Thackeray indulges in the bad practice of commenting on the conduct of his *dramatis personæ*. He is perpetually pointing out to us the generosity of Dobbin, the brutality of the Osbornes, the vanity of Joseph Sedley, and so on, instead of leaving us to find out their qualities from their actions. And in the course of this running commentary he keeps repeating that Amelia was adorable; that she was the idol of all who approached her, and deserved to be so; in short, that she was the perfection of womanhood. Now we will not deny that she had qualities which would make her agreeable as a plaything, and useful as a slave; but playthings or slaves are not what men look for in wives. They want partners of their cares, counsellors in their perplexities, aids in their enterprises, and companions in their pursuits. To represent a pretty face, an affectionate disposition, and a weak intellect as together constituting the most attractive of women, is a libel on both sexes.

We must now take up Amelia's pendant, Becky: the character, among all that Mr. Thackeray has drawn, which has received the most applause.

When we said that she was the impersonation of intellect without virtue, we used the word virtue in perhaps too narrow a sense, as indicating the qualities which we love, the qualities which arise from the sympathy of their possessor with others, and therefore occasion *them* to sympathise with him. Now, of these qualities Becky is devoid. She has no affection, no pity, no disinterested benevolence. She is indeed perfectly selfish. She wants all the virtues which are to be exercised for the benefit of others. She has neither justice nor veracity. She treats mankind as mankind treats the brutes, as mere sources of utility or amusement, as instruments, or playthings, or prey. But many of the self-regarding virtues she possesses in a high degree. She has great industry, prudence, decision, courage, and self-reliance. These are the qualities which, when under the direction of a powerful intellect, unbiassed by sympathies, and unrestrained by scruples, have produced many of the masters of mankind. In a higher sphere Becky might have been a Semiramis or a Catherine. As might be expected in a person of her good sense and self-control, she is mistress of the smaller virtues, good temper and good nature; she always wishes to please, because it is only by pleasing that she can subjugate. She is not resentful or spiteful, because she despises those around her too much to waste anger on them, and because she knows that petty injuries are generally repaid with interest. . . .

[Senior traces and discusses Becky's career.]

But with her success all the charm of Becky disappears. Even Mr. Thackeray turns his back upon her. He no longer supplies her with the sagacity and presence of mind which carried her triumphantly through the storms and among the quicksands of her London life. He allows her to sink from degradation to degradation, without an effort on his part, or even on hers, to extricate her, until she loses her identity, and the brilliant Rebecca turns into a vulgar swindler. At length, he seems to relent, and to take pity on the distresses of an old acquaintance who has afforded so much amusement. He throws Amelia and her brother across her path, and gives up to her the rich Joseph as a prey. And here we think her changes ought to have ended. As the ruler, and, as soon as the climate of Coventry Island rendered her a widow, the wife, of Joseph Sedley, she might have passed the tranquil, decorous middle age to which he at length dismisses her,— 'busied in works of piety; going to church, and never without a footman; the subscriber to every charity; the fast friend of the destitute orange girl, the neglected washerwoman, and the distressed muffinman; a patroness and stall-keeper in every benevolent bazaar in Cheltenham and Bath.' Instead of this, he blackens her with the vulgar commonplace crimes of making Sedley's will in her favour, insuring his life, and poisoning him.

This we venture to think a mistake. Comic characters are intended to amuse, not to frighten. They may be as vicious as the author pleases; they may be utterly heartless, they may swindle, they may rob; but they must not kill. The extent to which tragi-comedy is allowable may be undefined; but this we think is clear, namely, that the comedy must be an accessory to the tragedy, not the tragedy to the comedy. The intermixture of a few cheerful spots among gloomy or frightful scenes is felt as a relief. The intrusion of the terrible among gay images is an interruption. It is like a gibbet as the background of a Watteau. We are pleased to enjoy a respite from the continued contemplation of suffering or danger. We are shocked at being disturbed in our laughter by wailings and screams. All Shakspeare's tragedies have a mixture of comedy; none of his comedies contain any thing that is tragic. Hotspur, Henry the Fifth, and Richard are tragic. Their powers for good and for evil are gigantic; the fate of kingdoms depends on them. They can afford to trifle; their wit and humour, though sometimes pushed to buffoonery, does not lower them. Richard may smile, because he can murder while he smiles. But what should we think of Shakspeare if he had made Falstaff an assassin, or had engaged Shallow, Slender, and Poins in a murderous conspiracy? Hatred is to most men a painful emotion. There are undoubtedly torpid dispositions which require strong excitement, which enjoy pictures of murderers, tyrants, and oppressors just as they enjoy the taste of garlic, and the smell of tobacco; but these coarse intellectual palates are rare. In most minds the indignation produced by the description of great crimes requires to be soothed by the exemplary punishment of the offender, or to be diverted by withdrawing from him the reader's attention, and fixing it on the heroism of the sufferer, on the courage with which he resists violence, or on the patience with which he bears it. But these are the materials of tragedy; and when they are introduced into a work of which the basis is comic, they recall us painfully from the sunny scenes among which we have been wandering to the gloomy regions of danger and endurance. . . .

Pendennis has generally been thought inferior to *Vanity Fair*, and we are not inclined to dispute the verdict of the public. It wants the grand historical background of *Vanity Fair*. Mr. Thackeray never was more happily inspired than when he removed his theatre to Belgium. Every reader will admit that the events in Brussels are those which are the most strongly imprinted on his memory. Every one recollects, as well as if he had witnessed them, the perplexities of Lady Bareacres, the undaunted self-possession of Becky, and the terrors of Joseph Sedley. But it is not merely to the exquisite truth with which these scenes are imagined that they owe their apparent reality. The solid foundation of fact by which all that is invention is supported, gives to it a stability which no pure fictions can possess. We know that thousands must have been startled at their mid-day meal, like Sedley and Mrs. O'Dowd by the dull distant mutterings of Quatre Bras. We know that tens of thousands felt Amelia's terrors when the cannon of Waterloo began to roar. Every Scotchman who visited the British Institution last year, and admired Drummond's charming picture of John Knox bringing home his second wife, felt what probability was given to its imaginary details by the curious gable ends and projecting windows and outside staircase of the still existing house at the head of the Netherbow, which the serious bridal procession is reaching.[1]

It has been objected to the historical novel that it carries untruth on the face of it. First, because we already know all that can be known of the departed great, and feel that any additional actions or speeches must be attributed to them falsely. And secondly, because the reader has always formed to himself a conception of the language and conduct of every historical person in whom he is interested, and is disgusted when the author's conception of them differs, as it almost always must, from his own.

There is much foundation for these objections, and Mr. Thackeray,

[1] James Drummond (1816–77) painted many scenes from Scottish history.

in *Vanity Fair*, has skilfully avoided them, by excluding from his novel historical characters, though he admits historical events. He has not given us a sketch, or even a side view, of any actor in the great drama of 1815, whose name was ever heard of before. Isidor and Pauline, and the O'Dowds and Regulus, are all the delightful creations of the author. But we know that there must have been such persons in Brussels in June 1815, that they must have witnessed the wonders of that memorable month, and that they must have talked and acted in the same manner, though not quite so amusingly, as their representatives are made to do in the pages of *Vanity Fair*. Now all this is wanting in *Pendennis*. As far as can be inferred from any historical allusions, it might have been written at any time during the present, or indeed during the last century. The old and the young, the Londoners and the provincials, all act and talk as if the fortunes of the country had no connexion with theirs. Even the professional writers deal with politics with the impartiality of indifference. They put one in mind of Chatterton's computation on a great man's death. 'Lost by not being able to dedicate to him, ten guineas. Gained by writing his life, 12*l*. Am glad he is dead, by thirty shillings.' . . .

Fictitious characters may, we think, be conveniently divided into three classes—the Simple, the Mixed, and the Inconsistent.

By simple characters, we mean the persons to whom no qualities are attributed by the poet, except those which are subservient to one another, and co-operate in the main work which the person in question has to do. By mixed characters, we mean the persons who are endowed by him with different attributes, independent of one another, some of which are essential to the principal parts which they have to perform, and others have no connexion with them. By inconsistent characters, we mean those who possess discordant qualities,—qualities which counteract or modify, or even neutralise, one another. The test whether a character is simple, mixed, or inconsistent is, to try what would be the effect of removing any one of its attributes. If that removal would leave it incomplete, unfit to execute the duties assigned to it by the poet, it is a simple character. If the quality supposed to be removed would not be missed, the character is mixed. If that removal would render the rest of the character more harmonious, more efficient for the performance of any one or more of its parts, it is not only mixed, but also inconsistent. . . .

Mr. Thackeray's Blanche is . . . an inconsistent character. Her desire of power is constantly interfering with her desire of sympathy.

She cannot help teasing those whom she wishes to please. In her pursuit of immediate admiration she loses permanent esteem, and becomes a plaything when she aims at being an idol. When she sits between two admirers, she flirts alternately with each, and thus betrays to them both the emptiness of her kindness. Becky, we repeat, is a simple character. Numerous as her qualities are, they are not discordant. Not one of them could be taken from her without damaging her powers of worldly advancement.

Rawdon Crawley is one of Mr. Thackeray's best inconsistent characters. He is a gambler, indeed a blackleg, and would be an actual swindler if a swindler could be tolerated in society. He approaches as near to swindling as the law will allow. He preys on the young and the inexperienced, contracts debts which he knows never can be paid, and lies whenever it suits his convenience. Yet this degraded nature has its amiable and its respectable side. He is fond of his wife and of his child. He is brave, and he is grateful. He has an honour of his own, which, though its province is narrow, reigns there supreme. He knows that his only chance of escaping ruin is through the friendship of Lord Steyne. But the instant that he suspects how that friendship has been purchased, he breaks with his patron, sends back, poor as he is, the thousand pounds which he believes to have been Steyne's present to Becky, and is with difficulty restrained from shooting him.

Arthur Pendennis is a mixed character. He is a poet grafted on a dandy. So far as he is a dandy, he is vain, conceited, and extravagant. So far as he is a poet, he is inflammable and inconstant, easily attracted and easily repelled. Having scarcely any seriously adopted opinions, or principles, or plans, he is at the mercy of those around him. It is a defect in the story that his conduct recurs in a sort of circle. He falls in love with an actress, and is jilted; makes love to Blanche, is well received by her, and then cast off, and to please his mother offers himself to Laura; she refuses him, and so ends the first volume.

In the second volume he falls in love with a porter's daughter, and is cured by a fever; to please his uncle he proposes himself again to Blanche, and is engaged to her. She jilts him again, and again he offers himself to Laura; and, as it was necessary to end the novel, this time she accepts him.

There is nothing very attractive in such an outline, but many of the details are full of beauty. The wonder with which, after he is cured of an attachment, he revisits its former object, is admirably described. So is his last courtship of Blanche at Tunbridge Wells, where the *blasé* dandy and *blasée* flirt, after mutual attempts, all ineffectual, to be fond and sentimental, confess to one another that the marriage is not of their own seeking, but has been arranged for them by their mammas and uncles, and that they must submit to it like a good little boy and girl.

We have said nothing about the tragical parts of the story—about Colonel Altamont and his frightful secret and mysterious threats; or Warrington's discarded wife. They are tacked so slightly to the comic portions, that they might easily be detached altogether. And if Mr. Thackeray should think fit hereafter to lighten *Pendennis*, and so improve its chances of floating down to posterity, we recommend that these be the portions of its rigging that are first cut away.

Esmond is a reproduction of the manners, feelings, thoughts, and even style which prevailed from 180 to 140 years ago. It is a wonderful *tour de force*. Without doubt, one of the charms of art is the triumph over difficulty. But the triumph must not be a barren one. The value of what is gained must bear a considerable proportion to the labour that has been expended. The epic in twenty-four books, from each of which a letter was eliminated, was not more but less pleasing than if the author had allowed himself free use of the alphabet. Taken at the best, the task of a novelist is difficult. It is no easy thing to invent a plausible story, a story which shall have a beginning, a middle, and an end,—a beginning which shall raise expectation, a middle which shall continue it, and an end which shall satisfy it. Neither Richardson nor Fielding has succeeded in doing so more than once. It is less difficult, but still far from easy, to people that story with characters, distinct, natural, and amusing; and to make them talk and act like the living models supplied by the author's experience. If to the obstacles which nature has thrown across his path, the poet thinks fit to add fresh ones of his own; if he builds up walls in order to jump over them, the reader always suspects that what is supplied to him is not the author's best; that some real merit which he would have enjoyed is sacrificed to an imaginary one which he does not care about.

Now the amount of the self-imposed burden which Mr. Thackeray has undertaken to bear may be estimated, when we consider how few have been the writers who have ventured to submit to it. For at least 3000 years poets have taken their principal characters from history or mythology. But they have seldom borrowed more than the names, and perhaps one or two of the most notorious qualities, and one or two of the most notorious adventures, of their heroes. Everything else they have generally copied from what they saw around them. All

Homer's men and women, whether they be Europeans or Asiatics, Greeks or Phœacians, Trojans or allies, speak the same language, use the same weapons, amuse themselves with the same games, worship the same gods, believe in the same legends, are in fact identical in habits and manners. All those of Virgil, whether natives of Ilium, or Carthage, or Sicily, or Latium, are Romans of the Augustan age. Four great tragic poets, perhaps the four greatest that ever wrote, have brought on the stage Theseus. In the *Œdipus Coloneus*, he is an Athenian statesman; in the *Supplices*, an Athenian rhetorician; in *Phèdre*, a courtier of Louis Quatorze; and in the *Midsummer Night's Dream*, a highly educated English gentleman. Not one of these great writers thought himself bound to reproduce the Theseus of tradition, half-savage, half-divine, the first cousin and imitator of Hercules, who roamed over Greece destroying robbers, killing wild beasts, and carrying off women; a mixture of giant and knight-errant; raised, according to one legend, for his virtues, to be a god; according to another, for his crimes seated for ever in hell. Even Walter Scott, though, in order to please critics who are intolerant of anachronisms, he endeavours to copy the manners and feelings of a past age, does not try to speak in its language or in its style. His events may be mediæval, but he relates them like any other novelist of the nineteenth century. Though the scene of *Rob Roy* is laid 140 years ago, and though Osbaldistone is his own biographer, he tells his story as if he had just finished his education in the new town of Edinburgh. The courage, the diligence, and the skill of Mr. Thackeray have enabled him to avoid this inconsistency. Colonel Esmond writes as one of the best of her wits might have written in the reign of Queen Anne.

We cannot, however, avoid thinking that this merit has been purchased too dearly. The reader feels always that he is listening to falsetto tones; that he is looking at the imitation of an imitation. If Esmond had been confined within as short limits, it might have taken rank with the 'Defence of Natural Society.'[1] But a parody three volumes long becomes tiresome. We want the author to throw aside the fetters which impede his movements, though we require him to keep the costume which disguises his person. We wish to hear Jacob's own voice, though the hands be the hands of Esau.

The period at which Mr. Thackeray has laid his scene was scarcely a matter of choice, when once he had determined to imitate antiquated

[1] Edmund Burke's *Vindication of Natural Society* (1756) was a parody of some of Bolingbroke's philosophical writings.

forms of thought and expression. Those who succeeded the wits of Queen Anne's days were moderns. Thomson, Goldsmith, Adam Smith, and Hume, all remembered Pope and Swift; but they wrote as we do; —better, perhaps, so far as they took more pains, but with no other perceptible difference. The giants, indeed, who ruled the literary world between the Reformation and the Restoration used a style and a language sufficiently different from our own; but they were unfit for domestic narrative. No one could have tolerated the loves of Beatrix and Esmond enveloped in the grand periods of Bacon or Milton, or even in the quaint, loose verbiage of the *Arcadia*. The school which Mr. Thackeray has imitated was remote enough to be peculiar, and near enough for its peculiarities not to offend.

But that period had little else to recommend it. It was one to which every Englishman must look back with disgust. Up to the Restoration the English, at least in the higher classes, had been a serious people. Primogeniture as respects land, and the exclusion of the younger branches of even the greatest houses from nobility,—the happy accident from which so many of our peculiarities flow,—had prevented the existence among us of the idle, frivolous caste which, during the 16th, 17th, and 18th centuries, formed the aristocracy of the greater part of the Continent; a caste excluded by its prejudices from commerce, from the bar, from medicine, and, except in its high dignities, from the church, and naturally led, with the exception of the small portion of it that could find employment in arms, to dedicate its ample leisure to place-hunting and amusement. From the Conquest until the Restoration the rich and the noble of England had had duties to perform. The rich were great merchants or feudal proprietors; the noble were statesmen or soldiers; all the members of the younger branches, and the younger members of the eldest branch, who in France would have thronged the court of the sovereign, or lived in the *ruelles* of the capital, were actively engaged in business or in professions.

But during the sixty or seventy years which immediately followed the Restoration, London seems to have been the headquarters of a fashionable crowd which, in numbers, in wealth, in idleness, in dissoluteness, in every thing, in short, except education and refinement, rivalled the *grand monde* of Paris. Of course we cannot now dwell on the causes of this phenomenon. The increased wealth of the unemployed class was probably connected with the abolition of the feudal tenures, and the facilities thereby given to mortgages and sales, the increased occupation of land by tenants instead of by proprietors, the enormous augmentation of trade, and the large incomes, indeed, the large fortunes, that could be made in the public service, or squeezed from the royal bounty. Its dissoluteness was partly a reaction against the austerities of Puritanism, and partly a coarse imitation of the polished dissipation of France; but it would probably have shown itself, even if there had been no Puritans, and no French: in fact, it was the necessary result of wealth wanting occupation and literature. There were, of course, literary circles as brilliant as those of any other period, the circles in which the great writers of that age were formed; but every thing shows that the mass of the fashionable world was then deplorably ignorant. The women knew nothing, and professed to know nothing. The men passed many of their mornings, and almost all their evenings, in clubs, and at the theatres; smoking, drinking, and playing at cards, or listening to stilted tragedies or indecent comedies.

This levity was made hideous by the intermixture of ferocity not more savage, indeed, perhaps less so, than that of the previous century, but horrible in itself, and still more horrible as the cruelty of careless voluptuaries. A sanguinary penal code was enforced with unrelenting severity. Temple Bar and London Bridge were fringed with human heads. With not one-fourth of the present population, there were probably fifty times as many executions every year as there are now. The whippings of females, as well as of males, were perpetual, and were paraded up and down the most public thoroughfares; and yet these punishments were as inefficacious as they were cruel. The roads around London were beset by highwaymen; the streets were infested by footpads; amateurs in crime, who have been immortalised in *The Spectator* under the name of Mohocks, insulted and injured passengers by way of amusement. No one seems to have engaged in politics who was not sooner or later, and generally more than once, guilty of treason; the basest and the most unscrupulous traitors being those whom their crowns placed above the law. Duels were frequent and ferocious; the seconds fought as well as the principals, and victory was often obtained by treachery. Other aristocracies may have been more contemptible, but none can have been less attractive or amiable, than that of the English court from the return of Charles the Second down to the death of Queen Anne.

Over-indulgence, except indeed to the whimpering little goddess whom he deifies in every novel, is not Mr. Thackeray's weakness. His *dramatis personæ* are as black as their originals could have been. The only prominent male character who is not an habitual drunkard is the hero. Three Lord Castlewoods are introduced. The first is described as passing his early life abroad, where he was remarkable only for duelling, vice, and play,—and where he marries and then deserts the mother of the hero. He passes his middle age in London, a hanger-on of ordinaries, and a brawler about Alsatia and Whitefriars;[1] marries during his first wife's life an old maid with money; and is killed at the battle of the Boyne. The second is a drunken sensualist, who ill-treats and insults his wife, spoils his children, gambles away his property, and is killed in a duel. The third turns Roman Catholic, marries ill, quarrels with his own relations, and is left, at the end of the story, the slave of his wife's family of German adventurers.

The hero, of course, possesses the ordinary heroic qualities of courage, generosity, and affectionateness. But even *he* conspires for the purpose of occasioning a new revolution, though he strongly suspects that his success will be mischievous to his country. He is not seduced by the entreaties of any friend; he is not driven on by the blind, instinctive, spaniel-like loyalty, which leads a legitimist to throw his fortunes, his life, his family, and even his patriotism at the feet of him whom he adores as his sovereign. He is himself the originator of the scheme; he estimates calmly the results; 'has his own forebodings as to what they may be, his usual sceptic doubts as to the benefit which may accrue to the country by bringing a tipsy young monarch back to it.' The motive which, in spite of all these doubts and forebodings, impels him to endeavour to inflict, at the hazard of a civil war, such a master on his country, is merely the hope that by doing so he may please his cousin Beatrix Esmond, one of the heroines of the novel, a violent Tory, who for ten long years has been the object of Esmonds' unsuccessful adoration. . . .

When an author has been long and repeatedly before the public, the verdict of that great tribunal is likely to be a fair one. We believe its judgment on Mr. Thackeray—a judgment which we are not inclined to question—to be this:

That he is a bad constructor of a story; that his openings are tedious and involved, his conclusions abrupt and unsatisfactory; and that the intervening space is filled by incidents with little mutual dependence, and sometimes, as in *Pendennis*, repetitions of one another. On the other hand, it is admitted that these incidents, taken separately, are often admirable, well imagined, and well told, and amusing

---

[1] The district of London which until 1697 was a sanctuary for debtors and criminals.

exhibitions of the weaknesses or the vices of those who take part in them.

We say 'weaknesses or vices,' because this is the second reproach addressed to Mr. Thackeray. It is said that his men, if they are not absurd, are tyrants or rogues: that his women, if they are not fools, are intriguers or flirts. This accusation, if it be an accusation, is true as respects his men; and nearly true as respects his women.

If the *dramatis personæ* of *Vanity Fair* were average samples of the two millions who form the nation that inhabits London, or even if they were samples of what an American would call the Upper Ten Thousand of the Londoners,[1] the London world would be a detestable one. It would be as black morally as it is physically.

Now we are ready to admit that the darkness of Mr. Thackeray's patterns is an artistic defect: that is to say, we think that their texture and general effect would be improved by the introduction of a few threads, not as milkwhite and as superfine as Sir Charles Grandison or Clarissa, but of good average quality and colour; such as Belford, or Colonel Morden, or Miss Howe, or Lady G.[2] But if the objection be not to the artistic effect but to the truth of Mr. Thackeray's characters, if he be accused of giving not merely an unpleasant but a false view of human nature, the answer is this: that in *Esmond* the scene is laid in what we have already described as the period in which the English character was most demoralised; and that in *Vanity Fair* the characters are taken almost exclusively from two classes—the pursuers of nothing but wealth, and the pursuers of nothing but pleasure. Mr. Thackeray paints the former as vain, greedy, purseproud, oppressive, and over-bearing in prosperity, and grovelling and base in adversity, and envious and suspicious at all times. He describes the latter as frivolous, heartless, and false, with as much selfishness and vanity and malignity as their Russell-Square neighbours, though concealed under a smoother exterior. And who can say that these pictures are false?

The persons who form the *élite* of London society, the men whose objects are great and whose pursuits are ennobling, the politicians and men of science, the lawyers and physicians, the men of literature and taste, the poets and artists—all these are as much ignored as if the writer were not aware of their existence. The only allusion to such a class is old Osborne's complaint that his daughter, Mrs. Frederic Bullock, 'invites him to meet damned littery men, and keeps the earls and honourables to herself.' *Vanity Fair* is not a fair sample of the Lon-

[1] See above, p. 72.
[2] Characters in Richardson's *Clarissa Harlowe* (1740) and *Sir Charles Grandison* (1753).

don world taken as a whole, but is a not very exaggerated picture of two portions of it.

We have less to say in defence of *Pendennis*, for there the field is wider, and yet the result is nearly the same. Even in *Pendennis*, however, though the hero and his friend Warrington are literary men, their literature is of an humble kind. It is not the literature of statesmen, historians, or philosophers, of those who write for the purpose of influencing, or instructing, or improving mankind; it is not the literature of those whose object, though more selfish, is still magnanimous and splendid, of those who aim at widely diffused and permanent fame;—it is the literature of those who write for bread, who use their pens as a labourer does his spade, or a weaver his shuttle. Unless there be some reason for believing that hack writers in general are better than those whom Mr. Thackeray has described, we have no right to quarrel with his descriptions. There are too in *Pendennis* one or two persons whom we neither laugh at nor hate. There is Laura, who is intelligent and amiable, though indeed she behaves shamefully to the poor girl from the porter's lodge. There is a Mr. Pynsent, in whom there is no harm. There is a Lady Rockminster, who is sensible and kind, though rather *brusque*. In fact, however, we must admit that *Pendennis* is open to the reproach that it professes to be a fair specimen of English morality, and is not so.

Lastly, Mr. Thackeray is accused of lavishing on his heroines undeserved praise. It is said, that having with great skill put together a creature of which the principal elements are undiscriminating affection, ill-requited devotion, ignorant partiality, a weak will and a narrow intellect, he calls on us to worship his poor idol as the type of female excellence. This is true. Mr. Thackeray does all this; it is one of the greatest blemishes in his books. Happily it is a blemish that can be removed with ease. Nothing more than a pair of scissors is necessary. Let him carefully cut out every puff which he has wasted on Amelia, and Helen, and Laura, and Rachel; let him leave them, as all the characters in a novel ought to be left, to the reader's unbiassed judgment, and they would take their proper rank among his *dramatis personæ*, though it may differ from that to which their inventor thinks them entitled.

So much for Mr. Thackeray's faults. As to his merits, it is admitted that he is unrivalled by any living writer as an inventor and a describer of character; that he has penetrated into the lowest cells of pride, vanity, and selfishness, and laid open some of the secrets of the human prison-house which never were revealed before. Every reader admires the ease and vigour of his dialogue, its sparkling wit and its humour, sometimes broad, sometimes delicate, but always effective.

The few extracts which we have made from the serious portions of his works are sufficient to show that he has great tragic powers. Nothing can be more exquisitely imagined or described than the parting of George Osborne and Amelia. His natural tendency, however, is towards comedy, or rather towards satire. He

Shines in exposing knaves and painting fools.[1]

But his favourite amusement is the unmasking hypocrisy. He delights to show the selfishness of kindness, the pride of humility, the consciousness of simplicity. If any of Mr. Thackeray's characters had been copied from real life, and the originals could recognise themselves in his imitations, they never would tremble more than when some apparently good act was ascribed to them. They would expect to see in the next page the virtue turn into a vice or a weakness. . . .

37. [Mrs. Oliphant], from 'Mr. Thackeray and his Novels', *Blackwood's Magazine*

January 1855, lxxvii, 86–96

Margaret Oliphant (1828–97) was the author of nearly a hundred publications, including novels, biographies and semi-historical literature. She frequently contributed to *Blackwood's Magazine*, in which several of her works of fiction first appeared, and wrote two volumes of a history of Blackwood's publishing house (1897).

. . . Future generations will speak of Dickens and Thackeray as we speak of Pepys and Evelyn, and they are quite as dissimilar; but if aught of evil should befall the regnant sovereign of this realm of fancy, we will have a civil war forthwith to decide which of these pretenders shall mount the vacant throne. In the mean time, it is premature to agitate the question; there is no just ground of comparison between

[1] Pope, 'Of the Characters of Women' (1735), 119.

these two whose names are so commonly pronounced together. Perhaps there are no two men among their host of readers who are further apart from each other than Mr Dickens and Mr Thackeray; but instead of unnecessarily enlarging upon the difference, we count it better wisdom to take up this pretty pink volume, patiently waiting the conclusion of a rambling preamble, to remind us, that it has nothing to do with Mr Dickens, but in every page of it is solely Mr Thackeray's own.

And the *Rose and the Ring* is not a political satire, though one of its princes is of Crim Tartary; and we are afraid that those who look for one of Mr Thackeray's wicked and witty comments upon the world in general, will be disappointed in this book. He is not in the vein of teaching either; his Christmas carol does not treat of a magical dream and a wonderful transformation, like some other Christmas carols of our acquaintance. Thanks to Mr Thackeray, this fairy tale is a pure flash of mirth and laughter, and knows no moral. The little children and the great children may venture for once to enjoy their sport in peace, without being called upon to square up into a row with humility and receive their lesson at the end. There are two princes, and two princesses, and two fairy gifts, endowing the fortunate possessors with unlimited beauty and loveableness; and, like a skilful artist, after a few complications, Mr Thackeray contrives to bestow those fairy tokens upon the two poor souls who require to be attracted to one another, and leaves the true lovers to the inalienable glamour of their love. If Angelica loses her rose, or Bulbo his ring, the domestic happiness of this royal pair is not greatly to be calculated upon; and the public peace of the realms of Paflagonia and Crim Tartary may very possibly be disturbed once more; but magnanimous Giglio deprives *his* queen of the enchanted jewel with his own hand, and finds her quite as lovely without its magical influence;—and so Mr Thackeray, who is by no means apt to rhapsodise on this subject, makes a very seemly obeisance to True Love, the oldest of all the witchcrafts. We will not do our readers the injustice to tell them at second-hand how poor little Betsinda danced before their majesties in her one shoe—or how, by means of this little slipper, the persecuted Rosalba attained to her throne—or of Prince Giglio's infatuation with the grim old Countess Gruffanuff—or the magical bag which supplied him with everything he wanted, from blacking for his boots to armour for his battle;—but we have no doubt that everybody who has not read the *Rose and the Ring*, will be satisfied to know that Mr Thackeray dispenses poetic

justice with an unfaltering hand—that the exile has his own again—
and that the usurpers are sent upon their travels. We will not pause to
point out the catastrophe of Gruffanuff, and the lesson it impresses
upon the brethren of that unfortunate servitor; but we will promise
the fireside circle, which has the *Rose and the Ring* read aloud for its
general edification, one hearty laugh at the great and unlooked-for
discomfiture of the Countess Gruffanuff.

We are bound to say, that while Mr Thackeray has been disporting
himself among the family of Newcomes, Mr Michael Angelo Titmarsh, in his episodical existence, has made great use of his time since
his last appearance before the Christmas-keeping public. Mr Titmarsh may rest assured that no thunder will sour the beer which has so
little acid in it by nature. The fairy Blackstick is a much more agreeable
presiding genius than Lady Kicklebury;[1] and Mr Titmarsh has never
before produced so pleasant a picture-book, nor one whose pictures
were so worthy of the text. These illustrations are greatly superior to
all their predecessors by the same hand; they are so good that the artist
is fairly entitled to rank with the author in this pleasant production;
and altogether, amidst our wars and our troubles, in this Christmas
which is darkened and shadowed over to so many households, and at
a time when common tribulation and anxiety put us in charity with
all our neighbours, we are glad that we have to thank Mr Thackeray
for the honest laugh which is not at any one's expense.

Mr Thackeray, in his own proper person, has not made less progress
in kindness and good humour than has his *alter ego*, if we trace his
course from *Vanity Fair* to the *Newcomes*. Everybody praises Becky
Sharp, and the history in which she fills so important a place. Does
everybody like that clever, unbelieving, disagreeable book? But there
is nothing to be said on the subject of *Vanity Fair*, which has not been
said already—that all its rogues are clever and amusing, and all its good
characters fools—that Amelia is a greater libel upon womankind than
Becky herself, and that there is a heated crowded atmosphere in the
story which has scarcely any relief, seeing that the good people are by
no means a match for the bad, and cannot even pretend to balance the
heavy scale of evil. There is no one in the book who has the remotest
claim to our affection but Dobbin—good Dobbin, with his faithful
heart and his splay feet. Why should the Major have splay feet, Mr
Thackeray? Must the man who is not distinguished by moral obliquity
have some physical misfortune to make amends? But the splay feet

---

[1] In *The Kickleburys on the Rhine* (1850), one of Thackeray's 'Christmas Books'.

carry their owner into the heart of our regard, despite their unloveliness. The warmest admirer of Miss Rebecca Sharp is not moved to bestow his affection upon that amiable young lady; and though poor, little, silly Amelia may chance to touch a heart for a moment as she watches in Russell Square for a glimpse of her boy, she is quite too insignificant a person to insure any regard for herself. Mr Thackeray made a very clever book; and Mr Thackeray's book made a great sensation and success. There are many admirable things in it—a great sparkle of sayings and happy turns of expression; and the scenes are cut sharp and clear in their outline, and dullness is not within these pages. Nevertheless, we carry but one personage with us in real kindness when we close the volume. Of all its men and women, only Major Dobbin is worth the least morsel of love.

In Mr Thackeray's second grand exposition of his own principles, and of the human panorama of which he is a spectator and historian—in *Pendennis*—we find a little more to commend. There is Warrington, who has no splay feet; there is sweet Mr Pendennis, whom we consent to accept as an angel. It is a sad thing to think of Warrington, such a man as he is, spending his life in those chambers in Lamb Court, with nothing to do but to write articles, the fate of which he cares nothing for, only the Haunt to solace that great heart of his when the day's work is done, and no particular motive for living except the custom and habit of it. Few can paint a wasted life, and great powers wearing down with the continual dropping of every day, better than Mr Thackeray; but we are glad to think that he has still the means of rescue for this character in the exhaustless resources of fiction. Will not Mr Thackeray take into his gracious consideration ways and means for disposing of the graceless unknown Mrs Warrington, and leave Bluebeard free to make his fortune once more? We will answer for the entire satisfaction of the general population of these British Islands with any proceeding of the kind; and we do not doubt that Mr Warrington, when he is a free man, will find some one more faithful than Laura, and will not be forsaken a second time for such a coxcomb as Pen. Pendennis himself, though he is good-looking and fashionable, and writes a successful novel, is but a very poor fellow after all—not only falling far short of an ideal hero, but not much to brag of for a very ordinary man. Mr Thackeray avowedly scorns the loftiness of common romance, and will not have an exalted personage for the principal figure on his canvass; but Mr Arthur Pendennis does not possess a single feature of the heroic. Unfortunately, when we ought to admire, we are a great deal more likely to despise; and this, though it may be original, is neither true art nor noble; it is not original either; but Mr Pen is a meaner sinner than Tom Jones.

Leaving Pen—and leaving Laura, who is a very doubtful person, and whom we do not profess to make much of—if Pen is not the best husband in the world, popular opinion, we are afraid, will pronounce that popular sentence, 'Served her right!'—there is much more satisfaction in meeting with Harry Foker, who is Mr Thackeray's special property, the type of a class which our novelist has brought out of the shadows into the clearest and kindliest illumination. Good Harry Foker, who has no great share of brains—who does not spell very well, perhaps—whose habits are not what they ought to be, but who is the soul of honour, of unpretending simple courage and kind-heartedness. Some score of Harry Fokers, doing, with simple straightforwardness, what their commander ordered, have ridden with open eyes, and without a moment's faltering, right into the open-mouthed destruction, and made heroes of themselves upon the wintry heights of Sebastopol. Not a refined gentleman by any means, it is only genius that can commend this brave good-hearted simpleton to all our affections. A lesser artist might have been afraid of a character so little intellectual, and felt its defective points a reproach to his invention; but Mr Thackeray has been able to seize upon the genuine sparkle of this uncut jewel, upon the reverence for goodness, the humble self-estimation, the tender-heartedness, and the unsuspected pathos which lie in its depths. It is strange, when he has proved himself so capable of its exercise, that Mr Thackeray should so much overlook his true alchemy of genius. Is it best to drag the veil of decorum from a hidden evil, or to disclose a vein of native excellence—a secret even to its owner? Mr Thackeray, who scares his innocent readers with vague intimation of pitfalls round about them, and shocks mamma with terrific hints of the unmentionable ill-doing familiar to the thoughts of her pretty boy at school, does better service when Harry Foker, and Jack Belsize, and even Rawdon Crawley, show their honest hearts to us, than when he produces Mr Pendennis, with all his gifts, as a specimen of modern education, and the civilisation of the nineteenth century. What a simple noble gentleman is Lord Kew, who rises just above the strata of the Belsize formation! Such a hero as he is would leave us little to desire.

Only in one respect does *Pendennis* sin more grossly than *Vanity Fair*. Blanche Amory is more detestable, because she is less clever than

Becky. How much does Mr Thackeray owe to the world of woman-kind, by way of reparation for foisting into their ranks such a creation as this! Nothing less than a Desdemona can atone for such an insult. Can Mr Thackeray make a Desdemona? He has added some few pleasant people to our acquaintance in his day—Warrington may make amends for Pen, but who is to make amends for Blanche?

And here we touch upon our author's greatest imperfection. Mr Thackeray does not seem acquainted with anything feminine between a nursery-maid and a fine lady—an indiscriminate idolater of little children, and an angler for a rich husband. The 'perfect woman, nobly planned,' has no place in the sphere of Mr Thackeray's fancy. Perhaps the secret of this may be, that Mr Thackeray's world is a conventional world; and that even while he attacks its weak points, 'society,' the sphere with which he is best acquainted, represents this many-sided globe in our historian's eyes. The mother and the cousin in the little country-house, weeping and adoring as they read the hero's letters, telling each other of his childhood, those blessed days when Pen was in petticoats, seeing in all this heaven and earth only the bit of conse-crated soil under his shadow and the sky over his head, and furious at every other pretender for his gracious favour—that is one side of the picture. On the other is Miss Amory, with that bad leer in her eyes, which we are rejoiced to see has disappeared from the sketches of Mr Michael Angelo Titmarsh, calculating her chances of a husband, amusing Mr Pen into that last resource of idleness—falling in love; weeping 'Mes Larmes' in public, and in private cuffing her little brother; and Blanche is the other side of the golden shield, the obverse of the coin, the completion of Mr Thackeray's circle of female character. It is not a flattering estimate of Englishwomen which will be formed from the pages of this author, whom, of all others, we should fancy our neighbours over the Channel most likely to form their judgment from. Though Blanche has expanded into Beatrice, and Beatrice progressed to Ethel, the character is still far from satisfactory. And we must once more assure Mr Thackeray, that he owes his countrywomen an Isabella or a Desdemona to make amends.

In the one other creation of *Pendennis*, Mr Thackeray puts forth all his power. The Major rescues *his* class still more clearly out of the shadows than Harry Foker does; henceforward, instead of wordy de-scriptions of this old gentleman of the clubs, it will be quite enough to say that he is like Major Pendennis. This impersonation is so broad and clear that there is no mistaking it or its identity. There are certain portraits which convince us that they are admirable likenesses, though we are perfectly unacquainted with the original; and even those to whom 'society' is an unknown country, must recognise, as an un-mistakable individual, this specimen of the aborigines of 'the world.' Getting on in 'society' is the chief end of man to Major Pendennis—it is the grand vocation and duty of life. You must be moderately good, moderately brave and honourable, because the want of these qualities is apt to endanger your success in life; and with all the perse-verance and ardour which wins battles or makes fortunes, the Major devotes himself to securing an invitation to Gaunt House, or a gracious recognition from the Marquis of Steyne. It would be a pure waste of sympathy, in author or readers, to condole with the loveless, joyless condition of this old man of fashion. Loves and joys are out of the Major's way—they would simply embarrass and annoy him, these troublesome emotions; the Major has his pleasures instead, and his place in society, which he fills in a manner perfectly becoming the high end he has in view.

When we leave *Pendennis*, we find that Mr Thackeray takes a great leap out of his ordinary domain. It is no longer the English of the present day, careless and easy, just touched with the slang for which our author has a special gift, but it is English of the Augustan age, English which is balanced with antithesis, and polished into epigram, the English of those dainty people who wore bag-wigs and ruffles, patches and powder. Though we have serious fault to find with the story of Esmond, we are constrained to admit, at the outset, that the execution of this story is exquisite. In comparison with this, almost every other historical work we are acquainted with, except the romances of Scott, is a mere piece of masquerade. The age is not a great age, we confess, in spite of its Blenheim and its Ramillies, its Steele and its Addison; but such as it is, we have it here, a picture which is not merely paint, but is about the best example of absolute reproduction which our literature possesses. Nothing can be more real or touching—more like a veritable page of biography, if biographers were usually endowed with such a style as Mr Thackeray confers upon Harry Esmond—than the story of the solitary boy at Castlewood, his patrons and his teachers. The picture is perfect in its truth to nature, which is universal, and to manners, which are limited and transitory. Harry Esmond is not a boy of Queen Victoria's time, in the little cavalier's suit proper to Queen Anne's—he is not in advance of his age, nor has any conscious-ness of Waterloo dimming the glory of Blenheim. We never find ourselves deceived in him through all his history—the mask does not slip aside for a moment to show a modern face underneath. This book is a marvellous historical picture; in this point of view it is an unrivalled performance, and worthy of all the plaudits which a work, attended by so many difficulties, has a right to claim.

Nevertheless, with so much in its favour, this admirable production carries failure in it as a story, as a piece of human life represented for the sympathy of all humanity—our most sacred sentiments are outraged, and our best prejudices shocked by the leading feature of this tale. It is not only that Lady Castlewood is the confidant of the hero's passionate love for her daughter, yet compensates his disappointment in that quarter with her own hand—but it is the intolerable idea that this woman, who is pure as an angel, and as severe in her judgment of the back-sliding as a pure woman may be—a wife—and, still more, a mother, defended by the spotless love of little children—nevertheless cherishes for years a secret attachment to the boy to whom she gives the protection of her roof! This error is monstrous and unredeemable. If we do not count it among the affronts which Mr Thackeray puts upon his countrywomen, it is because it is too gross an error to look like truth; but it is not less disagreeable on this score. Mr Thackeray has spent all his pains to make this character a loveable and womanly one, and Rachel, Lady Castlewood, is a very 'sweet' person we confess, and would be worthy the idolatry of her historian but for this unaccountable blunder. The Love of the poets is young for a necessity. If it is fashionable to have a hero of discreet years, it requires nothing less than a long, constant, single attachment to make a heroine of middle age in any respect tolerable. A woman who loves two men must always condescend to a little derogation from her primal dignity—and the woman who contracts two marriages must be excused, in romance, by either a forced match, in the first instance, or the saddest and completest disappointment. In any way it is degradation to the heroine of our fancy—but Mr Thackeray must thrust *his* lady still further down. What had Lady Castlewood done that she should be compelled to fall in love with Harry Esmond, her daughter's adorer, her husband's faithful attendant, her own devoted and respectful son?

The hero himself is a hero in the proper acceptation of the word. It is not the faulty modern young gentleman any longer, but the antique ideal which Mr Thackeray has resorted to, in consent, perhaps reluctant, but certainly complete, to the old canons of his art. Harry Esmond has all the generosity, all the unselfishness, all the unrewarded and unappreciated virtues of genuine romance. When your hero is an ordinary sinner, it is possible to make him a more distinct personage than your ideal excellence can be—so that Esmond does not always stand quite clear from his background, and has not perhaps such a crisp sharp outline as Mr Arthur Pendennis. To make up for this, there is rather more distinctness than is desirable in the character of Beatrice. This bold, unscrupulous, and daring beauty, in whom the passion for admiration and the delight of conquest seem to possess the full power of passions more gross in their nature, is another of Mr Thackeray's special belongings. Her triumph in her own dazzling charms, and the mischief they make everywhere—the impetus with which her magnificent vanity carries her on—the trickery to which she stoops, and the intrigues into which she enters—never because her own heart is interested, but solely from an insatiable longing to madden every one about her—are combined with a singular power. This splendid creature not only obeys her natural impulse to destroy, but glories in the havoc she makes, and goes forth to new conquests in exulting power over the graves of her victims. For the good of humanity, we may venture to hope that, except within the pages of *Esmond*, the world knows few Beatrices; but it is impossible to deny the power and strength with which this cruel syren is drawn.

And what shall we say to Ethel Newcome? Ethel is not Beatrice, yet she is little better than a proper nineteenth century development of that all-conquering beauty. For our own part, we confess to being in the most perfect bewilderment as to the conclusion of the loves of these cousins, whose fate Mr Thackeray has yet to seal. Though the Bumbelcund bank confers a fortune on Clive, will it confer upon Ethel suitable dispositions to make the young gentleman happy? or is it consistent with the dignity of Mr Clive Newcome to be accepted as a *pis aller?* or must Clive marry Rosey after all, and sink down into humdrum domestic happiness, and leave the brilliant star for which he sighed to sparkle into a still brighter firmament, or to shoot and fall into the unfathomable darkness which swallowed Beatrice? We flatter ourselves that, in twenty years' experience of novel-reading, we have attained to as clear a prescience of a *dénouement* as most people; but Mr Thackeray, with his tantalising interviews, and all his hints of the future, puzzles and outwits our ordinary penetration. While the conclusion is not as yet, and everything is possible, we do not even find ourselves in a position to advise Mr Thackeray; we can but assure him honestly, that we see no outlet for him, though we expect he is to make himself a brilliant one. If Clive marries Ethel, how shall we vindicate the dignity of these young people, who cannot marry each other without a mutual sacrifice of pride and propriety; and if Clive marries Rosey, alas for Clive! Solemnly assuring Mr Thackeray of this dilemma, we leave him to make the best of it, only warning him of a storm of universal dissatisfaction if Clive marries no one at all—a miserable expedient, to which, we fear, *we* should be driven were the conclusion of the *Newcomes* left to our inventive powers.[1]

There is no book of Mr Thackeray which is so worthy of a great reputation as this uncompleted story. As full of character as its predecessors, it redeems their errors gallantly; and we could almost fancy that, in the scorn of genius for that accusation which pronounced him unable to manage the ideal, Mr Thackeray has showered a glory of manliness and goodness upon the inhabitants of this little world. There has never been a nobler sketch than that of the Colonel. The innocent heart and simple honour of this old man, and his horror of all falsehood and impurity, are enough to cover a multitude of Mr Thackeray's sins. We can understand how every individual worth caring for in the story or out of it rejoices to gain the acquaintance of Thomas Newcome. We are grateful to Lady Anne, and like her ever after, for her true apprehension of our Colonel's courtly manners, and old-fashioned chivalrous politeness. We are as ready to adopt him into our heart as Mr Pendennis and Mr Warrington can be; and Ethel herself gains an additional attraction when we see her beautiful eyes shining with pride for her noble old uncle. The key-note of the story is struck high and sweet in this character, which is at once so lofty and so childlike; and we cannot pass it by without once more admiring Mr Thackeray's skill in the retrospective story—the record of Thomas Newcome's misfortunes and troubles in his boyhood, which is almost as well done as the corresponding period in the history of Henry Esmond.

It is not easy to thread at a glance the lively maze of Mr Thackeray's story—to tell how pretty Ethel is engaged to Lord Kew by family arrangement, and how the young lady filches a green ticket from the Suffolk Street Gallery, with Sold upon it, and comes down to dinner wearing this label, like a wilful and rebellious young lady as she is; nor how good Colonel Newcome, whose great ambition it was to marry Clive to Ethel, and be a happy man in his old age, is balked by this engagement, and goes away sadly to India, to grow rich, if he can, for his dear boy's sake; how Clive is a painter, and varies between

[1] The monthly serialization of *The Newcomes* was not completed until August 1855.

ostentation of his art and the least morsel of shame for being engaged in it; how he makes a brave effort, and tears himself away from Ethel, and has almost got the better of his passion; how, of a sudden, the spirit of his dream is changed by hearing that Lord Kew and Ethel have broken off their engagement, at the first intimation of which poor young Clive finds out that he has not forgotten her, and comes home post-haste to try his hopeless chance once more; how there is a most noble Marquis of Farintosh in the field before him; how the hero and the heroine have little sparring-matches of courtship, but never come any nearer a conclusion; and how last month brings us to the climax of a farewell, which we, for our own part, have no faith in. Ethel Newcome, like Beatrice, is sometimes intoxicated with her own beauty, and the applauses it brings—sometimes carried off her balance with the *afflatus* of conquest and victory; but Ethel, we are glad to say, is much improved from her forerunner, and is a much less hopeless character than the beautiful tormentor of Harry Esmond. Is Ethel to consume what remnants are left to her of that fresh girl's heart she had when we first knew her—when she first fell in love with her good uncle—and be a great lady, and blaze her youthful days away in barren splendour? She likes being a great lady, you perceive—such a being was not born for love in a cottage, or for Clive's five hundred a-year, and odd position. Has Mr Thackeray prepared this beautiful victim for Moloch, or is there hope for Ethel still? The oracle preserves inexorable silence, and smiles upon our queries. We are quite as curious as you are, young lady; but we venture to predict that Miss Ethel Newcome, even though Mr Thackeray may have compunctions on her behalf, can never 'settle down' to romantic happiness. She will have to fulfil her destiny, and marry a most noble marquis. She is surely not for Clive the painter, whether he is to be made a Crœsus or a beggar, by means of the Bumbelcund Bank.

Clive himself, the handsome, dashing open-hearted young fellow, is an admirable hero. He is not called upon for feats of extraordinary generosity or self-sacrifice. His circumstances do not require Clive to take upon himself other people's burdens, or other people's penalties. He has only to enjoy himself, to paint when he pleases, and when he does not please, to draw his father's remittances, and look handsome, and be as happy as he can. There is no great demand made upon Clive's goodness throughout the story; yet we are quite content with him, and willing to believe that he will be equal to an emergency when it comes. We cannot refrain from making one quotation to illustrate the character of Clive, and the quality which, of all other qualities, Mr Thackeray expounds best. Clive is talking to his father:—

'At Newcome, when they go on about the Newcomes, and that great ass, Barnes Newcome, gives himself his airs, I am ready to die of laughing. That time I went down to Newcome, I went to see old Aunt Sarah, and she told me everything, and showed me the room where my grandfather—you know; and do you know, I was a little hurt at first, for I thought we were swells till then. And when I came back to school, where, perhaps, I had been giving myself airs, and bragging about Newcome, why, you know, I thought it was right to tell the fellows.'

'That's a man,' said the Colonel with delight; though, had he said, 'That's a boy,' he had spoken more correctly. [Ch. vii.]

This is a very delicate touch, and shows the hand of a master. Mr Thackeray's young hero, who is so honest and truthful in his boyish days, does not degenerate as he grows a man.

Lord Kew, too, simple, noble, and manful, is a further example of Mr Thackeray's most felicitous vein. These young men, who have no great intellectual elevation, and whose rank only makes them perfectly humble, unpretending, and free of all temptations to exaggerate themselves, seem characters on whom our author dwells *con amore*. Then there is the Vicomte de Florac, with his amusing French English, and his middle-aged princess, and that witch and malignant fairy, old Lady Kew, and Barnes Newcome the disagreeable, and the various family circles of this most respectable kindred, with all their nicely-touched gradations of character. There is no mist in this book; every one is an individual, pleasant or otherwise, and detaches himself or herself clearly from the background. The story is not in very good order, broken up as it is by retrospections and anticipations; and it is not good taste of Mr Pendennis to appear so frequently before the curtain, and remind us unpleasantly that it is fiction we are attending to, and not reality; but we think the great mass of his readers will bear us out in our opinion, that the *Newcomes* is not only the most agreeable story, but the cleverest book which Mr Thackeray has yet contributed for the amusement and edification of the admiring public.

When all this is said, there still remains a great deal to say which is less complimentary to our novelist. It is not, perhaps, the most agreeable information in the world to understand that our innocent school-boys must plunge into a very equivocal abyss of 'pleasure,' before they can come forth purged and renovated like Lord Kew. We are not very glad to hear that somebody could make revelations to us of our brothers and sons and fathers, such as the Duchesse d'Ivry did to Miss Ethel Newcome. We cannot acknowledge that between the innocence of youth and the goodness of matured life, there lies a land of darkness through which every man must pass; nor do we perceive the advantage of convincing Mr Thackeray's youthful audience that this is a necessity. The religious circles of our community have of late very much devoted themselves to that class of 'young men' for whom so many lectures, and sermons, and 'means of improvement,' are provided. We are not quite sure of the wisdom of thus making into a class the exuberant young life, which is, in fact, the world. When boys have ceased to be boys, they become human creatures of the highest order of existence. It is no compliment to their discernment to prepare for them mental food which is not suitable for their fathers or their teachers. They are men, with a larger inheritance of hope than their seniors; but their pride is not to be piqued into rebellion, by thrusting them into a half-way position between the man and the boy. But Mr Thackeray has a natural vocation in respect to his youthful countrymen. If he should happen, in fact, to be a grandfather, in disposition he is a young man continually—it is the life and pursuits of young men in which he is most skilled. Manliness, truthfulness, honour, and courage, are the qualities which he celebrates; and though Mr Thackeray is a favourite in countless households, it is not to be disputed that his stronghold is among those whose portraits he draws so truthfully, and whose life he describes with so much zest. Now here is scope and verge enough for any amount of genius; but surely it is not advisable that our teacher should lead his pupils to great harm on the way to great good. Is not that the loftiest purity which does not find it needful to fall?

We are afraid Mr Thackeray is beyond the reach of advice in respect to his female characters. Ethel is very attractive, very brilliant; but we would rather not have our daughters resemble this young lady, it must be confessed; and poor pretty Rosey, with all her goodness, is nobody, and Mr Thackeray intends that she should be so. If this is not good morals, it is still less good art. Providence has exempted woman from the grosser temptations, and romance has gifted her with a more ethereal life. If we do not bid Mr Thackeray create a woman of the highest order, or if we are doubtful of his capacity for this delicate formation, we may still beg him to add a little commonsense to his feminine goodness. When these tender pretty fools are rational creatures, the world of Mr Thackeray's imagination will have a better atmosphere; for besides marrying, and contriving opportunities to give in marriage, besides the nursery and its necessities, there are certain uses for womankind in this world of ours, and we are not so rich in good influences as to forfeit any of them. A coronet is certainly not an idol the worship of which gives much elevation to the spirits of its adorers; but when Lord Kew is so little ostentatious of his decoration, why should Ethel, and her friends for her, compass heaven and earth to obtain such another? Does not Mr Thackeray think this is too hackneyed a subject for his fresh and unexhausted invention? Might not the next Ethel do something better by way of novelty, and leave this field to Mrs Gore and Mrs Trollope, and the host of lesser ladies who devote their talents to the noble art of making matches?

We are not sure how far the English language will be benefited by the dialogues of Mr Thackeray; they are very clever, very entertaining, and their slang is admirable; but it is very doubtful if it will be an advantage to make these Islands no better than a broad margin for the witticisms and the dialect of Cockaigne. Our light literature begins to have a great savour of the Cockney in it. Our noble ally on the other side of the Channel does not seem so much the better of making Paris France, that we should repeat the experiment. London is the greatest town in existence, but it is not England, though the dialect of its many vagabonds seems in a fair way for beoming the classic English of our generation. Mr Thackeray's narrative is so pure and vigorous in its language, and his colloquial freedoms are so lively and entertaining, that there are no real exceptions to be taken to him; but every Thackeray and every Dickens has a host of imitators, and it is not an agreeable prospect to contemplate the English of Shakespeare and Bacon overwhelmed with a flood of Cockneyisms—a consummation which seems to approach more nearly every day.

Mr Thackeray is no poet; for one of the highest of the poet's vocations, and perhaps the noblest work of which genius is capable, is to embody the purest ideal soul in the most lifelike human garments; and this is an effort which our author has not yet attempted. Perhaps the title which Mr Thackeray would rather choose for himself would be that of an historian of human nature. In his sphere he is so eminently. Human nature in its company dress, and with all its foibles on, is the subject he delights to treat of; but Mr Thackeray is not great in home scenes, where the conventional dress is off, and the good that is in a man expands under the cheerful glow of the domestic fire. Mr Thackeray does not drape his hero in the purple, or make pictures of him as he walks loftily among suffering men; but takes him to pieces with wicked mirth, calling upon all men to laugh with him at the idol's demolition. We are no advocates for idol or for hero worship; but when we remember that there was once in this world a Man who was at once divine and human, whom we are all encouraged to make our example, and following whose wonderful footsteps some have attained to a life grander than that of common humanity, we feel that the highest ideal of the poets is but a fit and seemly acknowledgment of the excellence which has been made possible to our favoured race; and that the circle of life and manners is not complete, till we have admitted into it the loftiest as well as the lowest example of human existence— the saint no less than the sinner.

THE NEWCOMES

1853–5

---

38. Thackeray, *The Newcomes*, the beginning of ch. xxiv and the end of the novel

Works, xiv, 296–7, 1007–9

This narrative, as the judicious reader no doubt is aware, is written maturely and at ease, long after the voyage is over, whereof it recounts the adventures and perils; the winds adverse and favourable; the storms, shoals, shipwrecks, islands, and so forth, which Clive Newcome met in his early journey in life. In such a history events follow each other without necessarily having a connexion with one another. One ship crosses another ship, and after a visit from one captain to his comrade, they sail away each on his course. The *Clive Newcome* meets a vessel which makes signals that she is short of bread and water; and after supplying her, our captain leaves her to see her no more. One or two of the vessels with which we commenced the voyage together, part company in a gale, and founder miserably; others, after being wofully battered in the tempest, make port; or are cast upon surprising islands where all sorts of unlooked-for prosperity awaits the lucky crew. Also, no doubt, the writer of the book, into whose hands Clive Newcome's logs have been put, and who is charged with the duty of making two octavo volumes out of his friend's story, dresses up the narrative in his own way; utters his own remarks in place of New-come's; makes fanciful descriptions of individuals and incidents with which he never could have been personally acquainted; and commits blunders which the critics will discover. A great number of the descriptions in *Cook's Voyages*, for instance, were notoriously invented by Dr. Hawkesworth, who 'did' the book:[1] so in the present volumes,

---

[1] John Hawkesworth (1715?–73) published his account of voyages to the South Seas, including Cook's, in 1773.

where dialogues are written down, which the reporter could by no possibility have heard, and where motives are detected which the persons actuated by them certainly never confided to the writer, the public must once for all be warned that the author's individual fancy very likely supplies much of the narrative; and that he forms it as best he may, out of stray papers, conversations reported to him, and his knowledge, right or wrong, of the characters of the persons engaged. And, as is the case with the most orthodox histories, the writer's own guesses or conjectures are printed in exactly the same type as the most ascertained patent facts. I fancy, for my part, that the speeches attributed to Clive, the colonel, and the rest, are as authentic as the orations in Sallust or Livy, and only implore the truth loving public to believe that incidents here told, and which passed very probably without witnesses, were either confided to me subsequently as compiler of this biography, or are of such a nature that they must have happened from what we know happened after. For example, when you read such words as QVE ROMANVS on a battered Roman stone your profound antiquarian knowledge enables you to assert that SENATVS POPVLVS was also inscribed there at some time or other. You take a mutilated statue of Mars, Bacchus, Apollo, or Virorum, and you pop him on a wanting hand, an absent foot, or a nose, which time or barbarians have defaced. You tell your tales as you can, and state the facts as you think they must have been. In this manner, Mr. James, Titus Livius, Professor Alison, Robinson Crusoe, and all historians proceeded. Blunders there must be in the best of these narratives, and more asserted than they can possibly know or vouch for.

Two years ago, walking with my children in some pleasant fields, near to Berne in Switzerland, I strayed from them into a little wood: and, coming out of it presently, told them how the story had been revealed to me somehow, which for three-and-twenty months the reader has been pleased to follow. As I write the last line with a rather sad heart, Pendennis and Laura, and Ethel and Clive fade away into fable-land. I hardly know whether they are not true: whether they do not live near us somewhere. They were alive, and I heard their voices; but five minutes since was touched by their grief. And have we parted with them here on a sudden, and without so much as a shake of the hand? Is yonder line (——) which I drew with my own pen, a barrier between me and Hades as it were, across which I can see those figures retreating and only dimly glimmering? Before taking leave of Mr.

Arthur Pendennis, might he not have told us whether Miss Ethel married anybody finally? It was provoking that he should retire to the shades without answering that sentimental question.

But though he has disappeared as irrevocably as Eurydice, these minor questions may settle the major one above mentioned. How could Pendennis have got all that information about Ethel's goings-on at Baden, and with Lord Kew, unless she had told somebody—her husband, for instance, who, having made Pendennis an early confidant in his amour, gave him the whole story? Clive, Pendennis writes expressly, is travelling abroad with his wife. Who is that wife? By a most monstrous blunder, Mr. Pendennis killed Lord Farintosh's mother at one page and brought her to life again at another; but Rosey, who is so lately consigned to Kensal Green, it is not surely with *her* that Clive is travelling, for then Mrs. Mackenzie would probably be with them to a live certainty, and the tour would be by no means pleasant. How could Pendennis have got all those private letters, &c., but that the colonel kept them in a teak box, which Clive inherited and made over to his friend? My belief then is, that in fable-land some-where, Ethel and Clive are living most comfortably together: that she is immensely fond of his little boy, and a great deal happier now than they would have been had they married at first, when they took a liking to each other as young people. That picture of J. J.'s of Mrs. Clive Newcome (in the Crystal Palace Exhibition in fable-land) is certainly not in the least like Rosey, who we read was fair; but it represents a tall, handsome, dark lady, who must be Mrs. Ethel.

Again, why did Pendennis introduce J. J. with such a flourish, giving us, as it were, an overture, and no piece to follow it? J. J.'s history, let me confidentially state, has been revealed to me too, and may be told some of these fine summer months, or Christmas evenings, when the kind reader has leisure to hear.

What about Sir Barnes Newcome ultimately? My impression is that he is married again, and it is my fervent hope that his present wife bullies him. Mr. Mackenzie cannot have the face to keep that money which Clive paid over to her, beyond her lifetime; and will certainly leave it and her savings to little Tommy. I should not be surprised if Madame de Montcontour left a smart legacy to the Pendennis children; and Lord Kew stood god-father in case—in case Mr. and Mrs. Clive wanted such an article. But have they any children? I, for my part, should like her best without, and entirely devoted to little Tommy. But for you, dear friend, it is as you like. You may settle your fable-land

in your own fashion. Anything you like happens in fable-land.
Wicked folks die à propos (for instance, that death of Lady Kew was
most artful, for if she had not died, don't you see that Ethel would
have married Lord Farintosh the next week?)—annoying folks are
got out of the way; the poor are rewarded—the upstarts are set down
in fable-land,—the frog bursts with wicked rage, the fox is caught in
his trap, the lamb is rescued from the wolf, and so forth, just in the
nick of time. And the poet of fable-land rewards and punishes absolutely. He splendidly deals out bags of sovereigns, which won't buy
anything; belabours wicked backs with awful blows, which do not
hurt: endows heroines with preternatural beauty, and creates heroes,
who, if ugly sometimes, yet possess a thousand good qualities, and
usually end by being immensely rich; makes the hero and heroine
happy at last, and happy ever after. Ah, happy, harmless fable-land,
where these things are! Friendly reader! may you and the author meet
there on some future day! He hopes so; as he yet keeps a lingering
hold of your hand, and bids you farewell with a kind heart.

39. From an unsigned review, 'Thackeray's Newcomes', the *Spectator*

18 August 1855, xxviii, 859–61

The striking characteristics of Mr. Thackeray's novels have been so
often and so clearly pointed out, and the novels resemble each other so
much in general features—have such a strong family likeness—that it
becomes with each novel more difficult for the newspaper critic to
say anything that shall be at once new and true, if he confine himself
to his proper task of reviewing the book and fixing the literary position
of the author. Our limited space, and our obligation to say something
of every book as it comes to us, prevent us from following the example
of our brethren of the quarterlies and giving once for all a comprehensive survey of an author's writings; while in the case of a novel
that has been published in monthly parts, and with which the public
is already for the most part familiar, we are debarred from the common
resource of interesting our readers by recapitulating the leading incidents of the story and describing the principal characters. Ethel

Newcome and her cousin Clive—the brave, honest, affectionate Colonel—the cold-blooded, cowardly, cruel Barnes—Lady Kew, 'the wickedest old dear in all England'—Paul Florac and his group of relatives—Rosa Mackenzie and 'the old Campaigner'—and a crowd of clearly conceived vigorously drawn characters besides,—the public knows them as well as it does the faces of Disraeli and Lord John Russell, and has been much more interested about them for two years past. What can we say that has not been said over hundreds of dining-tables, in countless drawingrooms, students' chambers, under-graduates' rooms? Has not London for months been in consternation lest Ethel should waste her fair youth and noble heart in fruitless repentance, and that benevolent auntism we all respect so much, owe so much to, but so shudder at as a fate for our favourites in life and books? Was there not even a moment when a single hint about the importance of 'baptismal regeneration' made the profane throw the number violently to the other end of the room, as a vision rose of Venus-Diana with shorn tresses and close white cap, her bow straitened to a ferule, her cestus cut up for the personal adornment of her Anglican director, and all her little loves, all the bevy of nymphs, turned into smugfaced choristers and demure village schoolmistresses?[1] Has not the failure of the Bundlecund Bank hung over town with a prescient gloom, only lightened by the consciousness that Colonel Newcome's nobility of heart and mind could never be insolvent, come what run upon it there might? Has not Rosey Mackenzie's removal, by childbirth or any natural cause, and, that wanting, by poison administered so as to save Clive's neck and reputation, been almost prayed for in the churches? Were we not all present at the case of 'Newcome, Bart. *v.* Lord Highgate,' and did we not clap our inward hands with keen applause as the defendant's counsel painted, as only that distinguished mover of juries can paint, the character and brutal conduct of the injured husband? And now when the play is over, and the curtain down, the brown-holland thrown over the boxes, the lights out, and the audience gone home to supper, is it not rather a dull task and a superfluous, that we should be expected to retire to our sanctum and tell how interested and delighted they have been, how clever and how good the author is, and how often we hope they and we may have the pleasure of witnessing other performances from the same 'able and talented hand'?

Well, but we may at least congratulate the public that their favourite

[1] Presumably a reference to Ethel's breaking with the world, first described in ch. xxiv.

Ethel comes out of her trials and temptations not only wiser for her experience, but purer and nobler for her victory over her false-self; and that the happiness to which we have together looked doubtfully forward for her and Clive is theirs at last, though not till long after the fifth act is over, and seen only in prophetic vision from the authorial Pisgah. The play itself only moves through the wilderness, occupies itself with the murmurings of the people, with their idolatries, with their plagues—more than once we think the land of promise will never be reached: but far off from that mountain-top we spy the shining of its streams of milk and honey, and we see in spirit the wilderness cleared, the Jordan passed, and our wayworn and sorely-tried ones at rest beneath their vine. The dear old Colonel, too, finds rest. Like those herbs which emit their richest perfume when crushed, his character sweetens as his spirit breaks: his little absurdities, his Don-Quixotism, his magnificence of tone and manner, his high temper and irritability, all go, beneath the giant heel of the fate that tramples him. He rises from the blow weak and staggering, acknowledging his fault, deploring the misery he has brought upon others, giving up everything he has to repair it so far as may be: he is stern towards himself, patient towards those who persecute him, remorseful towards those he has injured, more affectionate and loving than ever to those who show him love and affection. He accepts his penalty like a brave, a kind, a humble man. We laugh at him no more; we love and admire him beyond expression; we bow before him in his bedesman's gown as we would not before a prince of the blood; and we follow his body to the tomb with a heartier belief in the power of simple goodness, a deepened reverence for it wherever we find it among men, and a sublimer confidence that in the still garden of souls its consummate flower goes on to bloom in eternal beauty. Dear old Colonel! since Lefevre[1] died more generous tears have not been wept over a book than have fallen for you—tears which have their source in noble thoughts and strengthen the hearts from which they flow. . . .

[1] Lieutenant Lefevre in Sterne's *Tristram Shandy*, vol. vi.

40. Unsigned review, *The Times*

29 August 1855, 5

This may have been written by Samuel Lucas (1818–68), who in an article in *The Times* on Thackeray's *Miscellanies* (1856) mentions 'reviewing *The Newcomes*' (*Eminent Men and Popular Books* (1859), 149).

Of course we all know the Newcomes. We may not visit at Park-lane or Bryanston or Fitzroy squares. We may have been too late a summer or two since to meet them at Baden. We should not bow nor perhaps recognize them individually if we did meet. But they are people with whose habits and motives we are familiar—about whom we have talked pleasantly for months—who have been more, perhaps, to each of us than many families of his or her acquaintance. If we question our respective impressions, we may even find that to many intents we have looked upon these 'Newcomes' as real personages, as helping to people our world, to attract or repel us, and to point or adorn our moral speculations.

Arthur Pendennis, *alias* Mr. Thackeray, to whom we are indebted for their introduction, may reasonably pride himself on their hearty reception. By the interest they have excited his own position is marked, and one of its incidents made sufficiently clear. It is plain that he can fashion a world like the real world, and characters the equivalent of those we meet in life, and can make them walk, talk, and do his bidding—to what purpose we shall consider presently—but with an ease which we at once admit to be admirable, with a clear conception and a broad handling which indicate the master. He has now proved to the satisfaction of all who are worth satisfying that he has creative vigour and singular dexterity; and he is justly celebrated for the reason that he is so accomplished.

To specify his peculiar talents we must consider the nature of his task. Time was when the novelist's function was more single and simple, and the critic could distinguish it by as simple a phrase. Of Richardson and Fielding Dr. Johnson could remark, that the one painted 'characters of nature,' and the other 'characters of manners.' But this distinction no longer serves to identify Mr. Thackeray, nature having become so polished and manners so natural that their confusion precludes a clear election between them. Mr. Thackeray, like Richardson, paints society, but society no longer narrowed to the axis which lies between the poles of a Lovelace and a Grandison. Society now-a-days is more large and complex, and includes a greater variety of elements. It is no longer exclusively fashionable, but political, religious, mercantile, professional, literary, artistic, and with an out-lying fringe of a Bohemian tendency which carries it to the verge of pure undisciplined nature. As these various circles combine and inter-sect, the ideas and sentiments derived from their different centres act and react upon each other. Our social, like our solar system admits of remote influences which require an enlarged survey; the orbit of our Kews is deflected by a Duchesse d'Ivry, just as Uranus is found per-turbing the satellites of Jupiter; and the aggregate becomes a difficult study in proportion as it is vast and complicated. The old novel is no more adequate to present a picture of life now-a-days than the old orrery to show us our planetary relations. If it be, as the poet sings, 'that the thoughts of men are widened with the process of the suns,'[1] it has become a larger function to comprehend and a more elaborate work to note and register them.

It is at the same time less easy because they have so modified each other as to obliterate the broad distinctions of class and character. Single passions no longer predominate; simple virtues and simple vices are out of date. If nature, as we said, has corrected manners, there is also less rigidity in conventional forms. The real and artificial are becoming blended; we are frank and noble amid frivolities, and sincere notwithstanding our partial pretences. Even *Vanity Fair* is traversed by its 'shining ones,'[2] though their wings are restrained under modern habiliments. Thus the eye wanders in doubt and perplexity, while the hand is puzzled how to portray. The differences are so fine as to be almost elusory; the confusion is so great that the inferior artist may well lay down his implements in despair.

As complexity is the prominent feature of the scene, he who would paint it must, at all events, spread forth an ample canvas; and his view must be panoramic, for cabinet pictures with a few simple figures would include but a part of the prospect of life. Such an one must forego the

[1] Tennyson, 'Locksley Hall' (1842), 138.
[2] Bunyan's term for the Angels in *The Pilgrim's Progress* (1678).

finish essential to a close inspection, and the dramatic interest which is compatible with a limited number of characters. He had better not seek, for he will surely miss the miniature perfection of such a picture, for example, as that of the family of Wakefield. He cannot compete in unity and intensity with the interest which attaches to the fortunes of the shipwrecked mariner cast upon his own resources, and self-sustained upon the rocky shore of his desolate isle. Another excellence he must forego is that minute analysis and constructive ingenuity of the French school, of which M. Balzac was such a great exemplar, and which consists in the dissection of a passion or relation, and the exhaustion of all its consequences, till the result is worked out and presented like a preparation of morbid anatomy. He must be content to make a sacrifice of points, of construction, contrast, and all the close effects which are barely, indeed, consistent with his object; and, if he attain this object at no greater cost, both he and his audience will have reason to be satisfied.

The question is, have they from this point of view occasion to be satisfied with the *panorama* of Mr. Thackeray? Is it in its main incidents like nature? Does it present a fair and lifelike transcript of the surface of society? If these questions can be answered affirmatively—and we are inclined so to answer them, with certain reservations—then has the writer accomplished a remarkable work. How rich must be the experience which could furnish its materials, and how wide the sweep of arm which could bring them together. In its power and ease we see his maturity; in its fulness the fruits of his previous exertions. He has availed himself, it is true, of his former conceptions with a liberty which was, perhaps, measured by his convenience; but, if he has reproduced and amplified these, it was clearly not for want of other resources. If, indeed, there is any one attribute of a fiction in which the present work surpasses its predecessors, it is assuredly in the number and variety of its characters, in the fertility and even opulent prodigality of its invention.

To render Mr. Thackeray his due in this respect, we should bear in mind that his characters are not mere eccentricities, but the types and symbols of class varieties, though somewhat exaggerated by a sense of fun and humour. It is this which renders them available, like counters, to signify certain values—to be taken up, employed, or put aside at pleasure. They are generalizations as well as portraits, and it is this distinction which makes it remarkable that they should be coined with such profusion; for be it observed that they also bear indubitable marks of individuality, and a Gandish is no more to be confounded with a Smee than Major Pendennis could be mistaken for Colonel Newcome.

Examine Mr. Thackeray's story, and how slight is its construction, yet how numerous are the characters which contribute to its *dénouement!* What a variety even of *groups* it winds through on its way. Commencing in the Clapham vineyard, that Goshen of spiritual grace and worldly prosperity, among awakened clothiers and black footmen, tracts, and seedcake,—what a contrast to this is afforded, for instance, by the Indian miscellany collected in Fitzroy-square, the good Colonel, with his cheroot, Sir Thomas De Boots, James Binnie, and the Mackenzies, down to the snares of Rummun Lal and the fall of the cocoa tree! Miss Ethel, at the instigation of Lady Kew, carries it into the regions of pure fashion to be the sport of the Kews and the Farintoshes, the Dorkings and the Roosters. Now it advances a little by the help of Sir Brian Newcome's wife and invalid children; now it stagnates among the Rudges, Pennifers, and other lions of Mrs. Newcome's scientific *soirées* in Bryanston-square. They use it roughly and vehemently enough at Baden Baden, with the help of the Queen of Scots and her retinue of equivocabilities. But it gathers fresh strength in ranging the Roman studios and carrying its cross to the foot of Vesuvius, whence it returns to set Newcome borough in an uproar, to unseat Mr. Barnes, deprive him of his wife, and to marry poor Clive himself into the clutches of the Campaigner. Concurrently with these events, how many subordinates are affected by its course. Little Miss Honeyman, in her Brighton apartments, the Gandishes, the Ridleys, the Sybarite incumbent of Lady Whittlesea's chapel, the hot-coppered and hilarious 'orphan' F. B., down to the songs in the Cave of Harmony and the Marsala in Sherrick's cellars. Even now we have skipped over the French group—including De Florac, Leonore, &c., and many scenes artistically contrasted, such as those at Grey Friars, of Clive in his youth and the Colonel on his dying bed. It is impossible at a glance to do justice to its extraordinary variety.

Per contra, we could note plenty of minor blemishes, but we don't care to do so with any great emphasis. Rosey, for instance, is too like in conception to Mr. Dickens's Dora. The Campaigner is liable to an imputation of a similar character. Mr. Thackeray occasionally writes slovenly English. He provides what Commodore Trunnion, or some such celebrity, terms 'unnecessary gum' for the Household Brigade.[1]

---

[1] 'Gum' is 'impertinent talk, chatter, "jaw"' (*OED*). The expression is used by Commodore Trunnion in Smollett's *Peregrine Pickle* (1751), ch. xvi.

His so-called hero is weak, and his heroine is worse. She has the further discredit to a heroine of being widely unpopular. But these abatements to Mr. Thackeray's skill as a novelist we account as trivial, and they are nothing in comparison with his happier delineations. Lady Kew outweighs them all, especially in her tournaments with Jack Belsize or the Queen of Scots. Kew and Honeyman are beyond praise; and a page of Florac's English atones for all Mr. Thackeray's abuse of his mother tongue. Last of all, the real hero of his story, Colonel Newcome, is conceived and executed in a spirit that has never been excelled. He is a noble creation, worthy of any age, or of any reputation, present or past. He never bores, or flags, or proses, and notwithstanding the evident care which Mr. Thackeray takes of him, we are solicitous for the great-hearted gentleman to the last; and, when the last does come, and he is discovered in the robes of a poor brother of the Charterhouse, we may say what Scott said of certain scenes in *Clarissa Harlowe*, that 'few, jealous of manly equanimity, should read them for the first time in the presence of society.' Upon the creation of this character Mr. Thackeray may rest his fame.

It would be affectation, after this, not to try him as a writer of fiction by the very highest standard; and, with this view, we have run over the catalogue of names from Fielding, 'the father of the English novel,' to Charles Dickens, its prodigal son. But, for the reasons we have mentioned, the means of comparison fail. We could mark differences without number, but no distinction that we could insist on would indicate the attributes of a genius which is original. We can only suggest the qualities it comprises by glancing as we have done at the nature of its work. We have shown that we regard Mr. Thackeray as a star of superior magnitude, and it only remains to note his chief and important defect, which is, that he fails on the side of imagination. He is always restricted to the domain of pure facts. He has no dreams, no superstititions, no tentative aspirations to the unseen. What he can see, hear, smell, touch, and taste he can describe, and even idealize, but he can go no further than the range of his five senses. His spiritual sense is either wanting or in abeyance, and the 'night side of nature' is entire night to him.

> He hears no voice we cannot hear,
> He sees no hand we cannot see,
> To beckon him away.[1]

Though his brilliancy cannot for a moment be questioned, yet he

[1] A confused version of a stanza from Thomas Tickell's 'Colin and Lucy' (1725).

moves on his orbit in a half eclipse. He has fancy, taste, humour, pathos, philosophy, but of one supreme faculty of genius he is destitute; and this will exclude him from the highest place to which genius might raise him in the world's estimation. But enough will still remain for a classical renown.

We make this admission of Mr. Thackeray's powers as a novelist all the more freely and cordially that we have now to question his teaching. What is the moral which he strives to convey after taking up his parable to this generation? 'Vanity of vanities all is vanity,' is a text fitted for the inspired preacher who is to elevate our thoughts above mortality. It is well for him who can suggest a substitute, who has someting to put in contrast with earthly good, to cry out continually against the foolishness of knowledge, the feebleness of power, and the frivolity of sensual or sentimental affections. But we should remember that Mr. Thackeray is not required to preach, and that he does not attempt it. It is something altogether foreign to his function; and in his position he is not entitled to play at football with our moral confidence. He has nothing, as we said, to offer us in exchange. He mars and distorts our little world without directing us to any other.

Happily, Mr. Thackeray's novels are of that rich and ripe flavour which commends itself to persons of age and experience. They are not crude enough for the youthful palate and the free digestion, or they might deaden and repress some of our early aspirations. It may not be well, as it is, to insist so continually, so searchingly, and emphatically on the selfishness of our nature. If the colour and gradations of the picture were correct they would cast too sombre a hue over the landscape of life; we should doubt and suspect at every turn, and walk on in gloom and apprehension. But there is an antidote to the belief which we have elsewhere characterized as amounting merely to this—that 'nothing is new, nothing is true, and it don't much signify;'[1] and that antidote is supplied by the moral nature of man—that moral nature which is thus calumniated. Motioned by this, man abhors the doctrine, and instinctively reverts to a more generous creed, and if he finds—as experience will find—that the world and some of its fashions are hollow, he knows that a cynical contempt for them is hollower still. Such contempt is at best but a self-delusion. It cannot for a moment sustain itself under question and examination. It betrays its inconsistency—the inconsistency, for example, of Mr. Thackeray, who has taken more pains and written more careful books than almost any

[1] See above, p. 134.

of his contemporaries to convince the world that human pains and human motives are worthless.

It is only fair to Mr. Thackeray to account for this difference between himself and the more cautious and reflecting of his readers. His impressions appear to have been derived from that age which he himself calls 'the old fogeyfied times,' but of which the pretence and selfish worldliness were more than usually prominent. We will not evoke ghosts who have not the graces, to couple with the obloquy, of Meyerbeer's nuns;[1] but there was a time, and that not long past, when the tone of society was the disgrace of England. To the skirts of that society clung certain parasites, especially of a literary class, who were pre-eminent as 'shams.' To them belonged the specious pretexts and affectations and the professed creed that 'no good could come out of Bloomsbury;' and we suspect that Mr. Thackeray, following their trail, remarked the emptiness of their maxims and the tinsel of their fashions. He may have studied nature, even worldly nature, in an inferior school, and may not have been able to rid himself of his impressions. But is society still what society was at that time? Is it as false in its relations and as hollow beneath the surface? For our own part we gladly believe in an improvement of which Mr. Thackeray appears to be still unconscious.

To take for illustration the social distinctions to which he refers with such continual scorn; if social distinctions must exist, when were they less oppressive than now? As compared with the times we mentioned, all ranks and all classes come under the control of public opinion. Not only is there more decency, but there is also, or we greatly mistake, a more immediate and independent appreciation of worth. We try the claims of all men by the best tests in our power, and we sift, as far as we can, their various pretensions. Certain classes may possess an organized influence on public affairs, but exemption from the just judgment of their contemporaries is as rigorously denied to them as to the meanest of their fellow citizens. Society now is more equitable; it has wider plans and loftier objects, and it no longer deserves the censure of the satirist for setting such store upon outside show, and insisting too much upon petty distinctions. We are far enough from social and moral perfection, but we should be ashamed of belonging to this generation if they did not leave the world somewhat better than they found it.

[1] The ghosts of renegade nuns dance in *Robert de Diable* (1831), frequently performed in London.

To return to our commentary. Be the world as empty and worthless as it may, there are two modes of reproving its errors and its vices. There is the spirit of Rasselas and the spirit of Candide. The philosopher and the fool may go through the world from Dan to Beersheba and agree that all is barren. But the fool only will make no suggestion for its culture, and will evince no preference for a better state of things. Mr. Thackeray is no fool, for he is a great humorist, and we only regret that he is not a great moralist also. If he views life in too gloomy a spirit, and sees all its objects, even lisping childhood and buoyant youth, through an atmosphere of regret and saddened experience, he ought not to be far from the lessons which follow. From one who had himself fathomed the 'vanity of human wishes' he may borrow the moral appropriate to his theme:—

> Pour forth his fervours for a healthful mind,
> Obedient passions and a will resigned;
> For love, which scarce collective man can fill;
> For patience, sovereign o'er transmuted ill;
> For faith, that, panting for a happier seat,
> Counts death kind Nature's signal of retreat.
> These goods for man the laws of Heaven ordain;
> These goods He grants who grants the power to gain;
> With these celestial Wisdom calms the mind
> And *makes* the happiness she cannot find.[1]

41. [Whitwell Elwin], from a review in the *Quarterly Review*

September 1855, xcvii, 350–78

Elwin (1816–1900), who became a friend of Thackeray about this time, was a country rector for over fifty years, and a contributor to the *Quarterly Review*, of which he was editor from 1853 to 1860. He edited five volumes of Pope's works (1871–2).

This is Mr. Thackeray's masterpiece, as it is undoubtedly one of the masterpieces of English fiction, if fiction is the proper term to apply to

[1] Johnson, *The Vanity of Human Wishes* (1749), 359–68, slightly misquoted.

the most minute and faithful transcript of actual life which is anywhere to be found. The ordinary resource of novelists is to describe characters under exceptional circumstances, to show them influenced by passions which seldom operate in their excess with each individual, and to make them actors in adventures which in their aggregate happen to few or none. It is the picked passages of existence which they represent, and these again are often magnified and coloured beyond the measure of nature. Mr. Thackeray looks at life under its ordinary aspects, and copies it with a fidelity and artistic skill which are surprising. Men, women, and children talk, act, and think in his pages exactly as they are talking, acting, and thinking at every hour of every day. The same thorns, the majority of them self-planted, are festering in myriads of bosoms; the same false ambition and crooked devices are fermenting in a thousand hearts; the same malice, lying, and slandering in all their grades, petty and great, are issuing from legions of mouths, and the same mixture of kindness and generosity are checking and tempering the evil. You find yourself in the saloon where upon gala days you are a guest; in the house you frequent as a familiar friend; in the club of which you are a member; you meet there your acquaintance, you hear again the conversation which you have often heard before, and it is by no means unlikely that among the assembled company you may be startled by coming upon the very image of yourself. Truth is never sacrificed to piquancy. The characters in *The Newcomes* are not more witty, wise, or farcical than their prototypes; the dull, the insipid, and the foolish, speak according to their own fashion and not with the tongue of the author; the events which befall them are nowhere made exciting at the expense of probability. Just as the stream of life runs on through these volumes, so may it be seen to flow in the world itself by whoever takes up the same position on the bank.

A notion prevails that to keep thus close to reality precludes imagination, as if it was possible to furnish an entire novel—plot, persons, and conversations—exclusively or even mainly from memory. The difference between him who wanders in fancy's maze, and him who stoops to truth,[1] is not that one creates and the other copies, but that the first goes further than nature and the second invents in obedience to its laws. Nor is it necessary to this end that every character should have its living counterpart. The diversities of men and women are

[1] 'That not in Fancy's maze he wander'd long,
But stoop'd to truth, and moraliz'd his song' (Pope, *Epistle to Dr. Arbuthnot* (1735), 340–1).

like the infinite number of substances in the material world, which are made up of a few elementary bodies in varying proportions. In the case of our own kind familiarity with the elements enables the novelist to frame fresh compounds, and the reader to judge of their fidelity to nature. Though we may never have set eyes upon the identical personage, we can pronounce upon his qualities, and determine whether they are separately consistent with truth and in harmony with each other. For all the exactness with which Mr. Thackeray follows life, it will be found that each character is usually in its aggregate an original conception. The range is unusually wide, and from the most noble the Marquis of Farintosh down to little Miss Cann, the humble governess who gives lessons by the hour, the many persons of every degree who compose the miscellaneous group are marked by traits as distinctive as the features of their faces. Some of them appear and re-appear at long intervals, some grow up before the reader, and in all the stages of their progress, and the various attitudes under which they are represented, there is still not a line out of drawing, not a touch out of place. There is always the same individuality, but it is modified by the changes which time and circumstances produce.

> So much the more our carver's excellence,
> Which lets go by some sixteen years.[1]

It is indeed a marvellous perception of truth of character which can thus keep every member of the crowd so continuously faithful to his own nature, a rare tact which, without the least exaggeration, can impart interest to so much which in society is wearying and commonplace as well as to that which is intrinsically winning.

'However the exaltedness of some minds, or rather, as I shrewdly suspect, their insipidity and want of feeling or observation, may make them insensible to these light things, I mean such as characterise and paint nature, yet surely they are as weighty and much more useful than your grave discourses upon the mind, the passions, and what not.' So wrote Gray of the novels, French and English, of his day,[2] but to no work of fiction is the opinion more emphatically applicable than to *The Newcomes*. A writer who depicts life with perfect fidelity, and indulges in no corrupting descriptions of vice, must, whether he

---

[1] *The Winter's Tale*, V, iii, 30–31. And cf. Trollope: 'On the last day of each month recorded, every person in his novel should be a month older than on the first' (*Autobiography* (1883), ch. xii).

[2] In a letter to Richard West, 8 April 1742 (*Correspondence of Thomas Gray*, ed. Toynbee and Whitley (Oxford, 1935), i, 192).

designs it or not, be a powerful moralist. The gloss which men put upon their motives, the meanness, the selfishness, the deceit which they endeavour to hide from the world and from themselves, are as palpable as the actions they have prompted, when the complete transaction is recorded in plain terms, with as little extenuation as malice. What a transparent device is a juggler's trick when the petty mechanism by which he works has been exposed to our gaze! But Mr. Thackeray has not left his moral to be inferred. He has taken care to point it for himself, and to show that he has a direct purpose of exposing the foibles and misdoings which most easily beset mankind. In the days of the *Spectator*, Addison, with exquisite humour, laughed away many of the social follies of his age. Alongside the papers in which his delicate pencil had drawn with such refined satiric touches the weaknesses of beaux, belles, and country squires, were graver essays recommending industry, truth, and cheerfulness. Mr. Thackeray disclaims the assumption of the preacher's office, but in reality, while eschewing all hacknied discourses on virtue and vice, he enforces maxims as serious and as important, as any that are contained in the didactic parts of the *Spectator*, and much more impressive and profound. If he had flourished in the reign of Queen Anne he would have been a celebrated member of the group of wits who furnished such delightful miniatures of life, and such graceful little lectures for the reading public of that generation. He would have dealt out his knowledge of men and manners in fragments, cut his pictures to fit the diminutive frame of a daily sheet, and alternated social sketches with moral admonitions. He would have put Mrs. Hobson Newcome and her *soirées* into one number, and a formal dissertation upon hypocrisy into another. In obedience to the taste of the age, he now writes novels instead of essays, paints a large piece, crowded with figures, instead of a long line of single portraits, and blends together grave and gay, light railleries and stern upbraidings. The censors of Queen Anne's fashionable subjects paid particular attention to externals, to the fopperies of dress and the offences against good breeding; Mr. Thackeray, without neglecting these, goes a vast deal deeper, and in this respect is a more interesting and forcible castigator of the pomps and vanities, the licensed artifices and flagrant trickeries of the world. If the bad are not made good by the lesson, the good will at least be made better. Those who are not too dull or too hardened to learn will rise up from these volumes with an increased scorn of everything ungenerous, sordid, and deceptive, and there is no one so perfect that he will not stumble in his progress upon infirmities which are his own. Even Colonel Newcome himself, if he could have read his history, would have found something to mend.

To reduce what is loathsome and contemptible to its native deformity is only a part of the duty which devolves upon the faithful chronicler of human life. He has to make amiability attractive, and to win sympathy for modest worth. Mr. Thackeray has nobly redeemed in *The Newcomes* the defect alleged against his former novels—that they were more employed in satirising evil than in setting forth excellence. His present production gains by the change. The larger infusion of benevolence, honour, and disinterestedness into the story makes it pleasanter to read, and gives, we think, a juster notion of the world. Though every character he has drawn has undoubtedly its counterpart, —the worthless, the crafty, the insignificant, and the foolish, much as they flourish in particular soils, are not, we will hope, so thick set as a rule as they appear in *Vanity Fair*. Nor probably did Mr. Thackeray intend them to be considered as equitable representatives of the human race any more than he meant Charles Honeyman for an average sample of English divines. A novelist selects the characters which he conceives to be best suited to the turn of his talents, and describes the double-dealing of Tartuffe without the least purpose of impeaching the rectitude of Mr. Abraham Adams.[1] To this we must add, that much as bad and good people are mixed up in the world, and many as are the points at which they come into contact, those who strive for particular objects chiefly associate with the persons through whom they can get what they desire. They avoid the rest and are avoided by them. 'The poor and the deceitful man meet together,' says Solomon; 'the Lord lighteneth both their eyes.' The discrimination, that is to say, with which Providence has endowed them shows each that what he seeks is not to be obtained from the other, and they recognise that their course is by different ways. Thus when Mr. Thackeray undertakes in *Vanity Fair* to follow the black sheep in their wanderings, it is not unnatural that their path should never lie long together with the whiter portion of the flock. Altogether the charge of cynicism, so often urged against him, was always exaggerated, and is now become an anachronism. Some asserted, in spite of a hundred signal and touching proofs to the contrary, that he had no belief in goodness. Others mistook his delicate and often subtle irony for grave injunctions to practise the misdeeds he condemned. With many more, the objection was not the indignant remonstrance of virtue, but the angry cry of vice surprised

[1] Parson Adams in Fielding's *Joseph Andrews* (1742).

in its ambush. People found themselves turned inside out,—their frailties hung as badges about their necks, written upon their backs, pinned upon their sleeves. The natural impulse was to deny the resemblance, and declare the exposure a calumny.

> Fiction holds a double mirror,
> One for truth, and one for error:
> That looks hideous, fierce and frightful:
> This is flattering and delightful;
> That we throw away as foul,
> Sit by this and dress the soul.[1]

Another indictment preferred against Mr. Thackeray is that he encourages the notion that to go certain lengths in sinning is our appointed course, and that it is necessary to wade through polluted streams to get into clear waters. Novelists may fairly, if they please, exercise their fancy in framing beings of ideal perfection, though, contrary to a common opinion, we believe that it requires a stronger effort of genius to represent men and women as they are than as they ought to be. It demands no great knowledge of human nature to personify the virtues. But because a novelist declines this course and depicts the existing world, instead of drawing from its abstract notions of morality, it is a perverse and unwarrantable reading of his intentions to say that he holds up licentiousness for imitation. To state, and state truly, that particular things *have* been, and according to all experience *will* be, is not to maintain that they *must* be,—to assert that they are usual is not to insist that they are inevitable. Mrs. Opie wrote a book called *Illustrations of Lying*, to show how pervading was the vice.[2] Was this to constitute her a patron of falsehood? Far from being obnoxious to the charge which has been made against him, no writer of fiction has surpassed Mr. Thackeray in the force with which he sets forth the beauty of pure hearts, and the contempt which he casts upon everything evil, however gilded by success. It is the very loftiness of his sense of the power of goodness which has sometimes laid him open to misconstruction. An able critic who admires 'good Dobbin with his faithful heart,' asks, 'Why should the Major have splay feet, Mr. Thackeray?'[3] Why should he not? They have the low notions of the rightful supremacy of worth who can only appreciate it when it

---

[1] Source untraced.
[2] *Illustrations of Lying, in all its branches* (1825).
[3] This was Mrs. Oliphant. See above, p. 204.

comes recommended by well-turned feet and a handsome face and figure. He is the true moralist who asserts its superiority over corporeal attributes, and refuses to believe that a virtuous man is less deserving of admiration because his limbs are clumsy, as certain Athenians considered Socrates an object of ridicule because he had prominent eyes, thick lips, and a protuberant belly. But there is another answer to the question. Although there is not an invariable connexion between men's persons and their virtues, it frequently happens that those whose appearance is the least advantageous are remarkable for amiability, from the simple cause that they escape many of the temptations and vanities which beset the well-favoured. If Dobbin had had nothing to keep him humble, if he had been an Apollo or an Adonis, he would probably have ceased to be '*good* Dobbin with his *faithful* heart.' The notion is not peculiar to Mr. Thackeray. No one has had a clearer perception of this truth than the fellow-genius who drew Tom Pinch and Traddles and a score of other examples of uncouth worth. If ever anybody was free from the reproach of attempting to lower the respect for moral excellence through bodily defects, Mr. Thackeray is that man. In his present tale, J. J. Ridley, the most contemptible in appearance, is the one genius of the book. With all his tendency, in fact, to satire, Mr. Thackeray has nowhere employed it in his novels upon improper objects. 'Surely,' says Fielding, 'he has a very ill-framed mind who can look on ugliness, infirmity, or poverty as ridiculous in themselves; but when ugliness aims at the applause of beauty, or lameness endeavours to display its agility, it is then that these unfortunate circumstances, which at first moved our compassion, tend only to raise our mirth.'[1] The author of *The Newcomes* has never forgotten this canon of good taste and good feeling. Calamity, physical and mental, is safe from his lash; he would as soon think of striking a woman. False pretension and imposture, the affectations and the hypocrisies, the duperies and the greediness of life, are his chosen and legitimate prey, and well may the daws with their peacock strut and plumage begin to chatter and scream when a hawk of the Thackeray tribe is with beak and talons plucking them bare.

Mr. Thackeray, beyond all other novelists, loves to comment upon his own text—to stop in his story, indulge in reflections, analyse the motives of his characters, and cross-examine his readers upon their individual propensities. His book is in many parts a discourse upon human nature illustrated by examples. These disquisitions would be

[1] Preface to *Joseph Andrews* (1742).

blemishes if they were not signal beauties; but the skill with which he unravels the complex windings of the heart, the art with which specious and conventional malpractices are shown under their proper aspects, the pensive tenderness of the sentiments, the charm of the composition, has won general admiration for passages which, were they less perfect, would cumber the tale. As it is, there is nothing which could so little be spared. It is by this means that the reader, who is condemning the proceedings of the personages in the story, finds himself unexpectedly accused of a like crime, and the virtuous juror has hardly delivered his verdict before he is dragged to the bar. Ethel Newcome is represented as riding with Clive in a railway carriage to Brighton, under circumstances which the novelist is aware will provoke the censure of rigorists. The minutely described journey is over, and the chapter is ended all but a single question addressed to those austere judges who search for black hairs in the ermine of their neighbours. 'I ask any gentleman and father of a family, when he was immensely smitten with his present wife, Mr. Brown, if he had met her travelling with her maid, in the mail, when there was a vacant place, what would he himself have done?' [Ch. xli.] Thus the mouth of Mr. Brown is perpetually stopped, and he suddenly drops the stone he was about to fling.

Many of these moralisings and reflections are pervaded by a mild and tranquil melancholy, which give them a strong hold upon the heart. Mr. Thackeray has shown himself in a hundred passages of his story a consummate master of genuine pathos. To draw tears is a vulgar art; it can be done by the clumsiest workmen, and the most unnatural fictions, for there are some distresses which always work upon the feelings, and the more morbid and melo-dramatic the scene the larger the tribute of sobs from the idle devourer of romances. Mr. Thackeray's pathos is of a higher and purer kind. By a line, or an allusion, he recalls a train of tender recollections, and stirs up sleeping sadness into life. So delicate is the touch by which he awakens sorrowful emotions, that we are apt to imagine that we alone have entered into his meaning until we learn how many have been affected by the same passage in the same way. In the longer scenes of misfortune and grief his tact never forsakes him; there is a chasteness of description, a skilful and sparing selection of details, a manliness of tone which it would be difficult to overpraise. He knows what to relate, and what simply to indicate; he understands the sacredness of sorrow, and never rends away the veil from weeping faces.

Mr. Thackeray is a humourist, as every writer of fiction must be who takes an extended view of human nature. There are few persons who do not deviate in some particular from common forms or common sense; who are not guilty of some vanity, affectation, whim, or inconsistency, which, however far, perchance, from promoting mirth among those who have to bear with them, are comic in the description. The simple Colonel Newcome, when he fancies himself an adept in the wiles of the world, though, 'if he had lived to be as old as Jahaleel, a boy could still have cheated him;' Mrs. Hobson worshipping rank, and pretending to despise the society she cannot obtain; the airs and cowardice of Barnes; the self-importance and primness of Miss Honeyman, who, instead of feeling ashamed at being a gentlewoman reduced to let lodgings, is proud to be a lodging-house keeper who was once a gentle-woman; the clerical impostures of her bland brother, the French-English of Paul de Florac, and his efforts to personate John Bull; Mr. Gandish insisting upon the indifference to 'igh art' as shown in the neglect of his monster pictures, and talking of the heroic in his vulgar language, afford a hundred examples of the ridiculous. Most of the actors in the Newcomes are tinged with it, but the quality is always in subjection to truth. There is none of the farcical extravagance which calls forth peals of laughter, always easy to be provoked by absurdity and caricature. In Frederick Bayham there is a two-fold source of merriment, for besides the smiles produced by unconscious infirmities, there is a fertile vein of fun in his expedients and vivacity. It is a peculiar charm of the light and pleasant wit which sparkles through the narrative that it never has the air of being studied. It shines forth in a name, an epithet, a parenthesis, in numberless undefinable ways, and always as if it sprung out of the subject, and had not been introduced for the sake of being facetious.

The exception of the work is not below the conception. Mr. Thackeray is deeply imbued with all our best literature. Numerous phrases and fragments of sentences attest his familiarity with the classic authors of his country—a familiarity which is not less surely shown by the perennial flow of his easy and graceful language. There is no appearance of effort, no studied artifice of composition, but neither is there any approach to baldness in the simplicity of his phraseology, or to carelessness in the freedom of his style. The narrative runs on in a rich abundance of strong, idiomatic, sterling English, often applied in a novel and felicitous manner, and sufficiently adorned by occasional metaphors of the same masculine stamp. He even manages to give additional raciness by the not unfrequent use of colloquial vulgarisms. which if they were introduced with less skill would debase his style, It is with reluctance we confess that he has turned language to good account which in all other hands has hitherto revolted every person of cultivated mind, for we fear the evil effects of his example, and are sorry the black patches should heighten the beauty.

'The stories he reads,' says Mr. Thackeray, speaking of the objections urged by the critic, 'and the characters drawn in them, are old sure enough. What stories are new? All types of all characters march through all fables.' [Ch. i.] It may be so; but it is equally certain that these points of resemblance do not necessarily interfere with the claim to originality. It is not, as we have already intimated, the crude passions with which the novelist works that constitute him a copyist, any more than the beauties of Sir Joshua Reynolds can be said to be copied from the virgins of Raphael because both have noses, eyes, and mouths. Colonel Newcome has several leading qualities in common with Uncle Toby—both are soldiers, both simple as children, both overflowing with benevolence—but they differ as widely as did the costume of Marlborough's hero, the cocked hat, Ramillies wig, and scarlet breeches, from the blue swallow-tail coat and duck trousers of the Indian dragoon. Though human nature is always the same, propensities contract a certain individuality from their owner, and are modified in their expression by those accompaniments and manners which are perpetually changing. The world of 'fable-land' will never be exhausted; each generation will supply new materials for the novelist no less than for the historian, and whoever has the cunning to reproduce truly what is passing before his eyes will by that very circumstance be an original writer. In *The Newcomes* we have 'the form and pressure of the very age and body of the time' as regards huge masses of society; and the author not having been forestalled by contemporaries, is safe from the rivalry of predecessors. But more than this, he is, in the whole construction of his story, in his style, in his sentiments, unlike any other novelist; there is not one of whom it is truer to assert that he is a voice and not an echo.[1] Fielding is the genius whom he most nearly resembles—for there is the same manliness, the same fidelity to nature, the same deep and precise knowledge of the mixed motives which influence mankind; but there is little similarity in the application of these qualities, which, if a comparison were instituted, would be found to have produced rather a contrast than a parallel.

[1] Goethe's famous image for the distinction between genius and talent.

Although Mr. Thackeray is not an imitator of others, it has sometimes been objected that he repeats himself. This is a charge which
may be preferred against every master of the craft. What novelist who
has written more than a single great work has not in some degree re-
trodden the circle in which he first walked with success? Is it Fielding,
Richardson, Smollett, or Scott? In truth, it is to complain that genius,
in itself so rare, is not multiplied indefinitely in the same individual,
that a man has one mind instead of fifty, and that a dozen dissimilar
fruits cannot be gathered in successive crops from the same tree.
Those who, ambitious of the praise of variety, have endeavoured
altogether to change their hand, have usually failed in the attempt,
or have been reduced to copy from existing models. The fair test to
apply to each succeeding production of an author is, whether it has
enough of novelty and excellence to give pleasure to the reader, and
make him feel that he would have been a loser by its suppression.
Who, when future generations speak of *Vanity Fair* and *Pendennis* as
we now talk of *Tom Jones* and *Joseph Andrews*, of *Roderick Random* and
Humphry Clinker, would be willing that *The Newcomes* should have
been wanting to the series? Mr. Thackeray sometimes dips his bowl
into the old well; but the new springs he has opened are many in
number, deeper in their source, and the waters that flow from them
more fresh and sparkling. The goad which is applied too freely by
contemporary criticism to abate the pride, or stimulate the flagging
imagination of popular authors, is at any rate not called for in the
present instance. Posterity, which adopts another standard, and
measures rather by depth than superficies, would not be likely to
depreciate Mr. Thackeray even if he had confined himself to far
narrower bounds. Sir Walter Scott had a genius more facile, fertile,
and various than Fielding, but there is nothing so perfect and profound
in the multifarious romances of the author of *Waverley* as the first
half of *Tom Jones;* and by virtue of this superiority of excellence most
would consider that 'the father of the English novel' still retained his
title to be called the greatest of English novelists. Tried by this rule
The Newcomes alone would ensure Mr. Thackeray a lofty pedestal.

There are not many defects in the work to set against its merits.
Rapidity of movement, a throng of incidents, is never a characteristic
of Mr. Thackeray's stories; and such is the interest he excites by the
development of his characters, that we do not usually desire that he
should quicken his pace. Sometimes, however, he lingers too long,
and we are only surprised that in a copious novel, of which the precise

length is fixed at starting, and of which the beginning is given to the world before the middle and end are composed, there should not be more than two or three scenes which have been unduly drawn out to fill their ample frames. A more substantial fault is the part which is assigned to Laura Pendennis—a portrait in itself as true to life as any in the book. There is a pragmatic assumption about her goodness, an air of prudery and self-conceit—the strings by which she leads her pliant husband, who esteems her the more for her pretension—but which render the praises bestowed upon her, and the general confidence reposed in her, somewhat distasteful. Pendennis himself is, to be sure, the ostensible writer, and the admiration he entertains for his wife, and his parade of her virtues before the public, are, as far as he is concerned, consistent traits in his character; but then again we are by no means reconciled to this exhibition of uxorious weakness in the reputed author of the book, who does not even offer the usual apology,— 'though I say it that shouldn't.' In fact, Arthur Pendennis becomes an excrescence. As long as he was kept in the back-ground he was neither an ornament nor a blemish, but when he comes forward as an actor in the story, as well as the narrator of it, we wish him away, and should prefer that Mr. Thackeray would tell his own tale without the unnecessary interposition of an Editor. The advantage of the auto-biographical novel is, that where the hero and the historian are the same, an appearance of reality can be given to events, as may be seen in the *Gulliver* of Swift, and the *History of the Plague*, the *Robinson Crusoe* and *Colonel Jack* of De Foe, which almost amounts to a perfect illusion. But when the bulk of the story is related in the ordinary way, and the auto-biographical method is too sparingly employed to secure any of its benefits, a pretended editor, thrusting himself from time to time upon the notice of the reader, appears an officious and offensive personage. It has the additional drawback that the fictitious author is quite unworthy to hold the pen of the veritable master. However modest it may be in Mr. Thackeray to ascribe his writings to a person of no greater calibre than his very inadequate representative, the incongruity is too glaring, and no one can for an instant bring himself to believe that the intrusive Mr. Pendennis could have written *The Newcomes*.

That there is little plot, in the strict sense of the word, and that little of no very exciting kind, is not to be numbered, in our opinion, among the defects of the tale. To be hurried on in breathless suspense distracts the attention from the merits of style, sentiment, and character, and appeals chiefly to minds which are incapable of appreciating more sterling qualities. Mr. Thackeray has simply been faithful to the instincts of his genius. The true and the probable are his domain, and he intuitively casts aside whatever offends against his theory of his art. Few lives would furnish the outlines of romantic stories, but every person has his hopes and fears, his passions and trials which are unceasingly in play beneath the smooth routine which scarce presents a salient point to the common observer. The merit of the plan can only be fully estimated by those who are aware how much easier it is to imagine marvels than to devise details, which shall be at once unhacknied, attractive, and consistent with the ordinary realities of life. The weak part of the plot is the clumsy and now stale device by which Clive and Ethel are brought together at last. The earliest author, whoever he may be, did not gain in originality what he lost in propriety of design, when to vary the old and approved method by which lovers are carried through tortuous paths and much suffering to the foot of the altar, he involved the hero in a preliminary marriage with somebody who was not the heroine, and afterwards brought in Death to cut the knot it was impossible to untie. The relentless tyrant is not usually so accommodating as to kill off the first wife in time for the much-enduring husband to contract a second marriage with the first love. When the contrivance has not even novelty on its side, it has nothing to recommend it, though we willingly admit that Mr. Thackeray has managed it with his usual skill. In one particular we miss the word of rebuke which nobody knows better how to administer with effect. It is consistent, no doubt, with nature that Clive, finding he had made a mistake in wedding Rosa, should pine after Ethel when it became evident that with a little further patience the prize might have been won. But though there are precedents for the course, they appertain to the evil side of humanity, and we wish that Mr. Thackeray had marked his consciousness of the wrong done to an unoffending girl by the neglect of her husband and the passion he continues to indulge for Miss Newcome. If Clive had not been the hero of the story, we should have inferred the condemnation without its being expressed. When however he is represented as a manly, and, in the main, a worthy fellow, we look for some exception to be made to the almost dastardly abandonment of every attempt to do his duty to the well-meaning puppet he had taken to wife, leaving her harsh mother to jerk the wire at the bidding of her low-minded passions. 'The shoe,' says Mr. Thackeray, 'was a very pretty little shoe, but Clive's foot was too big for it.' He might not the less have attempted to guide the little foot, and kindly helped it to keep step with his own. The one occasion in which this unresisting victim exhibits any emotion is at the close of the history, when a visit from Ethel calls forth those pangs of jealousy which agitate hearts that everything else has ceased to stir. 'Ah me! what a story was there; what an outburst of pent-up feeling! what a passion of pain!' But there are no struggles on the part of Clive, no subsequent remorse to alleviate the selfishness with which he plucked the flower and then flung it aside to wither, because the perfume it yielded was not that which he preferred. Nevertheless we must add Mr. Thackeray's apologetic reflection, which, if it does not altogether absolve his hero, is too good to be omitted.

The little ills of life are the hardest to bear, as we all very well know. What would the possession of a hundred thousand a-year, or fame, and the applause of one's countrymen, or the loveliest and best-beloved woman,—of any glory, and happiness, or good-fortune,—avail to a gentleman, for instance, who was allowed to enjoy them only with the condition of wearing a shoe with a couple of nails or sharp pebbles inside it? All fame and happiness would disappear, and plunge down that shoe. All life would rankle round those little nails. [Ch. lxvi.]

Duration is of more importance than intensity. No ill is great of which the painful effects are brief, none is small of which the irritation is perpetual. To be pricked for a life-time with pins would be worse than a single cut from a sabre, a never-ending tooth-ache than the amputation of a limb.

When we turn from the specks in the story, and they are nothing more, to the group of characters with which Mr. Thackeray has covered his thickly-peopled canvass, we must repeat our admiration at the unerring hand with which they are drawn. The real, though not the nominal hero, is Colonel Newcome. The story begins with his birth and ends with his death, and it is he that is the principal object of interest throughout. He is the very soul of modesty, honour, and benevolence—in every inch an officer and a gentleman. His scorn of everything ungenerous and ignoble gives a rare dignity to his simple nature so happily set off by his old-fashioned courtesy, and we know of no other character in fiction which is at once more thoroughly estimable and thoroughly human. With an expansive kindness of heart he has, what is not always found in company with it, an extraordinary fervour and stability in his individual attachments. Thus his early affection for the daughter of his French master, an *emigré* noble, is never obliterated. As no second object can take her place, it is out of the stock of his general benevolence, and not from love, that he marries in India the forlorn widow of a brother officer. Being unworthy his compassion, she makes him a bad wife; and the sole benefit he derives from a union, happily terminated by her death, is a son upon whom to bestow the overflowing stores of his fond nature. It is for him that the Colonel lives, and returning from India to England, whither the lad has been sent long before, he knows scarce any other pleasure than that which is reflected from the beaming countenance of his boy. The first part of their intercourse has no alloy, but Clive is at an age when a single stride forwards carries him from his constant place at his father's side into the larger companionship of young men like himself. The Colonel now discovers that love does not return upwards with the same force it flows downwards, and that he must be content to possess a divided property in the advancing youth. In this frame of mind he goes back to India to complete his service, his attachment unabated, and still resolved to make the road of life as smooth as a garden-walk to his son, who is left to saunter over Europe, and, since he has chosen to be an artist, to work or play at painting as he will. The Colonel is again in England, having made his fortune by taking shares in a bank, and must now put the crowning-stone to his schemes by marrying Clive, and establishing him in wealth and happiness. As Ethel, the lady of the young man's heart, is not to be had, the Colonel endeavours to bring about a match with Rosa Mackenzie, the niece of an old friend; and to this pretty, insipid girl Clive gives his hand, partly from the apathy produced by the extinction of better hopes, and partly to gratify his doating father. The fabric thus built up proves to be a house of painted cards, gaudy and unsubstantial. The prosperity of Clive is not the natural growth of circumstances; it has been forced upon him by the impatient love of his father, who is irritated when he sees that all his sacrifices and exertions have only resulted in the moodiness and discontent of the object of his idolatry. The history is unfolded with a thousand refined and natural strokes of character, but nothing is more delicately shaded than the picture of the Colonel under the combined influence of his domestic disappointments and worldly grandeur. He is injured in just the degree that so excellent a person would be by riches and fine living; and though the metal remains the same, spots of tarnish begin to show upon its surface. 'If it cannot be said that his new life had changed him, at least it had brought out faults for which there had hitherto been no occasion, and qualities latent before.' In this interlude of his history he stands upon the liberal interest for Newcome out of hostility to his nephew, Sir Barnes, and his nature is admirably developed upon the occasion. He is totally ignorant of politics and has compounded a system out of his feelings. With military loyalty to his sovereign, traditional reverence for the constitution, and benevolent sympathy for the labouring classes, he is a contradictory medley of the high tory and the socialist.

He was for having every man to vote; every poor man to labour short time and get high wages; every poor curate to be paid double or treble; every bishop to be docked of his salary, and dismissed from the House of Lords. But he was a staunch admirer of that assembly, and a supporter of the rights of the crown. He was for sweeping off taxes from the poor, and as money must be raised to carry on government, he opined that the rich should pay. [Ch. lxvii.]

He is preserved from the further effects of the corrupting and confusing atmosphere into which he is plunged by the breaking of the bank, which with a chivalry that scorns all mercantile considerations he refuses to abandon when it is tottering to its fall, and devotes every sixpence he possesses to the attempt to prop it up. The fortune of Rosa is swallowed up in the same gulf; and her penurious, greedy, and despotic mother, has also trusted her accumulations, by the advice of the sanguine Colonel, to the Bundelcund bubble. This coarse, passionate, hardened woman never ceases reproaching the noble-minded old man with her own and her daughter's ruin, and repeatedly tells him to his face that he is a swindler. The Colonel, as we have said, is the soul of honour; he feels an imputation upon it like a wound; to this honour he falls a martyr. Because it was through him that the loss was incurred, he writhes under her invectives, and does not venture to raise a finger to ward off blows which strike him to the dust. In spite of the offers of assistance, and the sympathy of friends, his mind begins to break down under the cruel scourgings of his mean and brutal task-mistress. When he has endured them for a while he finds a new home. Annuities are pressed upon him; doors are thrown wide open to receive him as a life-long guest; but he was educated, and his son after him, at the Cistercian school, or, to call it by its true names, the Charter-house, and he prefers to be appointed one of the 'poor brothers,' and end his race where it began. Like the stag represented in the initial engraving of one of the chapters, he goes to die where he was roused. It was a happy thought to conduct him to this asylum, recommended by old associations, the humility of his nature, the independence which will not permit him to be a burthen to others, and the appropriateness of the place for a wounded and prostrate spirit, unfitted for society and anxious to escape its notice and turmoil. To a superficial eye it might seem a melancholy close to a benignant career, but true nobility is in the mind and not in the trappings external to the man. It is here that his better self gains undivided sway; that, elevated above frivolity and false aspirations, he devotes himself to his prayers, to his Bible, to Heaven. To have been daily more and more leavened by the world, to have had his finest impulses stifled in crowded rooms, to have been drawn deeper and deeper into the whirl of ambition, jealousies, and petty rivalries—this is what would have been melancholy indeed, however encompassed by outward prosperity; and it was impossible for Mr. Thackeray, who discriminates so acutely between what is solid and what is specious, to have committed such treason against his exquisite creation. The solemn parts of his subject are passed gently over with a reverent abstinence. He has not thought fit in a work intended for general amusement to bring religion into a prominence by which the sacred might be profaned by its proximity to the secular, but he has said enough to indicate his opinions and to enable the imagination to fill up the outline. The last days of the Colonel at the Charter-house supply the climax to the moral, which is as plainly stamped upon the Newcomes as the name upon the title-page that all is vanity except goodness and love, that the highest employment of man is the service of his Maker. The concluding scenes are masterly in the extreme; the description of the good man's depth simple and sublime. Fiction affords no more beautiful page.

As Hazlitt was riding in a public conveyance from Paris to Versailles, one of the passengers spoke of the marriage of a couple that morning who had been ten years engaged. A second person remarked that they had at least this advantage, that they were thoroughly acquainted with each other. A third dissented from the conclusion, and shrewdly rejoined that perhaps the wife would appear next day in a different light from what she had ever been seen in the ten years of courtship.[1] The case is common; and Mr. Thackeray has furnished in Mrs. Mackenzie a forcible illustration of it. Her object is to win Colonel Newcome for herself, which she soon discovers to be hopeless, and Clive for her daughter. She appears an active, gay, obliging widow —affectionate to Rosa, and kindly to everybody. In that probationary period she kept her violence to the bedroom, where she boxed her

[1] William Hazlitt, 'On the Knowledge of Character', *Table Talk* (1821–2).

poor girl's ears in secret. The sobbing over, she put her arm about her darling's waist, and led her fondly to the drawing-room, where she talked to the company of her maternal solicitude, and prayed Heaven to provide for the happiness of her dear child, 'who had never known an instant's sorrow.' She has gained her end. Clive is married; Rosa gives birth to a son, and her mother has arrived for the interesting occasion. 'Assuming the command of the household, whilst her daughter kept her sofa, Mrs. Mackenzie had set that establishment into uproar and mutiny. She had offended the butler, outraged the house-keeper, wounded the susceptibilities of the footmen, insulted the doctor, and trampled on the inmost corns of the nurse. It was surprising what a change appeared in the campaigner's conduct, and how little in former days Colonel Newcome had known her.' The power of self-control vanishes with the motive for it; but the mask is not wholly dropped till the family reverses, when she stands revealed a furious scold, a grovelling schemer, an avaricious cheat, who charges her own vices upon probity and honour. ' "What a woman that Mrs. Mackenzie is," cries F. Bayham. "What an infernal tartar and catamaran! She who was so uncommonly smiling and soft spoken, and such a fine woman, by jingo! What puzzles all women are". F. B. sighed, and drowned further reflection in beer.' Who does not remember that maxim of Swift—'The reason why so few marriages are happy is because young ladies spend their time in making nets, not in making cages.'[1] How deep a response must the deceased Captain Mackenzie have sighed if he ever chanced to hear of the pithy saying of the Dean.

The manhood of Clive does not sustain the expectation raised by the description of his early days. He has spirit, truthfulness, the gener-osity of youth, and not a little of the selfishness which grows out of boyish thoughtlessness. His subsequent want of self-control, his inability to cope with the annoyances of his position, or, to say the truth, his entire subjection to them, destroy our respect for him. Ethel, on the contrary, is a charming example of the force of resolute virtue. Mr. Thackeray is not, for the most part, a flattering painter of women. The clever are artful and wicked; the good are insipid. Ethel is a great exception, and has no counterpart in *Vanity Fair* or *Pendennis*. There are three stages in her career, and each is distinguished by the nicest traits of nature. In the first she is a blooming girl, endowed with beauty, talent, and artlessness, and blessed with an independent mind which lifts her above the sordid atmosphere in which she is bred—

[1] *Thoughts on Various Subjects.*

the latent haughtiness of her disposition, softened by her feminine gentleness, and gracefully blending with it. She sympathises with whatever is good, has the instinct to discriminate, the courage to countenance and uphold it. In the second stage she figures under the influence of her match-making grandmother, Lady Kew, in that world of fashion

Where looks are merchandise, and smiles are sold.[1]

Here the admiration she receives, the language she hears, the dazzling attractions of rank and wealth to one so young, coupled with the lessons of her overbearing, satirical, wily chaperon, begin to spoil her. She grows coquettish and wayward; but retains her generous impulses, her proud spirit and indomitable will, and would marry her cousin Clive in spite of angry relatives, if, upon the whole, she did not prefer a nobleman she despised to affection and a commoner. In a word, she yields to the exaggerated importance attached to social distinctions by all who approach her, and commits the crime of becoming no better than her neighbours. Yet as she had too much conscience to act avowedly from the usual motives, she persuades herself that she is chiefly influenced by the desire to obtain a position in which she can promote the interests of her family. There are two events for which the story prepares us—the elopement of the wife of her eldest brother, and her own marriage with Lord Farintosh. The completion of the first tragedy is ingeniously contrived to prevent the second. Ethel is now alarmed by the fatal consequences of mercenary alliances; the opportune death of Lady Kew releases her from the control of that evil genius; she sees the peril and degradation of her course, her subsiding worth regains an immediate ascendancy, and, with the determination inherent in her character, she breaks through the artificial network which had held her in bondage, dismisses Lord Farintosh on the eve of their marriage, and appears under her third and abiding aspect. If a nature like hers has the strength to shake off its toils, it is no half goodness which results. Shame at the past, the necessity to recover her own self-respect, the native nobility of her disposition, unite to make her a pattern of self-denial, and diligence in the discharge of humble duties. When she breaks with Lord Farintosh, she is ignorant of the marriage of Clive. To have lost him through her folly at the moment she was about to welcome his suit is a new source of vexation—the severest of the taxes which she pays for past weakness; but she who has played so long with

1 Johnson, *London* (1738), 180.

the hearts of others surpasses them all in schooling her own; and a more estimable being than Ethel Newcome, when she emerges purified from the stains contracted in her worldly time, cannot well be imagined.

This book will open the eyes of many a girl who is dimly conscious of her position, and lead some, perhaps, to avoid the error of Ethel, or, more difficult still, enable them, like her, to retrace their steps. *The Newcomes*, by precept and example, is designed above all to shame a debasing traffic, which is carried so under so thin a veil that 'a good match' has long ceased to mean anything good in the contracting parties, but stands only for money or station. 'God forbid,' said Lord Kew, when he drew back from his engagement with Miss Newcome, 'that she and I should lead the lives of some folks we know; that Ethel should marry without love, perhaps to fall into it afterwards.' Ill-assorted unions abound in the story; and they flow so naturally out of the circumstances, are so varied and arranged, that there is no appearance of a wish to force a moral by the arbitrary collection of cases, after the fashion which was sometimes practised by Hogarth in his department of art, as when, to aggravate the distresses of his 'Enraged Musician,' he gathers under his window every discordant sound which was scattered throughout the length and breadth of London. Mademoiselle Léonore resigns Thomas Newcome to marry, in obedience to her father, the Comte de Florac, who is older than her father himself. What is begun in duty is carried on in the same spirit to the end. In being a martyr she becomes a saint. By piety, resignation, and the rigorous discharge of every obligation she has contracted, she attains to the peace which the earnest execution of our appointed task never fails to bring. Her meek acceptance of her part, her faithful performance of it, her angelic disposition, and the subdued sadness which hangs about her perpetually—the effect of that old love-wound never healed—are brought out by those ethereal touches in which Mr. Thackeray excels, and which, light and almost incidental as they seem, leave a perfect image upon the mind. Madame de Florac is an example how a wise and worthy woman may make, under disadvantageous circumstances, the happiness she does not find. Colonel Newcome, after his manly fashion, is not behind her, as we have seen, in accommodating himself to his mistaken marriage. Clive, with far better materials at his disposal, and in a kindlier situation, resigns himself to chagrin, and passes the period of his wedded servitude in moaning over his fate. The weak Lady Clara, repelled by a worthless, tyrannical husband, and solicited by the lover her parents obliged her to refuse for the sake of a monied lump of selfishness, suddenly snaps the tie she can endure no longer, and elopes with Lord Highgate. These are the several fruits of the misalliances introduced into *The Newcomes*. Notwithstanding the energy with which he denounces them, Mr. Thackeray reminds us, through the mouths of some of his characters, that love-matches have constantly as unprosperous an issue. But how many of these deluded adorers would have been happy with anybody? The qualities for the purpose are wanting; and whether the marriage was suggested by calculation or passion, the issue would be vexation and strife. If the blind god, at an age when affection is strongest and judgment weakest, misleads some who were worthy of a better lot, the majority of them do but end where the traffickers begin. Because, argue the Lady Kews, there are blanks in the lottery of love, therefore let us ignore love altogether, crush it in young bosoms, compel them to do violence to it, and put all our trust in venal and sordid marriages.

There are many characters in these volumes subsidiary in the space they occupy, or in their action on the main story, which are not inferior in execution to the central figures. Such is Lord Kew, high-minded, unassuming, with a disposition naturally turned to rectitude, flinging aside his youthful vices, and settling down upon his paternal estate, where his virtues and good sense, backed by his station, have a diffusive influence throughout and beyond his domain; an improver of land, a builder of churches and schools, a friend to his tenants, and a benefactor of the poor. Such is the oily Charles Honeyman, a fop vain of his person, who, without truth or seriousness, turns clerical actor, plays his sanctimonious part with sleek hardihood, his doctrines fashioned to the varying hour, a parasitical pastor fawning and fawned upon, and who, notwithstanding Mr. Thackeray's assurance that he has removed to India, still, we fear, preaches at Lady Whittlesea's chapel. Such is Sir Barnes Newcome, a banker on his father's side, and connected on his mother's with the aristocracy, who blends the meanness of a covetous trader with the vulgar insolence of an upstart moving in the outer circle of fashionable society; a bully, who strikes his wife, and turns pale at the cane of Colonel Newcome; a man without a heart or conscience, and whose only check is the fear of being thought a scoundrel by the world, yet a man who believes himself knowing in his generation, who considers life to be a game of selfishness, and who, without supposing himself to be a saint, would be surprised to find what an ugly portrait he made. Such is jovial Frederick Bayham, a large consumer of meats and drinks, a frequenter of all societies where good cheer is on the way, with empty pockets and inexhaustible spirits, a confident presence and rattling vivacity, not over-nice in the methods by which he builds up his own or other people's fortunes, but one of the staunchest and most zealous of friends as well as one of the liveliest of companions. Such is Paul de Florac, a *roué*, with a heart full of kindness and generosity, who comes before us under various phases, the result of new situations and increasing years, and whose attempts, in acts and conversation, to graft the Englishman upon the French stock are a surprising specimen of exact observation and humour. Exceedingly beautiful, too, is his reverence for his religious mother, his deference to her feelings, and his assumption of the out-ward sobriety of dress and deportment which will be most grateful to her solemn and chastened spirit. 'Shall not I,' he says, 'who have caused her to shed so many tears endeavour to dry some?' Rawdon Crawley, with his warm fatherly affections, Harry Foker, with his vivid sense of honour, are questionable characters of the Paul type, and we are half-ashamed of the favour they find in our eyes till we observe that there is a healthy spot in full play in their hearts amid the surrounding contamination, and that it is by this alone that our sympathy is won. . . .

'Happy, harmless fable-land,' exclaims Mr. Thackeray.[1] The fable-land of his creation is more than this. Those who have traversed it leisurely have found it as healthful as it is beguiling, and it is through its more sterling qualities that he has won for his book a loving admira-tion in many a home where genius alone would have been faintly welcomed. It is a proud privilege to have been able, month by month, for nearly two years, to interweave his fictions into the daily existence of his readers, and bring his mimic characters into competition with the living world, till forgetting they were shadows, we have followed their fortunes, and discussed their destinies and conduct as though they had been breathing flesh and blood. 'What a wonderful art!' so we may suppose some future critic of the English humourists to say— 'what an admirable gift of nature was it by which the author of these tales was endowed, and which enabled him to fix our interest, to waken our sympathy, to seize upon our credulity, so that we believe in his people, speculate gravely upon their faults or their excellences, and talk about them as if we had breakfasted with them this morning in their actual drawing-rooms, or should meet them this afternoon in

[1] See above, p. 220.

the Park! What a genius!—what a vigour!—what a bright-eyed intelligence and observation!—what a wholesome hatred for meanness and knavery! What a vast sympathy!—what a cheerfulness!—what a manly relish of life!—what a love of human kind! What a poet is here!—watching, meditating, brooding, creating! What multitudes of truths has that man left behind him! What generations he has taught to laugh wisely and fairly! What scholars he has formed and accustomed to the exercise of thoughtful humour, and the manly play of wit!'[1] Such is Mr. Thackeray's character of Fielding—such to the letter is the character, as a novelist, of the author of *The Newcomes*.

42. [Edward Burne-Jones], from his 'Essay on the Newcomes', *Oxford and Cambridge Magazine*

January 1856, i, 50–60

The magazine was founded by Morris and Burne-Jones. The religious tone of the essay is explained by Burne-Jones's youthful ambition to enter the church.

This last and greatest work of Mr. Thackeray has been completed now some six months, and, in the meantime, has been subjected to both public and private criticism with, I believe, one unvarying judgment of commendation, that he has indeed performed his labour excellently, and done a good work for society in giving us this story of our manner of life so faithfully and tenderly. One looks now, at last, for an escape from that old imputed charge of bitterness and wayward choosing of the evil only in his delineation of life; it was fast becoming meaningless from its very frequency, and I fear also an occasion sometimes for the most pitiful twaddle and conversational hypocrisy. Alas, those brilliant formulas in which we sometimes fold our criticisms and condemnations, and suffer them to pass from mouth to mouth, without question or gainsay, how are they not the cause of infinite injustice to others, and to ourselves of loss irreparable? It is but a little time ago that the

---

[1] From Thackeray's lecture on Hogarth, Smollett and Fielding (*The English Humourists* (1853); *Works*, xiii, 652–3).

name of Thackeray seemed an accepted text *in perpetuum* for gravest homilies upon evil speaking, satire, and slander; and, as if to counteract any latent consciousness of truth, that would be present sometimes, there would follow much self-complacency and congratulation upon our many social virtues and national character; for it is observable that men who will volunteer the most abject confessions of their own shortcomings,—and if self-depreciation were only humility, would afford an example of grace, edifying to all Christendom,—yet do nevertheless betray a strange impatience if their confessions are believed by others and accepted against them; do become, after a marvellous fashion, indignant when their Church confessions of unworthiness are granted by their neighbours as not improbable. Yet, verily, if this our daily humiliation, is not the veriest hypocrisy and climax of our iniquity; if we are not altogether committed to a sham worship, how comes this inconsistency of ours, that we reject our own testimony against ourselves in the mouth of a brother; that we do perseveringly seek to turn into a charge of spleen and sneering against a writer his faithful picturing of an evil we cannot deny, and a life of broken promises we are ever confessing. It is time now to have done with this silly, because untrue assertion that Thackeray gives only the evil that he sees, and gives that bitterly, for now at least he has vindicated for himself a name of truthfulness and widest sympathy unsurpassable; and it is time also for the critic altogether to take up a new position, descend from his seat of judgment to one of testimony; for, although it be well for him at the first appearance of a teacher among men, to prove and examine the spirit from whence it is, administering counsel, and at times correction, blaming gently and not unwisely, remembering that so God has tempered our hearts and intellects together, that wheresoever we render praise it will never be wholly undeserved, but in our condemnation it may be we were ourselves wanting in know-ledge and comprehending sympathy. I say, though it is good for the critic to take his allotted place then, to try every beginning and prove it; yet, when once this is done, and a great creative spirit has become manifest from the trial, then our place also is with the many that look on and listen, our duty to proclaim its honour, rejoice in its light un-selfishly; so only may we hope to understand its teaching, and the symbol of understanding in neither the unbridled tongue nor the supercilious lip, nor the mocking jest, but the hand closed upon the mouth.

Finding, therefore, in this story a wonderfully faithful picture of the great world as it passes daily before us, many-sided, deeply intricate;

finding so much mystery of our manifold human life unfolded, and the veil of its complexity drawn aside, not without deepest awe and veneration; how should we do other than listen reverently, and be thankful for the gift, and speak unlimited praise of it, heeding neither charge of extravagance, nor custom of detraction. . . .

I shall abstain altogether from quotation or digest of the history in *The Newcomes*, both from want of space, and chiefly because, of the unsatisfactory nature of such custom: for the many who have read the book, what has been or shall be said of it, will find at least ready understanding, if not assent; for those who have not such quotations, however selected and voluminous, would convey little idea of my meaning; for those again who read reviews only for the sake of their quotations, (and there are confessedly many such,) I shall warn at once; and for those still more unfortunate knowledge hunters who are satisfied to claim acquaintance with an author through his reviewers and such selections as they may of their bounty give, I extend the same warning—that they must seek elsewhere: even as it is I shall be unable to do more than merely point out the chief moral design of the book, as it seems to me, and even this cursorily; leaving all collateral and minor aims which are manifest throughout, to the reader's own suggestions.

And first of the central purpose of the book for which I imagine it was mainly written, reaching to the very heart and core of social disease, unhappy wedded life—the marriages that are not made in heaven, but if anywhere out of this strange world, why least of all in Heaven. Of all marvels in this same universe that pass our poor philosophy I doubt not this of marriage is the very strangest, seeing to what end it has arrived at last, and from what beginning! Were one to ask the sober question now at this late hour, why was it first ordained, how would he be answered? would it solve the problem we see before us daily? Suppose he should answer to this result—'It was ordained to bear the burden of a great mystery, the secret of the marriage of the Lamb, that we might not be without a continual symbol whereby to comprehend that holy union, that when the Bridegroom came we might know him and receive him worthily.' Mysticism! say you: not so, but forgotten truth. What if it should indeed be found at last that not mere palpable finite evil is the harvest of godless marriages, not broken hearts nor spotted life nor dishonoured children only, but that we have done infinite dishonour and despite to the holy thing it signified? How will it be then? Who shall lay damages and plead and give sentence then? Does that story of Christ's marriage with his people come home to us pure and holy? is there no darkness in our comprehension of the type? If men would learn to believe of all things here that they are but dim revelations of a hidden glory, that every finite thing in this vast universe is linked by ultimate relation to some eternity, is bound indissolubly to the feet of God; that not an act nor law nor visible thing whatever but has its greater counterpart out of space and Time—there would be less mockery and jesting in the world and more earnestness, less doing for fashion's sake and more for Christ's.

The plot of the story teems with marriages that should never have been made, differing in extent of subsequent misery, according to the degree of good or evil natures brought together. There is Madame de Florac, holy, prayerful, self-sacrificing—her life has been a painful vigil; she has been dying daily; hardly after forty years can she say tranquilly, 'when the end comes with its great absolution I shall not be sorry.' How then shall it be with Clive, paired, but not matched with his foolish little wife? she cannot understand him, has no companionship for him; after all our indignation she is perhaps thoughtless more than selfish, or if selfish, capable of transformation; she deserved at least a better fate; yet they might have lived not unhappily, spite of all this. But Clive was not in love with her—loved some one else too surely, and, knowing this, it was an evil step to take—thoughtlessly, carelessly cruel; in the sight of their elders it seemed an excellent match—money and youth, and beauty and amiable indifference— and behold the end! But what shall be said of the marriage in high life? what of the domestic hearth and family bosom of Sir Barnes Newcome, Bart. of Newcome? if the last was sufficiently heart-rending, what shall be said of this? Too truly it is an old story; we have seen it elsewhere also: above all others, one is before me in all the memory of its painted horrors—Hogarth's Marriage à la Mode, which seems its painted counterpart.

It is a subject of regret that the narrow limits of a single essay do not admit of a fuller investigation into these social questions; so shallow and void it seems to name them only and pass on, but it must be so. There is one more great social problem, however, set forth and answered in the lives of the actors of the book, which must share in this hasty sketch—a wofully neglected subject of thought, to the evil results of which oblivion one can place no definite bounds; but in this case I the less regret the brevity of what must be said, because the question, and much more that appertains to it, is embodied in a pamphlet on pre-Raphaelitism, by Ruskin, and continually in other portions of his works, to be hereafter commented on in these pages.

I refer principally to that episode in Clive's life where he makes known to his father the desire of his heart to become a painter, and dedicate his life to that end; and the good Colonel loving his son so that he would gladly die for him, cannot be brought to see it with the eyes of his son. Can understand him adopting it for amusement's sake, refined *dilettantism;* but to be a painter by profession—to live by the labour of his hands so, this he cannot comprehend, this society and immaculate respectability cannot endure. So poor Clive has a hard battle to fight; even Ethel can give him no sympathy, views his dreamland through a London fog. After all our rhapsodies about soul, what do we really sacrifice for it? We, men who have written so many volumes upon it and its immortal nature, who have called it by such high-sounding names for the sake of naming it, though none should ever express it worthily save with lips covered and deep silence, calling it Shekinah, and the articulate voice of God, heard louder than thunder and the voice of waters; sweeter than any wind. And yet for that evil genius Fashion, we could darken this Shekinah, close our ears against that clear-sounding voice for ever. Respectability? When shall we waken from this nightmare and dream of phantoms to a knowledge of the true dignity of work in any kind; to a confession of the majesty of soul in any form? I wish that the primal question at the setting out of life were not *what* is the best thing to do, and the most thought of, but rather *how* and in what manner and degree of excellence it is to be done. I claim at once an express assent to the position, that the work we do we do not for ourselves, nor our own pleasure nor advancement, but in the name of Christ, according to his commandment; and then for our children's sake, that we may make them better, happier; and then for the sake of all who have gone before us, that the travail and sorrow of their hard battle may not be unfruitful, may not become the desolation of wasted energy. It is the only premise upon which I can worthily found the conclusion that our work, whatsoever it be, must be the best of its kind, the noblest we can offer. So the former question frames itself anew: 'What is the best that any man can give?' And God has given us an answer, 'that in which he finds most happiness,' for this testimony he has sealed with truth.

And is this the question, O fathers, that you ask your children, and teach them to ask themselves, 'what they have most happiness in?'—

not transitory, idle pleasure, but enduring happiness; hence what they are most fitted for, what they can do best, what they can honour God most by doing. If this were the first inquiry, and were made the law and final cause in all our choice of action, I think we should meet less and less with those palpable signs of hurry and indifference, and listlessness and utter weariness, which face us at every turn, and paralyse alike art and government, and social relations,—a wide and fruitful subject for after development. Here, unhappily, is room only for hasty notice, and a promise that the question shall be taken up at some future time.

Of Thackeray's manner and style of writing a few words, the characteristics, I conceive, to be principally two, Humour and Pathos, most noble in combination: and first, of his humour, we meet it continually in gentle irony and glancing satire, as well as more directly in his open, laughing cheerfulness: it is for this, chiefly, that he is no favourite with religious parties; being such as they are, we will not regret it too severely: thus at least one agrees with them that it is a hard thing to be laughed at, and thus far with him also, that it is a hard thing not to laugh. Perhaps people differ more about jesting, and its proper conditions of object, manner and place, than about really serious things: this Babel of laughter sadly wants a music-master—one to strike the key-note and lead off the noisy chorus; for people will laugh, and who shall refuse them? 'Laughter is like sunshine,' says Carlyle; only let us keep in memory that story of the Apes by the Dead Sea. Like all else in Babel it lacks a reasonable soul at times, and in want of this will have to be taught roughly its proper whereabouts, lest it trespass upon holy ground; for laughter is not first nor best: love and faith, and hope and long-suffering, and self-sacrifice are raised high above its inarticulate din. For the sake of Him who gave them we will never laugh at these, and because we read not ever that He laughed while dwelling among men; but at whatsoever is mean and proud, and selfish and over-reaching, and hypocritical, laughter long and loud that shall strike the stars.

Sin truly is very foul and fearful; in its effects terrible, crushing the heart of man with overwhelming hopelessness, and oftentimes the terror of wickedness cannot but be uppermost in thought; yet it were a good thing also, and a sign of greater constancy and stronger faith, to feel how utterly contemptible it is, how laughable and ridiculous its miserable existence, and it is here that I imagine Thackeray has done good service to truth of morality and fact:—of morality, because he sets up crime in a kind of pillory for universal laughter and derision: no catastrophe and fearful overtaking of punishment to make his villains martyrs after all; loud laughter only and utter scorn, such as becomes men to feel, for who can calculate the folly of sin? and truth of fact in his account of retributive justice and fidelity to its general fate. His is not that fair land of romance and faërie, where the good are rewarded after sorrows, and the evil punished after short success, but rather the life we live, a fretful, sore, and envious life for many who behold the wicked in high places, and the throne of iniquity set up, and themselves cast out.

Of his pathos what shall I say? so true, so musical, one would not think that human speech were so very musical; it exalts him everywhere into highest poetry; as colour glorifies everything it overlays, so does the great sympathising heart everywhere it comes near and dwells with. In those scenes between the Colonel and his son, chiefly in that one after Clive knows of Ethel's betrothal, and his father's noble offer of sacrifice, and again in the reconciliation at the close of the book; they speak like man to man, in the very simplest words, because of the agony of the hour, but there is sweetest music in every word. And those letters of Madame de Florac, so full of the memory of an ancient sorrow, and a life that has been dying daily, 'One supports the combats of life, but they are long, and one comes from them very wounded: ah! when shall they be over?' Alas! for ill-fated, unforgotten love, colouring all the background of their lives with a melancholy twilight gloom, beautiful, profound: in all story I remember not anywhere the like, from that first parting for life to that last shriek, Léonore, how full is it of the anguish of enduring memory! 'Did it not seem once as if two hands never could unlock, so closely were they enlaced together? ah! mine are old and feeble now; forty years have passed since the time when you used to say that they were young and fair. How well I remember me of every one of those days, though there is a death between me and them, and it is across a grave I review them.' [Ch. liii.] This is like the melody of an old song we have not heard for years, like that burden of the song of tears, 'O death in life! the days that are no more!' Some time we shall meet Clive and Ethel again, and J. J. also, when all the letters and life-passages about him have been collected, and then we shall be admitted to his dream-land; weak, deformed, and silent, he is the genius of them all, the most inspired amongst them; *au revoir*, J. J., it is not for long.

So let us end, not as having completed the half of our task, nor spoken that half well, as became the subject, but withal faithfully.

This book has gone forth now upon a great embassy, gone forth from us into the future, bearing with it the seal and signature of truth; for even while the memory of its sweet pages is yet abiding, and we think upon all these things, the gain, the suffering, and the loss, and all the tumult of our life, even now the days are gathering in and closing upon us, and presently, very shortly, we shall be called the past, and our deeds good or evil will be judged of men in other years. This book also will be a record of us; flesh of our flesh will read it, and see what manner of men their fathers were. Will they speak lovingly, kindly of us, remembering the good to our account, the evil to their own? Will they stretch forth hands of blessing, not remembering the sorrow nor the curse we have handed down to them, so much heavier than we received ourselves, by the weight of all our evil days? Will they forgive us all these things? Is it also our wont so to deal with our fathers' memory, to speak mercifully, gratefully of them? too truly this lack of reverence must go down also in the catalogue of our great sins.

Thackeray will, I doubt not, one day be numbered with the great naturalists in all time, a lesser Shakespeare in golden and coloured chronicles, in a goodly company of painters, poets, and musicians, all who have ever burned with consuming love for men, or struck the key-note of human triumph and lamentation into loud pæans and enduring song. . . .

43. [Henry Theodore Tuckerman], from 'Mr. Thackeray as a Novelist', the *Christian Examiner*

Boston, January 1856, lx, 102–21

Tuckerman (1813–71), critic, essayist and poet, wrote numerous books, notably on travel, art and biography. His article on Thackeray was suggested by the publication in New York of *The Newcomes* in two volumes.

. . . We regard the popularity of Mr. Thackeray's writings as a note-worthy sign of the times. Earlier in the history of the English novel, superiority of execution would not have atoned for such a dearth of sentiment, a piquant social Dunciad could not have taken the place of romantic and impassioned creations, and pleasantry and sarcasm would have been deemed quite inadequate substitutes for heroism, mystery, and adventure. The fact that such writings succeed proves how little the age is attuned to enthusiasm, and how exclusively it seeks amusement; it demonstrates, in a peculiar manner, how entirely the scientific has eclipsed the chivalric era, how cosmopolitan, locomotive, and generalized has become the life and the taste which, prior to steam, telegraphs, and cheap printing, embosomed so much hallowed ground for wonder, ideality, and reverence to construct their unchallenged and endeared shrines. The novelist who can deal best with the familiar, who can make studies of the every-day life of the hour, who can lead his reader a lively dance from scene to scene of metropolitan and Continental experience, and weave a farce or a melodrama, a spectacle or a vaudeville, from the men, women, and facts of to-day, is the public favorite. Knights exist only as effigies on tombs; ghosts hold intercourse with mortals through quite a vulgar mechanical process; gas-light quells 'the palpable obscure'; Cupid has turned broker; war has such vast engines as almost to preclude the display of individual bravery; national, religious, and political zeal is no longer fiercely incarnate, hereditary, and localized so as to furnish ready to the limner's hand pictures and scenes that yield a world of meaning at a glance; handicraft, professional vocations, domesticity,—a uniform tenor reduces human life to the more comfortable but less inspiring level of respectability, insight, and social order; so that, as the Dutch painters found in dikes, tulips, and domestic interiors, compensatory scope for art, the word-painter of our epoch looks keenly about him, and sedulously works up the adjacent material, trusting to mastery of details, vividness of coloring, and skilful exaggeration, to awaken the interest once derived from profound sentiment, marvellous events, and heroic characters. Our social landscape thus assimilates with the natural one familiar to the Lowland artist, and the modern author, like the old Flanders limner, is a kind of Dr. Syntax in search of the picturesque under difficulties.[1] And if the legitimate triumph of modern novel-writing is to amuse without exciting, to substitute crude though keen observation for imaginative power and earnest sentiment, satire for sympathy, the familiar and immediate for the marvellous and the

---

[1] The three 'tours' of Dr. Syntax—verses by William Combe to illustrations by Rowlandson—were published in 1809, 1820 and 1821.

traditional, the conventional for the romantic, the pangs of domestic tyranny for the satisfaction of mutual love, the wilful for the intuitive in woman, and the indifferent for the intrepid in man,—and to do this in a way to command readers, guineas, and praise,—Mr. Thackeray has achieved a signal victory.

The significance of a work is to be estimated by the final impression, the positive tenor, and not according to an arbitrary infusion of mitigating sentiment. Thus Mr. Abbott fails to obviate the glorification of Bonaparte in his so-called Life of that remarkable man, by the occasional insertion of an evasive disclaimer, as, for instance, 'Such are the horrors of war!'[1] And in ascribing to Mr. Thackeray's writings a tone and *morale* which has the effect of a lamentable disenchantment of life, and an unphilosophical exaltation of worldliness as a subject of literary art, we are not insensible to the frequent and clear intermingling of 'glimpses that make us less forlorn.' Ethel's repentance, the Colonel's reconciliation with his son and final resignation and forgiveness, Madame de Florac's constancy and her son's filial love, the benevolent activity of Mr. Pendennis, J. J.'s devotion to Clive, the sweet pathos of Thomas Newcome's exit, and many other soft, humane, and benign episodes, lessen the harshness of the satire, and brighten the record of inanities and violence. But these are exceptions only, and for the most part indifferently conceived. The talent of the Newcomes is reserved for its ironical sketches; the final impression is such as we have described, the actual lesson is not one that exalts or cheers; 'the show of things' is not conformed 'to the desires of the mind,' nor is emotion sublimated by 'terror and pity.' Some of the maxims scattered through the narrative are worthy of Rochefoucauld: 'What a man has to do in society is to assert himself'; 'The pleasure of life is to live with your inferiors'; 'I believe what are called broken hearts are very rare articles indeed'; 'The sarcastic dodge is the best.'

A novel so graphic, spirited, alive to the real, cognizant of fact, and abounding in artistic excellence, is, indeed, a vast improvement upon the intense and the sentimental romance. There is nothing high-flown or maudlin; it is manly in its very tartness; and if unideal and unheroic, it is, at least, neither vapid nor bombastic. What we demur to is its reliability as a picture of English fashionable life, of which it is more properly a caricature; what we regret is, that so well-written and voluminous a book, 'about all the world and a most respectable family

[1] John Stevens Cabot Abbott's *Life of Napoleon Bonaparte* had just been published (New York, 1855).

dwelling in it,' should not enshrine one character we can dwell upon with strong interest and enduring satisfaction; that the good people in it are so weak, the bad so absurd, and that no one of the many *dramatis personæ* seems thoroughly in earnest, except a vixen and a little painter; that filial and parental love was not, if delineated at all, made holy by something like dignified consistency; that the hero was not more of a man, and the heroine more of a woman, so that the reader might honestly sympathize in their affection and their misfortunes. Many of the scenes through which we pass are entertaining, many are instructive, and nearly all well painted; but the actors therein keep us on the lowest range of sympathy; they provoke, amuse, repel, disgust, bore, and pique, and by turns leave us so unable either to love, admire, or hate, that we infer the gist of Mr. Thackeray's satire on modern English society to be, that it yields no character capable of exciting any strong, unmixed, and permanent interest.

It is peculiar to this class of books, that they appeal directly to the sympathies; in fact, the chief benefit to men of grave pursuits, to the care-worn and the elderly, derived from novel-reading, is its vivifying effect upon the sensibilities. Through the fresh delineation of early life, devoted affection, local, traditional, and social charms, the dormant faith in humanity and obscured perspective of time are renewed to the vision and the heart. In the hands of genial artists, patriotic like Scott, ardently intellectual like Madame de Stael, overflowing with humane fellowship like Dickens, this moral refreshment is sure to be imparted through the characters, the scenery, or the incidents of a novel; and it is because this is the legitimate end of fiction, considered as a department of literature, that we are justified in testing the worth of such productions by their companionable qualities. And has not the well-conceived and thoroughly executed romance a positive sphere, like that which defines a family, a clique, or a local society? If so, it may fairly be judged, as we estimate individuals, by the 'spirit they are of.' Now the radical objection to Mr. Thackeray's pictures of life is, that they are utterly devoid of earnestness; he leads us through a routine which is mechanical, outward, and artificial,—one we have more or less tried and found wanting, the memory of which it is wholly undesirable to revive, whose conventionalities are stereotyped, and their relative importance and actual significance in the drama of human existence fixed in the opinion of every man of reflection. We have wasted time enough at dreary banquets, observed the phenomena of balls, realized the folly of the gambler and the heartlessness of the coquette, seen the wickedness of mercenary marriages, recoiled from snobs, hypocrites, and bores, too often to resume our acquaintance with these blots on the scutcheon of social life, in the pages of a book we take up for the very purpose of meeting fellow-creatures of a more satisfactory type. There must, of course, be a sprinkling of the former to give truth to the whole; but Mr. Thackeray makes them the staple of his books. We know people of the order Major Pendennis, Becky Sharp, the Countess of Kew, Barnes Newcome, and the Rev. Charles Honeyman,—people to a degree like them; but we do not seek their intimacy; we feel so repelled by such company that we instinctively avoid it; familiarity therewith would not only breed contempt, but misanthropy, and therefore a slight acquaintance, a passing cognizance, is enough; equally distasteful is the predominance of these hardened incarnations of selfishness, equally acrid the influence of this perpetual atmosphere of wordliness, in a book as in life. Enough meets us in every walk of duty and intercourse to blunt the fine sensibilities, and to deaden the normal faith in human truth and love; in literature, at least, let us find these confirmed or quickened; there let us escape awhile the blight of indifference and the corrosion of scorn; let the inevitable shadows of the social panorama be there redeemed by those exquisite and true compensations of Shakespearian art, whereby the darkest traits and the most hopeless phases of our common destiny are warmed and purified by soulful flashes of tenderness, sacrifice, and aspiration. The power of Mr. Thackeray's characterization is expended on the monsters and the flats; their opposites are depicted in such tame colors as almost to disappear in the background. It is impossible to admire his good women and his pleasant fellows in the same degree with which we detest his *intrigantes*, his cowardly brutes, and his selfish old egotists. The tide of feeling, if it ever rises above the level of mere quiet, cynical amusement, is in the direction of impatience, contempt, and utter distrust of humanity. It is true, the heart warms towards such an epitome of kindness and parental love as Colonel Newcome, and we think Uncle James, Warrington, Fred Bayham, and De Florac good-hearted chaps, as the world goes; but they inspire simply good wishes, and no sentiment comparable in intensity with that which makes us recoil from the shallow, mean, detestable company around and through which they vibrate. But, exclaims an admirer of Thackeray's skill, consider the worldly knowledge, the sifting of human nature, the disrobing of vanity, the exposure of shams, the satire upon modern society, the wholesome irony and caustic truth of these sketches! We do consider them, and in as far as such anatomical preparations serve to unveil the mysterious laws of social health, and probe the diseases of modern English life to the quick, we do recognize and applaud them. Yet let them be rated at their just value, and pass for exactly what they are,—magnified daguerrotypes of a few prominent figures, not representative types of universal application;—the extreme results of club-life, aristocratic folly and egotistical wealth, as seen through the mephitic air of artificial society; not portraits of human nature as it unfolds under the free sky, in the patient struggles of honest toil, amid the pure magnificence of nature, in the battle for truth, beside the hearthstone of domestic happiness, or in communities where honorable enterprise is man's destiny, and respect woman's birthright.

THACKERAY'S ART AND
MORALITY

44. [W. C. Roscoe], from 'W. M. Thackeray, Artist and Moralist', *National Review*

January 1856, ii, 177–213. Reprinted in *Poems and Essays by the late William Caldwell Roscoe*, ed. Hutton, R. H., (1860), ii, 264–308

Roscoe (1823–59), the son of a poet and the grandson of an historian, was called to the bar in 1850. He wrote two tragedies, poems and essays. His general estimate of Thackeray's work was suggested by the publication of *The Newcomes* and the first two volumes of *Miscellanies: Prose and Verse* (1856).

We are not among those who believe that the 'goad of contemporary criticism' has much influence either in 'abating the pride' or stimulating the imagination of authors.[1] The human system assimilates praise, and rejects censure, the latter sometimes very spasmodically. A writer or labourer of any sort rarely profits by criticism on his productions; here and there a very candid man may gather a hint; but for the most part criticism is only used by an author as a test of the good taste of his judge. It is a fiction, in fact, long religiously maintained in the forms of our reviews, that we write for the benefit of the reviewee. In most cases, and at any rate in that of a mature and established author, this didactic figment would be as well put aside. A new work, a body of writings, by a man who has attained a wide audience and produced a considerable impression on his times, constitutes a subject for investigation; we examine it as we do other matters of interest, we analyse, we dissect, we compare notes about it; we estimate its influences; and as man is the most interesting of all studies, we examine what light it throws on the producing mind, and endeavour to penetrate through the work to some insight into the special genius of the writer;

[1] See above, p. 240.

—and all this for our own pleasure and profit, not because we think our remarks will prove beneficial to him who is the subject of them. Mr. Thackeray has outgrown even the big birch-rod of quarterly criticism. A long and industrious apprenticeship to the art of letters has been rewarded by a high place in his profession. He is reaping a deserved harvest of profit and fame; he can afford to smile at censure; and praise comes to him as a tribute rather than an offering. We propose, then, simply to say what we have found in the books we have read, and what light they appear to us to throw upon the genius of the author, more particularly in the two capacities we have indicated in the heading.

As an Artist, he is probably the greatest painter of manners that ever lived. He has an unapproachable quickness, fineness, and width of observation on social habits and characteristics, a memory the most delicate, and a perfectly amazing power of vividly reproducing his experience. It is customary to compare him with Addison and Fielding. He has perhaps not quite such a fine stroke as the former; but the *Spectator* is thin and meagre compared with *Vanity Fair*. Fielding has breadth and vigour incomparably greater; but two of his main excellencies, richness of accessory life and variety of character, fly to the beam when weighed against the same qualities in Thackeray. Fielding takes pride to himself because, retaining the general professional identity, he can draw a distinction between two landladies. Thackeray could make a score stand out—distinct impersonations. It is startling to look at one of his novels, and see with how many people you have been brought into connection. Examine *Pendennis*. It would take a couple of pages merely to catalogue the *dramatis personæ;* every novel brings us into contact with from fifty to a hundred new and perfectly distinct individuals.

When we speak of manners, we of course include men. Manners may be described without men; but it is lifeless, colourless work, unless they are illustrated by individual examples. Still, in painting of manners, as distinguished from painting of character, the men must always be more or less subsidiary to their clothing. Mr. Thackeray tells us of a room hung with 'richly carved gilt frames (with pictures in them).' Such are the works of the social satirist and caricaturist. He puts in his figures as a nucleus for his framework. A man is used to elucidate and illustrate his social environment. This is less the case with Mr. Thackeray than with most artists of the same order. He might almost be said to be characterised among them by the greater use he makes of individual portraiture, as he certainly is by the fertility of his invention. Still, at bottom he is a painter of manners, not of individual men.

The social human heart, man in relation to his kind—that is his subject. His actors are distinct and individual,—truthfully, vigorously, felicitously drawn; masterpieces in their way; but the personal character of each is not the supreme object of interest with the author. It is only a contribution to a larger and more abstract subject of contemplation. Man is his study; but man the social animal, man considered with reference to the experiences, the aims, the affections, that find their field in his intercourse with his fellow-men: never man the individual soul. He never penetrates into the interior, secret, *real* life that every man leads in isolation from his fellows, that chamber of being open only upwards to heaven and downwards to hell. He is wise to abstain; he does well to hold the ground where his preëminence is unapproached,—to be true to his own genius. But this genius is of a lower order than the other. The faculty that deals with and represents the individual soul in its complete relations is higher than that which we have ascribed to Mr. Thackeray. There is a common confusion on this subject. We hear it advanced on the one side, that to penetrate to the hidden centre of character, and draw from thence,—which of course can only be done by imagination,—is higher than to work from the external details which can be gathered by experience and observation; and on the other hand, that it is much easier to have recourse to the imagination than to accumulate stores from a knowledge of actual life,—to draw on the fancy than to reproduce the living scene around us. The answer is not difficult. It is easier, no doubt, to produce faint vague images of character from the imagination than to sketch from the real external manifestations of life before our eyes; and easier to make such shadows pass current, just because they are shadows, and have not, like the others, the realities ready to confront them. But take a higher degree of power, and the scale turns. It is easier to be Ben Jonson, or even Goethe, than Shakspere. In general we may say, that the less elementary the materials of his art-structure, the less imagination does the artist require, and of the less creative kind;—the architect less than the sculptor, the historian less than the poet, the novelist less than the dramatist. Reproducers of social life have generally rather a marshalling than a creative power. And in the plot and conduct of his story Mr. Thackeray does not exhibit more than a very high power of grouping his figures and arranging his incidents; but his best characters are certainly creations, living breathing beings, characteristic not only by certain traits, but by that atmosphere of individuality which only genius can impart. Their distinctive feature and their defect, as we have before stated, is this, that not one of them is complete; each is only so much of an individual as is embraced in a certain abstract whole. We never know any one of them completely, in the way we know ourselves, in the way we imagine others. We know just so much of them as we can gather by an intercourse in society. Mr. Thackeray does not penetrate further; he does not profess to show more. He says openly this is all he knows of them. He relates their behaviour, displays as much of the feelings and the character as the outward demeanour, the actions, the voice, can bear witness to, and no more. It is exactly as if you had met the people in actual life, mixed constantly with them, known them as we know our most intimate friends. Of course this is all we can *know* of a man; but not all we can imagine, not all the artist can, if he chooses, convey to us. We don't know our nearest friends; we are always dependent on our imagination. From the imperfect materials that observation and sympathy can furnish we construct a whole of our own, more or less conformable to the reality according to our opportunities of knowledge, and with more or less completeness and distinctness according to our imaginative faculty; and every man, of course, is something really different from that which every man around him conceives him to be. But without this imaginative conception we should not know one another at all, we should only have disconnected hints of contemporary existence.

It is perhaps the highest distinguishing prerogative of poetry or fiction, or whatever we choose as the most comprehensive name for that art which has language for its medium, that it gives the artist the power of delineating the actual interior life and individual character of a living soul. It is the only art that does so. The dramatist and the novelist have the power of imagining a complete character, and of presenting before you their conception of it; and the more complete this is, and the more unmistakably they can impress you with the idea of it in its fullness and in its most secret depths, the nearer they attain to the perfection of their art. Thackeray leaves the reader to his own imagination. He gives no clues to his character, as such; he is not leading to an image of his own. He probably has a very distinct, but no complete conception of them himself; he knows no more of them than he tells us. He is interested more in the external exhibitions of character and the feelings than in character itself; his aim is not to reproduce any single nature, but the image that the whole phenomenon of social life has left impressed on his mind. . . .

Individual character, however, is the deeper and more interesting study; and the writings prompted by genius which delights more in the habits and qualities and casual self-delineations of man than in man himself, always disappoint us by our half-acquaintance with the personages of the story. As for the subsidiary middle-distance people, this matters little. We know as much as we wish to do of Sir Pitt Crawley, of Lord Steyne, of the Major, of Jack Belsize, of Mrs. Hobson Newcome, of Mrs. Mackenzie; but how glad should we be to see more into the real heart of Major Dobbin, of Becky, even of Osborne, of Warrington, of Laura! Even of shallow and worldly Pendennis, how partial and limited, how merely external, is our conception! What do we know really of the Colonel, beyond that atmosphere of kindliness and honesty which surrounds one of the most delightful creations poets ever drew? But why complain? Distinctness and completeness of conception are two qualities divided among artists; to one this, to the other that; rarely, perhaps never, has any single man been gifted with a large measure of both. If Mr. Thackeray's genius is not of the very highest order, it is the very highest of its kind. The vividness, the accuracy of his delineation goes far to compensate for a certain want of deeper insight. Let us be grateful for what he gives us, rather than grumble because it is not more. Let us take him as that which he is—a daguerreotypist of the world about us. He is great in costume, in minutiæ too great; he leans too much on them; his figures are to Shakspere's what Madame Tussaud's wax-works are to the Elgin Marbles—they are exact figures from modern life, and the resemblance is effected somewhat too much by the aid of externals; but there is a matchless sharpness, an elaborateness and finish of detail and circumstantiality about his creations. He has an art peculiarly his own of reproducing every-day language with just enough additional sparkle or humour or pathos of his own to make it piquant and entertaining without losing *vraisemblance*. His handling of his subject, his execution, are so skilful and masterly, that they for ever hold the attention alive. He takes a commonplace and makes a novelty of it, as a potter makes a jug out of a lump of clay by turning it around in his hands; he tells you page after page of ordinary incident with the freshness of a perennial spring. He is master of the dramatic method which has of late preponderated so much over the narrative. Perhaps the greatest attraction of his writings consists in the wonderful appropriateness of the

language and sentiments he puts into the mouths of his various characters; and he not only makes them express themselves, but he manages,
without any loss of dramatic propriety, to heighten the tone so as to
give some charm or other to what every one says; and not only this,
but with an ease which veils consummate dexterity, he makes these
dramatic speeches carry on the action and even convey the author's
private innuendo. He has no scruple about this. He alters a woman's
thought just enough to make it the vehicle for a sarcasm of his own.

On this the two ladies went through the osculatory ceremony which they
were in the habit of performing, and Mrs. Pendennis got a great secret comfort
from the little quarrel, for Laura's confession seemed to say: 'That girl can
never be a wife for Pen, for she is light-minded and heartless, and quite unworthy of *our noble hero*. He will be sure to find out her unworthiness for his
own part, and then he will be saved from this flighty creature and awake out
of his delusion.' [*Pendennis*, ch. xxiv. Roscoe's italics.]

If the power of producing the impression of reality were the test
of the highest creative power, Thackeray would perhaps rank higher
than any one who has ever lived,—higher than Defoe. But Thackeray's
mode of creating an impression of reality is more complicated than
Defoe's. It is not that simple act of force by which the latter identifies
himself with his hero. It arises in great measure from his way of knitting
his narrative on at every point to some link of our every-day experience. His fiction is like a net, every mesh of which has a connecting
knot with actual life. Many novelists have a world of their own
which they inhabit. Thackeray thrusts his characters in among the
moving every-day world in which we live. We don't say they are
life-like characters; they are mere people. We feel them to be near us,
and that we may meet them any day. Dickens creates a race of beings
united to us by common sympathies and affections, endeared to us by
certain qualities, and infinitely amusing in their eccentricities. Still,
we all know perfectly well they are not really human beings; though
they are enough so for his purpose and ours. No one supposes that
Carker ever really rode on that bay horse of his to the city with those
shining teeth; that Traddles' hair really had power to force open a
pocket-book. We know that the trial of Bardell *v.* Pickwick is an
imaginary contribution to our judicial records, and that Edith Dombey
exists only in highflown language and the exigencies of melodrama.
But the Major frequents Bond Street, Mrs. Hobson Newcome's virtue
is a thing of this life and of London, and it is but one step from question-
ing the existence of Becky's finished little house in Curzon Street to

admitting the philosophy of Berkeley. All artists have an ultimate aim which shapes their working. Miss Brontë wishes to depict marked character; Dickens bends himself to elicit the humorous element in things; Bulwer supposes that he has a philosophy to develop; Disraeli sets himself to be himself admired. Thackeray only desires to be a mirror, to give a true but a brilliant reflection; his vision is warped, no doubt, by peculiarities of his own, but his aim is to reproduce the world as he sees it.

His conception of a story is, like his conception of a character, incomplete. There is no reason why he should begin where he does, no reason why he should end at all. He cuts a square out of life, just as much as he wants, and sends it to Bradbury and Evans.[1] In *Vanity Fair* and *Pendennis* the characters are at large, and might at any moment be gathered in to a conclusion. *The Newcomes* begins with the history of Clive's grandfather, and the reasons are independent of art which cause it to conclude before the death of his grandchildren. This, however, is little more than a technical shortcoming, and in all that belongs to execution he shows a mastery that almost makes us think he has some secret peculiar power, so effortless is his brilliancy, so easy his touch. His tale is like a landscape growing under the instinctive rather than conscious hand of a master.

The novelist who draws the external life of men is subject to this disadvantage: he is more dependent on his experience than the one who makes individual character his end. It is true, we apprehend, that a poet can, by the force of imagination, and the excitement of particular parts of his nature so as to produce temporary identification, create a character which he has never seen. Goethe bears witness to the fact in his own case. He tells us he drew in his youth characters of which he had no experience, and the truthfulness of which was justified by his mature observation. His evidence is peculiarly valuable, both because no man estimated observation more highly, and because his great skill in it would enable him to apply an adequate test to the accuracy of the delineations which he speaks of as springing ready-formed from the resources of his own nature. Of course, even granting that a man could be entirely independent of observation in his conception of a character, he would still require it in order to find a field for the display of that conception; and the more knowledge he commands, the better can he develop his idea. Less, however, will suffice for such an artist than for one who works like Thackeray or Fielding. These are absolutely

[1] Thackeray's publishers. See above, p. 130.

bounded by the limits of their observation, and consequently in constant danger of self-repetition. Mr. Thackeray is remarkable rather for his exhaustless ingenuity in making the most of the knowledge he possesses than for any very wide range. His fertility becomes the more remarkable when we survey the resources on which he draws. His field is not an extensive one. He stands on the debateable land between the aristocracy and the middle classes—that is his favourite position—and he has evidently observed this form of life mainly from dining-rooms and drawing-rooms. He surveys mankind from the club-room and from country-houses; he has seen soldiers chiefly at mess-dinners; is not familiar with lawyers, though he is with the Temple; has seen a good deal of a painter's life, and must of course have had a considerable knowledge of the professional world of letters, though he is shy of profiting by this experience. He is not at home in provincial life in England, especially town-life, nor has he any extensive acquaintance with the feelings and habits of the lower classes. His knowledge of men about town is profound, exhaustive; his acquaintance among footmen vast. He may have more materials in store; but he begins to indicate a check in the extent of his resources. We know the *carte du pays* pretty well now, and have a notion where the boundary fence runs. The extraordinary thing is the immense variety of the surface within it.

There is one direction, however, in which Mr. Thackeray's resources have always been remarkably limited. It is curious how independent he is of thought; how he manages to exist so entirely on the surface of things. Perhaps he is the better observer of manners because he never cares to penetrate below them. He never refers to a principle, or elucidates a rule of action. There is a total absence in his books of what we usually call ideas. In this respect Thackeray is as inferior to Fielding, as in some others we cannot help thinking him superior. Fielding, you cannot help seeing as you read, was a reflecting man; you feel that his writings are backed by a body of thought, though it is far from an intrusive element in them. De Foe always leaves the impression of an active, vigorous intellect. The force of Thackeray's writings is derived from the strength of his feelings; great genius he has, and general vigour of mind, but not the *intellectus cogitabundus*. Read his charming and eloquent Lectures on the Humorists. You would suppose that thought would ooze out there if any where; but there is no trace of it. He simply states his impressions about the men; and when he speaks of their personal characters, every deference is to be paid to the conception of one who has so sensitive an apprehension of the distinguishing traits of various natures. We are far from wishing for a change in the method of the book; we believe the sort of quiet meditative way in which Mr. Thackeray touches and feels about and probes these men is more valuable and instructive than any elaborate reasonings on them would be, and infinitely better calculated to convey just impressions of what they really were like. But the omission of thought is not the less a characteristic feature; and on one of the pages, where a note of Coleridge is appended to Thackeray's estimate of Sterne, it is curious to see two such utterly opposite modes of approaching a subject brought into juxtaposition. Thackeray never reasons, he never gains one step by deduction; he relies on his instincts, he appeals to the witness within us; he makes his statement, and leaves it to find its own way to the conviction of his readers; either it approves itself to you, and you accept it; or it does not, and you leave it. The highest moral truths have been thus enunciated, perhaps can only be thus enunciated; but Mr. Thackeray does not enunciate great truths. The most he does is to generalise on his social observation. He is not absolutely destitute of some of those distilled results of a wide knowledge of men which properly come under the head of wisdom; but they are very disproportioned to the extent and penetration of his perception. He occupies a good deal of space in half-meditative, half-emotional harangues on the phenomena of life. Where these do not immediately deal with the affections, they owe their novelty and value to their form alone; and it would not be difficult to enumerate his chief ideas, and count how often they occur. He impresses on us very constantly that 'the Peerage' is the upas-book of English society; that our servants sit in judgment on us below stairs; that good wages make a better nurse than love; that bankers marry earls' daughters, and *vice versâ;* that the pangs of disappointed passion stop short of death; that no man making a schedule of his debts ever included them all. We need not go through the list; and trite as such sayings seem when stripped bare for enumeration, the author for ever invests them with some fresh charm of expression or illustration, which goes far to preserve them from becoming wearisome. It is with the feelings and the affections that Mr. Thackeray is at home. They supply with him the place of reasoning power. Hence he penetrates deeper into the characters of women than of men. He has never drawn, nor can he ever draw, a man of strong convictions or thoughtful mind; and even in women he deals almost exclusively with the instinctive and emotional side of their nature.

This feature gives a certain thinness and superficiality to Mr. Thackeray's works. He nowhere leaves the mark of a thinker. Even his insight is keen and delicate rather than profound. But his deep and tender feeling makes him sensitive to those suggestions which occupy the boundary land between the affections and the intellect, the country of vain regrets and tender memories, of chastened hopes and softened sadness, the harvest-field in every human soul of love and death. The voice of Mr. Thackeray's tenderness is at once sweet and manly; and when he will allow us to feel sure he is not sneering at himself, its tone is not unworthy to speak to the most sacred recesses of the heart. Is there in the range of fiction any thing more touching than the conception which took the shattered heart of the old Colonel to rest among the pensioners of Grey Friars?

Mr. Thackeray's pathos is good; but his humour is better, more original, more searching. He never rests in the simply ludicrous or absurd. Irony is the essence of his wit. His books are one strain of it. He plays with his own characters. In the simplest things they say the author himself gets a quiet backstroke at them. It is not enough for him to depict a man ridiculous, he makes him himself expose his own absurdities, and gathers a zest from the unconsciousness with which he does so. He treats his *dramatis personæ* as if he were playing off real men. His wit is not a plaything, but a weapon, and must cut something wherever it falls; it may be a good-natured blow, but it must touch some one. He never fences against the wall. His satire is most bitter when he is most cool. He is skilful in the management of sneer and innuendo, and can strike a heavy blow with a light weapon. For his broadest absurdities he chooses the form of burlesque, and then he likes to have a definite something to parody. He is one who does not laugh at his own story. It is not often he makes his reader laugh; but he can do it if he will. Foker is the best of his more laughable creations. In general he is grave, composed, even sad, but he is never uninterested in the personal adventures he is engaged in narrating; his sympathies are always keenly alive, though often he prefers to conceal how they are enlisted. At bottom he has a warm, almost a passionate interest in his own creations. They are realities to him as to the rest of the world.

His peculiar powers must tempt him to personality, but in any open form of it he does not now indulge. The early days of *Blackwood* and *Fraser* are gone by. There was a time, however, when he gave 'Sawedwadgeorgeearllittnbulwig' a very severe, though not ungenerous shaking; and when himself attacked by *The Times* he turned and bit fiercely and sharply.[1] He is apt to wear the forms of his wit to tatters. Jeames, with his peculiar dialect, in the *Yellowplush Papers* and elsewhere, was entertaining and instructive, but has been allowed to grow wearisome. Orthographical absurdity is an exhaustible subject of merriment, and Mr. Thackeray's wit is somewhat too much dependent on his nice appreciation of distinctions of pronunciation, and the slavish subserviency he compels from the art of spelling. He can mimic in print as well or better than Dickens. His sense of humour differs from that of the latter, however, in being almost exclusively called forth by the peculiarities of persons themselves or personal relations. He very rarely is struck with the ludicrous in things alone, as Dickens often is; his description of Costigan's hairbrush, as 'a wonderful and ancient piece,' stands almost by itself; he rarely even makes fun out of a man's personal appearance, except so far as his dress or air indicate some mental trait or characteristic. The mode of his caricaturing, too, is quite different. Dickens collects all the absurdities and laughter-moving elements in a thing, and heaps them together in a new image of his own. Thackeray pictures the thing as it is, only bringing out its ludicrous or contemptible features into sharp relief.

His genius does not lead him to the poetic form; he has just that command of verse which one would expect from a man of his great ability; he can make an able use of it, and his power of language gives him great command of rhyme and sufficient facility. . . .

His sense of beauty is warm and lively. If he had as much of the negative sense of good taste which discards the ugly and jarring elements as he has of the positive sense which detects and appreciates the beautiful, his works would be far pleasanter reading. He sees beauty everywhere; his love of it mingles with the affectionateness of his nature, and throws a softening grace over his pages, relieving a bitterness which without it would sometimes be scarcely sufferable. . . .

Of his bad taste his works furnish only too abundant evidence. It was a happy idea to look at society from the footman's point of view; but a very little of that sort of fun suffices. And Mr. Thackeray does not scruple to surfeit us. We have rough Warrington's excellent authority for the assertion, that 'Mrs. Flanagan the laundress, and Betty the housemaid, are not the company a gentleman should choose for permanent association;' and we are not surprised at that 'most igstrorinary' burst of indignation with which Jeames's career draws to its close in the *Yellowplush Papers*.

[1] See the biographical note on Samuel Phillips, above, p. 129.

The advantage of using such a mouthpiece, if it be an advantage, is this, that it gives an opportunity of saying things more vulgar, biting, and personal, than a man's self-respect or shame would allow him to say out of his own mouth. It is a *quasi* shifting of the responsibility. But if we give Sheridan credit for his wit, we must give Thackeray credit for his vulgarity. This feature greatly disfigures his works, and shows itself not only in the gusto and ease with which he enters into the soul of a footman, but in a love of searching out and bringing into prominent view the more petty and ignoble sides of all things. We don't quarrel with a humorist for exposing the vulgar element in a vulgar man, and in taking all the fun he can out of it. Self-delineative dramatic vulgarity, used in moderation, is one of the fairest and readiest sources of laughter. What we quarrel with is vulgarity in the tone of the work; a charge for which it is not very easy to cite chapter and verse, as it is a thing which is felt by the instinct rather than detected by observation; but we will adduce one instance of the sort of thing we allude to. In the first volume of *The Newcomes* we are told how Warrington and Pendennis gave a little entertainment at the Temple, including among their guests little Rosey and her mother. It is a very pleasant charming picture, and the narrator speaks of the 'merry songs and kind faces,' the 'happy old dingy chambers illuminated by youthful sunshine.' What unhappy prompting, then, makes him drop this blot on his description: 'I may say, without false modesty, that our little entertainment was most successful. The champagne was iced to a nicety. The ladies did not perceive *that our landress, Mrs. Flanagan, was intoxicated very early in the afternoon.*' And before the end of the description we are not spared another allusion to 'Mrs. Flanagan in a state of excitement.' It is vulgar, surely, to mar the pure and pleasant impression of the scene with this image of the drunken laundress not only introduced, but insisted on. [Ch. xxiii; Roscoe's italics.]

Not from false taste, but from something deeper,—a warp in the very substance of his genius,—arises another unwelcome characteristic. *Vanity Fair* is the name, not of one, but of all Mr. Thackeray's books. The disappointment that waits upon human desires, whether in their fulfilment or their destruction, the emptiness of worldly things, the frailty of the affections, the sternness of fate, the hopelessness of endeavour, *vanitas vanitatum,*—these are his themes. The impression left by his books is that of weariness; the stimulants uphold you while you read; and then comes just such a reaction as if you had really mingled closely in the great world with no hopes or ambitions outside it; you feel the dust in your throat, the din and the babbling echo in your ears. Art may touch the deepest sources of passion: awe and grief and almost terror are as much within her province as laughter and calm; she may shake the heart, and leave it quivering with emotions whose intensity partakes of pain; but to make it unsatisfied, restless, anxious,—this is not her province. To steep it in the turmoil, the harass, the perpetual shortcomings of actual life, may possibly be sometimes permissible. But this must only be for a brief period—it is a very exceptional source of excitement; and to drop the curtain and leave the mind jaded with small discontents, perplexed with unsolved difficulties, and saddened with the shortcomings of fruition,—this is to be false to the high and soothing influences of Art, and to misuse the power she gives. Those old story-books show a deeper sense of her true province who marry a couple and tell us they lived happily till they died, than Mr. Thackeray, who cannot forbear from turning over one more page to show us the long-beloved and hardly-won Amelia scarcely sufficing to her husband, and who brings back the noble-hearted Laura to teach us that she cannot escape the consequences to her own demeanour and character of having married a man so far inferior to herself.

As a Moralist, Mr. Thackeray's philosophy might be called a religious stoicism rooted in fatalism. The stoicism is patient and manly, kindly though melancholy. It is not a hardened endurance of adverse fate, so much as an unexamining inactive submission to the divine will. . . .

His fatalism is connected with a strong sense of the powerlessness of the human will. He is a profound sceptic. Not a sceptic in religious conviction, or one who ignores devotional feeling,—far from it; but a sceptic of principles, of human will, of the power in man to ascertain his duties or direct his aims. He believes in God *out of the world*. He loves to represent man as tossing on the wild sea, driven to and fro by wind and waves, landing now on some shining fortunate isle, where the affections find happy rest, and now driven forth again into the night and storm; consoled and strengthened now and then by the bright gleams above him; dexterous with his helm to avoid or conquer the adverse elements; but destitute of all knowledge of navigation, and with no port to steer for and no compass to guide his course. Pleasure, he tells you, may and perhaps should be plucked while you are young; but he warns you that the zest will fail; he warns you that gratified ambition will taste like ashes in the mouth that fame is a delusion, that the affections, the sole good of life, are often helpless under the foot of adverse fortune, and neither so powerful nor so permanent as we dream; and he can only recommend you to enjoy honestly, to suffer bravely, and to wear a patient face. He speaks to you as one fellow-subject to another of the Prince of this world. He has no call to set things right, no prompting to examine into the remedy. His vocation is to show the time as it is, and especially where it is out of joint. His philosophy is to accept men and things as they are.

He is a very remarkable instance of the mode in which the force of the intellect affects the moral nature and convictions. We apprehend he never asked 'why?' in his life, except perhaps to prove to another that he had no because. With a very strong sense of the obligation of moral truthfulness, and the profoundest respect for, and sympathy with, simplicity and straightforwardness of character, he has no interest in intellectual conclusions. He would never have felt sufficient interest to ask with Pilate, 'What is truth?' Always occupied with moral symptoms, intently observing men, and deeply interested in their various modes of meeting the perplexities of life, he never attempts to decide a moral question. He rarely discusses one at all; and when he does so, he is studiously careful to avoid throwing his weight into either scale. Elsewhere ready enough to show in his proper person, he here shrinks anxiously out of sight. Sometimes he warns you expressly he will not be responsible for what he is putting into the mouth of one of his characters; or more often he treats the subject like a shuttlecock, raps it to and fro between two dramatic disputants, and lets it fall in the middle for those to pick up who list.

From this form of mind springs, in great measure, that scepticism to which we have alluded. A writer can scarcely help being sceptical who sees all sides of a question, but has gathered no principles to help him to choose among them; who has no guiding rules to which to refer, and whose instincts alone prevent the field of his conscience from being an absolute chaos. Only by these instincts he tests the characters of men and the propriety of actions; and wherever they alone can serve as guides, they do so faithfully, for in him they are honest and noble. . . .

He professes to paint human life; and he who does so, and who does not base his conception on that religious substructure which alone makes it other than shreds of flying dreams, is an incomplete artist and a false moralist. And Mr. Thackeray cannot be sheltered behind the assertion that a fitting reverence precludes the intermingling of religious ideas with light literature,—first, because what we ask for does not demand a constant presence of the religious element on the surface, or indeed that it should appear there at all,—only that the spirit of the work and the picture of life should recognise it as at the foundation, or even only not utterly lose sight of it as a fundamental element in the conception of this world; and secondly, because he does not scruple (and fitly, we think) reverently to introduce the topic of religion, and to picture a humble spirit looking upwards for consolation and support;—because, while he includes the *sentiment*, he excludes the *realities* of religion, and has no place for those aspirations of the higher life, only to form the field for which was this world he deals with created.

And this further quarrel we have with Mr. Thackeray's picture— that he gives a worldly view of the world; that through sarcasm and satire there shines every where a real undue appreciation of worldly things—most, of those things which he is most bitter against—money and rank; and above all, a debasing sensitiveness to the opinion of those around us, apart from any regard for them and independently of any respect for their judgment. He reads as if he had a consciousness in himself of too great an appreciation of these things, against which his moral indignation is always in arms, and to which his honesty compels him to give expression; as if the bitterness of his jests were founded on that temper the poet speaks of—

> Out of that mood was born
> Self-scorn, and then laughter at that self-scorn.[1]

Otherwise, by what strange distortion can a man of Mr. Thackeray's mind and heart have allowed himself to become absorbed in the contemplation of meanness and false shame, and the world's low worship of mere worldly advantages? How can he have permitted so unpleasant a subject to grow on him till it has become the atmosphere of his thoughts? As Swift rakes in dirt, so Thackeray in meanness. He loves to anatomise its every form, to waylay and detect it at every corner, to turn it inside out, to descant on it, to conjugate it. He sees English society worshipping a golden and titled calf, and he angrily dashes down the image; but that is not enough; he grinds it to powder, and mingles it in every draught he gives us. We know there are these things in the world; but the question is, whether an author is well employed in constantly forcing them on our attention. All will agree that the less a man can be affected by them the better; we know these meannesses and basenesses are in our own natures; but the true way to

[1] A misquotation from Tennyson's 'The Palace of Art' (1833).

deal with them is, looking upwards, to tread them under foot, not to go scraping about with our noses to the ground and taking credit for our humility and honesty when we lay them bare. . . .

Some of Mr. Thackeray's lesser works are pervaded throughout with a genial kindly spirit; such are the History of Mr. Samuel Titmarsh and the Great Hoggarty Diamond (which it is pleasant to hear is a favourite with the author), and The Kickleburys on the Rhine, Dr. Birch's School, &c. In these, foibles are pleasantly touched with cheerful happy raillery, and a light, gay, yet searching tone of ridicule, and a tender pleasing pathos, pervade the story: 'the air nimbly and sweetly recommends itself;' the wit plays freshly and brightly, like the sun glittering through the green leaves on the wood-paths. But in the mass of his works the tendencies we have before spoken of give a dark and unpleasing ground to the whole picture; and on it he draws in strong black and white. His general view of English society is a very low and unrelieved one. It is a true but a strictly one-sided representation, selected partly for its amusing elements, partly from an unhappy idiosyncrasy of the author. An opposite picture might be drawn as flattering as this is satirical; and neither, of course, would be complete. On this stage move many figures fair and dark. The author's skill by no means forsakes him when he chooses to draw upon our love and admiration: Dobbin and Amelia, Warrington and Laura, and Helen; Lady Esmond, Colonel Newcome, and the sweet, placid, tear-worn, but somewhat shadowy image of Madame de Florac, rise up at once before the mind. But he puts such characters apart; they shine like glowworms, brightly, but with no influence in the surrounding darkness. They are in his world, but scarcely of it; they are never allowed to leaven his general conception of society. A lump of sugar here and there cannot soften the bitterness of the whole cake. It would be unjust, perhaps, to say that his genius is more at home in his darker portraitures; but they certainly gain an undue significance, if only from this, that they are always represented in their proper sphere of activity, where their whole cleverness and energy is brought into light; whereas his fairer characters are invariably those whose excellence consists in the goodness of their instincts and emotions, and, with the single exception of Colonel Esmond, no external field of any interest is found for them to occupy. It is unfortunate, too, that Mr. Thackeray finds the main sources of wit and amusement in the most close connection with some form of vice or wickedness. How often is his laughter spun out of baseness, and crime, and misery! Degrading selfishness, heathen worldliness, abandoned honour, broken oaths, dice, drunkenness, every form of viciousness but one are made the subjects of sparkling satire, witty jests, the universal charity of mockery, and scorn tempered by scepticism. The company of bad men and women in the world is not elevating. How can they be elevating made amusing in books? The 'terrible death-chant of the contrite chimney-sweep,' in which Sam Hall conveys the lesson of his example, enforced by maledictions, has a grim humour about it true enough,—might almost be said to be a work of genius; but we don't take our daughters to hear it sung.[1] Wickedness has its funny side; but it grates on our ears to hear English ladies talking as they do sometimes of 'that charming wicked little Becky.' We don't say that a vicious or even a degraded nature is not a fit subject for the artist,—no doubt it is; we do not say it is an unfit subject even for comedy; but we do say it ought not to be comically treated. We do maintain that there is a sin against good taste and right moral influence in mingling too intimately real vice and the ridiculous; they may be alternated, but not mixed, still less almost chemically combined, after Mr. Thackeray's fashion. You sap the force of moral resentment when, by smiling raillery or farcical laughter, you make tolerable the stern realities of sin. We know no book with so repulsive a contrast between the broad farce, almost buffoonery, of its form, and the hideous and utterly unrelieved baseness and wickedness of its subject-matter, as is exhibited in the history of 'Mr. Deuceace,' told in the characteristic orthography of 'Jeames.' Mr. Thackeray has in his heart an eager hatred of baseness and hypocrisy. It bursts out unmistakably sometimes. It is hidden, no doubt, under all his air of persiflage; but it is part of his art to preserve a mask of neutrality; and an occasional protest has no weight against the tone of universal toleration, and the bantering mood which shakes these glittering sparks of wit out of the devil's devices. Sin is fire; and Mr. Thackeray makes fireworks of it. . . .

As a set-off against these unpleasing elements in Mr. Thackeray's writings, there is one whole side of his genius which casts a pure and pleasant sunshine over his pages. He has a heart as deep and kind as ever wrote itself in fiction. His feelings are warm and impetuous, his nature honest, truthful, honourable. Against cruelty, against baseness, against treachery, his indignation flames out quick and sudden, like a scorching fire. With what is manly, frank, and noble, he has a native inborn

[1] One Ross was famous for singing this song about Sam Hall, a chimney-sweep condemned to death, who hurls bitter defiance at the world.

sympathy. If his sense of the ludicrous, and his wit, are too often nourished upon wickedness and depravity, he is familiar with another and truer connection, and has an exquisite felicity and moving power in the mingling of humour and pathos. If his works as a whole want purpose and depth, and clearness of moral conviction, if they accept sin simply as part of what is, instead of as a departure from what should be, yet they preach throughout lessons of example more telling than precept, and contain many and many a passage well fitted to stir the spirit and to move the heart. If his wicked and mean creations are too predominant and too detailed, he has some at least whose great goodness and white purity relieve by fair gleams the dark and clouded landscape. They are emotional characters: but are not these the very ones which practically take the strongest hold on our affections; and the errors of impulse those which, however long the preacher may preach, we shall always the most readily excuse? Who ever painted a manly generous boy with so free and loving a pencil as the author of *Dr. Birch's School*, of Champion Major, and of young Clive Newcome? Who else has that fine touch that can picture us so delicately and so clearly the fresh innocence of girlhood, the tender passion of a loving woman, or the absorbing devotion of a mother? Who can trace in firmer strokes fidelity and courage and temperate endurance in a man? In every page, alternating with bitterness, and sometimes an unsparing cruelty of sarcasm, there shines out a kindly affectionate nature, soft compassion, and humble reverence. It is as if Mr. Thackeray's nature, like his writings, were full of strongly-contrasted elements, lying closely side by side. Whatever his defects,—and they are great,—he must always take his stand as one of the masters of English fiction; inferior to Fielding, because he wants his breadth and range, the freeness of his air, and the soundness of his moral healthfulness; but his rival in accuracy of insight and vigour of imagination; and perhaps, as we have before said, more than his rival in fertility. And since Fielding's time, though characters have been drawn more complete than any one of Mr. Thackeray's, no fiction has been written in the school to which his imagination belongs which can bear a moment's comparison with *Vanity Fair*. This is hitherto his masterpiece, and will probably always remain so. There is a *vis* in it greater than in any of his other works—the lines are more sharply, deeply cut, the whole more marked with the signs of special and peculiar genius. Our pleasure in it alternates vividly with dislike—almost repulsion; but our admiration is compelled by all parts of it, and our eagerest sympathy by some. Dobbin and Amelia will always remain living inmates of the English mind. They have both of them, Amelia especially, had much injustice done them by their author; but as their images lie longer in our breasts, and we meditate upon them, the sneers and innuendoes fade away, and we see them undefaced, and recognise that Dobbin's devotion was not selfishness, and Amelia's characteristic tenderness not weakness. Just as with living people small obscurations and accidents fall away, and we estimate the whole character better in absence, so it is with these: we know them better, and love them more trustfully in memory than on the actual page. Thackeray's genius is in many respects not unlike that of Goethe; and such another woman as Amelia has not been drawn since Margaret in *Faust*.

Of his other great works, *Pendennis* is the richest in character and incident, and the least pleasing; *The Newcomes* the most humane, but less vigorous and concentrated than any of the others; *Esmond*—the later parts at least—by far the best and noblest. We have no temptation to discuss the merits of its imitative style and scenery, observing only that though a modern mind shines through the external coat, yet probably no other man could have gathered so many minute and characteristic indicia of the times of which he writes, and so artfully have blended them together. It is as a tale we look at it; and though to most men such a subject, so treated, would have afforded more than ordinary temptations to an overloading of character with costume and external detail, with Mr. Thackeray the reverse is the case. He is freed from his devotion to the petty satire of modern conventions, and has fewer calls for the exercise of small contempts. The main characters, Esmond, his Mistress, and Beatrix, are the ablest he has drawn; they are not less vivid than his others, and more complete. Esmond is strong, vigorous, noble, finely executed as well as conceived, and his weakness springs from the strength of a generous and impulsive nature. He is no exception to the observation that Mr. Thackeray never endows a hero with principles of action. Esmond is true to persons, not to ideas of right or duty. His virtue is fidelity, not conscientiousness. Beatrix is perhaps the finest picture of splendid, lustrous, physical beauty ever given to the world. It shines down every woman that poet or painter ever drew. Helen of Greece,

> Fairer than the evening air
> Clad in the beauty of a thousand stars,[1]

is the only one who approaches her. And both her character and that

[1] Marlowe, *Doctor Faustus* (c. 1592), from 'Was this the face . . .'

of her mother are masterpieces of poetical insight; the latter blemished, however, here and there with the author's unconquerable hankering to lay his finger on a blot. He must search it out, and give it at least its due blackness. He will not leave you to gather that it must be there,—he parades it to the day, and presses it to your reluctant eyes. It comes partly from the truthfulness of his nature, which cannot bear that a weakness should be concealed, and partly probably from a mistaken apprehension of the truth that the artist must be true to nature. There was a time when a good deal of parade was made and some very diluted philosophy spun out of the distinction between 'the true' and 'the real.' But this simple fact there is, that a man may be true to nature and yet depart from all her manifested forms; and that it is a higher striving to be faithful to such an inborn conception than to mutilate and distort it for the sake of finding room in it for certain observed facts. Mr. Thackeray sometimes does this, oftener he does what is quite as unpleasing. When in a character, especially a woman's, he comes upon a defect, he does not allow it to speak itself, or show itself naturally, and sink with its own proper significance into the reader's mind. He rushes in as author, seizes on it, and holds it up with sadness or triumph: 'See,' he says, 'this is what you find in the best women.' Thus he gives it an undue importance and vividness, and troubles and distorts the true impression of the whole character.

In the same spirit he lays hold of the petty dishonesties and shams of social life. Almost all these have their origin in vanity, and in its hasty and habitual gratification the meanness of the devices is overlooked, at any rate not often wilfully adopted with a consciousness of its presence. Such contrivances are follies of a bad kind; but to stigmatise them as deliberate hypocrisies is to give a very false significance to the worst ingredient in them.

In *The Newcomes* 'the elements are kindlier mixed' than in any of the other fictions; there is a great softening of tone; a larger predominance is given to feeling over sarcasm. As before, the book is a transcript from life; but the life is more pleasantly selected, and the baser ingredients not scattered with so lavish a hand. If the execution be somewhat inferior, as perhaps it is, the characters of Clive and Ethel less clearly and vividly defined than we have by long use to high excellence begun to think we have a right to expect they should be, and the former unattractive in his feebleness; if the journey through the story be rather *langweilig*, sometimes from over-detail, sometimes from long and superficial moralisings over the sins of society,—yet there is much to reconcile us to these shortcomings in exchange, in some greater respite from the accustomed sneer. We have said before that the genius of Thackeray has many analogies to that of Goethe. He is like him, not only in his mode of depicting characters as they live, instead of reproducing their depths and entirety from the conception of a penetrative imagination, but also in his patient and tolerant acceptance of all existing phenomena, and his shrinking not merely from moral judgment but from moral estimate. The avoidance of the former springs in Thackeray from kindly feeling, from the just and humble sense we all should have that our own demerits make it unseemly for us to ascend the judgment-chair, and from a wide appreciation of the variety and obscurity of men's real motives of action; the latter, a very different thing, springs from this same wide insight, which makes the task more than ordinarily difficult,—especially to an intellect not framed to take pleasure in general conclusions,—and from his imagination being one which does not naturally conceive in separate wholes, and most of all from an insufficient sense of the duty incumbent on us all to form determinate estimates of the characters and moral incidents around us, if only to form the landmarks and bearings for our own conduct in life. These features remain in the *Newcomes*. There is the same want of ballasting thought, the same see-saw between cynicism and sentiment, the same suspension of moral judgment. The indignant impulse prompts the lash, and the hand at once delivers it, while the mind hangs back, doubts its justice, and sums up after execution with an appeal to our charity on the score of the undecipherable motives of human action, the heart's universal power of self-deception, and the urgency of fate and circumstance.

THE VIRGINIANS

1857–9

---

45. [Goldwin Smith], from a review in the *Edinburgh Review*

October 1859, cx, 438–53

Smith (1823–1910) was a classical scholar, a controversial writer on education and politics, a contributor to various periodicals (notably the *Saturday Review*), and Regius Professor of Modern History at Oxford from 1858 to 1866.

. . . To write a novel, laying the scene in a past age, and preserving the character of that age, is indeed a Herculean task. It requires a double effort of the imagination, the difficulty of which is a great deal more than double that of the single effort. To accomplish it successfully, the imaginative faculty must, as it were, be raised to the second power. First, the writer has to present to himself vividly the age he seeks to depict, to place himself mentally in it, and see everything as it was in that age; and, secondly, he has to create imaginary characters, and throw himself into them in the way necessary to give imaginary characters consistency and life. You may almost count on your fingers the men who have been able to do either of these things separately, and to do them both together is, we believe, a feat of which there is no example. Besides, the necessity of preserving antiquarian correctness must keep the critical judgment of the writer always in a state of vigilance incompatible with the intense and unshackled exertion of the creative imagination. How can even a Thackeray live, think, speak, and move in the creatures of his fancy, when he has at the same time to be asking himself whether every thought, speech, motion, and each of the surrounding circumstances, is in accordance with what we know of the lives of men of fashion, soldiers, and play writers of the time of George II?

There is, indeed, a kind of *antiquarian* rather than historical novel, which can scarcely be named in connexion with Mr. Thackeray's works, but which is sometimes successful in its small way. We mean such books as Bekker's *Charicles and Gallus*, where the sole object is to 'cram' us with antiquities, and the characters and incidents are only so many pegs whereon the contents of Adams and Potter may be hung.[1] Such novels are to be classed, not with works of imagination, but with historical games and geographic puzzles and the other *miscuit utile dulci*[2] devices for learning easily what perhaps is as easily forgotten. There is also that to which the name 'historical novel' is most strictly applicable; the novel in which the main action and the principal characters are historical, the details and subordinate personages, and perhaps some slight under-plot, alone being fictitious. This class can scarcely be called a legitimate species of composition, being in effect, not a novel but a loose kind of history, the outline of which is filled in with imaginary details, and which is to that extent false in fact; besides being generally perverted by some historical crotchet or prejudice, the free indulgence of which is apt to be, in truth, the leading object of the writer. It is, in a word, history written with the licence of fiction, an unsound kind of production and dangerous to the integrity of historic truth.

But *The Virginians* is neither antiquarian nor, in the strict sense, historical. It is an attempt to create a good story and good characters, and at the same time to call from its grave a past age, in which the writer happens, probably from his admiration and deep study of Fielding, to take a great interest. 'I have drawn the figures as I fancied they were; set down conversations as I think I might have heard them; and so, to the best of my ability, endeavoured to revivify the bygone times and people.' We can easily enter into the feeling which prompts the attempt. But we suspect that the pensive pleasure of brooding over the past, which Mr. Thackeray, and not he alone, desires to clothe with a tangible form and communicate to others, is in fact an intellectual sensation eluding expression, and incapable of being communicated otherwise than by just touching the chord which vibrates to it in our hearts. It is like the sensation felt in looking at the sea, and susceptible only of the same kind of embodiment.

---

[1] Immanuel Bekker (1785–1871) was a German classical scholar and novelist. Francis Adams (1796–1861) was a classical scholar and lexicographer. John Potter's *Archaeologia Graeca; or, the Antiquities of Greece* (1697–9) remained a standard reference book till well into the nineteenth century.

[2] Horace, *De Arte Poetica*, 343. '. . . Who has mingled usefulness and pleasure.'

Break, break, break
On thy cold grey stones, O Sea !
And I would that my tongue could utter
The thoughts that arise in me.[1]

The natural way of giving vent to a feeling of interest in a bygone time, and making others partake it, is to write a history of the time. And why should not Mr. Thackeray write a history of any time in which he feels interest? He possesses some of the highest qualities for such a task, provided the period he chooses be one in which individual character and action, rather than great movements or principles, would be the main subjects of description. His narratives of Marlborough's battles and his sketches of the characters of Marlborough and St. John in *Esmond* are excellent in their way, and his knowledge of the period of English history between the Restoration and the revolutionary war must be very great. Let him think of this if his mine of pure fiction is for the present somewhat exhausted, as the recurrence of old characters and incidents rather indicates, and as it may well be, considering what store of rare metal he has dug from it. He should remember that he is already Fielding's superior in fertility as well as his rival in excellence.

In this hybrid sort of composition, between history and fiction, we confess we think his powers misapplied. It is at best an expenditure of strength in a *tour de force*. The 'bygone time,' however skilfully 'revivified,' is bygone, and touches us, especially those of us who are not well read in history, far less than the time in which we live. Mr. Tennyson has chosen the remotest age of chivalry for the scene of his *Idylls of the King*. Milton had looked at the legends of Arthur, when casting about for a subject for his Epic, and, as it seems to us, with true poetic instinct, had rejected them, and chosen instead a great religious subject, of all times and of none, and the nearest of all subjects to the heart of his own generation. We desire to see in the hero of a novel our own ideal, as the Greek saw his own ideal in the heroes of the *Iliad* and the *Odyssey*, as the Knight of the Middle Ages saw his own ideal in the heroes of chivalrous romance; and we shall not be easily affected by the artificial reproduction of an ideal which is not ours. The living interest of the *Idylls of the King* is, in truth, produced by the blending of entirely modern ideas and sentiments incongruously, however beautifully, with the names and actions of the chivalry of the Round Table; as may be clearly seen, for instance, in 'Vivien,' where the dialogue between

[1] Tennyson, first stanza of 'Break, break, break' (1842).

Vivien and Merlin is impregnated with the spirit, not of the age of chivalry, but of the age of Goethe. If our age had ceased to afford good matter for narrative poetry or for novels, it would be a sign that narrative poetry and novels had reached the limit of their allotted reign, and that the time had arrived when the play of human imagination was about, Proteus-like, to assume another form. And if the value of an antiquarian novel is less than that of a living picture of ourselves to our own age, what will it be to posterity? What would be the value of Fielding to us, if instead of painting the squires and parsons of the pig-tail age, he had chosen to paint the Tudor court, or even the Round-heads and Cavaliers? He would be a sort of Chatterton of novelists, and lie with Chatterton on the shelf. And such is the fate which Mr. Thackeray must expect for *Esmond*, and *The Virginians*, compared with *Vanity Fair*, *Pendennis*, and *The Newcomes*. We would not have posterity too much considered. There is a good deal of affectation in writing as well as in acting for posterity. 'What glitters,' (says the poet in the prologue to *Faust*,) 'is born for the moment; what is genuine remains unlost to posterity.' 'If I could hear no more about posterity!' replies *Merryman*. 'Suppose I chose to talk about posterity, who then would make fun for contemporaries? *That* they will have, and ought to have it.' But the fact is, the claims of contemporaries and posterity coincide. The best fun for both is a lively picture of the humourist's own time.

And then, if a bygone time is to be exhumed, and a Thackeray is to be employed in the task, is the social epoch of the early Georges the one of all others peculiarly worth exhumation? Is it not rather the epoch which of all others might be most advantageously left to its repose? The general character of that epoch, perhaps, cannot be regar-ded as having been yet absolutely fixed. Lord Stanhope seems some-times inclined to consider it an Augustan Age, while Mr. Massey treats it as an unredeemed abyss of all moral, social, legal, political, and ecclesiastical evil.[1] That there *must* have been some good in it, with all its faults, is to us clear: or the nation could never have had the moral and spiritual energy to reform itself, and win its way back, as it happily has done, to better things. That there *was* some good in it is evident not only from the bright characters, the Chathams, Wolfes, Wesleys, Butlers, Johnsons, Berkeleys and Howards, which it produced; but

[1] The fifth Earl Stanhope (1805–75) wrote several historical works, including a *History of England, from the Peace of Utrecht* (1836–54). William Nathaniel Massey (1809–81) wrote *A History of England during the Reign of George the Third* (1855–63).

still more from the respect and affection these characters commanded among the people. A nation cannot be utterly depraved when patriotism, pure genius, religious and philanthropic heroism, however rare, are the objects of popular affection. The fact seems to be that, as Berkeley in his *Minute Philosopher* [1732] intimates, the upper classes were the worst, the corruption not having spread, at least in its most virulent form, to the middle and lower. The middle and lower classes thrust aside the political sharpers and caballers and bore Chatham on their shoulders to dictatorial power. The middle and lower classes received the religion which Wesley and Whitfield offered to their social superiors in vain. But as to the high society of the time, which is the society depicted in *The Virginians*, there can be no manner of doubt that it was profligate, frivolous, sensual, heartless, and atheistical in the highest degree. There intervened, in fact, between the great political and religious movement of puritanism and constitutional liberty which ended in 1688, and the equally great political and religious movement which commenced with 1789, one of those slack tides of opinion and principle, in which the surface at least of the waters is sure to become putrescent, and to produce noisome creatures. As in the dreadful calm in *The Ancient Mariner*,—

> The very deep did rot: O Christ!
> That ever this should be!
> Yea, slimy things did crawl with legs
> Upon the slimy sea.
>
> About, about, in reel and rout,
> The death-fires danced at night;
> The water, like a witch's oils,
> Burnt green, and blue, and white.

Certainly the Ancient Mariner saw nothing among the 'slimy things' and the 'death-fires' of his 'rotting deep' more diabolical than the orgies of Medmenham Abbey.[1] But we are not, like the Ancient Mariner, under a fatal necessity of repeating the story, much less of making fictitious additions to it.

The grand objection to revivifying the social era depicted in *The Virginians*, is that it has never died; it has been perpetuated for us by immortal artists. Those whose portraits you are laboriously endeavouring to paint after death from faint reminiscences, have already sat in life to great masters, beside whose breathing likeness yours will show

---

[1] Organized by Sir Francis Dashwood (1708–81).

like the shadow of a shade. Fielding, Smollett, Richardson, Hogarth, have already done that which the author of *The Virginians* undertakes to do; and they have done it with a truth, breadth, freedom, on which morality and decency forbid their imitator to venture in our age. Mr. Thackeray's hand is perpetually checked by moral considerations, and his picture is therefore timid and incomplete. He does not venture to introduce, but only to allude to, the gallantries which play so great a part in Fielding and Smollett, as they did in the evil life of those times. He has a hundred ingenious devices for denoting without actually expressing the blasphemies with which the fine gentlemen he is describing gave point and force to their conversation. That he should feel this necessary does honour to his sense of morality and religion and to that of the public for which he writes, but it spoils him as a novelist of the last century. He seems himself half conscious of the impossibility of his task. He owns that *Tom Jones, Clarissa, Roderick Random*, or *Peregrine Pickle*, would not be tolerated now, and even that it is to the credit of the age that they would not be tolerated; though he makes this last admission with reluctance, and not without wafting a sigh to the frank and masculine morality of Fielding. 'A hundred years ago,' he says, of a low drunkard and debauchee, 'his character and actions might have been described at length by the painter of manners; but the Comic Muse now-a-days does not lift up Molly Seagrim's curtain; she only indicates the presence of some one behind it, and passes on primly, with expressions of horror and a fan before her eyes.' If the Comic Muse now-a-days cannot lift Molly Seagrim's curtain, would it not be more discreet in her to avoid a subject for her art of which the lifting of Molly Seagrim's curtain is a principal portion?[1] Besides, we doubt whether the indicating the presence of some one behind the curtain is much less dangerous than the lifting it, as far as the effect on morality is concerned. The *pueri virginesque* who would not be allowed to read *Tom Jones* or *Roderick Random*, but who may be allowed to read *The Virginians*, are very likely to get a notion that what is funny behind the curtain would hardly be very vicious, though it might be rather shocking, before it. The grossness of a hundred years ago is grossness undisguised. It stands in its naked deformity. We look at it as a thing of the past, and thank heaven that it is past. But when it is reproduced under a gauze veil by a contemporary author, both the naked repulsiveness and the purifying effect of distance are removed. However, if we are right in these remarks, the

[1] Molly Seagrim is in Fielding's *Tom Jones* (1749).

fault lies wholly in the subject chosen, not in the intention of the author. England in our day may regard it as some proof of her moral soundness that her greatest novelist is in all his sentiments and sympathies the deadly enemy of hypocrisy, but the constant friend of virtue.

Of the plot of *The Virginians* we have only to say what the topographer said of the snakes in Iceland. There is none. There is only a string of incidents woven together, serving for the delineation of character and the expression of sentiment, carried on through the legitimate twenty-four numbers, and capable of being carried on *ad libitum*, or cut short at any earlier point if it had so pleased the author. We know Mr. Thackeray does this habitually and on principle; and we do not wish to be guilty of the ungracious platitude of quarrelling with one good thing for not being another. But it must be owned that a well-conducted plot is a pleasant thing; and that a story without a story wants a principal element of itself. It is the plot that prevents us from being too conscious of the art exercised in the delineation of characters, or exerting our critical faculties too keenly on the characters delineated. By the absence of a plot, the whole weight is thrown on the character-painting, and our critical acumen is always kept awake to observe whether the painting is correct. Of incident we have enough in *The Virginians*. It is necessarily contrived somewhat after the fashion of the antiquarian novels to which we have above referred, with the view of taking us the round of all the social habits and circumstances of the age. The resurrection of George after his supposed death is a little common, and his sudden appearance in England without any previous notice to his brother, struck us as rather unnatural. The facility with which people of quality are arrested for debt also appears to us exaggerated, though it shows us the sponging-house, one of the most characteristic institutions of the time. But the task of inventing incidents at once natural and surprising is so difficult that we must not be hypercritical in judging of the result. . . .

Besides these imaginary characters, however, a number of historical personages are introduced in *The Virginians*. Almost all the persons of note of the time, royal, political, ecclesiastical, social, and literary, are made to pass over the stage, and some take a considerable part in the action and dialogue. This use of real characters in fiction seems to us, as we have intimated above, rather a questionable habit. It can scarcely fail to taint history, which, it should be remembered, is not only a repository of facts but a school of right sympathies, and which for both purposes requires absolute adherence to the truth and nothing but the truth. Even Shakspeare's historical dramas have done mischief by fixing falsehoods respecting some historical characters in the popular imagination; for instance, the slanderous though poetically sublime account of Cardinal Beaufort's death-bed, and the legend, proved by Mr. Tyler to be as baseless as it is unnatural, of the debauched youth of Henry V.[1] Shakspeare's excuse is, not that as a man of genius he had a divine right to do wrong (though this is now becoming current doctrine); but that in his day the value of historical truth, and the obligation to preserve and respect it, were not so clearly seen as to make tampering with it a palpable offence.

But, moreover, the juxtaposition of real with imaginary characters is injurious to the object of the novelist's art. A novel, while we are reading it, is to us neither a *reality* nor a *fiction*, but an *illusion*—an illusion of which we are half conscious, unless we have the good fortune to be very young or very imaginative, but to which we surrender ourselves more or less completely in proportion to the skill with which the novel is written. The intrusion of realities obviously tends to dispel this illusion. The twilight of the land of dreams pales on the admission of the broad light of the day. The critical faculties are awakened by the presence of historical personages, which are their proper object, and the mood of passive belief and delight is broken and dispelled. We begin to think whether Dr. Johnson would really have said this, and whether General Washington would really have done that, instead of being absorbed in the adventures of Harry Warrington and the intrigues of the Baroness Bernstein. The reintroduction of characters from previous novels also breaks the illusion in another way. We know beforehand, and have it fixed in our minds, that these characters are fictitious, so that about *them* there can be no illusion any more. To give the action of a novel a background of real history, as is done in *Vanity Fair*, the background of part of which is Brussels in the campaign of 1815, is a different thing, it will be observed, from mixing up historical with imaginary personages in the action; it perverts no history, excites no criticism, and rather tends to make the illusion more complete by making the fiction more circumstantial.

In Mr. Thackeray's fictitious delineations of Washington and Wolfe there is nothing that either adds to or detracts from our historical notion of two of the greatest and purest heroes of that or any age; so that nothing is gained by those delineations either for history or fiction. But

---

[1] James Endell Tyler (1785–1851) wrote *Henry of Monmouth* (1838), which was reviewed by Thackeray in *The Times*.

we can hardly say as much for his portraits of Johnson and Richardson in the following passage.

[Quotation from ch. xxvi; *Works*, xv, 268–71.]

We will not say that there is no resemblance here, but we will say, that what resemblance there is was not worth producing.

The same remark applies to the counterfeit letter of Horace Walpole which Mr. Thackeray gives us in *The Virginians* as a pendant to the counterfeit number of *The Spectator* he gave us in *Esmond*. As might have been expected, the letter is overcrowded with instances of Walpole's mannerism, while it has little of the unique, though not lofty, merit of that feeble but delicate and penetrating mind. Mannerism, we repeat, can alone be adequately imitated; and to imitate mannerism is an employment which Mr. Thackeray may resign to meaner hands.

We are not aware what historical materials there are for the character of General Braddock, the unfortunate commander of the expedition against the French Canadians in 1755, but it is finely drawn in its way:—

. . . the stout chief, the exemplar of English elegance, who sat swagging from one side to the other of the carriage, his face as scarlet as his coat; swearing at every other word; ignorant on every point off parade, except the merits of a bottle and the looks of a woman; not of high birth, yet absurdly proud of his no-ancestry; brave as a bull-dog; savage, lustful, prodigal, generous; gentle in soft moods; easy of love and laughter; dull of wit; utterly unread; believing his country the first in the world, and he as good a gentleman as any in it. [Ch. ix.]

The historical scenes, again, show Mr. Thackeray's descriptive powers, though there is no subject for their exercise here equal to the battles of Marlborough in *Esmond*. In the details of manners, habits, and costume we have observed no flaw; and indeed it would be presumptuous to pretend to find flaws in a painter who is so thoroughly master of his subjects as Mr. Thackeray is of the social life of the last century. A doubt crossed us whether Lady Maria's angelic visitations of the poor, when she is angling for Harry's heart, are as much in keeping with the notions of that age as of ours. It also occurred to us in reading the Yankee speeches of the young American Countess of Castlewood to ask whether Yankeeism was at that time so full blown? —whether the Northern States were not still half Puritan in manner and phraseology, as the Southern were half Cavalier? But correct as the details may be, every one must feel that the ideas and sentiments thoughout are deeply tinged with a hue which is not of the eighteenth century, but of the nineteenth. Each century, each generation, has its own phase of thought and feeling, the result of all that has gone before as well as of all that exists, of which a writer can no more divest himself by any effort of intellect or imagination than he can put off the form of his own body or the peculiarities of his own mind. *Vanity Fair, Pendennis,* and *The Newcomes,* in which Mr. Thackeray has portrayed the living manners of his own age, as Fielding and his contemporaries did theirs, most nearly correspond, of all the works of our day, to *Tom Jones* and *Roderick Random;* and they bear a truer and deeper resemblance to their prototypes of the eighteenth century than is or can be borne by any artificial reproduction.

There is one point in which Fielding is a model for all times, and in which Mr. Thackeray is his worthy disciple, and we venture to think, perfectly his equal. That point is, style and beauty of composition. The last century was certainly more studious, generally speaking, of forms than ours. You may open any page of Fielding at random, and read it with pleasure, without reference to the story or context, merely as a piece of exquisite writing. The same may be said of Mr. Thackeray. It can hardly be said of any one else, among the novelists of our day, most of whom seem never to have apprehended beauty of composition as a distinct object to be aimed at, and one which requires a distinct effort of the intellect in order to its achievement. Let them, if they wish to please greatly and live long, study their great leader's art in narrative, description, and dialogue, and those beautiful miniature essays, perfect in form as crystals, in which the sentiment of his novels is here and there condensed.

If there is a weakness of style to which we should wish Mr. Thackeray to look before he launches his works on the stream of time, it is an occasional tendency to ride metaphors too hard. For instance, in [ch. xviii], Lady Maria's elderly orbs, with Harry's gaze poured into them, are compared to two fish-pools irradiated by a pair of stars; and this figure, which would hardly bear dwelling on, is laboured out till women become treacherous pools into which silly dogs of lovers drop their beef bones, and which are *dragged* for lovers' corpses; and at last a woman is the green-eyed naiad of the waters of her own eyes, luring the deluded Hylas under their surface.

The philosophy of life embodied in *The Virginians,* as in Mr. Thackeray's other novels, is sound and sensible rather than deep. Its ideal character, the young, good-looking, good-natured, high-spirited Harry Warrington, is a fair measure of its profundity. Deeper character can only be displayed in more serious action, and the more serious actions of life, excepting war, are repudiated by Mr. Thackeray as subjects for fiction, in a passage of this work, in which he seems to us rather to confound together the *serious* and the *prosaic*. We cannot accuse *The Virginians* of cynicism, if by cynicism is meant either want of geniality of sentiment, or a sour view of human nature. That author cannot be an unbeliever in human virtue who painted the Lambert family. Mr. Thackeray's characters are generally mixed. He marks the evil that is blended with the good; but he also marks the good that is blended with the evil, and if he finds some self-deception in our highest actions, he makes allowance for it in our lowest. On the whole, the impression we draw from him is that there is more weakness in the world than is commonly supposed, and less positive vice. It must be allowed, however, that whether from something amiss in his own spectacles, or from using those of Fielding too often, he sometimes exaggerates the number of people in the world who wear a mask. 'Daily in life,' he says, 'I watch men whose every smile is an artifice, and every wink is an hypocrisy.' With deference to the opinion of so great an observer of character, we doubt whether many men are even capable of sustaining such lifelong efforts of dissimulation; and suspect that Mr. Thackeray has put too harsh a construction on that ordinary social hypocrisy which springs partly from the mere desire to please, and which, though ignoble, does not go very deep into the heart.

In fine, if *The Virginians* is not perfectly successful, it is because its author, led astray, as we venture to think, by his admiration for Fielding, has attempted to do that which for the reasons we have given above cannot be done. To say that this novel will not rank with Mr. Thackeray's best works is very slight blame; to say that it will rank with those of his works which are less good is no slight praise. Milo has shown extraordinary strength in striving to rend the oak, though he is wedged in the oak he strove to rend.

46. Unsigned review, the *Saturday Review*

19 November 1859, viii, 610–12

Thackeray seldom commented on reviews, but in certain of the *Roundabout Papers* he showed that remarks in this article and others in the *Saturday Review* could cause him household embarrassment. See, for example, his comments in 'On Screens in Dining-Rooms', 'De Juventute' and 'Small-Beer Chronicle' (*Works*, xvii, 409–12, 423, 510–11). There is a full account of the relationship between him and the paper in M. B. Bevington, *The Saturday Review* (Columbia University Press, 1941), 167–74.

It is a peculiarity of imaginative writers that, after they have reached a certain point of eminence, it becomes almost impossible to criticise their works in a distinctive manner. When a man writes history, metaphysics, or theology, he has something to go upon. His subject constantly supplies him with new material; and though the probability is that the style, not only of language but of thought, will be uniform throughout, the impression of uniformity will not be produced. No man except the author of the *Middle Ages* could have written the *Constitutional History of England;*[1] but no one, we suppose, ever complained that the latter work was only the former over again. In the same way, Lord Macaulay's Essays and History are as easily recognised by the mental peculiarities of which they bear the traces as sovereigns by the likeness of the reigning monarch, but as each refers to a distinct set of facts or opinions, no one would say that they all amounted to very much the same thing.

With imaginative writers in general the case is altogether different. In their books, the style and the sentiment is so much more important than the specific subject-matter which is handled that, after a certain quantity has been produced, the literary value of subsequent works fails to keep pace with the rate of production, even if the author's powers of thought and composition show no traces of overwork.

[1] i.e. Henry Hallam (1777–1859).

For example, if Mr. Tennyson were to write ten poems on various subjects, each as good as the best of his *Idylls*, the ten taken together would not be ten times as valuable as any one of them. The thought which pervaded any one would be either the same, or nearly the same, as that which pervaded all the rest, and the differences between them would lie principally in the way of expressing that thought. There is, however, no class of books to which this observation applies so forcibly as to those novels in monthly numbers, which, through the agency of Mr. Thackeray and Mr. Dickens, have attained such remarkable popularity. The obvious tendency of the mode of publication which they have selected is to reduce the popularity of a novel almost entirely to a question of style and sentiment, and to teach people neither to expect nor to relish an interesting plot. A novel which is, in fact, the aggregate of twenty-four monthly pamphlets must always be disjointed and languid; nor would anything short of a superhuman energy, of which neither of these writers displays much trace, keep in lively motion waters which flow through a channel so very long and so much interrupted. The consequence of this is, that whilst Mr. Dickens's novels have come to be pamphlets on various subjects, hinted and insinuated through caricatures of imaginary people, Mr. Thackeray's are assuming the type of sermons, conversations, and miscellaneous remarks put into the mouths of personages who are constantly deducing all Mr. Thackeray's favourite conclusions from their observation of each other and from their reflections on the various events amongst which their author assigns them their local habitation. Thus the substance of each successive novel is precisely the same. Each is an embodiment of Mr. Thackeray's view of human life, and that view differs extremely little whether it is taken from one point or another. In order, therefore, to criticise any one of these works, it is more or less necessary to criticise them all, or at least to criticise that general temper of mind to which they all alike owe their origin.

We do not know that Mr. Thackeray has been more fortunate than his neighbours in obtaining from his critics a just estimate of what he really thinks and has really said; and, indeed, it has always appeared to us that neither his strong nor his weak points have been very fairly appreciated by them. They seem to us to have almost uniformly overrated his powers, or rather the character of his powers; whilst, on the other hand, they have underrated, or at least misapprehended, the moral value of his writings. We hope it may not be considered impertinent to say that one of the great leading features of

Mr. Thackeray's books—and one of their most honourable features—
is that they are the writings of a thorough gentleman and of a man of
high and liberal education. This is not only high but it is rare praise.
We do not allude to those constant denunciations and exposures of
social meanness and vulgarity which fill, in our judgment, much too
large a space in his works; for they suggest—like all very faithful
delineations of vice—the remark that what was painted so clearly must
have been studied sympathetically. We refer rather to the general
tone of self-restraint, modesty, and honesty which pervades his books.
Mr. Thackeray always knows how to respect himself and how to
respect his readers. He never takes that mean satisfaction which inferior
writers so constantly display in producing an effect by roughly handling
the most sacred and most delicate parts of our nature. There is no scene-
painting or death-hunting in his books. When anything horrible or
offensive comes in his way he turns aside from it, instead of making
capital out of a minute investigation and description of its details.
Thus, for example, Amory in *Pendennis* is allowed to escape the violent
death originally intended for him in consideration of his misdeeds, on the
ground that the subject was so horrible that to paint it truly would
have been disgusting, whilst to paint it untruly would have been wrong.

The same temper of mind is even more strikingly displayed in the
genuine modesty of all Mr. Thackeray's writings. They have not a
single trace of that intolerable arrogance which too often distinguishes
such works. The commonplace, ill-bred, uneducated, literary gentlemen who take to writing novels almost always assume that they and
their craft are not only the salt of the earth, but the natural rulers,
guides, and lights of mankind. They almost always assume that to be
able to write a popular tale is a gift so precious that its possessor has a
right to stand towards the prosaic part of human society in the same
sort of relation as that which the Hebrew Prophets assumed towards
the Jewish Kings. The *Græculus Esuriens* of modern literature is as
versatile as his predecessor in Juvenal, but infinitely less humble.[1]
Instead of going to the infernal regions when he is told, he expects the
rest of mankind to go there when he tells them, and nothing can equal
the satisfaction which he feels in issuing such orders to all persons who
have a recognised position or constituted authority. Mr. Thackeray
is absolutely free from this monstrous presumption. He uniformly
confines himself to his own legitimate sphere, and he never attempts to
write upon matters which he does not understand, and hardly ever

[1] Juvenal, *Satires*, iii, 76. The 'hungry little Greek' who was willing to do anything.

expresses any feeling but respect for those who administer the ordinary affairs of life. It is impossible not to trace in this temper of mind the effects of a really sound and liberal education. At the Charterhouse and at Cambridge, Mr. Thackeray must have learned that lesson which is, after all, one of the most important which any one can learn—that commonplace qualities which insure commonplace success are by no means matters of course—that, on the contrary, their possession and cultivation require strenuous, long-continued efforts, the results of which are thoroughly worthy of the respect and admiration of every man of sufficient understanding to appreciate their importance— and that it is a miserable fallacy to suppose that the mere sayer or writer of good things is entitled to treat with contempt the opinions or the practice of a person who has made a special study the object of his life. Few parts of the teaching of English schools and colleges are so valuable as the constant proof which they afford, to every student who has sufficient generosity and candour to feel it, of the fact that he is by no means the greatest man in the world, and that he cannot expose himself more effectually than by trying to teach mankind at large to suck eggs.

Mr. Thackeray's intellectual gifts have met, we think, with more justice than the moral tone of his books. In one particular art his skill is almost miraculous. He has the power of combining a constant flow of delicate satire with minute, though not grotesque, accuracy of portrait-painting which we do not think any other writer in the language possesses. What he knows and has seen and felt he can reproduce as no other man ever could reproduce it. This power, combined with that delicacy of phraseology and observation which it implies, places him very high indeed in the list of English novelists. Those who want to know how people amused themselves, what were the special foibles and hypocrisies of society, and, generally, what was the slight and weak side of the middle and upper classes of English society in the middle of the nineteenth century, and how all this presented itself to the mind of a man quite capable of viewing its pettiness in the light of something far higher and nobler—though from that something he preferred to turn away his eyes—will always find in Mr. Thackeray's works more abundant satisfaction for their curiosity than is usually supplied to any curiosity of the kind.

Such are, we think, the strong points of Mr. Thackeray's novels. Their weak points may almost be inferred from the strong ones without further explanation; but their principal weakness has perhaps not been so fully recognised as it might be. The view of life which they adopt is as shallow as it is accurate so far as it goes. It is no doubt a great thing that Mr. Thackeray himself is quite aware of its shallowness; but still it is systematically and consciously superficial. In one of the many 'asides' to the reader in which *The Virginians*, like all his other works, abounds, Mr. Thackeray not only avows this, but maintains that it is inevitable. Friendly critics, he says, have observed that the real business of life is not represented in his novels—that there is, after all, much more in the world than love-making, gambling, the giving of parties, and the little domestic tyrannies and hypocrisies which seem essential to his conception of the female character. This he admits is quite true; but how could anything so prosaic as real business be introduced into a work of fiction? How, he pleads, can I tell my readers how the lawyer and the doctor, by obscure toils and uninteresting opportunities, gradually worked their way in their profession—how the clergyman managed his parishioners, how the shopkeeper extended his business, or even how the author wrote his books—unless, indeed, like Mr. Pendennis, he spent his evenings at the Back Kitchen, and made amusing speeches about it to Mr. Warrington afterwards? War, he says, is the only branch of the common business of life which is sufficiently picturesque for the purposes of the novelist; and he accordingly scatters observations on the American War pretty freely through the second volume of *The Virginians*.

The answer to these questions appears to us to afford what is perhaps the broadest criticism that can be made, not only on Mr. Thackeray's novels, but on the modern practice to which he has so powerfully contributed, of writing novels without a plot. It is simply this—that novels ought to have plots, and that the development of those plots would afford opportunities for referring to the common business of life, and doing honour to the commonplace virtues which secure success in it. The strongest illustration of this is to be found in two writers, each of whom has powerfully influenced Mr. Thackeray's literary career—we mean Balzac and Charles de Bernard. Balzac's novels, as every one knows, form a sort of picture gallery, in which are contained portraits of members of every one of the classes which, taken together, made up the French society in which he lived. With a vanity and an affectation of omniscience equally characteristic of himself and of his nation, Balzac aimed at describing every pursuit and every rank of life, from the king to the beggar; and it cannot be doubted that a great part of his descriptions is altogether, or at least to a great extent, untrue. Still the interest and importance which his novels derive from this characteristic are exceedingly great. They give with wonderful point and effect the view which one of the cleverest and most inquisitive men in France took of the daily life and principal occupations of those amongst whom his life was passed. The mass of information (true and false) which his novels contain about every transaction of French life—about marriages, sales, bills of exchange, the investment of property, the army, the lawyers, the priests, the criminals, the doctors, the journalists, the landholders, the shop-keepers, and every other class of Frenchmen—is often untrustworthy and occasionally tiresome, but it is generally exceedingly interesting, and there is, at any rate, enough of it to satisfy the most gluttonous of human appetites.

The same, to a much smaller extent, is the case with Charles de Bernard. The *Gentilhomme campagnard* and *L'Homme sérieux* introduce us to large sections of everyday life.[1] They contain pictures of the ordinary routine of the business of a country lawyer—of the causes tried before a *juge de paix*—of the curious system of local administration which is so important an element of French life—of the Liberal deputies, Democratic journalists, and Legitimist noblesse who played their parts under Louis Philippe—and of an immense number of other things and persons belonging almost universally to the prose of life. These pictures are all introduced in the most easy and natural way, and, notwithstanding Mr. Thackeray's dictum, they form by far the most interesting and important parts of the books in which they are contained. How, then, do these French writers produce an effect which Mr. Thackeray despairs of producing? Simply by bearing in mind the truth that a novel is not primarily a set of descriptions of states of mind, but a story; and that, in order that it may be a good story, it is absolute-ly essential that it should have a plot. The complications of the events related bring the parties to a trial, and this gives an opportunity for showing how the judges and lawyers pass their time—or there is an illness, and this brings the physician on the stage. Every pursuit in life has its special transactions which are capable of being described in an interesting and striking manner. Balzac makes a whole novel turn upon the manner in which a perfumer carries on his business and speculates in a newly invented description of hair oil. If he had taken Mr. Thackeray's view of the duties of a novelist, and instead of the

---

[1] Charles de Bernard (1804–50), *Le Gentilhomme campagnard* (1847) and *L'Homme sérieux* (1847).

story of Cæsar Birotteau, his baths, and his perfumes, had given us a volume of meditations on life from the point of view of Birotteau, he would certainly have produced something neither readable nor intelligible. Mr. Thackeray has the less excuse, because he can make a plot when he tries; and, when he does so, he is insensibly carried out of his constant meditations on the astonishing truth that there really is a seamy side to human affairs, and that it is perfectly possible to confine one's attention to it. The *Hoggarty Diamond* and *Barry Lyndon* have each a story well contrived and well told, and the consequence is that we get in those works real characters, instead of accounts of the reflections suggested to Mr. Thackeray by his fictitious characters.

In *The Virginians*, as in *Esmond*, Mr. Thackeray appears to have caught sight of the necessity of having a plot for his novels; and though he has not kept it before him so steadily as might have been desired, he has considerably added to the interest of his work by giving it a semi-historical character. The pictures of Marlborough and Washington, which he has rather sketched than drawn, are remarkable exceptions to the generally superficial character of his subjects. The habit of adopting 'Scriberis Vario'[1] as his motto, and of leaving the great affairs of the world for others to handle, is, indeed, so inveterate that when he comes across a great man he indicates instead of painting his greatness; but he does so with a spirit of honourable respect, and with an eager acknowledgment and instinctive appreciation of the fact that the man with whom he is concerned really was great, which increase our regret that he did not adopt more worthy walks of literature at an earlier stage of his career. If he had acquired the knowledge and exercised the power necessary for such an undertaking whilst it was possible to do so, he might have written such a novel as haunts the dreams of most modern novelists. He might have produced a novel which would have been a faithful and not unworthy picture of some characteristic feature of the great epoch in which he lives—which would have shown not merely the petty, but the grand side of English life, and have enabled future generations to know what sort of limbs were still made in England in the age when all countries alike grew rich, and built railroads, and dug canals, and set up electric telegraphs, but when one country alone could reform ancient institutions without tyranny or bloodshed, could extend its empire without losing its freedom, and could show armies, second to none in courage and in glory, which had never fired a shot or levelled a bayonet in civil war. These are imperial

[1] Horace, *Odes*, i, 6, 1. 'Varius [an epic poet] will write [of your great deeds]'.

arts; and to show by what sort of persons they were cultivated would perhaps be the grandest enterprise which a writer of fiction could attempt. It has not been achieved by Mr. Thackeray, and we fear that it is now too late for him to achieve it. It is, however, much that he has felt and acknowledged the existence of greatness which he has not painted, and that he, at least, is free from the reproach of systematically debasing and insulting the generation in which he lives.

PHILIP

in the *Cornhill Magazine*, January 1861–August 1862

47. [Walter Bagehot], review in the *Spectator*

9 August 1862, xxxv, 885–6. Reprinted in *The Collected Works of Walter Bagehot*, ed. St. John-Stevas, Norman, ii (1965), 313–17

Mr. Thackeray has arrived at a peculiar distinction in the world of art. When we look at a new picture of any recognised school—suppose the Dutch School of Art—we do not expect to receive any entirely novel idea. We look at the pictures of Wouvermans' and we ask where is the White Horse; we look at Teniers or Ostade, and we expect to see our old friends, the old clay jug, the old merry boors, the old natural bourgeois life. Of each new picture, we judge, or attempt to judge, whether that new specimen of the familiar class is of the first excellence in that class. If a person says, 'Teniers is occupied with low subjects,' we answer, 'Of course he is! how young *you* are!' In the same way, when we read a new book of Mr. Thackeray's, we know precisely that which we have to anticipate. We are well aware that human life will be delineated in a certain characteristic way, and according to certain very peculiar and characteristic conventions. *That* is Thackeray, we say: we know what he is, and we do not expect him to change; we compare himself with himself; we only ask whether he is good to-day in comparison to what he was yesterday.

Mr. Thackeray is a writer to whom this peculiar sort of fame is especially natural and appropriate. His most obvious merit is an artistic expression. His words have a felicity in conveying what he means, which no other words would have. His delineation is inexplicably, but somehow certainly, better than any other sort of delineation of the same kind. You say those sentiments are low; they are, at any rate, not the highest; but if you try to express those sentiments yourself, you will find that you come to nothing, or that you become unendurable. The author of *Vanity Fair* can describe the world as if it were a vanity fair, and all men read him, and those who study the art of expression study him for that art; but we should laugh at a baby imitator. We should say, 'My dear young sir, it takes years of worldly study and years of deep feeling, at once worldly and unworldly, to know how to use these worldly words so spiritually and so nicely. You can hardly talk as yet. Do not try to imitate the delicate *finesse* of the practised *raconteur*, or the melancholy mirth of the Belgravian novelist. It is not for young enthusiasts, it is not for patient-thinking men so to dress thought or a near approach to thought, that the unthinking world will read and reread it.'

In this book, *Philip*, Mr. Thackeray is evidently trying to baffle his critics. They have said very often that he could never make a plot. He is now trying to show that he can. He has accumulated all the best traditional material. An eager, impetuous hero, who is skilful in getting into scrapes, and unskilful in extricating himself from them; a nice little heroine, gentle on all other matters, but biting like a tigress when her lover is attacked; a bad father, who commits forgery and seduction; a bad mother, who wishes to induce her daughter to abandon her lover, partly from a just belief that the match is a bad one, but partly also from a maternal impulse to bully and tyrannize; a professional nurse who is still not very old, and who was seduced in her youth, and who passes her life in doing good actions to a son of her seducer by a different woman; an old lord of diabolical principles and conversation to match; a marriage perhaps valid, perhaps invalid; a long period, during which the hero is interestingly poor; a sudden discovery of a lost will by which he is reinstated in comfort and opulence; these are good materials. They are the best part of the recognised stock in hand of narrative artists. If a writer could accomplish nothing with this capital apparatus, it is not likely that he will accomplish much with any other. He has as good a chance with this machinery as he is ever likely to have with any. Nevertheless as far as 'plot' is concerned, *Philip* is a failure. No one of all its most numerous readers has probably read it with eager interest as a story. You no more care what becomes of any of Mr. Thackeray's celebrated characters than you want a biography of a Dutch boor or a Dutch utensil in Teniers' pictures. There the characters are in 'Thackeray;' you contemplate them with pleasure and indulgence and satisfaction; and you watch them as you watch your companions at a party only that you feel that you understand them better. Thackeray is like the edited and illustrated edition of a great dinner; but as for caring what becomes of those people, of the adjacent crinolines and opposite white ties, no, you cannot do that. You see what they are but you cannot be interested in their future. Mr. Thackeray, as we know well, cares for the people in the book, and Providence (we suppose) will care for the people at the dinner, but we cannot in either case concern ourselves with the subject.

Mr. Thackeray evidently feels this himself. He has no great impulse to tell us what happened to his characters. He must have a story, he knows, to tell us, and, therefore, he concocts or adapts a story, and involves his characters in it as best he may, but he can do no more. His feeling is the opposite of Mr. Canning's knife-grinder; the latter had nothing to relate, and was sorry for it: Mr. Thackeray must relate something, and is sorry for that also. His characteristic exclamation is, 'Story! God bless you, I have one to tell you, Sir; but do not ask me to tell it, Sir; it *is* such a bore, Sir.'[1]

Mr. Thackeray likes to have a characteristic particular in every book, and he has one here. It is the relation of children to their parents. We do not mean the sentimental relation in which each is fond of the other, or the pecuniary relation in which one inherits from the other, but a more complex relation in which one of them is contrasted with the other. With a very peculiar watchfulness Nature has provided us with an instinctive aversion to what our parents do. '*I* won't do *that*, at any rate,' says the eager vanity, the improving conceit of youth. From the faults and vanities of our fathers we rush, angry and ardent, to follies of our own. Even with the very best children of the best parents it is so. The religious daughter of a Puritan mother has very early a latent weakness for the Virgin Mary. In the early self-will that accompanies second teeth, she peruses the *Christian Year* as a secret study, not being quite sure whether she enjoys most the overt excellence of the pure book or the latent flavour of her slight disobedience. All the Wilberforces are anti-Evangelical, and the Bishop of Oxford has very little anti-slavery fanaticism.[2] The good children of good parents are sure to have, at any rate, a very different sort of goodness from that of their parents. And the good children of bad parents feel the reaction too, and make a much better use of it. They are excellent with the very virtues which their progenitors missed, and loath all the offences in which those progenitors especially indulged. Philip is bold, outspoken, and unworldly, because his father is mean, cringing, and parasitical.

---

[1] See above, p. 99.
[2] Samuel Wilberforce (1805–73), the third son of William Wilberforce.

Nature won't have a monotonous world at any rate. With an impatience of what it has always seen, an antipathy to what it has always heard, and a frantic wish to be original, an eager youth flounders into life: 'May I be delivered from father and mother!' so begins his litany. And his prayer is granted. The world strikes him hard enough and often enough, but it has an insidious pleasure in exiling him far from his paternal home and driving him far from his ancestral creed.

We do not mean that Mr. Thackeray resembles Sir Archibald Alison.[1] His books are not sermons with narratives between them. Mr. Thackeray's favourite art is a sort of annotated picture. He describes to you Philip and Charlotte, the mother-in-law and the aunt-in-law, and then he likes to pause to analyse, to assure you that Philip was very impetuous and eager, which was a disadvantage to him generally in life; but an advantage to him in this case, for else he would never have been bold enough to seize that pretty little girl; and as to Charlotte, he tells you that she is a weak little thing, which is also a difficulty for her in the general course of life, but an advantage now, for if she had had any mind, she might have obtruded it during the courtship, and so disconcerted and startled her admirer. Any particular intellect in either party would rather, the commentator says, disenchant than enchant the other. And so he goes on volume after volume painting for us pretty scenes, and covering them with worldly remarks.

It is for these sort of half cynical, half true delineations that Mr. Thackeray's pen was meant. He looks at the spectacle of society, the *play* which is going on in the miscellaneous theatre of the world. He rather yawns at the great passions, and but torpidly wonders at its great efforts and troublesome events. The 'grand style' may be grand, but it is a little tiresome; it is rather a young notion to be taken in by all that. Some divines earnestly counsel us not to be busy about 'public matters which concern us not;' the true philosophy of this world is of the same mind. 'If you bore yourself, my son,' it says, 'you will become a bore; leave the great tasks of life to the few who are intrusted with them and paid for them; it is ridiculous to be an amateur statesman: if you have an opinion on such subjects secrete it; sooner or later it will bring you into trouble, and you will be laughed at for it.' Such is Mr. Thackeray's evident belief. He won't encumber himself with big ideas. If he should encounter a serious discussion, as will happen to the lightest writers, he will lounge through it if he can. He

1 See above, p. 177.

is great in minute anatomy. The subsoil of life—not the very surface, but just the next layer which one painful scratch will bring up—this is his region, and it is an immense one. The great passions are few and simple; lists of the best situations might well be drawn up, and categories of the highest characters even more easily. The peaks of great mountains are much like one another, and an artist who was celebrated only for painting them would have but few pictures to sell. Various art is, in its essence, sublunary. Do not be exaggerated, do not aim too low; do not take the worst of the world; extreme badness is as monotonous and of as few species as the best excellence. Live on the ordinary common follies of the ordinary common world; analyse most men as they stand before you, interested in most things and practising most things. By natural tact and studious pains Mr. Thackeray does so inimitably well, and therefore his art is copious as well as excellent.

48. Unsigned review, the *Saturday Review*

23 August 1862, xiv, 223–4

It is the popular belief that a popular writer can go on writing for ever. It would, of course, be conceded that old age, or illness, or great mental distress would render a favourite author incapable of doing again as he has done before. But it is taken for granted that, unless there is some special reason to prevent it, there is a power of composition in a man of genius and of practised skill which he can tap at pleasure. In reality, this belief, although it assures a popular writer fortune and fame, often causes a very severe drain on him, and tortures him into writing what, without this popular pressure, he would much rather have left unwritten. A writer may have great natural and acquired gifts, and yet have nothing more to say than he has said already. He may feel acutely that he has no call, except an artificial one, to say any more. But imploring publishers, and an expecting public, and the certainty of a splendid reward, impel him with a force he cannot resist. In return for his compliance, the public, it must be acknowledged, accepts with an admirable thankfulness and readiness whatever he is pleased to write. Mr. Dickens, when it was remarked that *Little Dorrit*, or *Bleak*

House, was hardly up to his level, replied, with real or affected innocence, that none of his books had sold so well. The public does not play fast and loose with its favourites. If it goads them into writing when they do not want, it at least takes care that their publications shall be pecuniarily successful. People always find something to like and wonder at—some jokes that remind them of other days, some touches that none but their favourite could have added. And, in some degree, they are right. The composition of a good writer is never wholly bad. It may be poor, as compared with other things he has written, or it may be substantially a repetition of what he has said before, but skill and lively thought and observation are never asleep in a man who possesses them, and he is sure to betray, in some respect or other, a casual superiority which shows that even his bad books are the bad books of a good writer.

No one knows better, or can see more clearly, than Mr. Thackeray, all the conditions of authorship. His works abound with traces that he has set before him what he can do and what he cannot. It is part of his habit of mind to look at his own books from the outside, to pass a continual judgment on them, and to state as frankly as possible what he means by writing them. He not only is not under any illusion about them, but he makes capital out of his own conscious freedom from illusions. The *Adventures of Philip* gains its most distinguishing peculiarity from the habit which the author has of reflecting on his own compositions. Mr. Thackeray seems to have been possessed with a humorous enjoyment of his position. He delighted in thinking over what was taking place. He appears to have said to himself that, if publishers and admirers and banker's books made him write when he did not want to write, and give old things as new, he would have the satisfaction of doing it frankly and completely. No author, we believe, ever sent up his cold mutton to table more frankly, or ever relished more keenly the operation of putting bits of parsley round it. He seems to be tickled with the joke of seeing his friends devour it. They ask him for something from his pen; what it is they do not care; and as he really has no other method of easily satisfying them, he gives them reminiscences of his old novels in profusion. In the first place, he uses up at random the characters of almost all his former compositions. We have the later days of Pendennis and Mrs. Pendennis, of Clive Newcome, of the Ravenswing, and of poor little Caroline Gann. All these old favourites are trotted out, and made to jog once more over the course for our amusement. 'If people,' the author seems tacitly to say, 'really want my old characters tossed up again, they shall have as many as they like.' Then, familiar characters of the old novels are reproduced, with the slightest possible variation. Barnes Newcome revives again in Ringwood Twysden, and is again the cousin of the hero. The Marquis of Steyne is now the Earl of Ringwood, but changes nothing whatever but his title. He is still a cynical, capricious, damnatory old sinner, the idol and terror of his relations, and full of a ferocious but lordly wickedness. Mrs. Baynes, the military mother-in-law of Philip, is precisely like Mrs. Mackenzie, the military mother-in-law of Clive Newcome. We may reverse the experience of Charles Lamb and say, 'All, all are come, the old familiar faces.' That we are glad to see them, or that we find them as amusing as they used to be, it would be insincere to assert. But the tedium of their appearance is certainly mitigated by the grim humour with which their author pushes them again on the stage. He is even, on one occasion, so diverted with the operation that he stops to calculate the amount per line he is paid for doing it, and to express an honest wonder that the transaction should be possible. He refines upon the thought, and invites his readers to ponder with him upon the marvel that even the half dozen lines in which he records his astonishment at the facility with which he coins money should themselves bring him in enough to provide a comfortable household with breakfast. The candour of authorship can scarcely go farther than this.

Mr. Thackeray has so honestly given the public exactly what it asked for that it may seem superfluous to speculate on the causes which might make it more difficult for him than for most authors of his ability to go on producing new works. Yet it is worth while remarking, as a general criticism on his writings, that his range is a limited one. He photographs with astonishing accuracy the objects which it has come in his way to observe, but these objects are confined in a narrow circle. He looks at society from one point of view. He regards it as it appears to a man who lives in London without professional occupation, who knows the great world but does not belong to it, and who also knows a certain number of other sets of people belonging to the upper or wealthier classes of great towns, or dependent on them. He knows the clubs, and theatrical society, and artists, and lodging-houses, and hotels, and the places of feasting for all kinds of queer people—from the gatherings of the finest butlers down to the resorts of the humblest footmen and adventurers. The peculiarity of Mr. Thackeray is, that he surveys all these ranks of London society from the position of a gentleman having a recognized status by birth and education, and too well placed to wish to pretend to be what he is not. We have had plenty of descriptions of high life from persons who belonged or pretended to belong to the fashionable world, and we have had plenty of descriptions of artists, and vulgar editors, and publishers, and actors, from inhabitants of 'Bohemia;' but Mr. Thackeray stands almost alone in surveying all these people, high and low, from the position of a man who is not a 'swell,' but who is a gentleman. What he thus observed he made his own by his great power of minute observation, by his prolific humour, and by his admirable command of English. But this section of life is a small one, and although it lives in London, and thus gains a sort of factitious importance, is really an insignificant one. Reprobate lords, and their toadies, and artists, and young barristers, and majestic butlers, and club-goers, and those who form the subject of the conversation of club-goers, are only a fraction of mankind, and by no means an edifying or attractive portion. The labour, and the lives, and the daily interests, and the highest thoughts of men at large belong to quite another sphere. The narrow circle of the prominent classes of London is quite worth describing, but it is a narrow circle. It is wearying to hear eternally of people selling their daughters to the richest bidder, and of every vice and cruelty being pardoned in a millionaire marquis, and of the pompous fatuity of the grand domestics of grand people. It is quite as wearying to hear too much of the shifts and pretensions of people who are only sham in their grandeur— of the plate that is not plate, of the greengrocers who wait, of the side-dishes that come in cold from the confectioner's. So far as these things are a necessity of people in moderate circumstances, there is nothing very funny in them. It would be rather hard that no one should be allowed to ask his friends to dinner who had not got half a dozen men servants. But so far as there is pretension in Baker Street, it is fair fun to laugh at and expose it. The only thing is, that the joke is soon over, and these follies of sham-grandeur are poor game for the satirist. It would be absurd to say that Mr. Thackeray occupies himself exclusively with the follies of the grand and the sham-grand; but a very large portion of his observation has been directed towards them, and they do not afford scope for very long or very repeated description.

Mr. Thackeray knows this better than any one can tell him, and he has tried to make other fields for himself. His literary predilections led him to the study of the eighteenth century, and it seemed that historical knowledge might open a door for the introduction of quite a new set of characters and thoughts. The results of his efforts in this line was the composition of *Esmond* and *The Virginians*. But the masterly writing of *Esmond* was appreciated only by a comparatively small number of readers, and *The Virginians* gained very little from the local colouring of America, and from the introduction of Dr. Johnson and Washington. If Mr. Thackeray wished to please the public, he was quite right, we think, to go back to his Pendennises and his wicked lords and big footmen. But besides historical research, Mr. Thackeray had another resource for getting away from his representations of a section of the London world. He would philosophize. He could reflect as well as observe, and speculate as well as describe. He could address the reader, and moralize, as between the reader and himself, over the proceedings of the characters he was painting. Perhaps these moralizings are natural to a mind that has the gift of observing minutely, and of remaining outside of the thing observed. Perhaps they are practically found to be not the least easy style of writing, and as quick a road to sixpence a line as any that can be hit on. At any rate we have much more of this sort of padding in *Philip* than we ever had before. The author even engages two special performers to take the two first parts in his philosophical episodes. Mr. Pendennis is there to do the cynical sensible man of the world; and Mrs. Pendennis represents a gushing, tender, half-religious sentimentalism. Mr. Thackeray's philosophy, stated shortly, seems to be something of this sort:—'Most men, or at least most London men, are full of worldliness and meanness, and conceal their faults under a very thin cloak. All are about like, and the author and his readers, and most people at most clubs, are pretty much birds of a feather. Still there is much kindliness among men, and a few friends are really to be trusted. There is, however, something beyond the vices and virtues of club men, for there is religion, which we see exhibited in women, and especially in women who are not very clever. These women are very good and loving, and will stand any tyranny, and have views about Providence which do not seem much like real life, but which may be true somehow.' These are the chief, if not the only, tenets of Mr. Thackeray's philosophical creed. It is not a creed which he is at all singular in holding; nor do we feel called upon in any way to attack it. But it does not seem to us to be new enough or true enough to be continually thrust upon us. It furnishes material for a sort of sermonizing which most men could command, but which they do not care to produce, partly, because no one will give them sixpence a line to produce it. We think it rather hard on the readers of *Philip* that there should be so much of it in these volumes. We know that no one can go on always narrating, and we are quite prepared to find that a writer who is busy hashing up his old characters into a new form should freely help himself our with moral remarks. But there are things which are simple outrages on critical patience, and Mr. Pendennis on Providence is one of them.

As we have said, the bad book of a good author is never wholly bad. There are many things in *Philip* which no one but Mr. Thackeray could have written. There are also scenes which are new and well contrived, and worthy of his best works. For skill in treatment, and dramatic vigour, and happiness of dialogue, nothing could be better than the encounter between the Little Sister and Parson Hunt, when the parson is gloriously robbed of his pocket-book. Those also who have had the pleasure of being acquainted with the diplomatic world will enjoy the excellent dialogue in which the attachés of the Paris Embassy are introduced, as recording their sentiments on men and manners. The whole of the Paris part of the book, with the sorrows of Charlotte, and the neat portrait of Madame Smolensk, and the melo-drama of the fury of General Baynes, and the great family fight in which the General only conquered to die, seems to us much the best and most entertaining in the book. But even in the worst parts we are amused, if not by the thing written, at least by the humorous attitude which the author assumes; and throughout we are cheered by the presence of that singularly pure and easy style which seems quite as much at Mr. Thackeray's command as it ever was.

OBITUARY TRIBUTES FROM FELLOW-AUTHORS

49. James Hannay, *A Brief Memoir of the late Mr. Thackeray*

Edinburgh, 1864, 7–8, 10–11, 18–26, 30–31. Reprinted from the *Edinburgh Evening Courant* (5 January 1864), 3

Hannay (1827–73), a friend of Thackeray's, was a novelist and journalist, and edited the *Edinburgh Evening Courant* from 1860 to 1864.

In after-life, he let most of his Greek slip away; but his acquaintance with the Latin language, and especially the Latin poets, was eminently respectable, and exercised a profound influence over his genius and his diction. The *Odes* of Horace he knew intimately well, and there are subtle indications of the knowledge—the smell of Italian violets hidden in the green of his prose—only to be truly enjoyed by Horatians. A quotation from Horace was one of the favourite forms in which he used to embody his jokes. If you bored him with genealogy, he would begin—

> Quantum distet ab Inacho,[1]

which was quite a sufficient hint; and when a low fellow in London hanged himself, he observed that it was a 'dignus vindice NODUS.'[2] Latin writers, French writers, and English eighteenth century men were the three sources at which his genius fed, and on which it was nourished. . . .

He was not *essentially poetical*, as Tennyson, for instance, is. Poetry was not the predominant mood of his mind, or the intellectual law by which the objects of his thought and observation were arranged and classified. But *inside* his fine sagacious common-sense understanding,

[1] Horace, *Odes*, iii, 19, 1. 'How far distant he is from Inachus . . .'
[2] Horace, *De Arte Poetica*, 191. 'A knot worth unravelling.'

315

there was, so to speak, a pool of poetry,—like the *impluvium* in the hall of a Roman house, which gave an air of coolness and freshness and nature to the solid marble columns and tessellated floor. The highest products of this part of his mind were the *Chronicle [of the Drum]*, the *Bouillabaisse*, the lines on Charles Buller's death at the end of one of his Christmas Books, and the 'Ho, pretty page with dimpled chin' of another of them. A song or two in his novels, and some passages in which rural scenery is quietly and casually described, might also be specified. But all this is chiefly valuable as showing that his nature was *complete*, and that there wanted not in his genius that softer and more sensitive side natural to one whose observation was so subtle and his heart so kind. He was essentially rather moralist and humourist,—thinker and wit,—than poet; and he was too manly to *overwork* his poetic vein as a man may legitimately work his mere understanding. This honourable self-restraint, this decent reticence, so natural to English gentlemen, was by some writers of the Gushing School mistaken for hardness. . . .

The man and the books were equally real and true; and it was natural that he should speak without hesitation of his books, if you wished it; though as a man of the world and a polished gentleman who knew the world thoroughly, literature to him only took its turn among other topics. From this point of view, his relation to it was a good deal like that of Scott. According to Lockhart, people were wrong in saying that Sir Walter declined at all markedly to talk about Literature, and yet his main interest was in active life. Just so, Thackeray was not bookish, and yet turned readily to the subject of books, if invited. His reading was undoubtedly large in Memoirs, Modern History, Biography, Poetry, Essays, and Fiction,—and, taken in conjunction with his scholarship, probably placed him, as a man of letters, above any other novelist except Sir Bulwer Lytton. Here is a characteristic fragment from one of his letters, written in August 1854, and now before us:—'I hate Juvenal,' he says; 'I mean I think him a truculent brute, and I love Horace better than you do, and rate Churchill much lower; and as for Swift, you haven't made me alter my opinion. I admire, or rather admit, his power as much as you do; but I don't admire that kind of power so much as I did fifteen years ago, or twenty shall we say. Love is a higher intellectual exercise than Hatred; and when you get one or two more of those young ones you write so pleasantly about, you'll come over to the side of the kind wags, I think, rather than the cruel ones.' [See *Letters*, ii, 553n.] Passages like this,—which men who knew him, will not need to have quoted to them,—have a double value for the world at large. They not only show a familiar command of writers whom it is by no means easy to know well,—but they show what the real philosophy was of a man whom the envious represented to the ignorant as a cynic and a scoffer. Why, his favourite authors were just those whose influence he thought had been beneficial to the cause of virtue and charity. 'I take off my hat to Joseph Addison,' he would say, after an energetic testimony to his good effect on English life. He was, in fact, even greater as a moralist than as a mere *describer* of manners; and his very hatred of quackery and meanness was proved to be real by his simplicity, humanity, and kindliness of character. In private, this great satirist, whose aspect in a crowd was often one of austere politeness and reserve, unbent into a familiar *naïveté* which somehow one seldom finds in the demonstratively genial. And this was the more charming and precious that it rested on a basis of severe and profound reflection, before the glance of which all that was dark and serious in man's life and prospects lay open. The gravity of that white head, with its noble brow, and thoughtful face full of feeling and meaning, enhanced the piquancy of his playfulness, and of the little personal revelations which came with such a grace from the depths of his kindly nature. When we congratulated him, many years ago, on the touch in *Vanity Fair* in which Becky '*admires*' her husband when he is giving Lord Steyne the chastisement which ruins *her* for life, 'Well,' he said,—'when I wrote the sentence, I slapped my fist on the table, and said "*that* is a touch of genius!"' The incident is a trifle, but it will reveal, we suspect, an element of fervour, as well as a heartiness of frankness in recording the fervour, both equally at variance with the vulgar conception of him. This frankness and bonhommie made him delightful in a *tête-à-tête*, and gave a pleasant human flavour to talk full of sense, and wisdom, and experience, and lighted up by the gaiety of the true London man of the world. Though he said witty things, now and then, he was not a wit in the sense in which Jerrold was, and he complained, sometimes, that his best things occurred to him after the occasion had gone by! He shone most,—as in his books,—in little subtle remarks on life, and little descriptive sketches suggested by the talk. We remember in particular, one evening, after a dinner party at his house, a fancy picture he drew of Shakspeare during his last years at Stratford, sitting out in the summer afternoon watching the people, which all who heard it, brief as it was, thought equal to the best things in his Lectures. But it was not for this sort of talent,—rarely exerted by him,—that people admired his conversation. They admired, above all, the broad sagacity, sharp insight, large and tolerant liberality, which marked him as one who was a sage as well as a story-teller, and whose stories were valuable because he was a sage. Another point of likeness to him in Scott was that he never overvalued story-telling, or forgot that there were nobler things in Literature than the purest creations of which the object was amusement. 'I would give half my fame,' wrote Scott, 'if by so doing I could place the other half on a solid basis of science and learning.' 'Now is the time,' wrote Thackeray, to a young friend in 1849, 'to lay in stock. I wish I had had five years' reading before I took to our trade.' How heartily we have heard him praise Sir Bulwer Lytton for the good example he set by being 'thoroughly *literate!*' We are not going to trench here on any such ground as Thackeray's judgments about his contemporaries. But we may notice an excellent point bearing on these. If he heard a young fellow expressing great admiration for one of them, he encouraged him in it. When somebody was mentioned as worshipping an eminent man just dead,—'I am glad,' said Thackeray, 'that he worships any body.'

After *Vanity Fair*, Thackeray's fame steadily increased. *Pendennis* appeared during 1849 and 1850, and though it was generally considered inferior in mere plot to its predecessor, no inferiority was perceived in the essential qualities of character, thought, humour, and style. The announcement in the summer of 1851 that he was about to lecture on the English Humourists gave a thrill of pleasure to intellectual London; and when he rose in Willis' Rooms to commence the course with Swift, all that was most brilliant in the Capital was assembled to hear him. Amidst a throng of nobles, and beauties, and men of fashion, were Carlyle, and Macaulay,—Hallam with his venerable head,—and Charlotte Brontë, whose own fame was just at its height, and who saw in the lecturer her ideal of an elevated and high-minded master of literary art. The lectures were thoroughly appreciated. Everybody was delighted to see the great masters of English of a past age brought to life again in their habits as they lived, and endowed with the warm human reality of the lecturer's Dobbins, and Warringtons, and Pendennises. It was this power, and not the literary criticism, which constituted the value of Thackeray's lectures, and will secure their place in the biographical literature of the country.

Towards the close of 1852, *Esmond* appeared, and Thackeray sailed for America. *Esmond* constituted a new epoch in his career. By this time his celebrity, and the impression made by his distinct and peculiar genius,—so different from that of the common sentimental schools,—had provoked a certain amount of reaction. Cads who disliked him as a gentleman,—Mechanics' Institute men who disliked him as a scholar,—Radicals who knew that he associated with the aristocracy,—and the numerous weaklings to whom his severe truth and perfect honesty of art seemed horrible after the riotous animal spirits, jolly caricature, and lachrymose softness of the style which he was putting out of fashion,—this crew, we say, was by no means satisfied with the undoubted fact that Thackeray was becoming the favourite writer of the cultivated classes. They accordingly began to call his honesty cynicism, and his accuracy reporting. They forgot that tears are pure in proportion to the depth from which they come, and not to the quantity in which they flow, and that the tenderness of a writer is to be estimated by the *quality* of his pathos. They also forgot that as what they called hardness was mere fidelity to truth, so what they called stenographic detail was mere finish of art. The richer imaginativeness of *Esmond*, and the freer play of feeling in which the author allowed himself to indulge when dealing with a past age, came in good time to rebuke cavillers, and prove that Thackeray's mind was rich as well as wide. . . .

Well, indeed, might his passing-bell make itself heard through all the myriad joy-bells of the English Christmas! It is long since England has lost such a son—it will be long before she has such another to lose. He was indeed emphatically English,—English as distinct from Scotch, —no less than English as distinct from Continental,—a different type of great man from Scott, and a different type of great man from Balzac. The highest purely English novelist since Fielding, he combined Addison's love of virtue with Johnson's hatred of cant,—Horace Walpole's lynx-like eye for the mean and the ridiculous, with the gentleness and wide charity for mankind as a whole, of Goldsmith. *Non omnis mortuus est.* He will be remembered in his due succession with these men for ages to come, as long as the hymn of praise rises in the old Abbey of Westminster,★ and wherever the English tongue is native to men, from the banks of the Ganges to those of the Mississippi.†

★ 'Dum Capitolium
Scandet cum tacita virgine Pontifex.'
† 'Dicar qua violens obstrepit Aufidus,' &c.[1]

[1] Horace, *Odes*, iii, 30, 8–9. These lines must be read in their context. Loosely, they mean: '(I shall continue to grow in the praise of posterity) as long as the Pontiff climbs the Capitol with the silent virgin. Where the fierce torrents of Aufidus rage and swell, men will speak (of my writings) . . .'

This humble tribute to his illustrious and beloved memory comes from one whom he loaded with benefits, and to whom it will always throw something of sadness over the great city where he first knew him, that it contains his too early grave.

50. Charles Dickens, 'In Memoriam'
Cornhill Magazine

February 1864, ix, 129–32

It has been desired by some of the personal friends of the great English writer who established this magazine, that its brief record of his having been stricken from among men should be written by the old comrade and brother in arms who pens these lines, and of whom he often wrote himself, and always with the warmest generosity.

I saw him first, nearly twenty-eight years ago, when he proposed to become the illustrator of my earliest book. I saw him last, shortly before Christmas, at the Athenæum Club, when he told me that he had been in bed three days—that, after these attacks, he was troubled with cold shiverings, 'which quite took the power of work out of him'—and that he had it in his mind to try a new remedy which he laughingly described. He was very cheerful, and looked very bright. In the night of that day week, he died.

The long interval between those two periods is marked in my re-membrance of him by many occasions when he was supremely humourous, when he was irresistibly extravagant, when he was sof-tened and serious, when he was charming with children. But, by none do I recall him more tenderly than by two or three that start out of the crowd, when he unexpectedly presented himself in my room, announcing how that some passage in a certain book had made him cry yesterday, and how that he had come to dinner, 'because he couldn't help it,' and must talk such passage over. No one can ever have seen him more genial, natural, cordial, fresh, and honestly impulsive, than I have seen him at those times. No one can be surer than I, of the great-ness and the goodness of the heart that then disclosed itself.

We had our differences of opinion. I thought that he too much feigned a want of earnestness, and that he made a pretence of under-valuing his art, which was not good for the art that he held in trust. But, when we fell upon these topics, it was never very gravely, and I have a lively image of him in my mind, twisting both his hands in his hair, and stamping about, laughing, to make an end of the discussion.

When we were associated in remembrance of the late Mr. Douglas Jerrold, he delivered a public lecture in London, in the course of which, he read his very best contribution to *Punch*, describing the grown-up cares of a poor family of young children. No one hearing him could have doubted his natural gentleness, or his thoroughly unaffected manly sympathy with the weak and lowly. He read the paper most patheti-cally, and with a simplicity of tenderness that certainly moved one of his audience to tears. This was presently after his standing for Oxford, from which place he had dispatched his agent to me, with a droll note (to which he afterwards added a verbal postscript), urging me to 'come down and make a speech, and tell them who he was, for he doubted whether more than two of the electors had ever heard of him, and he thought there might be as many as six or eight who had heard of me.' He introduced the lecture just mentioned, with a reference to his late electioneering failure, which was full of good sense, good spirits, and good humour.

He had a particular delight in boys, and an excellent way with them. I remember his once asking me with fantastic gravity, when he had been to Eton where my eldest son then was, whether I felt as he did in regard of never seeing a boy without wanting instantly to give him a sovereign? I thought of this when I looked down into his grave, after he was laid there, for I looked down into it over the shoulder of a boy to whom he had been kind.

These are slight remembrances; but it is to little familar things sug-gestive of the voice, look, manner, never, never more to be encountered on this earth, that the mind first turns in a bereavement. And greater things that are known of him, in the way of his warm affections, his quiet endurance, his unselfish thoughtfulness for others, and his muni-ficent hand, may not be told.

If, in the reckless vivacity of his youth, his satirical pen had ever gone astray or done amiss, he had caused it to prefer its own petition for forgiveness, long before:

> I've writ the foolish fancy of his brain;
> The aimless jest that, striking, hath caused pain;

The idle word that he'd wish back again.

[From 'The Pen and the Album'.]

In no pages could I take it upon myself at this time to discourse of his books, of his refined knowledge of character, of his subtle acquaintance with the weaknesses of human nature, of his delightful playfulness as an essayist, of his quaint and touching ballads, of his mastery over the English language. Least of all, in these pages, enriched by his brilliant qualities from the first of the series, and beforehand accepted by the Public through the strength of his great name.

But, on the table before me, there lies all that he had written of his latest and last story. That it would be very sad to any one—that it is inexpressibly so to a writer—in its evidences of matured designs never to be accomplished, of intentions begun to be executed and destined never to be completed, of careful preparation for long roads of thought that he was never to traverse, and for shining goals that he was never to reach, will be readily believed. The pain, however, that I have felt in perusing it, has not been deeper than the conviction that he was in the healthiest vigour of his powers when he wrought on this last labour. In respect of earnest feeling, far-seeing purpose, character, incident, and a certain loving picturesqueness blending the whole, I believe it to be much the best of all his works. That he fully meant it to be so, that he had become strongly attached to it, and that he bestowed great pains upon it, I trace in almost every page. It contains one picture which must have cost him extreme distress, and which is a masterpiece. There are two children in it, touched with a hand as loving and tender as ever a father caressed his little child with. There is some young love, as pure and innocent and pretty as the truth. And it is very remarkable that, by reason of the singular construction of the story, more than one main incident usually belonging to the end of such a fiction is anticipated in the beginning, and thus there is an approach to completeness in the fragment, as to the satisfaction of the reader's mind concerning the most interesting persons, which could hardly have been better attained if the writer's breaking-off had been foreseen.

The last line he wrote, and the last proof he corrected, are among these papers through which I have so sorrowfully made my way. The condition of the little pages of manuscript where Death stopped his hand, shows that he had carried them about, and often taken them out of his pocket here and there, for patient revision and interlineation. The last words he corrected in print, were 'And my heart throbbed with an exquisite bliss.' God grant that on that Christmas Eve when he

322

laid his head back on his pillow and threw up his arms as he had been wont to do when very weary, some consciousness of duty done and Christian hope throughout life humbly cherished, may have caused his own heart so to throb, when he passed away to his Redeemer's rest!

He was found peacefully lying as above described, composed, undisturbed, and to all appearance asleep, on the twenty-fourth of December, 1863. He was only in his fifty-third year; so young a man, that the mother who blessed him in his first sleep, blessed him in his last. Twenty years before, he had written, after being in a white squall:

> And when, its force expended,
> The harmless storm was ended,
> And, as the sunrise splendid
>   Came blushing o'er the sea;
> I thought, as day was breaking,
> My little girls were waking,
> And smiling, and making
>   A prayer at home for me.
> [From 'The White Squall' in *A Journey from Cornhill to Grand Cairo*.]

Those little girls had grown to be women when the mournful day broke that saw their father lying dead. In those twenty years of companionship with him, they had learned much from him; and one of them has a literary course before her, worthy of her famous name.

On the bright wintry day, the last but one of the old year, he was laid in his grave at Kensal Green, there to mingle the dust to which the mortal part of him had returned, with that of a third child, lost in her infancy, years ago. The heads of a great concourse of his fellow-workers in the Arts, were bowed around his tomb.

51. [Lord Houghton], 'Historical Contrast May, 1701: December, 1863', *Cornhill Magazine*

February 1864, ix, 133. Reprinted in *The Poetical Works of Lord Houghton* (1876), i, 302–3

> When one, whose nervous English verse
> Public and party hates defied,
> Who bore and bandied many a curse
> Of angry times—when Dryden died,

Our royal abbey's Bishop-Dean
Waited for no suggestive prayer,
But, ere one day closed o'er the scene,
Craved, as a boon, to lay him there.

The wayward faith, the faulty life,
Vanished before a Nation's pain;
'Panther' and 'Hind' forgot their strife,
And rival statesmen thronged the fane.

O gentler Censor of our age!
Prime master of our ampler tongue!
Whose word of wit and generous page
Were never wrath, except with Wrong.

Fielding—without the manners' dross,
Scott—with a spirit's larger room,
What Prelate deems thy grave his loss?
What Halifax erects thy tomb?

But, may be, He,—who so could draw
The hidden Great,—the humble Wise,
Yielding with them to God's good law,
Makes the Pantheon where he lies.

52. Anthony Trollope, 'W. M. Thackeray' *Cornhill Magazine*

February 1864, ix, 134–7

'Quis desiderio sit pudor aut modus Tam cari capitis?—What shame to wail with tears the loss of so dear a head, or when will there be an end to such weeping?'[1] Now, at the present moment, it is not so much that he who has left us was known, admired, and valued, as that he was loved. The fine grey head, the dear face with its gentle smile, the sweet, manly voice which we knew so well, with its few words of kindest

[1] Horace, *Odes*, i, 24, 1.

greeting; the gait, and manner, and personal presence of him whom it so delighted us to encounter in our casual comings and goings about the town—it is of these things, and of these things lost for ever, that we are now thinking! We think of them as of treasures which are not only lost, but which can never be replaced. He who knew Thackeray will have a vacancy in his heart's inmost casket, which must remain vacant till he dies. One loved him almost as one loves a woman, tenderly and with thoughtfulness,—thinking of him when away from him as a source of joy which cannot be analysed, but is full of comfort. One who loved him, loved him thus because his heart was tender, as is the heart of a woman.

It need be told to no one that four years ago—four years and one month at the day on which these words will come before the reader—this Magazine was commenced under the guidance, and in the hands, of Mr. Thackeray. It is not for any of us who were connected with him in the enterprise to say whether this was done successfully or not; but it is for us—for us of all men—to declare that he was the kindest of guides, the gentlest of rulers, and, as a fellow-workman, liberal, unselfish, considerate, beyond compare. It has been said of him that he was jealous as a writer. We of the *Cornhill* knew nothing of such jealousy. At the end of two years Mr. Thackeray gave up the management of the Magazine, finding that there was much in the very nature of the task which embarrassed and annoyed him. He could not bear to tell an ambitious aspirant that his aspirations were in vain; and, worse again, he could not endure to do so when a lady was his suppliant. Their letters to him were thorns that festered in his side, as he has told us himself. In truth it was so. There are many who delight in wielding the editorial ferule, good men and true, no doubt, who open their hearts genially to genius when they find it; but they can repress and crush the incapable tyro, or the would-be poetess who has nothing to support her but her own ambition, if not with delight, at least with satisfaction. Of such men are good editors made. Whether it be a point against a man, or for him, to be without such power, they who think of the subject may judge for themselves. Thackeray had it not. He lacked hardness for the place, and therefore, at the end of two years, he relinquished it.

But he did not on that account in any way sever himself from the Magazine. His *Roundabout Papers*, the first of which appeared in our first number, were carried on through 1862, and were completed in the early part of 1863. *Lovel the Widower*, and his *Lectures on the Four*

Georges, appeared under his own editorship. *Philip* was so commenced, but was completed after he had ceased to reign. It was only in November last, as our readers may remember, that a paper appeared from his hand, entitled, *Strange to say, on Club Paper*. In this he ridiculed a silly report as to Lord Clyde, which had spread itself about the town, —doing so with that mingled tenderness and sarcasm for which he was noted,—the tenderness being ever for those named, and the sarcasm for those unknown. As far as we know, they were the last words he lived to publish. Speaking of the old hero who was just gone he bids us remember that 'censure and praise are alike to him;—"The music warbling to the deafened ear, The incense wasted on the funeral bier!"' How strange and how sad that these, his last words, should now come home to us as so fitted for himself! Not that we believe that such praise is wasted,—even on the spirit of him who has gone.

> Comes the blind Fury with th' abhorred shears,
> And slits the thin spun life! 'But not the praise,'
> Phœbus replied, and touched my trembling ears.[1]

Why should the dead be inaccessible to the glory given to them by those who follow them on the earth? He, of whom we speak, loved such incense when living. If that be an infirmity he was so far infirm. But we hold it to be no infirmity. Who is the man who loves it not? Where is the public character to whom it is not as the breath of his nostrils? But there are men to whom it is given to conceal their feelings. Of such Thackeray was not one. He carried his heart-strings in a crystal case, and when they were wrung or when they were soothed all their workings were seen by friend and foe.

When he died he was still at work for this Magazine. He was writing yet another novel for the delight of its readers. 'Shall we continue this story-telling business and be voluble to the end of our age? Will it not be presently time, O prattler, to hold your tongue and let younger people speak?' These words, of course, were his own. You will find them in that Roundabout Paper of his, *De Finibus*, which was printed in August, 1862. He was voluble to the end;—alas, that it should have been the end! The leisure time of which he was thinking never came to him. That presently was denied to him, nor had he lived would it have been his for many a year to come. He was young in power, young in heart as a child, young even in constitution in spite of that malady which carried him off. But, though it was so, Thackeray ever spoke of

---

[1] Milton, *Lycidas* (1638), 75–77.

himself, and thought of himself, as of one that was old. He in truth believed that the time for letting others speak was speedily coming to him. But they who knew him did not believe it, and his forthcoming new novel was anxiously looked for by many who expected another *Esmond*.

I may not say how great the loss will be to the *Cornhill*, but I think that those concerned in the matter will be adjudged to be right in giving to the public so much of this work as he has left behind him. A portion of a novel has not usually much attraction for general readers; but we venture to think that this portion will attract. They who have studied Mr. Thackeray's characters in fiction,—and it cannot be doubted that they have become matter of study to many,—will wish to follow him to the last, and will trace with a sad but living interest the first rough lines of the closing portraits from his hand.

I shall not attempt here any memoir of Mr. Thackeray's life. Such notices as the passing day requires have been given in many of the daily and weekly papers, and have been given, I believe, correctly. I may, perhaps, specially notice that from the pen of Mr. Hannay, which appeared in the *Edinburgh Courant*.[1] The writing of his life will be a task, and we trust a work of love, for which there will probably be more than one candidate. We trust that it may fall into fitting hands,— into the hands of one who shall have loved wisely, and not too well,— but, above all things, into the hands of a true critic. That which the world will most want to know of Thackeray, is the effect which his writings have produced; we believe that effect to have been very wide, and beneficial withal. Let us hope, also, that the task of his biography may escape that untoward hurry which has ruined the interest of so many of the memoirs of our latter-day worthies.

Of our late Editor's works, the best known, and most widely appreciated are, no doubt, *Vanity Fair*, *Pendennis*, *The Newcomes*, and *Esmond*. The first on the list has been the most widely popular with the world at large. *Pendennis* has been the best loved by those who have felt and tasted the delicacy of Thackeray's tenderness. *The Newcomes* stands conspicuous for the character of the Colonel, who as an English gentleman has no equal in English fiction. *Esmond*, of all his works, has most completely satisfied the critical tastes of those who profess themselves to read critically. For myself, I own that I regard *Esmond* as the first and finest novel in the English language. Taken as a whole, I think that it is without a peer. There is in it a completeness of historical plot,

---

[1] See above, No. 49.

and an absence of that taint of unnatural life which blemishes, perhaps, all our other historical novels, which places it above its brethren. And, beyond this, it is replete with a tenderness which is almost divine,— a tenderness which no poetry has surpassed. Let those who doubt this go back and study again the life of Lady Castlewood. In *Esmond*, above all his works, Thackeray achieves the great triumph of touching the innermost core of his subject, without ever wounding the taste. We catch all the aroma, but the palpable body of the thing never stays with us till it palls us. Who ever wrote of love with more delicacy than Thackeray has written in *Esmond*? May I quote one passage of three or four lines? Who is there that does not remember the meeting between Lady Castlewood and Harry Esmond after Esmond's return. ' "Do you know what day it is?" she continued. "It is the 29th December; it is your birthday! But last year we did not drink it;— no, no! My lord was cold, and my Harry was like to die; and my brain was in a fever; and we had no wine. But now,—now you are come again, bringing your sheaves with you, my dear." She burst into a wild flood of weeping as she spoke; she laughed and sobbed on the young man's heart, crying out wildly,—"bringing your sheaves with you,—your sheaves with you!" ' [Book II, ch. vi.].

But if *Esmond* be, as a whole, our best English novel, Colonel Newcome is the finest single character in English fiction. That it has been surpassed by Cervantes, in *Don Quixote*, we may, perhaps, allow, though *Don Quixote* has the advantage of that hundred years which is necessary to the perfect mellowing of any great work. When Colonel Newcome shall have lived his hundred years, and the lesser works of Thackeray and his compeers shall have died away, then, and not till then, will the proper rank of this creation in literature be appreciated.

We saw him laid low in his simple grave at the close of last year, and we saw the brethen of his art, one after another, stand up on the stone at the grave foot to take a last look upon the coffin which held him. It was very sad. There were there the faces of rough men red with tears, who are not used to the melting mood. The grave was very simple, as became the sadness of the moment. At such times it is better that the very act of interment should be without pomp or sign of glory. But, as weeks pass by us, they, who love English literature, will desire to see some preparation for placing a memento of him in that shrine in which we keep the monuments of our great men. It is to be regarded as a thing of course, that there should be a bust of Thackeray in Westminster Abbey.

53. [Henry Kingsley], 'Thackeray', *Macmillan's Magazine*

February 1864, ix, 356–63

Kingsley (1830–76), a brother of Charles Kingsley, is best known as the novelist who wrote *Geoffrey Hamlyn* (1859) and *Ravenshoe* (1862). Concerning the present article, he complained to Alexander Macmillan, the publisher, that Masson, the editor, 'cut out the best part . . . the comparison between William M. T. and Smollett and Fielding; as it was the only important thing in the whole article, it was to be expected. It merely contained the highest tribute to the exquisite purity of Thackeray as compared with the eighteenth century novelists. Every word was carefully weighed; every idea had been carefully discussed with clever men. Masson did not agree, and so he has drawn his pen through it without one word of notice or apology' (S. M. Ellis, *Henry Kingsley* (1931), 126). In his *Fireside Studies* (1876), i, 13, Kingsley writes that 'It is extremely strange that both Mr. Dickens and Mr. Thackeray, two men whose writings were so singularly pure, should have quoted Smollett as such a witty writer, and have considered him, or affected to consider him, their master; it would puzzle any one to find a witty passage in Dickens or Thackeray with a *double entendre* in it; it would puzzle any man to find a funny passage in Smollett without one.'

Masson's tribute to Thackeray (No. 54) immediately followed Kingsley's in the pages of the magazine.

'Come children, let us shut up the box and the puppets, for our play is played out.'

Does any one remember the words which form the title to this article? They are the concluding words of *Vanity Fair*. Beneath them is a vignette as suggestive and as pathetic as the best of Bewick's. A boy and a girl are looking into a box of puppets, which one knows are the puppets which formed the characters of *Vanity Fair*. Dobbin and Amelia are standing up wishing us 'Good-bye'; Lord Steyne has tumbled out on the floor; and the boy has his hand on the lid, on which is inscribed 'Finis,' ready to shut it down. Now it is shut down for ever: And, alas! the master is shut in with his puppets.

How was it that we first came to know him? In recalling a lost friend to our memory, what is the first thing we think of? Almost always we try to bring back our first interview with him. How naturally it comes to our tongue to say, 'Well, I remember the day I first saw him.' Let us try to do this with the great one who is gone.

Does any one remember the time when one began to hear such sentences as these flying from mouth to mouth—'It is wonderfully clever.' 'It is so very strange.' 'One don't know whether to laugh or cry at it.' 'Is his name really Titmarsh?' 'No, his real name is Thackeray, and he wrote *Cornhill to Grand Cairo*! Not a very young man either, you say; how strange it is his bursting on us with such stuff as this. He *frightens* one at times.'

And so on. If you find in some long neglected Barathrum[1] of waste paper a yellow-coloured pamphlet, on the tattered covers of which is printed 'Vanity Fair; or, Pen and Pencil Sketches of English Society,' you may remember that these were the sort of remarks which went about among non-literary men when the educated world was taken by storm with the most remarkable novel in the English language; coming from the pen of a man, known certainly to some extent, but who was thought to have had sufficient trial, and to have found his *métier* as a clever magazine writer.

Some knew better, but the general world did not. *Vanity Fair* took the world by surprise. Its appearance was a kind of era in the lives of men whose ages were at that time within four of five years of twenty; and, for aught we know, in the lives of men older and wiser.

One's most intimate and dearest friends before this era were probably Hamlet, Don Quixote, Robinson Crusoe, My Uncle Toby, or, probably, for tastes vary, Mr. Tom Jones, or Mr. Peregrine Pickle. Latterly, also, we had got to love Mr. Pickwick, the Brothers Cheeryble, and dear old Tom Pinch; and were conceiving an affectionate admiration of Eddard Cuttle, mariner; but when these wonderful yellow numbers were handed eagerly from hand to hand, to be borrowed, read, re-read, and discussed, it became evident that the circle of our acquaintances had been suddenly and singularly enlarged; that we

[1] Literally, 'a bottomless pit'.

were becoming acquainted with people—strange people, indeed!—who forced themselves on our notice, and engaged our attention, to a degree which none of our former acquaintances had ever suceeded in doing.

These wonderful new people, too, were so amazingly commonplace. They were like ourselves in detail. There was nothing whatever about them except that we could not get them out of our heads; that we discussed their proceedings as we would those of the real people our neighbours; that we were amused with their foolishness, and intensely angry at some of their proceedings. Any fool could have written about such people as these: there was nothing worthy of notice in the book at all, except that it had taken entire possession of us, and of the world. Through the exquisite perfection of the art, the art itself was not only ignored, but indignantly denied.

How melancholy it is to look back at the long line of our sweethearts, loved so dearly for a time, then neglected, then cast off, and only remembered by their names, and by a dull regretful wonder at *that* having been so dear to us at any time. Were we ever so silly as to have wept over the death of Virginia, our first lady-love, when she was shipwrecked in the Mauritius? and how soon after were we furiously indignant at the treatment of Rosamund by her papa about the purple jar and the new shoes? Then it was that impertinent *espiègle* little thing, Julia Mannering; then Flora M'Ivor, and, then by a natural reaction from such overstrained sentimentalism, Evelina Burney.[1] And so we went on from one imaginary young lady to another, until we became so *blasé*, so used to the storms of the great passion, that we could love no more, at least, not in the old degree. We understood women. We had been through too much: when at last that queer old-fashioned, dear little body, Jane Eyre, married Fairfax Rochester, we merely said that the girl was a fool, and lit our cigar. We could love no more.

Fools that we were! we were just on the eve of a crisis in our lives, of the greatest passion of all (for an unworthy object certainly)—a passion different from, and more profound than, all which had gone before. At the time that these yellow numbers began to appear, we made acquaintance with one, Miss Rebecca Sharp, and from the moment she threw her 'dixonary' out of the window, we loved as we

---

[1] The heroines of Bernadin de St. Pierre's *Paul et Virginie* (1787), Maria Edgeworth's 'The Purple Jar' (1796), Scott's *Guy Mannering* (1815) and *Waverley* (1814), and Fanny Burney's *Evelina* (1778).

had never loved before. We were fully alive to that young lady's faults; indeed she did not take any vast trouble to conceal them; but in spite of this she simply gave a whisk of her yellow hair, and an ogle with her green eyes, took us by the nose, and led us whithersoever she would.

And did ever woman lead man such a dance as she led us? Never, since Petronius wrote the first novel eighteen hundred years ago. There was one Ulysses, and there is one Becky Sharp, the woman of many experiences and many counsels, the most of them far from satisfactory. There is no killing or shelving her; she always rises to the occasion, save once, and that one time is the only time on which she was really guilty. Then she is prostrated for a period, and shows you accidentally what you were hardly inclined to believe, that she had some sort of a heart.[1]

Is there anything like the rise, the fall, and the rise of this woman, in literature? It is hard to say where. Many other characters in prose fiction, and often, though far less often, in poetry, grow and develop; but we know of none which enlarges and decreases again, like that of Becky Sharp—which alters in quantity and degree, but never in quality, by the breadth of a hair. False, clever, shifty, and passionately fond of admiration in her father's studio, she carries those qualities and no others with her, using them in greater or less degree, according to her opportunities, through her life. One finds her sipping gin and water in her father's studio, and imitating Miss Pinkerton; one finds her entertaining a select audience of Lord Steyne and Lord Southdown, with a wonderful imitation of the Dowager Lady Southdown; and one finds her at last with the plate of sausages and the brandy bottle, entertaining two German students with an imitation of Jos. Sedley, in the later and not so prosperous times when she lived at Numero Kattervang doose. But it is Becky Sharp still. Her mind, her tact, her power, enlarge according to her circumstances, but her character never develops; the pupils of her green cat's-eyes may expand and contract according to the light, but they are cat's-eyes still. Becky Sharp was crystallized and made perfect by her drunken disreputable father and mother in early years; and whether you find her among drunken art-students, talking *their* slang, or among the dwellers in the gardens of the west, where the golden apples grow, talking *their* slang—whether she does battle with a footman or a marquis—she is still the same dexterous, unprincipled, brilliant, and thoroughly worthless Becky

[1] After Rawdon had found her with Lord Steyne (*Vanity Fair*, ch. liii).

Sharp of old. Any apprentice can make a more or less successful attempt to *develop* a character by circumstances; to make it 'grow under his hand,' as the slang goes. It required the hand of an almost perfect master to draw a character which politely declined to develop on any terms whatever. A sort of Lot's wife of a character, who, though changed into a pillar of salt, persisted in looking back to Sodom, and, what is more, succeeded in the end in getting back there—if not to the old place itself, at least to the most fashionable quarter of Zoar.

Yes, Rebecca Sharp, although she pitched one overboard for the next man she came across, although she debauched one's moral sense, and played the deuce with one's property, still holds the first place among one's ideal lady-loves. Competing even with the last and noblest of them all, with Maggie Tulliver: the girl who wore dark night on her head for a diadem.

And while one made acquaintance with this woman, one began to make acquaintance with other people quite as remarkable as she; with people of whom one had never seen the like exactly, and yet people who were evidently real, and yet could not be sketched from life— with Lord Steyne, for instance.

Some said that Lord Steyne was a sketch from life of Lord A, others of Lord B; the character suited neither. Lord A was accused of being the wicked nobleman, because his house was in a certain square, and Lord B, goodness only knows why. The fact was that Lord Steyne was a result of English History. He may have been as infinitely better than Lord A, as he was infinitely worse than Lord B. But he was the result of ever increasing wealth which passed without disturbance from generation to generation; of five or six centuries of family tradition— tradition which said that the human race was divided into men, women, and the British Peerage. It is perfectly impossible that Lord Steyne could ever have existed; absolutely perfect characters do not exist. Mr. Pitt must have had his failings (one says nothing of the port wine and water; that was a necessity), but they have not come down to us. Marat must have had his virtues, though we have not heard of them. There are no perfect characters in the world. Lord Steyne is a masterly creation, but he is too perfect a character ever to have existed; he is so perfect, that we have to argue ourselves out of the belief that he is drawn from life. The details are too probable—the bow legs, the red hair, the buck teeth; all telling of latent scrofula; his snarling godless scorn, telling of his familiarity with the delightfully choice spirits of the aristocratic revolutionary party of France—of the men who encouraged the revolution, *pour s'amuser*, and perished in it, with a smile of cynical good humour on their faces, as if their own ruin was the best joke of all; his intense admiration for Becky's lying, even when it was directed against himself. All these things, and many others, mark Lord Steyne as the imaginary representative of all the vices which proceed from irresponsible wealth, without one of the virtues which come from the desire to keep a great name spotless; able, sensual, witty, and heartless, without God in this world, not even dreading the Devil in the next. People have tried to represent the wicked nobleman often enough. Let them try the more. Lord Steyne is in the field.

If Rebecca Sharp is a perfectly original character, and if Lord Steyne has been often tried, but only now accomplished, we wish to ask, you whether there is not another character in the book as wonderful in its way as either of the two others. We allude to the Dowager Lady Southdown.

There never was anything like this old lady. Every one appreciated her; to those who were indignant that such people as our dear Becky Sharp, and Lord Steyne, should ever be mentioned, Lady Southdown appeared respectable, inimitably ridiculous, and, on the whole, good: those enjoyed the fun of Lady Southdown who had never spoken to a Countess in their lives. Some might fancy that one-half of the amusement one gets out of her proceeds from her pompous 'façons de parler;' but it is not so. People recognised Lady Southdown, who couldn't in the least appreciate such sentences as 'Jane, I forbid you to put pen to paper;' 'I will have my horses to-morrow morning;' they delighted in Lady Southdown on her own merits entirely. Other men might have known the habits of the British aristocracy as well as Thackeray, who was brought up among them, but it is Thackeray only who has taken one of the most peculiarly aristocratic of them— one of them whose every word and every thought was exclusive— and made her a character to be understood by every class and for all time.

And, besides the originality of these three great characters, any one of which would form the nucleus of a successful novel, there was another fact about this most wonderful story, which no man of humour can ever forget—we mean the names which the author gives his characters. There was an infinite field of fun and suggestive humour opened to us by those wonderful names. Each name in *Vanity Fair* suggest a history.

Marquis of Steyne, for instance. Not Earl of Steyne—that would be too Saxon; not Duke—that would be too personal, for, although there are more Dukes than Marquises, yet they are better known. Marquis, a title like Viscount, with a slight French smack about it, corresponding to his amateur rose-water whiggery; and then Steyne, a name which rings on the ear as true as Buckingham or Bedford, and yet one which instantly suggests to one Brighton, the Pavilion, George the Fourth and all his set. Then Lord Southdown, gentlest of beings, brought into the world to be shorn; second title Lord Wolsey; family name Sheepshanks; seats, Southdown, and Trottermore. Again, that gaunt and dreadful person, Lady Grizzle Macbeth, daughter of Lord Grey of Glowry; and the wonderful German dancer whom Becky dances off his legs, the Count Springbok von Hauhen-laufen. If one began to point out the fun of the names in *Vanity Fair*, one could write a book as big as *Vanity Fair* itself. Take the names of the exceedingly doubtful ladies, with whom Becky has to make it up in her fall, after having cut them in her prosperity, when she was attempting the to her impossible task of being good without three thousand a year. Here they are—the Marquise de la Cruche-cassée, Lady Crackenbury, and Mrs. Washington White. Were there ever three such names for slightly unfortunate ladies?

To follow him through the wild jungle of fun into which he gets when he takes us to the German Court of Pumpernickel, with all the infinitely suggestive absurdity of the names which it pleases him to use, would be impossible. The crowning point of this unequalled non-sensical wisdom, is the triumph of British diplomacy, in arranging the marriage between the Prince of Pumpernickel with the Princess Amelia von Humburg Schlippen-Schloppen—the French candidate Princess Potztausend Donnerwetter having been pitched triumphantly overboard, to the confusion of M. de Macabau the French minister. Schlippen-Schloppen must have been sister, one would think, to our own poor dirty, down-at-heels, Queen Caroline; and Princess Potztausend Donnerwetter (Deviltakeyou Thunder-and-lightning, it might be very loosely rendered), what sort of a lady was she?

Another point about this wonderful book—a point which we cannot pass over—is the way in which the author has illustrated it. For the first time we found a novelist illustrating his own books well. At times, nay very often, we could see that the great brain which guided the hand, in its eagerness to fix the images on the paper, made that hand unsteady; that, in seeking after the end also, there had been some impatient neglect of the means: in other words, that Thackeray sometimes drew correctly, but more often did not. But, notwithstanding this, there are very few of the vignettes in *Vanity Fair*, which, when once seen, can be forgotten.

One begins to wonder, on looking once more on these vignettes, whether Thackeray knew Bewick, the inventor of these tale-telling wood blocks. Bewick writes you the natural history of the cock-robin, and either the master himself, or Luke Clennell,[1] the great pupil, at the end puts you in, *apropos des bottes*, a little, exquisitely finished, inch-and-a-half vignette of a man who has hanged himself, in the month of June, on an oak bough, stretching over a shallow trout stream, which runs through carboniferous limestone. You can see, by the appearance of the hanging corpse, that everything has gone wrong with him. The very body has a dissipated and hopeless look; he has laid his hat and stick at the foot of the tree, and his dog is whining to get at him. We cannot help wondering whether Thackeray took his idea of introducing suggestive vignettes into *Vanity Fair* from having studied Bewick, and noticed the effects these 'tail pieces' in Bewick had upon those who took up a book upon snipes and cock robins, and found themselves face to face with a small school of great humourists; with the men who show us more of the domestic agricultural life at the end of the last century than any others. He most probably saw this—he most probably got from Bewick the idea of small pictures, which, from the very absence of any title, force one to think of them, and puzzle them out. If he got the idea from them, he used it in a way different from theirs. He used these wonderful woodcuts, as most novelists use the titles to their chapters, as a key to the text—as a means of forcing home his moral, not only on the ear but on the eye.

There is one of them lying before us now, and, as an illustration of what we mean, we will make, if the reader will allow us, a quotation—the only one we will trouble him with.

The great Lord Steyne, the short, bow-legged man of fierce animal passions, the man with the bald head, the red hair, and the prominent scrofulous buck teeth, had, as Dr. Elliotson or Dr. Bucknill would have told you, the instant they looked at him a tendency to hereditary madness. He knew it, and it was a spectre to him: he carried his remedy about with him, and defied death. The destroying angel had, for some inscrutable reason, passed over his head without striking, leaving him responsible for his own wickedness; but had stricken down Lord George Gaunt, his innocent son, who went to a madhouse. Lord George

---

[1] Luke Clennell (1781–1840), a wood-engraver trained by Thomas Bewick.

Gaunt had children, on whom, in all probability, the curse would fall. Now read what follows, and say where you will find such stuff elsewhere.

'Twice or thrice in a week, in the earliest morning, the poor mother went for her sins and saw the poor invalid. Sometimes he laughed at her (and his laugh was more pitiable than to hear him cry); sometimes she found the brilliant dandy diplomatist of the Congress of Vienna dragging about a child's toy, or nursing the keeper's baby's doll. Sometimes he knew her, and father Mole, her director and companion; oftener he forgot her, as he had done wife, children, love, ambition, vanity. But he remembered his dinner-hour, and used to cry if his wine-and-water was not strong enough.

★　★　★

The absent Lord's children meanwhile prattled and grew on, quite unconscious that the doom was over them too. First they talked of their father, and devised plans against his return. Then the name of the living dead man was less frequently in their mouths—then not mentioned at all. But the stricken old grandmother trembled to think that these too were the inheritors of their father's shame, as well as of his honours; and watched sickening for the day when the awful ancestral curse should come down on them.' [*Vanity Fair*, ch. xlvii.]

This is terrible enough, but it does not satisfy Thackeray; he must use both pen and pencil to drive his moral home. He must draw us a picture in illustration of his awful words; here it is:—

Lord George Gaunt's children, a pretty, highbred-looking pair, are crouched with their happy heads together, on the floor against the old oak wainscot, in a long-drawn corridor, talking merrily over a great picture-book, which they hold together on their knees. They have taken their place by some accident, under an old trophy of armour, under a cuirass and four straight cavalry swords, probably of Cavalier and Roundhead times. But the swords—the ancestral swords—the swords of Damocles, hang point downwards over the heads of the unconscious prattling innocents below.

What wonder is it that we, trying in our poor way, to lay our wreath on the grave of the great man just dead, should begin our work by trying to bring before you some points of excellence in his first great work. After all, *Vanity Fair* is the book by which he introduced himself to us—the book which first made us love him. We remember, in a later book, *The Newcomes*, meeting dear old Dobbin at a party at Colonel Newcome's, with young Rawdon Crawley; it was like meeting a dear and honoured old friend.

Our task is well-nigh done. It remains for others to write his biography; we only wish to speak of him as we knew him. We knew him first through his greatest work; and so we have affectionately recalled it. Of his later works we have nothing to say. No man could possibly be expected to write two *Vanity Fairs*; and yet *Pendennis* and *The Newcomes* are not much inferior. The highest compliment to his beautiful, singular style, lies in the fact that it became a necessity to the public. They demanded of him that he should write them something— anything, only they *must* have *him*. He complied with their demands. He latterly wrote the *Roundabout Papers;* sat down and wrote the first thing that came into his head, apparently. Many of them are about nothing, or next to nothing—for instance the first; but they are exceedingly charming; every word of them is read and admired by his thorough-going admirers; and certainly the worst of them is a pleasanter stop-gap for an idle quarter of an hour than one can easily find elsewhere.

The great accusation against him has been cynicism and hardness. In that charge most of us from time to time have joined. But, going into the more solemn and careful account which we must make with the dead, we think that charge should be withdrawn. The charge has been made and sustained, because in his fierce campaign against falsehood, meanness, and vulgarity, he did his work only too thoroughly, and hunted those vices high and low, into every hole and corner where they had taken refuge. If he found a mere soupçon of one of them in his own favourite characters; if, following out inexorably his own line of thought, he discovered in one of his own creations, one of his own pet children, what should not be there, he dragged it to the light; and then the world, or part of it, said, 'The man cannot understand a perfect character.' It was because he understood what a perfect character should be so well that the charge was made against him.

The charge cannot be sustained. To repeat it would be to say that the large majority of common-place people are without faults; or else to say that the pointing out of minor vices, the detection of a snake in the verandah, or a scorpion in the wood-basket, is the sign of a cynical and bitter mind. His private life is public enough just now; in that is the answer. His having fought bravely against poverty, after having been brought up in luxury, is no secret, for *The Times* has alluded to it. Other afflictions which he might have had are not the property of the public; but those who accuse him of cynicism and bitterness little think that they are accusing a man whose life was one long, splendid effort of unselfish devotion. He seems never to have lost a friend, and not to have left one single enemy.

How we devoured with amazed admiration this new view of life, *Vanity Fair*. How we wondered what kind of man it was who had written these wonderful words—who had poured out a flood of such strange experiences? To a raw boy of eighteen, we can remember that William Makepeace Thackeray was an awful and mysterious personage —a man whose very clothes would have been interesting even if he himself had not been inside them.

We remember a raw lad of this sort being asked to dine and meet the great man, by one who is gone also—the good and kind John Parker; and even now that lad remembers the day he was asked to meet him as a red-letter day. There was Goethe Robespierre; there was the Waterloo Chaplain; there was the Sanitary King; and there was somebody else entitled to great veneration; and, last of all, there was Thackeray.[1] But this lad had no eyes for the great men named first, though any one of them would have been a wonder to him at another time. There, before him, was the great man himself, at last; there was the head of hair so familiar afterwards, though not so grey sixteen years ago; there were the spectacles, and the wonderful up-looking face. There was an equal of the great man's at table, but this lad engaged himself entirely in watching Thackeray, and, as he did so, he came to this conclusion—that the man who had written the most remarkable tale he had ever read had the most remarkable face he had ever seen.

And we shall never look on that kind good face again! Just now, while we were writing this poor tribute to him, we were turning over the leaves of *Vanity Fair*, and, coming across the wonderful vignette of Lady Southdown bringing in the black dose to Becky Sharp, we burst into a roar of laughter; but it was checked in an instant, for we remembered that the hand which had drawn it was cold and still for ever, and the noble head which had designed it was bowed down to rise no more.

Yes, William Thackeray is dead. He was, as it were yesterday, in the prime of life, full of new projects, surrounded by friends, quite unexpectant of any change. But in the dull winter's night, while he

[1] John Parker (1820–60), Charles Kingsley's publisher; G. H. Lewes, who wrote biographies of Goethe and Robespierre; the Rev. G. R. Geig (1796–1888), who served in the Peninsular War and wrote *The Story of Waterloo* (1847), which is one of Thackeray's sources in *Vanity Fair*; either Edwin Chadwick (1800–90) or the Rev. Thomas Southwood Smith (1788–1861), sanitary reformers. Perhaps the person 'entitled to great veneration' was Carlyle.

was alone in his chamber, the Messenger came for him, and he arose and followed it. He had passed quietly from among us, without a word of farewell, and the riddle of this painful earth is redd to him at last.

And those who loved him are left lamenting because he is gone, and because they missed the few last priceless words which he might have spoken. We honour their grief, but let them remember that it is shared by others—that William Makepeace Thackeray has seventy millions of mourners.

Just now the mails are going out. A hundred splendid steamships are speeding swiftly over every sea, east, west, and north, from the omphalos called London, to carry the fortnight's instalment of British history and British thought into every land where the English language is spoken. But the saddest news they carry—sadder news then they have carried for many a month—is the announcement of the death of William Thackeray.

It will come first to New York, where they loved him as we did. And the flaneurs of the Broadway, and even the busy men in Wall-street, will stay their politics, and remember him. They will say, 'Poor Thackeray is dead.' Though they may refuse to hear the truth—though they choose to insult us beyond endurace, at stated times—let us keep one thing in mind; the flags at New York were hung half-mast high when Havelock died.[1] Let us remember that.

And so the news will travel southward. Some lean, lithe, deer-eyed, quadroon lad will sneak, run swiftly, pause to listen, and then hold steadily forward across the desolate war-wasted space, between the Federal lines and the smouldering watchfires of the Confederates, carrying the news brought by the last mail from Europe, and will come up to a knot of calm, clear-eyed, lean-faced Confederate officers (Oh! that such men should be wasted in such a quarrel, for the sin was not theirs after all); and one of these men will run his eye over the tele-grams, and will say to the others, 'Poor Thackeray is dead.' And the news will go from picket to picket, along the limestone ridges, which hang above the once happy valleys of Virginia, and will pass south, until Jefferson Davis—the man so like Stratford de Redcliffe—the man of the penetrating eyes and of the thin close-set lips—the man with the weight of an empire on his shoulders—will look up from his papers and say, with heartfelt sorrow, 'The author of *The Virginians* is dead.'[2]

[1] Sir Henry Havelock (1795–1859), the military hero of the Indian Mutiny.

[2] Jefferson Davis (1808–89), President of the Confederate states in the American Civil War, which was still in progress. Lord Stratford de Redcliffe (1786–1880) was one of the most prominent diplomatists of the time.

High upon the hill-side at Simla, there will stand soon a group of English, Scotch, and Irish gentlemen, looking over the great plain below, and remarking to one another how much the prospect had changed lately, and how the grey-brown jungle has been slowly supplanted by the brilliant emerald green of the cotton plant, and by a thousand threads of silver water from the irrigation trenches. They will be hoping that Lawrence will succeed poor Lord Elgin,[1] and that he will not be sacrificed in that accursed Calcutta; they will be wondering how it fares with Crawley. Then a dawk will toil up the hill-side with the mail; and in a few minutes they will be saying, 'Lawrence is appointed; Crawley is acquitted; but poor Thackeray is dead.'

The pilot, when he comes out in his leaping whaleboat, and boards the mail steamer, as she lies-to off the heads which form the entrance gates to our new Southern Empire, will ask the news of the captain; and he will be told, 'Lord Elgin and Mr. Thackeray are dead.' That evening they will know it in Melbourne, and it will be announced at all the theatres; the people, dawdling in the hot streets half the night through, waiting for the breaking up of the weather, will tell it to one another, and talk of him. The sentence which we have repeated so often that it has half lost its meaning, will have meaning to them. 'William Thackeray is dead!'

So the news will fly through the seventy million souls who speak the English language. And he will lie cold and deaf in his grave, unconscious, after all his work, of his greatest triumph; unconscious that the great, so-called, Anglo-Saxon race little knew how well they loved him till they lost him. Vanitas vanitatum! 'Let us shut up the box and the puppets, for the play is played out.'

54. [David Masson], 'Thackeray', *Macmillan's Magazine*

February 1864, ix, 363–8

While thinking it most fit that the duty of paying some tribute to the memory of the noble Thackeray should be performed by a contributor,

[1] Lord Lawrence (1811–79) succeeded Lord Elgin (1811–63) as Viceroy of India in 1863.

qualified for the duty no less by his practised perception in the subtleties of that species of literature in which Thackeray was a master than by his great reverence for the deceased, I cannot bring myself to part altogether with the right, which I may assume in these pages, of saying a word or two, in my own name, respecting a man whom it was my privilege to know personally of late years, whose writings had been familiar to me long before I saw his kingly form or shook his cordial hand, and the latest scraps from whose pen in the numbers of the *Cornhill* were read by me with something of that punctual avidity with which some scribbler in ancient Rome may be supposed to have bent over the inimitable Latin of each last-published copy of verses from Horace.

Thackeray's special place in British literature is that of a star of the first magnitude, but of a colour and mode of brilliancy peculiarly its own, in the composite cluster known as our Novelists, our Humourists, our Imaginative Prose-writers. As this is, however, a very numerous cluster, including writers of all degrees of importance, from the smallest up to some so great that we rank them among the chiefs of our total literature, and are not afraid to cite them as our British equivalents to such names of a larger world as Cervantes, Rabelais, and Jean Paul, so there are many ways in which, on our examining the cluster, it will resolve itself into groups. More especially, there is one way of looking at this large order of writers, according to which they shall seem to part, not so much into groups as into two great divisions, each including names of all degrees of magnitude. Now, although, if we view the cluster entire, without seeking to resolve it at all, Thackeray will strike us simply by his superior magnitude, and although, on the other hand, however minutely we may analyse the cluster, we shall find none precisely like Thackeray, and he will continue to strike us still by his intense peculiarity of hue, yet, if we do persuade ourselves to attend to such a general subdivision of the cluster into two main classes as has been hinted at, Thackeray will them on the whole, seem to range himself rather with one of the classes than with the other.

While all writers of fiction make it their business to invent stories, and by the presentation of imaginary scenes, imaginary actions, and imaginary characters, to impart to the minds of their fellows a more prompt, rousing, and impassioned kind of pleasure than attends the reading either of speculative disquisitions or of laborious reproductions of real history, and while most of them in doing so, strew a thousand incidental opinions and fancies by the way, and deviate into delightful and humorous whimsies, a considerable number of such writers are found to differ from the rest in respect of the constant presence in their fictions of a certain heart of doctrine, the constant ruling of their imaginations by a personal philosophy or mode of thinking. It is not always in the fictions of those novelists respecting whom we may know independently that they were themselves men of substantial and distinct moral configuration, of decided ways of thinking and acting, that we find this characteristic. Scott is an instance. He was a man of very solid and distinct personality; and yet, at the outset of his fictions, we see him always, as it were, putting on a dreaming-cap, which transports him away into realms far removed from his own personal position and experience, and from the direct operation of his own moralities. And so with others. When they begin to invent, they put on the dreaming-cap; and many cases might be cited in which this extraordinary power of the dreaming-cap might appear to have been all that the writers possessed—in which, apart from it, they might seem to have had no substantial personality at all. Whether Shakespeare, the greatest genius of the dreaming-cap that ever lived, had any coequal personality himself, of the features of which a glimpse is now recoverable, is, as all know, one of the vexed questions of literary history. We have an opinion of our own on this matter. In every case, we hold, there is an unseverable relation between the personality and the poetic genius, between what a man is and what he can imagine. Dreams themselves are fantastic constructions out of the *débris* of all the sensations, thoughts, feelings, and experiences, remembered or not remembered, of the waking-life; all that any power of the dreaming-cap, however extraordinary, can do, is to remove one into remoter wastes of the great plain of forgetfulness whereon this *débris* lies shimmering, and to release one more and more from the rule of the waking will or the waking reason in the fantasies that rise from it, and flit and melt into each other. Yet, just as some dreams are closer in their resemblance to waking tissues of thought, and more regulated by the logic of waking reason, than others, so, though in all cases the imaginations of a writer, the creations of his literary genius, are related by absolute necessity to his personal individuality, there are many cases in which the relation is so much more subtle and occult than in others, that we find it convenient in these cases to suppose it non-existing, and to think of the imagination as a kind of special white-winged faculty that can float off at any moment from its poise on the personality, move to any distance whithersoever it listeth, and return again at its own sweet will. Hence, for example, among our writers of prose-fiction, we distinguish such a writer as Scott from such a writer as Swift. The connexion, in Swift's case, between his fictions and his personal philosophy and mode of thought is direct and obvious. In his inventions and fancies he does not move away from himself; he remains where he is, in his fixed and awful habit of mind—expressing that habit or its successive moods in constructions fantastic in form, but of regulated and calculated meaning, and capable at once of exact interpretation. Even his Islands of Lilliput and Brobdingnag, his Laputa, and his country of the Houynhmns and Yahoos, are not so much visions into which he has been carried by any power of the dreaming cap, as fell Swiftian allegories of the stationary intellect. And, though Swift is almost unique among British writers in respect of the degree to which he thus made imagination a kind of architect-contractor for fixed moods of the reasons, he may yet stand as, in this respect, an exaggerated exemplar of a whole class of our writers of fiction. In other words, as has been already said, there is a class of our writers of prose-fiction, including writers of as great total power as are to be found in the class that arrive at their fancies by means of the dreaming-cap, but differing from that class by the presence in their fictions of a more constant element of doctrine, a more distinct vein of personal philosophy.

Thackeray was, on the whole, of the latter class. That he may be considered as belonging to it is one reason the more for maintaining its co-ordinate importance with the other class, and for not giving that other class, as has sometimes been proposed, a theoretical superiority as being more entitled, in virtue of their power with the dreaming-cap, to the high designation of creative or imaginative writers. One reason the more, we say—for might it not have been recollected that even Goethe, whose range of dream was as wide as that of most men, made his imagination but a kind of architect-contractor for his reason in his great prose-novel, and that, if we rank among our highest British artists a Sir Joshua Reynolds, we do not put our Hogarth beneath him? A creative writer! Who shall say that Thackeray did not give us creations? What reader of these pages, at all events, will say it, after his memory has been refreshed by our contributor with those recollections of a few of the wondrous creations that took flight from the single novel of *Vanity Fair* into that vast population of ideal beings of diverse characters and physiognomies with which the genius of imaginative writers has filled the ether of the real world? Nay, on the question whether Thackeray *should* be so decidedly attached to the class of writers of fiction with which at first sight we associate him, there may be some preliminary hesitation. In his smaller pieces, for example—some of his odd whims and absurdities in prose and verse—did he not break away into a riot of humour, a lawlessness of sheer zanyism, as exquisitely suggestive of genius making faces at its keeper as anything we have seen since Shakespeare's clowns walked the earth and sang those jumbled shreds of sense and nonsense which we love now as so keenly Shakespearian, and would not lose for the world? The dreaming-cap!—why, here we have the dreaming-cap, and bells attached to it. He moves to any distance out of sight, and still, by the tinkle, we can follow him and hear 'the fool i' the forest.' We are not sure but that in some of these small grotesques of Thackeray we have relics of a wilder variety of pure genius than in his more elaborate fictions. But, again, even in some of these larger and more continuous constructions of his genius in fiction, we have examples of a power which he possessed of going out of himself, and away from the habits and humours of his own time and circumstances, into tracts where the mere act of producing facsimiles or verisimilitudes of what he had directly seen and known was not sufficient, and he had to move with the stealthy step of a necromancer, recalling visions of a vanished life. When we think, for instance, of his *Esmond*, and of passages in his other novels where he gives play to his imagination in the historic, and assumes so easily a certain quaintness of conception and of phraseology to correspond, we seem even to catch a glimpse of what that marvellous dreaming-power of the so-called creative writers may after all in part consist in—to wit, a wide range of really historic interest in their own waking persons, and a habit of following out their trains of historic speculation and enthusiasm, rather than their passing observations and experiences, in their dreams. Thackeray, at all events, had a remarkable historic faculty within a certain range of time, which it was perhaps owing to the more paying nature of fiction than of history in these days that he did not more expressly use and develop. The Life of Talleyrand, which he once had in contemplation, before the days of his universal celebrity as a novelist, would have been, if done as Thackeray could have done it, a masterpiece of peculiar eighteenth-nineteenth-century biography. Nor is the story, jocularly spread by himself some years ago, that he meant to continue Macaulay's unfinished *History of England*, taking it up at the reign of Queen Anne, without a certain significance. One of the many distinctions among men is as to the portion of the past by which their

imaginations are most fondly fascinated and with which they feel themselves most competent to deal in recollection. Macaulay's real and
native historic range began where he began his History—in the interval
between the Civil Wars and the Revolution of 1688. Thackeray's began
a little later—at the date of Queen Anne's accession, and the opening of
the eighteeenth century. And, as within this range he would have been
a good and shrewd historian, so within this range his imagination moves
easily and gracefully in fiction. A man of the era of the later Georges
by his birth and youth, and wholly of the Victorian era by his maturity
and literary activity, he can go as far back as to Queen Anne's reign by
that kind of imaginative second-sight which depends on delight in
transmitted reminiscence.

As a Victorian, however, taking for the matter of most of his fictions
life as he saw it around him, or as he could recollect it during his own
much-experienced and variously-travelled career from his childhood
upwards, Thackeray *was* one of those novelists whose writings are
distinguished by a constant heart of doctrine, a permanent vein of
personal philosophy. Our long and now hackneyed talk about him as
a Realist, and our habit of contrasting him perpetually with Dickens,
as more a novelist of the Fantastic or Romantic School, are recognitions
of this. It would ill become us here and now to resort again to the full
pedantry of this contrast; but, in a certain sense, as none knew better
than Thackeray himself, there *was* a kind of polar opposition between
his method and Dickens's in their art as humourists and writers of
fiction. With extraordinary keenness of perception, with the eye of a
lynx for the facts, physiognomies, and humours of real life, and taking
the suggestions of real life with marvellous aptness for his hints,
Dickens does move away with these suggestions into a kind of vacant
ground of pure fancy, where the relations and the mode of exhibition
may be ideal, and there shapes such tales of wonder and drollery, and
holds such masques and revels of imaginary beings, as (witness how
we use them and how our talk and our current literature are enriched
by references to them) no genius but his has produced in our day. In
him we do see, after a fashion entirely his own, that particular kind of
power which we have called the power of the dreaming-cap, and which
is oftenest named ideality. Thackeray, on the other hand, is sternly,
ruthlessly real. Men and women as they are, and the relations of life
as he has actually seen and known them, or in as near approach to
facsimile of reality as the conditions of invention of stories for general
reading will permit—these are what Thackeray insists on giving us.

Fortunate age to have had two such representatives of styles of art the co-existence of which—let us not call it mutual opposition—is ever-lastingly possible and everlastingly desirable! Fortunate still in having the one master-artist left; unfortunate now, as we all feel—and that artist more than most of us—in having lost the other! For in Thackeray we have lost not only our great master of reality in the matter of prose-fiction, but also the spokesman of a strong personal philosophy, a bracing personal mode of thought, which pervaded all he wrote. Thackeray, it has been well said, is best thought of, in some respects, as a sage, a man of experienced wisdom, and a conclusive grasp of the world and its worth, expressing himself, partly by accident, through the particular modes of story-writing and humorous extravaganza. And what was his philosophy? To tell that wholly, to throw into systematic phrase one tithe even of the characteristic and recurring trains of thought that passed through that grave brain, is what no man can hope to do. But the essential philosophy of any mind is often a thing of few and simple words, repeating a form of thought that it requires no elaborate array of propositions to express, and that may have been as familiar to an ancient Chaldæan making his camel's neck his pillow in the desert as it is to a sage in modern London. It is that elementary mode of thought which comes and goes oftenest, and into which one always sinks when one is meditative and alone. And so may we not recognise Thackeray's habitual philosophy in a peculiar variation of these words of the Laureate, which he makes to be spoken by the hero of his *Maud*?—

> We are puppets, Man in his pride, and Beauty fair in her flower:
> Do we move ourselves, or are moved by an unseen hand at a game
> That pushes us off the board, and others ever succeed?
> Ah yet, we cannot be kind to each other here for an hour;
> We whisper, and hint, and chuckle, and grin at a brother's shame;
> However we brave it out, we men are a little breed.
>
> A monstrous eft was of old the Lord and Master of Earth;
> For him did his high sun flame, and his river billowing ran,
> And he felt himself in his force to be Nature's crowning race.
> As nine months go to the shaping an infant ripe for his birth,
> So many a million of ages have gone to the making of man:
> He now is the first, but is he the last? is he not too base?
>
> The man of science himself is fonder of glory, and vain,
> An eye well-practised in nature, a spirit bounded and poor;
> The passionate heart of the poet is whirled into folly and vice.

I would not marvel at either, but keep a temperate brain;
For not to desire or admire, if a man could learn it were more
Than to walk all day like the sultan of old in a garden of spice.

Such, in some form, though not, perhaps, precisely in this high-rolled
and semigeologic from, was Thackeray's philosophy, breathed through
his writings. That we are a little breed—poets, philosophers, and all
of us—this is what he told us. Nature's crowning race?—Oh no; too
base for that! Many stages beyond the Eft, certainly; but far yet from
even the ideal of our own talk and our pretensions to each other. And
so he lashed us, and dissected us, and tore off our disguises. He did it
in great matters and he did it in small matters; and, that he might draw
a distinction between the great matters and the small matters, he
generalised the smaller kinds of baseness and littleness of our time,
against which he most persistently directed his satires, under the mock-
heroic title of Snobbism. Anti-Snobbism was his doctrine as applied
to many particulars of our own and of recent times—Victorian or
Georgian. But he took a wider range than that, and laid bare the deeper
blacknesses and hypocrisies of our fairly-seeming lives. And we called
him a cynic in revenge. A cynic! No more will that word be heard
about Thackeray. How, in these few weeks since he was laid in Kensal
Green, have his secret deeds of goodness, the instances of his incessant
benevolence and kindheartedness to all around him, leapt into regretful
light. A cynic! We might have known, while we used it, that the word
was false. Had he not an eye for the piety and the magnanimity of real
human life, its actually attained and incalculable superiorities over the
Eft; and did he not exult, to the verge of the sentimental, in reproductions of these in the midst of his descriptions of meannesses? And did
he not always, at least, include himself far better or for worse in that
breed of men of which the judgment must be so mixed? Not to desire
or admire, but to walk all day like a sultan in his garden, was a dignity
of isolation to which he had never attained. He did not hold himself
aloof. Ah! how he came among us here in London, simply, quietly,
grandly, the large-framed, massive-headed, and grey-haired sage that
he was—comporting himself as one of us, though he was weightier
than all of us; listening to our many-voiced clamour, and dropping in
his wise occasional word; nay, not forbidding, but rather joining with
a smile, if, in hilarity, we raised his own song of evening festivity:—

Here let us sport,
Boys as we sit,

Laughter and wit
Flashing so free:
Life is but short;
When we are gone,
Let them sing on
Round the old tree.

[From 'The Mahogany Tree'.]

Ah! the old tree remains, and the surviving company still sits round it, and they will raise the song in the coming evenings as in the evenings gone by. But the chair of the sage is vacant. It will be long before London, or the nation, or our literature, shall see a substitute for the noble Thackeray.

55. [Walter Bagehot], from 'Sterne and Thackeray', *National Review*

April 1864, xviii, 523–53. Reprinted in Bagehot's *Literary Studies* (1879), ii, 106–45

This article was ostensibly a review of Percy Fitzgerald, *The Life of Laurence Sterne* (1864) and Theodore Taylor, *Thackeray the Humourist and the Man of Letters* (1864).

. . . Thackeray, like Sterne, looked at everything—at nature, at life, at art—from a *sensitive* aspect. His mind was, to some considerable extent, like a woman's mind. It could comprehend abstractions when they were unrolled and explained before it, but it never naturally created them; never of itself, and without external obligation, devoted itself to them. The visible scene of life—the streets, the servants, the clubs, the gossip, the West End—fastened on his brain. These were to him reality. They burnt in upon his brain; they pained his nerves; their influence reached him through many avenues, which ordinary men do not feel much, or to which they are altogether impervious. He had distinct and rather painful sensations where most men have but confused and blurred ones. Most men have felt the *instructive* headache, during which they are more acutely conscious than usual of all which goes on around them,—during which everything seems to pain them, and in which they understand it, because it pains them, and they cannot get their imagination away from it. Thackeray had a nerve-ache of this sort always. He acutely felt every possible passing fact—every trivial interlude in society. Hazlitt used to say of himself, and used to say truly, that he could not enjoy the society in a drawing-room for thinking of the opinion which the footman formed of his odd appearance as he went upstairs. Thackeray had too healthy and stable a nature to be thrown so wholly off his balance; but the footman's view of life was never out of his head. The obvious facts which suggest it to the footman poured it in upon him; he could not exempt himself from them. As most men say that the earth *may* go round the sun, but in fact, when we look at the sun, we cannot help believing it goes round the earth,—just so this most impressible, susceptible genius could not help half accepting, half believing the common ordinary sensitive view of life, although he perfectly knew in his inner mind and deeper nature that this apparent and superficial view of life was misleading, inadequate, and deceptive. He could not help seeing everything, and what he saw made so near and keen an impression upon him, that he could not again exclude it from his understanding; it stayed there, and disturbed his thoughts.

If, he often says, 'people, could write about that of which they are really thinking, how interesting books would be!' More than most writers of fiction, he felt the difficulty of abstracting his thoughts and imagination from near facts which *would* make themselves felt. The sick wife in the next room, the unpaid baker's bill, the lodging-house keeper who doubts your solvency; these, and such as these,—the usual accompaniments of an early literary life,—are constantly alluded to in his writings. Perhaps he could never take a grand enough view of literature, or accept the truth of 'high art,' because of his natural tendency to this stern and humble realism. He knew that he was writing a tale which would appear in a green magazine (with others) on the 1st of March, and would be paid for perhaps on the 11th, by which time, probably 'Mr. Smith' would have to 'make up a sum,' and would again present his 'little account.' There are many minds besides his who feel an interest in these realities, though they yawn over 'high art' and elaborate judgments.

A painfulness certainly clings like an atmosphere round Mr. Thackeray's writings, in consequence of his inseparable and ever-present realism. We hardly know where it is, yet we are all conscious of it less or more. A free and bold writer, like Sir Walter Scott, throws himself far away into fictitous worlds, and soars there without effort, without pain, and with unceasing enjoyment. You see as it were between the lines of Mr. Thackeray's writings, that his thoughts were never long away from the close proximate scene. His writings might be better if it had been otherwise; but they would have been less peculiar, less individual; they would have wanted their character, their flavour, if he had been able while writing them to forget for many moments the ever-attending, the ever-painful sense of himself.

Hence have arisen most of the censures upon him, both as he seemed to be in society and as he was in his writings, He was certainly uneasy in the common and general world, and it was natural that he should be so. The world poured in upon him, and *inflicted* upon his delicate sensibility a number of petty pains and impressions which others do not feel at all, or which they feel but very indistinctly. As he sat he seemed to read off the passing thoughts—the base, common, ordinary impressions—of every one else. Could such a man be at ease? Could even a quick intellect be asked to set in order with such velocity so many data? Could any temper, however excellent, be asked to bear the contemporaneous influx of innumerable minute annoyances? Men of ordinary nerves who feel a little of the pains of society, who perceive what really passes, who are not absorbed in the petty pleasures of sociability, could well observe how keen was Thackeray's *sensation* of common events, could easily understand how difficult it must have been for him to keep mind and temper undisturbed by a miscellaneous tide at once so incessant and so forcible.

He could not emancipate himself from such impressions even in a case where most men hardly feel them. Many people have—it is not difficult to have—some vague sensitive perception of what is passing in the minds of the guests, of the ideas of such as sit at meat; but who remembers that there are also nervous apprehensions, also a latent mental life among those who 'stand and wait'—among the floating figures which pass and carve? But there was no impression to which Mr. Thackeray was more constantly alive, or which he was more apt in his writings to express. He observes:

Between me and those fellow-creatures of mine who are sitting in the room below, how strange and wonderful is the partition! We meet at every hour of the daylight, and are indebted to each other for a hundred offices of duty and comfort of life; and we live together for years, and don't know each other. John's voice to me is quite different from John's voice when it addresses his mates below. If I met Hannah in the street with a bonnet on, I doubt whether I should know her. And all these good people, with whom I may live for years and years, have cares, interests, dear friends and relatives, mayhap schemes, passions, longing hopes, tragedies of their own, from which a carpet and a few planks and beams utterly separate me. When we were at the sea-side and poor Ellen used to look so pale, and run after the postman's bell, and seize a letter in a great scrawling hand, and read it, and cry in a corner, how should we know that the poor little thing's heart was breaking? She fetched the water, and she smoothed the ribbons, and she laid out the dresses, and brought the early cup of tea in the morning, just as if she had had no cares to keep her awake. Henry (who lived out of the house) was the servant of a friend of mine who lived in chambers. There was a dinner one day, and Henry waited all through the dinner. The champagne was properly iced, the dinner was excellently served; every guest was attended to; the dinner disappeared; the desert was set; the claret was in perfect order, carefully decanted, and more ready. And then Henry said, 'If you please, sir, may I go home?' He had received word that his house was on fire; and, having seen through his dinner, he wished to go and look after his children and little sticks of furniture. Why, such a man's livery is a uniform of honour. The crest on his button is a badge of bravery.' [From 'On a Chalk-Mark on the Door', *Roundabout Papers.*]

Nothing in itself could be more admirable than this instinctive sympathy with humble persons; not many things are rarer than this nervous apprehension of what humble persons think. Nevertheless it cannot, we think, be effectually denied that it coloured Mr. Thackeray's writings and the more superficial part of his character—that part which was most obvious in common and current society—with very considerable defects. The pervading idea of the 'Snob Papers' is too frequent, too recurring, too often insisted on, even in his highest writings; there was a slight shade of similar feeling even in his occasional society, and though it was certainly unworthy of him, it was exceedingly natural that it should be so, with such a mind as his and in a society such as ours.

There are three methods in which a society may be constituted. There is the equal system, which, with more or less of variation, prevails in France and in the United States. The social presumption in these countries always is that every one is on a level with every one else. In America, the porter at the station, the shopman at the counter, the boots at the hotel, when neither a Negro nor an Irishman, is your equal. In France *égalité* is a political first principle. The whole of Louis Napoleon's *régime* depends upon it; remove that feeling, and the whole fabric of the Empire will pass away. We once heard a great French statesman illustrate this. He was giving a dinner to the clergy of his neighbourhood, and was observing that he had now no longer the power to help or hurt them, when an eager *curé* said, with simple-minded joy, '*Oui, monsieur, maintenant personne ne peut rien, ni le comte, ni le prolétaire.*' The democratic priest so rejoiced at the universal levelling which had passed over his nation, that he could not help boasting of it when silence would have been much better manners. We are not now able—we have no room and no inclination—to discuss the advantages of democratic society; but we think in England we may venture to assume that it is neither the best nor the highest form which a society can adopt, and that it is certainly fatal to the development of individual originality and greatness by which the past progress of the human race has been achieved, and from which alone, it would seem, all future progress is to be anticipated. If it be said that people are all alike, that the world is a plain with no natural valleys and no natural hills, the picturesqueness of existence is destroyed, and, what is worse, the instinctive emulation by which the dweller in the valley is stimulated to climb the hill is annihilated and becomes impossible.

On the other had, there is the opposite system, which prevails in the East,—the system of irremovable inequalities, of hedged-in castes, which no one can enter but by birth, and from which no born member can issue forth. This system likewise, in this age and country, needs no attack, for it has no defenders. Every one is ready to admit that it cramps originality, by defining our work irrespective of our qualities and before we were born; that it retards progress, by restraining the wholesome competition between class and class, and the wholesome migration from class to class, which are the best and strongest instruments of social improvement.

And if both these systems be condemned as undesirable and prejudicial, there is no third system except that which we have—the system of *removable inequalities*, where many people are inferior to and worse off than others, but in which each may *in theory* hope to be on a level with the highest below the throne, and in which each may reasonably, and without sanguine impracticability, hope to gain one step in social elevation, to be at last on a level with those who at first were just above them. But, from the mere description of such a society, it is evident that, taking man as he is, with the faults which we know he has, and the tendencies which he invariably displays, some poison of 'snobbishness' is inevitable. Let us define it as the habit of 'pretending to be higher in the social scale than you really are.' Everybody will admit that such pretension is a fault and a vice, yet every observant man of the world would also admit that, considering what other misdemeanours men commit, this offence is not inconceivably heinous; and that, if people never did any thing worse, they might be let off with a far less punitive judgment than in the actual state of human conduct would be just or conceivable. How are we to hope men will pass their lives in putting their best foot foremost, and yet will never boast that their better foot is farther advanced and more perfect than in fact it is? Is boasting to be made a capital crime? Given social ambition as a propensity of human nature; given a state of society like ours, in which there are prizes which every man may seek, degradations which every one may erase, inequalities which every one may remove, —it is idle to suppose that there will not be all sorts of striving to cease to be last and to begin to be first, and it is equally idle to imagine that all such strivings will be of the highest kind. This effort will be, like all the efforts of our mixed and imperfect human nature, partly good and partly bad, with much that is excellent and beneficial in it, and much also which is debasing and pernicious. The bad striving after unpossessed distinction is snobbishness, which from the mere definition cannot be defended, but which may be excused as a natural frailty in an emulous man who is not distinguished, who hopes to be distinguished, and who perceives that a valuable means of gaining distinction is a judicious, though false pretension that it has already been obtained.

Mr. Thackeray, as we think, committed two errors in this matter. He lacerates 'snobs' in his books as if they had committed an unpardonable outrage and inexpiable crime. That man, he says, is anxious 'to know lords; and he pretends to know more of lords than he really does know. What a villain! what a disgrace to our common nature! what an irreparable reproach to human reason!' Not at all; it is a fault which satirists should laugh at, and which moralists condemn and disapprove, but which yet does not destroy the whole vital excellence of him who possesses it,—which may leave him a good citizen, a pleasant husband, a warm friend; 'a fellow,' as the undergraduate said, '*up* in his *morals.*'

In transient society it is possible, we think, that Mr. Thackeray thought too much of social inequalities. They belonged to that common, plain, perceptible world which filled his mind, and which left him at times, and at casual moments, no room for a purely intellectual and just estimate of men as they really are in themselves, and apart from social perfection or defect. He could gauge a man's reality as well as any observer, and far better than most: his attainments were great, his perception of men instinctive, his knowledge of casual matters enormous; but he had a greater difficulty than other men in relying only upon his own judgment. 'What the footman—what Mr. Yellowplush Jeames would think and say,' could not but occur to his mind, and would modify, not his settled judgment, but his transient and casual opinion of the poet or philosopher. By the constitution of his mind he thought much of social distinctions; and yet he was in his writings too severe on those who, in cruder and baser ways, showed that they also were thinking much.

Those who perceive that this irritable sensibility was the basis of Thackeray's artistic character, that it gave him his materials, his implanted knowledge of things and men, and gave him also that keen and precise style which hit in description the nice edges of all objects,—those who trace these great qualities back to their real source in a somewhat painful organisation, must have been vexed or amused, according to their temperament, at the common criticism which associates him with Fielding. Fielding's essence was the very reverse; it was a bold spirit of bounding happiness. No just observer could talk to Mr. Thackeray, or look at him, without seeing that he had deeply felt many sorrows—perhaps that he was a man *likely* to feel sorrows—that he was of an anxious temperament. Fielding was a reckless enjoyer. He saw the world—wealth and glory, the best dinner and the worst dinner, the gilded *salon* and the low sponging-house—and he saw that they were good. Down every line of his characteristic writings there runs this elemental energy of keen delight. There is no trace of such a thing in Thackeray. A musing fancifulness is far more characteristic of him than a joyful energy.

Sterne had all this sensibility also, but—and this is the cardinal discrepancy—it did not make him irritable. He was not hurried away, like Fielding, by buoyant delight; he stayed and mused on painful scenes. But they did not make him angry. He was not irritated at the 'foolish fat scullion.' He did not vex himself because of the vulgar. He did not amass petty details to prove that tenth-rate people were ever striving to be ninth-rate people. He had no tendency to rub the bloom off life. He accepted pretty-looking things, even the French aristocracy, and he owes his immortality to his making them prettier than they are. Thackeray was pained by things, and exaggerated their imperfections; Sterne brooded over things with joy or sorrow, and he idealised their sentiment—their pathetic or joyful characteristics. This is why the old lady said, 'Mr. Thackeray was an uncomfortable writer,'—and an uncomfortable writer he is.

Nor had Sterne a trace of Mr. Thackeray's peculiar and characteristic scepticism. He accepted simply the pains and pleasures, the sorrows and the joys of the world; he was not perplexed by them, nor did he seek to explain them, or account for them. There is a tinge—a mitigated, but perceptible tinge—of Swift's philosophy in Thackeray. 'Why is all this? Surely this is very strange? Am I right in sympathising with such stupid feelings, such petty sensations? Why are these things? Am I not a fool to care about or think of them? The world is dark, and the great curtain hides from us all.' This is not a steady or an habitual feeling, but it is never quite absent for many pages. It was inevitable, perhaps, that in a sceptical and inquisitive age like this, some vestiges of puzzle and perplexity should pass into the writings of our great sentimentalist. He would not have fairly represented the moods of his time if he omitted that pervading one.

We had a little more to say of these great men, but our limits are exhausted, and we must pause. Of Thackeray it is too early to speak at length. A certain distance is needful for a just criticism. The present generation have learned too much from him to be able to judge him rightly. We do not know the merit of those great pictures which have sunk into our minds, and which have coloured our thoughts, which are become habitual memories. In the books we know best, as in the people we know best, small points, sometimes minor merits, sometimes small faults, have an undue prominence. When the young critics of this year have grey hairs, their children will tell them what is the judgment of posterity upon Mr. Thackeray.

THACKERAY'S WRITINGS: AN HISTORICAL AND CRITICAL ESSAY

56. Leslie Stephen, from 'The Writings of W. M. Thackeray', *The Works of William Makepeace Thackeray*

Stephen (1832–1904), literary critic, historian, philosopher, first editor of the *Dictionary of National Biography*, and mountaineer, married as his first wife Thackeray's younger daughter. He wrote for many of the leading periodicals, and outstanding amongst his numerous books are his *History of Thought in the Eighteenth Century* (1876) and *Hours in a Library* (1874–9).

. . . Thackeray's work, like other people's, must ultimately be judged on its own merits and without reference to the personal history of its author. The question remains of his relation to contemporary literature. What were the moods of thought which were seeking to express themselves, and who were the authorised interpreters? What was the niche to be filled by the new aspirant? Thackeray does not appear to have been prepared with a distinct answer to such questions when he first took to literature as a profession. He had in great measure to feel his way, and certainly did not, like some more fortunate writers, burst upon the world as a fully-developed genius. He had passed five-and-thirty before his triumph was unequivocally achieved; and, though some earlier works might give a sufficient indication of his power to intelligent critics, he made various experiments before fully recognising his true sphere. The earlier writings, however, show what he thought of the men who were then at the head of his profession and so indirectly reveal the nature of his own impulses. The future literary historian of the nineteenth century will have to deal at length with topics which I can only touch in the most cursory manner. He will probably observe that the years in which Thackeray was growing to manhood mark a very distinct transition. Generations of mankind overlap; but it often seems as though the generations in literature succeeded each other without blending. A group of eminent men appears simultaneously, and then dies out to give room to its successors. So, for example, the groups which flourished (to use the time-honoured phrase) at the opening of the seventeenth, of the eighteenth, and of the nineteenth centuries respectively may each be marked off from their immediate followers by very definite limits of time. The era of the Reform Bill coincides with the extinction of a whole generation of eminent men. Scott, Coleridge, Wordsworth, Shelley, Byron, Keats, Lamb, Southey, and others, all either passed away or ceased to be productive within a few years of that date. Poor Colonel Newcome was quite bewildered when he returned from India and found the young men of letters provided with a new set of idols. Not to dwell upon other differences, it is remarkable that our grandfathers, the men who were stirred by the great revolutionary earthquake, were far more poetical than their children. We still have one or two great poets amongst us, and a very large number of moderate poets; but no poem which has appeared within the last half-century has taken the world by storm, like the *Lay of the Last Minstrel* or *Childe Harold*, or has produced so profound an effect upon thoughtful minds as the poetry of Wordsworth. At a time when such a writer as Crabbe—a man whom I heartily admire, but who certainly is not to be reckoned amongst great names—could receive 3,000*l*. for a new set of tales in verse, it is clear that there must have been a very large and inflammable public. On the other hand, Scott was the only man of very high or enduring reputation who made a great success in the department of fiction. Scott, to my thinking, is one of our very greatest names, but it is curious to remark how solitary was his empire. Miss Austen belongs to quite a different category, and, however admirable her art, was clearly not one of those writers who stamp a character upon the litera-ture of the time. But who were Scott's rivals or imitators? There must have been some, for people read novels then, though perhaps not so exclusively as now. But who were they? If Scott stands for Shak-speare, who were the Ben Jonsons, and Fletchers, and Chapmans, and Massingers of the period? I presume that a candidate in a competitive examination could answer, and indeed, after a little thought, I could suggest a name or two myself; but certain it is that they have sunk into oblivion, and that a novel of this period means for us a Waverley Novel. In the later period fiction seems to have succeeded to poetry, and one may perhaps assume that the difference is significant. A period of comparative calm was following a vehement outburst of sentiment. The strong emotion which could only express itself in lyrical out-bursts was passing away, and the world was to be content to resume a quiet jog-trot of prose for another generation. People were beginning to see the ridiculous side of Wertherism and Byronism; and nobody, except Mr. G. P. R. James, tried to carry on the style of Scott's romances.

This, of course, is only one aspect of a very complex process; but we see it very clearly represented in Thackeray. Byron, for example, was one of his favourite antipathies. He seldom speaks of him without a manifest dislike. He naturally thinks of him at Athens in connection with the beauty of Greek women, upon which subject, as we know, Byron had uttered various sentiments. 'Lord Byron,' observes Thack-eray, 'wrote more cant of this sort than any poet I know of. Think of the "peasant girls with dark blue eyes" of the Rhine—the brown-faced, flat-nosed, thick-lipped dirty wenches! Think of "filling high a cup of Samian wine;" small beer is nectar compared to it, and Byron himself always drank gin. That man *never* wrote from his heart. He got up rapture and enthusiasm with an eye to the public: but this is dangerous ground, even more dangerous than to look Athens full in the face and say that your eyes are not dazzled by its beauty. The great public admires Greece and Byron. The public knows best. Murray's *Guide-book* calls the latter, "our native bard!" Our native bard! *Mon Dieu!* He Shakspeare's, Milton's, Keats's, Scott's native bard! Well, woe be to the man who denies the public gods' [*From Cornhill to Cairo*, ch. v]. Warrington expresses a similar opinion to Colonel Newcome, though with less energy, for, in truth, less energy was required to meet the flagging tide of Byronic enthusiasm. His view of Scott is hinted a little further on in the same book. 'When,' he asks, 'shall we have a real account of those times and heroes—no good-humoured pageant like those of the Scott romances—but a real authentic story to instruct and frighten honest people of the present day and make them thankful that the grocer governs the world now in the place of the baron?' In fact, if we think of it, the grocer came in for his turn with Louis Philippe and the English Reform Bill; and the sham glorification of feudalism (the 'brutal, unchristian blundering feudal system,' says

Thackeray), which we now see to be the alloy which mixes with Scott's pure gold, and not, as his early readers imagined, the really valuable element, was growing threadbare like other affectations. The grocer, too, has his faults and may as well hear of them; but they are best portrayed in plain prose and with unflinching realism.

Two contemporaries of Thackeray's were rapidly growing famous; they were for him the representatives of the rival literary schools which were to supplant Scott and Byron. His views of their perform-ance is therefore interesting as indicative of his own position. Bulwer, afterwards Lord Lytton, was six years his senior, and had become conspicuous whilst Thackeray was still at college. This is not the place to attempt any estimate of Bulwer's merits. It is at least clear that he was a man of extraordinary versatility and energy, and with talents so great that they may easily be taken for genius. His early novels are perhaps less familiar to readers of the present day than the later books, *The Caxtons* and its successors, which differ rather curiously from his first performances. Amongst other changes, he became rather obtru-sively moral, and given to sing the praises of domestic propriety. It would therefore be difficult for any one, familiar with these stories alone, to appreciate the satire which Thackeray directed against him in the 'novels by eminent hands' and the Deuceace papers. I have reason to know that Thackeray materially changed his views upon this matter, and expressed some regret for the asperity of his early utterance. In youth we are all apt to be intolerant and dogmatic. But in those early days he evidently regarded Bulwer to a great extent as another avatar of the great spirit, of humbug. For not only did the new writer talk about the True and the Beautiful in capital letters, or, in other words, try to enliven British dulness by a liberal infusion of German mysticism and sentimentalism, but he applied this sham philo-sophy to point very immoral doctrines in such books as *Ernest Mal-travers* and *Eugene Aram*. He gave himself the airs at once of a dandy and a metaphysician, and tried to astonish British grocers and other respectabilities by an affectation as silly as it was offensive. If the public was tired of Byron's rant and Scott's romance, these new-fangled antics of a clever prig, who was trying to gain notoriety by insulting honest prejudice, and mystifying plain understanding, were at bottom an offensive continuation of fooleries which ought to be dead and buried. That, at least, is the light in which I take Bulwer to have appeared to Thackeray in early days. Certain it is that, though Thack-eray admits his rival to be a man of remarkable talents, he pours unsparing ridicule upon his pretensions, and regards his philosophising and his poetising with equal contempt. Dickens, one year junior to Thackeray, certainly did not offend in this way. He had no desire whatever to mystify or to shock. He was successful beyond any English novelist, probably beyond any novelist that has ever lived, in exactly hitting off the precise tone of thought and feeling which would find favour with the grocers. As Burke said of George Grenville and the House of Commons, Dickens hit the average Englishmen of the middle-classes between wind and water. Nor would Thackeray have been slow to declare, if any criticism of a writer generally considered to be in some sense his rival had been becoming, that Dickens won his amazing triumph not merely by an extraordinary and, in its way, quite unrivalled faculty for perceiving certain aspects of men and things, but also by appealing to the better nature of his hearer. The only question that can be raised in regard to Dickens concerns the intellectual depth of his perceptions. He may be accused of taking up too easily the obvious commonplace view of things, which commends itself to the class which he delighted because it makes little demand upon their power of thought. Some such view is perhaps indicated in Thackeray's reference to him in the *Paris Sketchbook*—a reference made before both men had become too famous and too much connected to speak freely of each other. The future student of history would do wrong, he says, 'to put that great contemporary history of Pickwick aside as a frivolous work. It contains true character under false names, and, like *Roderick Random*, an inferior work, and *Tom Jones* (one that is immeasurably superior), gives us a better idea of the state and ways of the people than one could gather from more pompous or authentic histories.' The scale of merit is interesting, though, of course, it can only be taken as representing Thackeray's impression at an early period of his own and Dickens's career.

Thackeray's admiration of Fielding is in many ways significant. He has often been compared to Fielding, and, in my opinion, the resemblance is close and important. That excellent critic, the late Mr. Bagehot, has indeed spoken of the annoyance with which readers who really appreciate Thackeray hear the comparison made, and has traced to his own satisfaction a closer parallel between Thackeray and Sterne. I am sorry to come under this anticipatory condemnation, and to submit to the implication that I do not rightly appreciate Thackeray. Yet I must take my chance, and can only say that, in this case, Mr. Bagehot seems to me to have been misled by a certain preference for paradoxical

views. Whether Thackeray most resembled Fielding or Sterne, there
can be no doubt which he loved. To Sterne he found it hard even to
render the praise which he saw to be just, so heartily did he abhor the
pruriency, the affectation, and the sham sentimentalism of that strange
compound of genius and baseness. But Fielding was not only a favourite
but in some degree a model. 'Since the author of *Tom Jones* was buried,'
he says, 'no writer of fiction among us has been permitted to depict
to his utmost power a Man.'[1] And I could not better describe what was,
in my opinion, Thackeray's conception of his proper function as an
author than by saying that it was his ambition to tread in the steps of
Fielding, though with more refinement and greater tenderness of sentiment. He had, as all that I have been saying tends to prove, an eye for
a humbug; a hearty scorn for sham sentiment in literature, for sham
loyalty in politics, for sham proprieties and sham improprieties in
social life. Mr. Carlyle himself could not entertain that creed more
severely or preach more vigorously from the Johnsonian text, 'Clear
your mind of cant.' This is indeed almost the only point of contact.
Thackeray and Carlyle differed as the prophet of a generation differs
from the artist in whose mind the dislike to cant takes the form, not
of a tendency to indignant rhetoric, but of a preference of realism
touched by humour to all strained sentiment. It is from this point of
view that Thackeray regarded the Scott romanticism as effete, detested
the dying affectation of Byronism, and looked upon Bulwerism as
merely a new phase of affectation, imported from Germany by a conceited dandy. The Dickens view, as represented in *Pickwick*, would
probably appear to him to sin by superficiality. It was infinitely amusing, more amusing than Smollett's best work, but did not imply that
unflinching resolution to set forth actual facts of life which he so heartily
appreciated in Fielding. Fielding was allowed a liberty of expression,
which he abused only too often so as to degenerate into the coarse,
and even the purely disgusting. But at least Fielding looked at the
world calmly, resolutely, and with a penetrating gaze, which refused
to be hoodwinked by fine phrases. He described men as he saw them,
unveiled hypocrites, and gave to the passions their real value and
meaning. He saw the man, not the clothes. In that sense, Thackeray
could follow him, so far as British decency would allow. He would not
deal in Scott's cavaliers in buff jerkins, nor in Byron's scowling corsairs
in Eastern petticoats, nor in Tom Moore's Peris and bulbuls, nor in
Bulwer's philosophic and dandified seducers and high-minded assassins,

[1] See above, p. 89.

nor in Dickens's grotesque figures, overflowing with milk-punch and maudlin philanthropy. He would draw to the life the world as he saw it, stripped of its pleasant disguises and solemn humbugs, as far as his powers could go; and try whether a downright realistic portraiture would not have a chance of success in the literary world then encumbered by the fashionable novel, and the highwayman novel, and the famous traveller's novel, as well as occupied by work of higher pretensions.

It is only by degrees, as I have said, that Thackeray came to put forth his power, on an adequate scale, whether self-distrust, or indolence, or other distractions, restrained him to less daring procedure. His first story of any serious pretensions shows, I think, that he was still taking a comparatively narrow view of the nature of the evil to be assaulted. *Catherine* is intended, as the author tells us very frankly, as an attack upon some of the rising idols of the day. Bulwer, Harrison Ainsworth, and Dickens, are the objects of his rather naïf indignation. 'The public will hear of nothing but rogues,' he says, 'and the only way in which poor authors, who must live, can act honestly by the public and themselves, is to paint such thieves as they are; not dandy poetical rose-water thieves; but real downright scoundrels, leading scoundrelly lives, drunken, profligate, dissolute, low, as scoundrels will be. They don't quote Plato, like Eugene Aram, and live like gentlemen, and sing the pleasantest ballads in the world, like Dick Turpin;[1] or prate eternally about τὸ καλὸν like that precious canting Maltravers, whom we all of us have read about, and pitied, or die whitewashed saints like "Biss Dadsy" in *Oliver Twist*' [ch. iii], and some good honest indignation follows as to the error of weeping over the criminal population. Certainly, the devil ought to be painted black, and with his full complement of horns and hoofs; only we are a little surprised to see Dickens charged with this fault, for it cannot be denied that *Oliver Twist* is in intention as moral as a tract; and we feel still more that the offence is scarcely worth the powder and shot. The immorality which tries to make highwaymen and murderers interesting is easily exposed, and not very seductive; it is by a much more subtle intermixture of good and evil that poisonous literature is commended to the palate. We might also doubt whether in any case the mode of demonstrating the ugliness of villany is not a little too elaborate. The author confesses to weariness of his own creatures, and we are inclined to sympathise. *Catherine*, however, is interesting, not only as an early

[1] In Harrison Ainsworth's *Rookwood* (1834).

specimen of the master's hand, and showing many of the qualities of style and types of character which were afterwards more fully developed, but as manifesting, even in a comparatively crude form, his strong conviction of the value of downright realistic honesty of portraiture. I venture to guess that besides his desire to expose a contemporary evil, Thackeray was more or less prompted by a wish to try his hand at an imitation of Fielding's 'great comic epic,'—as he calls it in the *Paris Sketchbook*—the *History of Jonathan Wild the Great*. That powerful satire is perhaps the closest literary parallel to *Catherine*, and the coarse vigour of its execution had excited Thackeray's hearty admiration. Fielding is indeed able to be still more realistic in his discussion of the unmitigated brutality of a thorough-paced ingrained villain; and the immediate purpose of his satire is rather different from that of *Catherine*. The moral of *Jonathan Wild* appears to be the doctrine popular with the philanthropic philosophers of Fielding's time, that the difference between a conqueror and a murderer is simply the difference between a wholesale and a retail occupation. Thackeray himself was presently, as we shall see, to preach more or less from that text. Meanwhile *Catherine*, whatever the merits of the story, was necessarily liable to the objection that the more vigorous the performance, the more disagreeable it must be to average readers. It could only be attractive whilst the tendency which it caricatured was sufficiently obvious to make a caricature intelligible; and English novelists did not long continue to sing the praises of the heroes of Newgate. Its chief interest is now for the critic who wishes to examine the development of its author's powers.

This curious study of the blackguard element may possibly have helped to interest Thackeray in a problem to which novelists pay less attention than it deserves. A virtuous person—by a virtuous man I mean any one possessed of a conscience not habitually outraged—is often puzzled to interpret to himself the state of mind of the systematic scamp. A certain degree of self-complacency seems to be almost a necessity of life. A man who is always condemning his own actions, and whose existence depends upon conduct which he regards as shameful, seems to be barely intelligible. Everybody commits at times actions which he regrets, and tries perhaps to atone for them by repentance. But how can a man live in a continuous atmosphere of self-disgust—loathing the very bread which supports his life—feeling more humiliated in proportion to the success of his schemes? A thorough villain and even a thorough hypocrite is intelligible; so far as we can suppose a man to have simply no conscience; to disbelieve in the possession of a conscience by any one; and to put on a merely external mask of moral or religious sentiment, as a pickpocket puts on a decent coat. Most novelists are satisfied with such a type of character, and are content to draw a man simply and radically bad—a devil incarnate, entirely composed of mean, cruel, or sensual instincts. Such people exist, I fancy, and perhaps are more common than is sometimes said. But they scarcely represent the normal case, and certainly not the most puzzling case. When a respectable banker or clergyman turns out to have been living upon downright cheating for years, we do not suppose that he was entirely without a conscience, but that it was smothered and hoodwinked. How did he manage it? How did he soothe the pain of constant remorse? How did he comfort himself under the constantly recurring reflection, I am a liar and a villain? And so of the average rogue; the man who knows that every gentleman scorns him, and every honest man sees through him, and who yet lives 'infamous and contented;' how does he manage to put such a colour upon his conduct in his own private reflections as to make life tolerable?

To consider the question fairly requires a certain impartiality which most novelists lose. They hate their villains so as to make them—not perhaps unnatural, but abnormally base. They tear away every shred of excuse which might blind not only the spectator, but the criminal himself. Thackeray, however, seldom loses his temper with his characters, and he had evidently looked at this problem with his usual calmness. In several of his pictures we have the curious study of a villain seen from within. Mr. Brough in the *Hoggarty Diamond*, and Mr. Brandon in *Philip*, are sketches of one variety of impostor, and we can see in each case, how they have imposed upon themselves. But a more extreme case is taken in one or two of the earlier stories. *The Fatal Boots*, for example, is a study of the thorough sneak, the utterly mean and contemptible knave, whose miserable cunning and selfishness has overreached itself, and who is quite unable to understand why Mr. Titmarsh should find any moral in his story. To him it appears to be a melancholy proof that in this world the most scrupulous devotion to the best object—one's own interest—may often fail, from some unaccountable perversity in the nature of things, to meet with its due reward. A villain of a more heroic type is depicted with more intensity in the story of *Barry Lyndon*. I will take, says Thackeray, in effect, a man who lives by roguery; he shall be a braggart, a liar, a thoroughly selfish and unprincipled scoundrel; he shall be a spy and a pander, ready to consent to the meanest services in order to attain the means of sensual gratification; he shall live, during the most respectable part of his career, as a professional gambler, cheating whenever he thinks that cheating will not be detected; he shall be prepared to take advantage of any secret scandals which may come to his knowledge, in order to extort money from the unfortunate victims, or compel them to further his scheme of forcing a rich heiress into marriage; when that fails, he shall by sheer bullying and blustering, and enormous lying, become the husband of a widow with a fortune, whom he heartily despises for her weakness; when married, he shall treat her with brutality, be openly unfaithful to her, bully her son, squander her fortune, and make himself the laughing-stock of good society, in spite of his vulgar swagger, and console himself by buying the attention of the lowest parasites; at last, after alienating the affections of every one concerned in him, except his old mother, who sticks by him to the last, he shall fall into the lowest decay, be deservedly thrashed by his stepson, and die in the Fleet of *delirium tremens*. A few good impulses may be allowed to him; he shall be fond of his boy, and have a certain courage and buoyancy which would conciliate us in a better cause. So much is necessary in order that he may be possessed of some feelings capable of doing duty for a conscience; and, in spite of all the unutterable baseness of the man, you shall see how he not only reconciles himself to his position, but is sincerely proud of it; how he has a genuine conviction that he is really a most meritorious and estimable person, and can, on occasion, preach edifying sermons, regret the decay of the fine old spirit of the ancient noblesse, and consider himself as an eminent member of the aristocracy of nature, as well as a worthy descendant of the ancient kings of Ireland.

This is clearly a far more effective exposure of villany than the method adopted in *Catherine*. Nobody can read *Barry Lyndon* without the heartiest disgust for the hero, and a perception that even the rags and tatters of virtuous spirit in which he delights to array himself are probably manufactured in part out of downright lying; and yet we can also see how at every turn in his history Mr. Lyndon has an unfeigned admiration for his own fine qualities, and can speak with pathetic indignation of the ingratitude which he has received from the world. The story has never been so popular as others—not so popular, I imagine, as the *Hoggarty Diamond*, which is a more straightforward and normal fiction; and for the simple reason that no art can make such a narrative agreeable to the ordinary reader. It is of the nature of a *tour de force;* but, taken on that understanding, it is certainly amongst the most remarkable efforts of its author's imagination. Undoubtedly his intellectual power had reached its full development when *Barry Lyndon* was written—and read, as it seems, with little attention. He never made a villain (I must not ask whether any one else ever made a villain) more supremely hateful and yet more thoroughly intelligible. It is not merely as giving the skilful anatomy of a corrupt heart that the story deserves the study of Thackeray's admirers. The style shows a quality which changes,—as his mental attitude changes,—in his later productions. In them he is fond of turning aside from his characters and his story to address his readers or indulge in a kind of public soliloquy. He makes his own reflections, and the reflections are often amongst the most interesting passages of the story. But in *Barry Lyndon* he is more occupied with the direct presentation of telling facts. The style is intense, vivid, and compressed; especially in the description of his hero's military adventures and the striking story of the tragedy in the Duchy of X——. I have remarked that Thackeray, though sharing Mr. Carlyle's antipathy to humbug, gives a very different version of the creed. Those early chapters of *Barry Lyndon* give a very compressed view of the reverse side of history, which, short as it is and fictitious in its form, would be a very effective antidote to some eulogies upon the great king of the eighteenth century. Mr. Barry Lyndon is a knave of the purest water; but he has human feelings when his interests are not concerned on the other side. 'Whilst we are at present admiring the "Great Frederick," as we call him,' he says, 'and his philosophy and his liberality and his military genius, I, who have served him and been, as it were, behind the scenes of which that great spectacle is composed, can only look at it with horror. What a number of items of human crime, misery, slavery, go to form that sum-total of glory! I can recollect a certain day, about three weeks after the battle of Minden, and a farm-house, in which some of us entered, and how the old woman and her daughters served us, trembling, to wine; and how we got drunk over the wine, and the house was in a flame, presently; and woe betide the wretched fellow afterwards who came home to look for his house and his children!' [End of ch. iv.]

Thackeray was not a hero-worshipper, as we shall have occasion to observe; and in *Barry Lyndon* he preaches very energetically that doctrine about the great men of history which his favourite Fielding had expressed in *Jonathan Wild.* His other stories of the same period deviate less from the ordinary track, and may be considered as preparatory studies for the more important works which followed. They seem to have attracted less attention than the papers which he was then contributing to *Punch*, which first made his reputation general. Yet I must refer to one proof that his genius was meeting with recognition from readers of penetration. 'I got hold of the first two numbers of the *Hoggarty Diamond*, says John Sterling, writing to his mother in December, 1841, 'and read them with extreme delight. What is there better in Goldsmith or Fielding? The man is a true genius, and, with quiet and comfort, might produce masterpieces that would last as long as any we have and delight millions of unborn readers. There is more truth and nature in one of these papers than in all ——'s novels together.' 'Thackeray,' remarks Mr. Carlyle, 'will observe that this is dated 1841, not 1851, and have his own reflections on the matter!'[1] The fresh hearty nature of the *Hoggarty Diamond* was, however, unable to arrest public attention as the sterner force of *Barry Lyndon* was likely to repel it; but in the 'Snob Papers' Thackeray for the first time achieved a distinct popular success with readers of perceptions less keen than Sterling's. The moral essay or lay sermon has been popular under a great variety of forms in English literature. The 'Snob Papers' contain as many lively sketches of character as are to be found in any collection of the kind; and we see that Thackeray is an essayist by accident, and would prefer concrete pictures of life to abstract discussions. Perhaps he has nowhere drawn a more lively character by a few touches than Major Ponto, and some other brilliant vignettes show almost equally his skill in graphic portraiture. But the speciality of the little book (which first appeared as a separate collection in 1848, when he was becoming known as the author of *Vanity Fair*) is the central social doctrine which it is intended to enforce. I am not prepared to give a philological discussion upon the origin of the word snob, which, as we have already seen, he had used as an undergraduate. Anyhow in Thackeray's hands it now received a new connotation. 'Snob,' as he says, meant, in the Cambridge days, a youth who wore 'high-lows[2] and no straps'—symptoms of an inferior social grade, which have now become obsolete;—whereas the true snob was the youth who despised his strapless comrade. I resist the temptation to

---

[1] Thomas Carlyle, *The Life of John Sterling* (1851), Part III, ch. iii. The unnamed novelist is probably Bulwer.

[2] Boots fastened in front and reaching up over the ankles, and therefore neither 'high' boots nor 'low' shoes.

dwell upon this illustration of one process by which words change their meanings. The meaning, in any case, was virtually new; and there is some truth in Thackeray's humorous description of himself in the first chapter as the being predestined to describe the snob, and therefore provided with an eye for the species. Great physicians have been immortalised by giving their name to some new or previously unclassified malady, and we may venture to say that the morbid condition of society known as snobbishness might as well be called Thackeray's disease. The servile love of rank has indeed been pretty well known in all ages, but that special form of servility which is manifested in England by the association of the 'Peerage' with the Bible had never been contemplated as a distinct variety or ticketed by a class name.

Opinions may of course differ as to the prevalence and importance of this disease. To some people it may seem that the worship of lords is neither so widely spread in English society as Thackeray supposed, nor so serious a symptom; and they may think that, as usually happens, the zeal of the early discoverer led him to exaggerate the importance of his discovery. My own view would be that snobbishness in Thackeray's sense is a special manifestation of an evil tendency much more easily underrated than exaggerated. He satirised the special symptoms which came most frequently in his way, or described one variety of a widely spread genus. If he incidentally lost sight of the underlying conditions which generate snobbishness, his conception was so far superficial. He erred in an artistic sense, as a man would err logically who attacked a particular corollary from an erroneous doctrine without striking at the radical fallacy. On the other hand, a novelist must of necessity proceed by giving typical and concrete instances, and not by abstract discussion of principles. Thackeray, limiting himself to the society with which he was most familiar, laid most emphasis upon the form of the evil which came most frequently under his notice. The question for a critic would be whether he so treated it as to show insight into deeper springs of conduct. Does he denounce snobbishness as a mere superficial fashion, an absurd eccentricity amenable to gentle treatment, or does he show how it arises out of profound defect of character and an unwholesome stage of social development? An intellectual treatment gives the true genesis of the evil where a superficial treatment gives only the accidental absurdity and inconvenience.

That, I take it, is the criterion by which Thackeray's works should be tested: though I shall not attempt to apply the test myself. This much, however, I will venture to say. Thackeray gives in his second chapter his own definition of snobbishness. 'He who meanly admires mean things is a snob.'[1] He illustrates the proposition in the same essay by one of his favourite examples, the 'fat old Florizel,' the 'bloated pimplefaced Gorgius,' or in plain English, George IV. The theory of snobbishness is pretty well exemplified by the worship paid to that broken idol. Loyalty is a noble emotion as long as it is genuine; as long, that is, as it implies a generous spirit of self-devotion to the constituted representative of the great principles of order and national unity. Nothing could be more generous and deserving of all respect than the loyalty of an old English cavalier, who would die without a thought of self in the cause of his king; or the loyalty of a modern American republican who died with an equally generous devotion in the cause of the constitution. Loyalty turns into snobbishness when it is selfishness or meanness disguised; when we reverence the king or the mob as the distributor of places or pensions, or when our souls are overpowered by the gorgeous outside without being touched by any generous emotion. If the idol which you venerate is a mere sham, made up of wigs and robes and plush, or of mere buncombe about the rights of man, your veneration is the product of your lower nature, and is so far grovelling and degrading. The vice of snobbishness, then, is the outcome of a state of society in which the dead form has survived the living spirit, and men go on their kness before wealth and rank without considering them as symbols of some loftier principles. It is not wrong to be respectful to a king or a noble, if the custom of the time requires respect, and to refuse the conventional homage would imply nothing better than a peevish petulance. But it is contemptible to proportion your respect simply to the outside magnificence or the bigness of the phrases without a thought of the ultimate basis upon which all respect must repose which is not dishonourable to both giver and receiver.

That, I fancy, roughly stated, would be the true theory of snobbishness; and would account for the prevalence and significance of the fashion in a time and country where there are so many decaying survivals of old superstitions that have lost their genuine vitality.

[1] It may be compared with Mr. Ruskin's definition of poetry; which is, he thinks, the suggestion by the imagination of noble grounds for the noble emotions—and, if so, it would seem the poetic is the antithesis of the snobbish and vulgar. I think both definitions excellent, though a little wide [Stephen's note].

Why is poor Major Ponto so pathetic an instance of misplaced veneration? Because he has no purpose in life worth the sympathy of an
intellectual being; because he is dropping the substance for the form;
because he is striving to keep up a social status as an ultimate end,
without its ever crossing his mind that social status is really useful
only as a means; because (one may perhaps say) his life is regulated
throughout, down to its smallest details, by the same mysterious
principle which decides that his daughters are to be incessantly strum-
ming on the piano. They have no love of music or power of enjoying
it, but it is part of their whole theory of life that they are to acquire
certain accomplishments as a badge of social respectability. Music
is admirable for musicians, but the queer superstition which sacrifices
the lives of so many girls to a task which is for them as lively as a
performance upon the treadmill is beginning, one may hope, to reveal
its absurdity. It is merely a particular case, however, of that senseless
process by which so many inhabitants of Thackeray's Mangelwurzel-
shire, and Baker Street, are drilled in a ceaseless round of mechanical
repetition of performances which have ceased to have any intelligible
meaning whatever. This particular case of the general fetish worship
may imply nothing more than a waste of time; other observances are
worse than ridiculous; but there are many modes of paying court to
the great Mumbo-jumbo, and innumerable human lives are made
barren and wretched by the superstition. The family of the De
Mogynses, whose whole aim is to fight their way into drawing-
rooms; Lieutenant Grig, who passes his life as a magnificent flunkey
in a cuirass and top-boots, and in marches from Knightsbridge to
Regent's park; Mrs. Botibol, who crams hundreds of perspiring
wretches into three little rooms to enjoy a literary conversazione,
and stare at Abou Gosh from Syria; and poor Ponto, trying desperately
to pay young Ponto's bills for his pelisses and overalls required in
the Queen's old pyebald hussars; these and any number of other British
types, are equally illustrative of the narrow mechanical millround in
which so many lives are passed. The struggle for social position, the
mean subservience to those who can bestow it, is one outgrowth of
the system, and one upon which Thackeray has laid particular stress.
But the common characteristic of all such lives is that the true end of
human existence, the gratification of the domestic affections, of intellectual or artistic impulses, of any of the deepest instincts of our nature,
is neglected and despised in the senseless competition for things whose
only intrinsic worth would be in their applicability to loftier purposes.

It is an old story—as old as human nature—as old, certainly, as the day when the weary philosopher uttered his 'Vanity of vanities.' But the idol to which men sacrifice their lives and the mode of worship which is regarded as likely to propitiate him varies from age to age, and in Thackeray's day and station the most popular cult seemed to him to be mainly describable as 'snobbishness.' It is the form characteristic of a social atmosphere in which shams flourish, in which no man can say precisely what he believes, or what he respects, or what are the ultimate grounds for respecting or believing in anything. When life goes out of a religion it becomes an organised hypocrisy, and when institutions have nothing better to say for themselves than that they still occupy the ground, the respect for them becomes snobbishness. The times are ripe for satire and the satirist will be denounced as a cynic. What is to be thought of a man who does not see the intrinsic beauty which a livery possesses even when it signifies no reciprocation of respect and confidence?

To hint at such a theory of the natural history of snobbishness is to go a little beyond my sphere. Thackeray saw that certain symptoms were ugly. He did not, so far as I know, give any scientific diagnosis of the complaint which caused them, and it is probable enough that he would not have sanctioned mine. At any rate, the ordinary public was impressed chiefly by the phrase snobbishness, and was content to admire or be amused at his skill in portraying various phases of the passion. Probably they thought him, as perhaps he may have been, rather too sensitive on this matter. So long as dukes exist, it is said, easy-going people will be flattered by walking arm-in-arm with them; and if the existence of dukes is a first principle in philosophy, there is of course no more to be said. The probability of that hypothesis lay beyond Thackeray's subject. An essayist is bound to be light in the treatment of his topics, however serious may be the questions which he incidentally raises. But Thackeray, who must have been growing in consciousness of his power, was about to give a more serious picture of society from a higher point of view. Of *Vanity Fair*, which began to appear in January, 1847, I may at least say this much, that no novel has ever been better christened. The title is what a title ought to be— a brief summary of the whole book. And here, I may speak briefly of a parallel already suggested. Balzac gave to a series of novels the analogous name of the *Comédie Humaine*. He professed to be drawing a faithful portrait of the French as Thackeray of the English society of the day. Balzac is, I think, one of the very greatest masters of his art;

and there is at least one case in which Thackeray is said to have taken
him to some extent as a model. In speaking, however, of a parallel, I
do not mean to compare the merits of the two writers, or to imply any
similarity except that of general aim. Parallel drawing is generally a
childish amusement; I venture to make the comparison here because
the contrast between the two men appears to me to show better than
anything the true nature of Thackeray's artistic aims. His taste was
shocked, as I remarked, by the extravagant horrors of some French
writers, by their delight in painting the darkest passions and selecting
situations in which those passions might be represented as triumphant.
Balzac is the great master in this school of art. The vividness of his
painting is unrivalled; he seems to be rather suffering from halluci-
nation than imagining in the ordinary sense; his creatures dominate
his fancy instead of being in subjection to his will. He combines the
minute photographic reality of Defoe with the intensity of Dante's
vision. He produces absolute illusion, and is therefore supposed by some
readers to represent the truth. Nothing but a real perception, it is
thought, could generate such vivid images. If we admitted this, we
must also admit that French society was more corrupt than any state
of society that ever existed. The most cold-blooded selfishness, the
most grovelling sensuality, the most contemptible greed and venality
would be the normal springs of action, and virtue would be invariably
dragged in triumph at the wheels of vice. The truth is, I fancy, much
simpler. It is simply that Balzac was anxious to produce the most
poignant sensation, whether painful or agreeable; and made the great
discovery that an inversion of the old-fashioned canons of poetical
justice was as piquant to the ordinary reader as their observance. Nothing is more pathetic than a story of goodness bound hand and foot by
victorious evil; and though Balzac aimed constantly at this effect, and
often produces it with astonishing power, unconditional admirers
assume too easily that it implied extraordinary penetration, and, using
the worn-out metaphor of the scalpel, describe him as dissecting with
unequalled skill that hideous organ, a 'naked human heart.' The
assertion that all successful men are rogues and all successful women
harlots is made very easily, and, if true, certainly entitles a man to be
called a most penetrative observer; but if the case is simply that he
calls the world corrupt because he has found out that a description of
corruption is more impressive than a description of the natural state
of things, in which honesty is the best policy and rogues have a
tendency to the gallows, we must so far withdraw our approval. He has

undoubtedly marvellous power, but it shows skill in morbid pathology rather than in observing the organism in its normal condition.

A good deal has been said about Thackeray's use of this same 'scalpel,' his merciless dissection of the selfishness and meanness of human nature, and so on. At any rate, his aim differs radically from that of Balzac; and he diverges just at this point. Thackeray's ultimate aim always appears to have been not the production of a vivid sensation, but the faithful portraiture of actual society. He will not represent virtue as always triumphant, for virtue does not always triumph; still less will he make vice the invariable conqueror, for vice generally fails to succeed in the long run. He does not see many great heroes or many great criminals in actual life; and therefore there shall not be many in his books. Fine phrases cover a vast amount of selfishness, narrowness, and stupidity; and the true nature of the qualities so veiled by cant and hypocrisy should be exposed; but neither is it true that to pierce below the surface of society is to come upon unmixed cruelty and vice; and therefore he will not deal in thrilling revelations, however delicious may be the horrors which they profess to expose. No, life is on the whole a commonplace affair, with a queer and intricate blending of motives; kindly feeling is often to be found in the bad, and a dash of selfishness in the good; we will have the normal and not the exceptional cases, even at the price of making our stories, like our lives, rather commonplace. There is interest enough in the facts if we will open our eyes boldly and see them honestly, without trying to distort them so as to gratify a morbid love of the horrible, or to avoid an occasional chock to the sentimentalist. The faithful picture may be less exciting than that which represents exceptional events as natural, but, at any rate, Thackeray despises any claims inconsistent with a rigid adherence to fidelity of portraiture. How far his portrait is correct is another question; but fidelity, not the production of a powerful effort, is the ultimate end, and a desire to see things as they are, the governing and regulating principle of his work.

I may briefly notice one striking story in which Thackeray seems to have taken a hint from Balzac's method. The *Yellowplush Papers*, which appeared in *Fraser*, were apparently amongst his first experiments in literature. They show, however, that he was already a master of that 'peculiar, unspellable, inimitable, flunkefied pronunciation which,' as he observes in the 'Snob Papers,' 'forms one of the chief charms of existence.' But beginning with mere comedy or farce, he rapidly slid into one of the bitterest tragedies which he ever composed.

The concluding page of the history of Mr. Deuceace is more in the taste of Balzac than anything which afterwards followed. We leave off with a picture of a villain crushed, but crushed by the more cold-blooded and malicious villany of his father, and crushing the one tender heart which clings to him faithfully in spite of everything. Certainly, a strong impression is produced, and one with a curious complexity of horrors. A ghastly sort of comic effect arises from the story being put into the mouth of the absurd Yellowplush, who was calmly looking on with an eye to possible effects upon his own perquisites. The effect is as though a painter should introduce a grotesque gargoyle looking down upon a scene of assassination. Thackeray never, I think, resorted afterwards to this means of moving his readers, though 'Dennis Haggarty's Wife' is a short study in the same vein. He would, I fancy, have despised it as unworthy. Anybody, he probably thought, can be more or less effective who is not afraid of being disgusting. But, whatever his theory, he confined himself to more normal manifestations of human passion without seeking such effects as are certainly most attractive to readers with an itch for the horrible. . . .

Colonel Newcome is a most admirable and attractive character. We love him with all our hearts—as we love Parson Adams or Uncle Toby or the Vicar of Wakefield. But does not the very fact seem to show that virtue is something rather too good for this world? Does not Thackeray substantially preach that a very good man has too much of the dove and too little of the serpent for practical use; and that gentleness and simplicity and tenderness of heart are apt to generate a certain intolerance when he is somehow awakened to the harsh realities of life? Are they not, in short, qualities adapted for some imaginary Arcadia, which are rather out of place in Mayfair as in the neighbourhood of the Bank?

This, I fancy, is what was meant when Thackeray was called a cynic. He recurs to the subject once or twice in *Philip* and seems to have been hurt by the imputation and by the reported advice of some well-meaning mothers to daughters not to read his works lest they should imbibe 'dangerous' notions. I cannot, as I have said, speak impartially in this matter, nor will I undertake to argue the case as an advocate. After all, the question must be, what impression do the books make upon you? No special pleading on either side will settle the point. But it is clearly desirable that the point at issue should be fairly understood. By a 'cynic,' when the word is used in its fullest condemnatory sense, is meant, as I understand, one who does not believe in virtue or who regards tender feeling as a fair object for ridicule. Anybody who should use the name in this sense of Thackeray would be altogether beyond my reach. His writings seem to be everywhere full of the tenderest sensibility, and to show that he valued tenderness, sympathy, and purity of nature, as none but a man of exceptional kindness of heart knows how to value them. In short, his writings mean, if they mean anything, that the love of a wife and child and friend is the one sacred element in our nature, of infinitely higher price than anything which can come into competition with it; and that Vanity Fair is what it is precisely because it stimulates the pursuit of objects frivolous and unsatisfying just so far as they imply indifference to these emotions. A warm and generous heart is the one great possession which alone gives any interest to the struggle of life. If he refrains from frequently drawing pathetic pictures, it is not because he feels too little but too much. He fears to trust himself upon such tender ground. If that is not the impression made by Thackeray's writings upon any reader, I think that he had better not read them; but I am certain that I cannot agree with him. But beyond this lies a question of fact. A man may be called a cynic not as disbelieving in the value of virtue, but as disbelieving in its frequency. He may hold that the tender emotions have a smaller influence in actual affairs than easy-going people maintain, and that a purely virtuous person is a very rare phenomenon indeed. The sentimentalist is a man who exaggerates the accessibility of mankind at large to good feeling, and supposes that revolutions can be made with rosewater and villains converted by a few pretty speeches: as the cynic is (in this sense) a man who holds that, as a matter of fact, selfishness is the general rule even with people who profess and call themselves Christians, and that it is much too deeply ingrained and cunningly disguised to be overcome by superficial remedies.

To settle which picture of the world is accurate, whether pessimists or optimists are right, whether men are naturally good or naturally bad, is beyond the power of any man, whatever his pretensions. I will only point out that the darker view need not, though it perhaps may, arise from any want of apprehension of virtue. It may be due to a melancholy temperament, to hard experience, or to a simple desire to see facts without the ordinary masks of fine phrases. Many of the greatest reformers and most powerful preachers of the world have taken the darkest view of the actual facts of human nature. Taken in this sense, I can understand the opinion that Thackeray was cynical; and I can even share the view to some extent, though I should prefer to use the word 'ironical.' He looks at the world, not with a savage or misanthropical spirit, as the true cynic is supposed to do; nor with the passionate anger of a reformer, but with a half-tolerant contempt, with indignation at times, but with indignation toned down by humour, and therefore passing into irony. I do not think, as I have already said, that he believed very much in heroes. He was clearly no enthusiast by nature; he was always ready to ask whether the heroes of history had not a weak side, and to insist that it should be fully taken into account. And, further, I am clear that he had a very strong conviction indeed of the shallowness and heartlessness prevalent in the society which he described. If indeed he had simply denounced it by painting the devil as black as his colours would allow, he might not have been called cynical; it was his awkward determination to do justice even to the poor devil, and not to paint even his saints with rose-colour, which procured for him the unfavourable name. It is this impartiality which is unfairly interpreted into indifference. He always recognises the weak side of the more uncompromising character. He saw and accordingly represented what we may call the impracticability of saints. He thought that they might be too rigid for the world in which we actually live, too apt to condemn it in a lump, too unforgiving, and too apt to resist the dispersion of their allusions; and that a simple-minded and honourable man like Colonel Newcome may have cause to regret that he ever mixed in affairs in which simplicity is not a sufficient armour. But we may draw the moral for ourselves. We may say that a world for which men like Dobbin or Warrington or Colonel Newcome are more or less unfitted in proportion to the nobility of their character is so far condemned and in want of thorough reform; or prefer with Pendennis to make the best of it, and mix in the Fair even at some risk to our own delicate sense of honour as well as to our pockets. The problem is a difficult one, as many people have found; and the man who would undertake any profession has often to solve many such scruples of conscience for himself. But, whatever the solution, there the problem is. The prizes offered by the world are not of the Montyon kind—rewards for simple virtue[1]; and we can neither join in the competition nor stand

---

[1] Baron de Montyon (1733–1820), the French economist, instituted several prizes including an annual award made by L'Académie française for a literary work of high moral tone.

aside from it except at our peril. Only a saint can join in the struggle without being stained; and yet only a coward would keep altogether apart. The saint is too apt to preserve his purity by intolerance and one-sidedness; and most of us will find that our best heroism consists in judicious running away from temptation. Many women are good, perhaps because women have their nurseries for a refuge; but very few men have the finely-tempered nature which can resist effectually the corroding influences of the struggle. It is sad: life is sad to all who think; but we can make a tolerable world of it, if we do not expect too much, if we will be tolerant and kindly to the tempted and travel-stained amongst our fellow-pilgrims, and be careful above all to preserve the springs of tender domestic affection from all danger of defilement.

I have dwelt at some length upon these views, and, indeed, have very likely moralised too much, because I felt that after all the interest which we take in Thackeray's writings must depend chiefly upon the congeniality to our own temperaments of his teaching. As I am writing to those who are already familiar with them, I have insisted more (if I may say so) upon the nature of the soil than upon that of the harvest —upon the underlying sentiment everywhere implied than upon the characteristics of the literary art by which that sentiment is interpreted. A criticism which should deal with the last alone might be more interesting for many purposes, but would often fail to reveal to us the causes of our sympathy with or alienation from the author. We may read *Vanity Fair* and the rest simply for amusement or to admire their technical skill; but we shall make them part of the permanent domain of our fancy in proportion as we feel ourselves in harmony with their implicit teaching. This is not so true, however, of the books of which I must now speak briefly. Many critics have spoken of *Esmond* as the most perfect of Thackeray's performances. I shall not attempt to decide the question; but I think that the decision will turn chiefly upon the degree in which we are impressed by technical skill, by the general harmony of tone and proportion between the different parts of a work of literary art; or, on the other hand, by the vigour with which it embodies the strongest feelings and convictions of the writer. If you read in order to feel yourself in contact with the author's deepest nature, you will unhesitatingly prefer *Vanity Fair* to *Esmond*. If you read chiefly to enjoy his style and to sympathise with the free play of his imagination, not consciously directed to any moral or social purpose, you may probably prefer *Esmond*. If it has no passages of such intensity as its fellows, it is more harmonious and carefully constructed. . . .

Burlesque came as naturally to Thackeray as the mock-heroic to Fielding. To analyse his impressions as a prosaic critic was not his method, though he had a certain leaning to art-criticism, as is shown by his papers on Cruikshank and Leech, and in many passages of his books. But burlesque is a kind of criticism which is not the less effective because it is indirect; and it would be easy enough to conjecture Thackeray's serious opinions of the authors whom he caricatured from these ludicrous imitations. Compare, for example, Thackeray's version of Cœur-de-Lion with Scott's *Knight of the fetterlock*, and you can see as plainly as if he had written it down in black and white what he thought of the romantic business. No man, to paraphrase Johnson, is a hypocrite in his laughter, and when you know what strikes him as absurd, you know a great deal as to his general sentiments. But it would be unfair to both critic and criticised to read the burlesques in this fashion, whatever reflections may be afterwards extracted from them. They are primarily amusing, and the test of their success is the degree in which they make you laugh. The most successful of all the books which may be classed amongst burlesques is, I suspect, the *Rose and the Ring*. Written to amuse a child, it ought to be read in the childish spirit; and yet one cannot read it, I fancy, without having in one's mind the thoughtful and kindly face of the writer,—than whom no one ever loved children better,—as well as the eager delight of his audience. The drawings, I think, which illustrate it, and which appear to have been the nucleus of the whole, are amongst his happiest; and show, like innumerable vignettes scattered through his books, how tenderly sensitive he was to the beauty of childhood. They are not the less touching because little Betsinda-Rosalba is contrasted with the broad farce of Valoroso and Gruffanuff. And I must venture the confession that Prince Bulbo—with all the undeniable weaknesses of which that young gentleman can be fairly accused—is one of my favourite heroes of fiction. He is not beautiful, but I am sure that he was good.

The sentiment, varying from pretty sharp satire to unmixed playfulness, which is to be found in the burlesques, animates also the last class of writings of which I must speak. The *Roundabout Papers* are ostensibly mere trifling; and perhaps to the unexperienced reader they have the air of being perfectly easy. You have nothing to do but to sit down after dinner, fold your legs comfortably, and talk easily and gracefully about any topic that turns up, to indulge in a little harmless fun, a complaint about servants or the woes of an editor, or a generous word for some old friend, or a bit of gossip about childish memories, just as one topic or the other happens to come uppermost. I need not tell any one who is not inexperienced of the extreme difficulty of such a performance or the rarity of any tolerable success. The *Roundabout Papers* have so much special Thackeray flavour that one cannot well compare them with any closeness with the *Essays of Elia* or Hazlitt's *Table-talk*, or other specimens of the voluminous literature which has grown up since Montaigne first gave popularity to this form of art. They belong, of course, to the lightest variety of their species, and cover none of the profound reflections on philosophy or life which have sometimes been hidden in similar work. The degree in which they are felt to be charming will vary with individual taste; but no competent reader can amuse himself with them in an occasional leisure hour without recognising the skill of the writer's hand and the felicity with which he converts the merest trifle into a topic for pleasing meditation. Nothing, if one may judge from experience, is more difficult than to trifle gracefully without being flippant or vulgar or grotesque. The talents of composing such essays and of writing really good drawing-room verses are almost as rare as the talents required for metaphysical speculation or for epic poetry and tragedy; though, of course, they are very far indeed from having the same intrinsic value. And, finally, the mention of poetry suggests that, in this department too, Thackeray had a power which often suggests a regret that it was not more fully exercised. His poetry was evidently regarded by himself as an amusement, and he did not value the results sufficiently to labour after any high polish or to attempt any exalted task. Such trifles as the 'Ballads of Policeman X' and the 'Lyra Hibernica' are curious proofs of his mastery over the cockney and Irish dialects—to say nothing of their intrinsic fun. We are amused by them as we should be amused by some eminent painter drawing caricatures with a bit of charcoal on a whitewashed wall, and showing his singular facility of hand as distinctly as in his most serious work, though for a humbler purpose of momentary amusement. Mere facility of versification and dexterity in manipulating quaint slang dialects are of course no proof of high poetic power. Nor was Thackeray's success in more serious attempts of such a kind as to suggest that he was deserting his natural vocation in making so little use of the poetic form. He has written half-a-dozen songs, and one ballad of considerable length which will,

I think, be remembered much longer than much poetry of higher aims and reputation. But they are the kind of work which cannot be made to order. They were products of an occasional inspiration, and he would have been wrong to force a vein, the charm of which depends in great measure upon the obvious spontaneity of the thought. They certainly give the impression of being comparatively slight efforts of a man who had a great reserve of power; but the power thus indicated was actually expended in a different direction, and there is, I think, every presumption that it was expended in the direction most congenial to his talent. The 'Chronicle of the Drum,' originally written in 1841, contains some of those ringing and hard-hitting stanzas which are appropriate to the style adopted; they have stuck to my memory since I read it first, with a persistency which convinces me at least of their picturesque power. The old drummer telling his old tales on the sunshiny bench of the tavern, warming his old blood with memories of victories and defeats and revolutionary triumphs, is as vividly drawn as Wilkie's or Mr. Herkomer's Chelsea Pensioners.[1] The dramatic force is often quite admirable; as in the stanzas which describe the Reign of Terror, and the son of St. Louis silenced at the bidding of Santerre by a tap of the old ruffian's drum; if ruffian be not too harsh a word for a mere bit of military machinery. But, though I love the 'Chronicle,' it seems to me that, though the easy-going verse is a very fit vehicle for the rough-and-ready eloquence of the drummer, the more serious treatment of the same theme would require rather prose than poetry. The drummer would fit into one of MM. Erckmann-Chatrian's novels,[2] and scarcely ventures further than the outskirts of poetry. To compare small things with great, one feels, in reading the *Lay of the Last Minstrel*, that though William of Deloraine—whose morality was pretty much that of the drummer and his Emperor applied on a large scale—is a delightful portrait, his creator could express himself to still better purpose in prose; and so I think that the 'Chronicle'—excellent in itself—is more suggestive of the future novelist than of an incomplete poet.

The short lyrical pieces which we remember in Thackeray's poetry are perhaps suggestive of something more: at least of a wish that they could have received a little higher polish. And yet, though

---

[1] For Wilkie see above, p. 115n. Hubert von Herkomer (1849–1914) had achieved fame in 1875 with his 'The Last Muster—Sunday at the Royal Hospital, Chelsea'.

[2] The most famous novel by Emile Erckmann (1822–99) and Louis Chatrian (1826–90) is *Histoire d'un consrit de 1813* (1864).

apparently thrown off without very much care, they hit the mark so easily and gracefully that we are well content as they stand. The ballad of 'Bouillabaisse' and the 'Cane-bottomed Chair,' the little song 'At the Church Gate,' originally published in *Pendennis*, the 'End of the Play', and the 'Vanitas Vanitatum', do not profess to go very deep; they are half humorous as well as tender; but they seem to have in them so complete an infusion of the author's characteristic mood, that they affect me at least more than the more exquisite performances of recognised poets. There is the same kind of charm as in Lamb's 'Old Familiar Faces', and in some other poems which appear to be all the more genuine because they have a certain stamp as of amateur work. The carelessness seems appropriate to the sincerity of feeling. Certainly, one could not express the doctrine which he has expounded so often more pithily than in the comment on the *vanitas vanitatum*:—

> Though thrice a thousand years are past,
>   Since David's son, the sad and splendid,
> The weary King Ecclesiast,
>   Upon his awful tablet penned it.—
>
> Methinks the text is never stale,
>   And life is every day renewing
> Fresh comments on the old, old tale
>   Of Folly, Fortune, Glory, Ruin.
>
> Hark to the Preacher, preaching still,
>   He lifts his voice and cries his sermon,
> Here at St. Peter's of Cornhill,
>   As yonder on the Mount of Hermon:
>
> For you and me to heart to take
>   (O dear beloved brother readers)
> To-day, as when the good King spake,
>   Beneath the solemn Syrian cedars. . . .

[From 'Vanitas Vanitatum.']

Index

2 TOPICS